Joy for Millions!

From his impoverished youth to the great years when he kept breaking his own records in stroke after stroke of hard-working genius—this the incredible Disney story. It is also a wonderful inside picture of nearly half a century of Hollywood.

"Lively . . . entertaining . . . surprisingly informative . . . documents his biography with memorandums, letters, and photographs, all of which lend the book richness of detail."
—*The New York Times*

"I don't for a moment believe that Uncle Walt can be explained, but . . . this book is a fine way to find out about this amazing man."
—*Chicago Sun-Times*

WALT DISNEY

AN AMERICAN ORIGINAL

BOB THOMAS

PUBLISHED BY POCKET BOOKS NEW YORK

POCKET BOOKS, a division of Simon & Schuster, Inc.
1230 Avenue of the Americas, New York, N.Y. 10020

Published by arrangement with Simon and Schuster
Library of Congress Catalog Card Number: 76-13028

ISBN: 0-671-62870-4

First Pocket Books printing May, 1980

10 9 8 7 6 5 4 3 2

POCKET and colophon are registered trademarks
of Simon & Schuster, Inc.

Printed in the U.S.A.

To my daughters,
Nancy, Janet and Caroline,
with sweet remembrance of their Disney years

CONTENTS

FOREGROUND

"DISNEYLAND ISN'T designed just for children. When does a person stop being a child? Can you say that a child is ever entirely eliminated from an adult? I believe that the right kind of entertainment can appeal to all persons, young or old. I want Disneyland to be a place where parents can bring their children—or come by themselves and still have a good time."

Walt Disney was talking to me as he drove his convertible along a wide boulevard lined with fragrant groves of orange trees. The car's top was down, but he scarcely seemed to notice the cool April morning. Nor did he appear to be cognizant of the route he had taken from his Burbank studio to downtown Los Angeles and through the sprawling orchards of Orange County; he had traveled the same freeway and streets with regularity for a year. He was intent on describing the pleasure park he was building in Anaheim.

"It all started when my daughters were very young, and I took them to amusement parks on Sunday," he told me. "I sat on a bench eating peanuts and looking around me. I said to myself, dammit, why can't there be a better place to take your children, where you can have fun together? Well, it took me about fifteen years to develop the idea."

The convertible turned off Harbor Boulevard and entered the vast black expanse which was the Disneyland parking lot. It stretched almost immeasurably, with fresh white hashmarks indicating spaces for future parkers; at the extremities, steamrollers were gliding back and forth, smoothing the steaming asphalt. Disney brought his car to a halt in front of the entrance, over which a newly painted railroad station loomed. One of the men awaiting his arrival was Joe Fowler, a plain-spoken ex-admiral who was construction boss for Disneyland.

"How's it going?" Disney asked.

"Okay," Fowler replied. "I took a look all around the park this morning, and I think we'll make the opening all right. Just barely. But we'll make it."

"Well, I hope so," Disney said with a wry grin. "Otherwise we'll have to paint a lot of signs saying, 'Watch for the grand opening of this exhibit.' "

"I don't think we'll have to do that, Walt," Fowler assured.

"Just in case, I've ordered a lot of bunting for the opening," Disney said. "That'll cover up what isn't ready."

A handsome young Texan, Earl Shelton, said he would fetch a jeep for the inspection tour. Disney leaned against his car and pulled off his shoes and replaced them with brown cowboy boots. He was wearing gray slacks, black sport coat and a red checked shirt with a neckerchief bearing the symbol of the Smoke Tree Ranch of Palm Springs. He completed the costume with a white Western-style hat.

Disney strode through the passageway under the railroad tracks, glanced around the town square, then climbed the stairs to the train station, with me following him. "This will be a nice shady place for the people to wait for the train," he said, looking about the bright, airy station. "Look at that detail in the woodwork. We got hundreds of photographs and drawings of railroad stations in the last century, and we copied all the details." He stood on the platform for a minute and seemed to be envisioning the locomotive huffing into the station with breaths of steam, the passengers anxious to climb aboard.

Shelton was waiting with the jeep at the bottom of the stairs, and Disney and I climbed in. The jeep swung around the square and started idling down Main

Street. The buildings were half-painted, and some of the steel superstructure was exposed. But to Walt it seemed the small-town Main Street of his youth, in turn-of-the-century Missouri.

He described what the stores would be like. An ice-cream parlor with marble-topped tables and wireback chairs. A candy shop, where taffy would be pulled and chocolate fudge concocted in view of the patrons. A music store with Gramophones and player pianos and a silent-movie house with six screens.

He talked in flat, matter-of-fact tones that were unmistakably middle-American. When he described how a part of Disneyland would dramatize itself to the customers, he seemed almost transported. The right eyebrow shot up, the eyes gleamed, the mustache waggled expressively. He had used the same persuasion in making fairy tales come to life; now he was telling how the half-finished buildings would soon contribute to the enjoyment of patrons making their way through the park.

The jeep came to a circular park where workmen were straining to lower a huge olive tree into the ground. "This is the hub of Disneyland, where you can enter the four realms," Disney said. "Parents can sit in the shade here if they want, while their kids go off into one of the other places. I planned it so each place is right off the hub. You know, when you go to a world's fair, you walk and walk until your feet are sore. I know mine always are. I don't want sore feet here. They make people tired and irritable. I want 'em to leave here happy. They'll be able to cover the whole place and not travel more'n a couple of miles."

He went first into Fantasyland, which he admitted was his favorite. The jeep passed over a bridge and through Sleeping Beauty's towering, blue-turreted castle. The courtyard of the castle was a jumble of lumber and packing crates and newly painted signs, but Walt saw the place as it would be: "A splash of color all around —reds, yellows, greens. Each ride will have a mural eight feet by sixty feet. In the middle, King Arthur's carousel with leaping horses, not just trotting, but all of them *leaping*. The rides will be like nothing you've ever seen in an amusement park before." He described each one in detail. In Peter Pan's Flight, you would fly out the window of the Darlings' house, over Big Ben and the Thames and on to Never-Never Land; in Mr. Toad's Wild Ride, your ancient automobile would crash through haystacks and fences; in Snow White's adventures, you would visit the Dwarfs' diamond mine, then travel through the Enchanted Forest to meet the terrifying witch; in the Mad Tea Party, you would twirl in giant teacups that revolved around each other.

Then to Frontierland through Davy Crockett's stockade, built of real logs and foot-long nails. The jeep bounced along a dusty road; soon, Disney said, stagecoaches would pass this way, trundling through the Painted Desert and skirting the bank of the river, only a dry ditch now. Resting on the bottom was the steel hull of a boat, with a steam engine inside and wooden planking on the deck. The superstructure was being built at the studio, Disney explained, and he described how the *Mark Twain* would paddle through these future waters like the great Mississippi steamers of another century. In warehouses behind Frontierland, Disney displayed some of his treasures: two steam engines of five-eighths scale for the Disneyland and Santa Fe Railroad; surreys, stagecoaches, trolley cars, all constructed new at the studio; automatic organs and pianos, hand-crank kinetoscopes and penny-arcade machines, collected by Disney scouts from all over America; rows of hand-carved carousel horses, bought in Coney Island and Toronto, all of them leaping.

Adventureland was a rambling ditch with the suggestion of a tropical jungle on its banks. Disney stepped down from the jeep and walked along the riverbed, describing to me what the jungle ride would be like. A pilot would take the visitor down the great rivers of the world, past ruined temples and through rain forests. Dangers were everywhere: hippos charging at the boat, ears twitching; crocodiles with mouths agape; cannibals dancing on the shore; a waterfall that threatened to inundate the explorers. The adventures became a vivid reality in Disney's recounting.

The jeep drove on to Tomorrowland, where a massive rocket pointed skyward. Inside, Disney said, visitors would enjoy the fantasy of being transported to the moon and back. Kids who dreamed of driving would be able to do so on a miniature freeway, operating gasoline-fueled cars.

The tour was over, and Disney conferred with some of his construction men about the day's problems. Then he took off his walking boots and hat and prepared for the drive back to Los Angeles. He took a final look down the unpaved Main Street toward the castle. "Don't forget," he said to me, "the biggest attraction isn't here yet."

"What's that?"

"People. You fill this place with people, and you'll really have a show."

The year was 1955, and Walt Disney was fifty-three years old. He had already developed the animated film into an art form and had made a massive contribution to the folklore of the world. Now he was on the threshold of another achievement. Disneyland proved to be an unparalleled success, as innovative in the field of outdoor entertainment as the Disney cartoons had been in the world of film.

Disneyland, together with the television series that helped finance and publicize the park, brought fiscal security to the Disney enterprise for the first time in its thirty years of existence. Roy Disney no longer needed to importune bankers for money to meet the payroll and fulfill his brother's dreams. Financial jeopardy had never worried Walt, and release from it did not lessen his creative drive. Far from it. In the last decade of his life, Walt Disney pushed himself and his co-workers to new plateaus of creativity. He seemed to consider his time limited, and his impatience to get things done sometimes made him hard to work for. He had little patience with those whose thinking was earthbound.

One of his writers observed: "When Walt dropped an idea, he didn't expect you to pick it up where he left it; you were supposed to move a couple of steps beyond. God help you if you took his idea and ran in the wrong direction. If you did, one eyebrow would rise and the other would descend, and he'd say, 'You don't seem to get it at all.'"

Disney possessed a remarkable skill for drawing the best from those who worked with him. Many of them were astonished at what they could accomplish under his prodding; Disney never was. He expected the best and would not relent until he got it. The bright sharpness of his vision compelled his workers to achievement. "Walt is the best gag man around here," his cartoonists said in awe. It was their highest compliment; not only could he devise moments of hilarity, but he could blend character and action into prodigious feats of story-telling. Above all, he was a storyteller, whether he was spellbinding a half-dozen animators in the studio "sweatbox" or providing entertainment for a packed Radio City Music Hall. The communication was the same; he had an uncanny capacity for reaching the human heart, hence causing nervousness and distrust among intellectuals. They exulted in the Disney failures —and he had some. No one could attempt so much and not fail. But he had an imperishable optimism that allowed him to overcome failure, condescending critics, foreclosing bankers, defecting employees, fraudulent distributors and other hazards of the motion-picture industry. By the end of his life, his vision had taken him beyond—to the planning of a university that would intermingle all the arts and to the shaping of a city that would prove a model for the future.

How could it happen? How could one man produce so much entertainment that enthralled billions of human beings in every part of the world? That is the riddle of Walt Disney's life. The answer can't be found in his background. His parents were plain people who moved from one section of the country to another in futile search of the American dream. Young Walt showed no brilliance as a student; he daydreamed through his classes. Cartooning proved his major interest, but his drawings were uninspired; as soon as he could hire better cartoonists, he gave up drawing entirely. It seems incredible that the unschooled cartoonist from Kansas City, a bankrupt in his first movie venture, could have produced works of unmatched imagination —and could even have undertaken the creation of a future city. In terms of accomplishment, he might be considered a genius, but the word has lost its impact in the movie world. And even true genius must have roots.

A large part of the answer to the Disney riddle, I believe, lies in the form of expression he chose for himself at the beginning of his film career. Cartoons are the most controlled of motion-picture mediums. The animator draws his own characters, makes them move, places them against a background that is complementary. Total control.

Before Disney, cartoons were slapdash—two-dimensional characters in bizarre movement before elemental backgrounds. Disney insisted on rounded, humanized figures. He wanted the humor to come out of character, not from outrageous action. His cartoon actors had to move convincingly and distinctly; there could be no vague or unsure motion.

In 1928, Walt Disney wrote instructions from New York to Ub Iwerks, his chief animator in Hollywood: "Listen—please try and make all action definite and pointed and don't be afraid to exaggerate things plenty. It never looks as strong on the screen as it appears on the drawing board. Always work to bring the GAGS out above any other action—this is very important." Over the years Disney repeated to his animators: "Make it *read!*" Meaning, make the action distinct and recognizable. No contradictions, no ambiguities.

Disney constantly strove to make the cartoon more convincing and more entertaining. He added sound and color. He pressed his animators to develop greater skills until they were able to sustain the cartoon to feature length. When he had developed animation to its fullest, he moved to new challenges—live-action movies, nature films, television entertainment, then Disneyland. It was a natural progression, changing the audience from spectators to participants. Walt Disney brought to Disneyland all the skill and showmanship he had learned in three decades as a film maker. He thought in movie terms: transporting his audience from one scene to the next with smooth transition, combining controlled elements for a total experience.

The designers of Disneyland were movie-studio art directors—artists who knew the technique of creating sets and backdrops to provide a storytelling experience. Their Main Street was unlike any small-town Main Street that ever existed. At Disneyland, all the shops and emporiums complemented each other; even the signs and paint colors were in harmony. The result was pleasingly believable to the visitor. They thought, "That's the way Main Street must have been in the old days!" But that was the way it *should* have been.

Although he was constantly reshaping it, Walt Disney was pleased with what he had wrought at Disneyland. His only discontent was with the peripheral neon jungle of motels and fast-food shops competing with each other for the tourist's attention and dollar. "Dammit, we should have had more land," he often muttered. "We could have done it so much better."

After Disneyland, Disney agreed to create exhibits for the New York World's Fair of 1964–65. His planners were puzzled. Why expend talent and time on attractions that would be shown for two years at a world's fair? It seemed illogical, especially since Disney for the first time would be entering a field in which he could not maintain total control. He would be building shows for other corporations and competing before millions of visitors with the efforts of nations, states, and giant companies.

During the World's Fair planning, Disney revealed his thinking in a remark to one of his designers, John Hench: "How would you like to work on a future city?"

It was said with a grin, and the matter was dropped. Later Hench realized that the World's Fair attractions were part of Disney's long-range scheme to work with industry to restore order to city living. The first step would be another park in Florida following the pattern of Disneyland. Then Disney would build a new kind of city.

From Mickey Mouse to the City of Tomorrow. The range of Walt Disney's talent was incredible. This biography will attempt to trace the development of his creative processes, together with a picture of the man and his time.

I
THE
MIDWEST
YEARS
1901–1923

1

ISIGNY-SUR-MER IS a small windswept village on the
Normandy coast, a few kilometers from the beaches
where Allied troops landed on June 6, 1944. Nine
centuries before, French soldiers sailed from the same
coast to invade England, and among them were Hughes
d'Isigny and his son Robert. The family remained in
England, their name becoming anglicized to Disney.
During the Restoration, a branch of the Disney clan
moved to Ireland, settling in County Kilkenny. Arundel
Elias Disney was born there in 1801, and in 1834 he
and his brother Robert sailed from Liverpool with their
families to begin new lives in America. After a month's
voyage, they arrived in New York on October 3. The
two brothers parted, Robert heading for a farm in the
Midwest, Elias traveling to the Canadian frontier in
mills, schools or churches.

The first white men had settled there only nine years
before. Other immigrants—Scottish, Pennsylvania-Ger-
man, Irish—were attracted to the land by promises of
roads and improvements and prices of seven shillings
and sixpence per acre. But the land company failed to
keep its promises, and the settlers found they had
brought their families to a wilderness without roads,
mills, schools or churches.

Elias Disney saw hope in the vast acreage, with its
rushing, trout-filled streams, forests alive with deer and
elk, meadows abounding with wild plums and berries.
He built a mill beside the Maitland River and prospered
by grinding wheat and sawing timber for his neighbors.
His wife, Maria, gave him sixteen children, the eldest

being Kepple Disney, born in Ireland in 1832. The Disney mill thrived for many years, then bad times descended on Goderich. Elias was forced to default on his mortgages.

Son Kepple married an Irish-born immigrant, Mary Richardson, and they settled in the nearby Bluevale district. Kepple was a strapping, black-bearded man who tried a variety of enterprises, from drilling for oil to operating a salt well. He disliked the Canadian winters, and in 1878 he took off for the California gold fields with his oldest sons, Elias and Robert. Passing through Kansas, Kepple Disney was convinced by a railroad agent to buy two hundred acres of Union Pacific land near Ellis. He sent for the rest of his family to join him on their new farm. Because he couldn't afford lumber, he built them a house made of sod. The farm began to thrive on cattle and wheat, but Kepple still resisted the high prices the railroad charged for lumber. He quarried rock and built a house of stone.

Elias Disney, eldest of Kepple's eleven children, became restless on the farm and left for a job as machinist in a railroad shop, where a co-worker was Walter Chrysler, founder of the automotive empire. Elias moved on to join the work crew pushing the Union Pacific line through Colorado. When the railroad reached Denver, his job as apprentice carpenter was over. Jobs were scarce in Denver, and Elias tried to earn a living by playing his fiddle with two other amateur musicians outside saloons. The returns were skimpy, and Elias returned to the family farm in Ellis.

Part of the reason for Elias's return to Kansas was Flora Call, the pretty daughter of the Disneys' neighbors, the Charles Calls. The Call family was Scottish and English. The first to emigrate, Thomas Call, arrived in Boston in 1636. A descendant, Eber Call, moved to Ohio in 1825, and his son Charles left Oberlin College to join the 1849 Gold Rush to California. He found no gold and returned to Ohio, later settling his wife, eight daughters and two sons in Ellis, Kansas, where he taught school. The prairie blizzards convinced Charles Call to move his family to Florida in 1884.

Kepple Disney also grew weary of the Kansas winters, and he and his son Elias accompanied their neighbors to Florida. Kepple decided against making the move permanent and returned to his Kansas farm. Elias remained in Florida. He bought a forty-acre farm at Kismet and continued his courtship of Flora Call, who had become a grammar-school teacher. They were married on New Year's Day, 1888, in her parents' home at Akron, Florida. Elias was twenty-eight, his bride nineteen.

Photographs of Elias and Flora Disney provide hints of their natures—he with starched collar and heavy woolen ready-made suit, big-eared with hawk nose, alert eyes in a stern face; she in high-necked dress, deep-set eyes, heavy-lidded, wide mouth pursed but with a hint of humor. They were a devoted couple, and she remained patient and understanding through his many misadventures in business.

First, Elias sold his farm and bought a hotel in Daytona Beach. But the tourist trade slumped and he was forced out of business. Now he had a son, Herbert, born December 8, 1888, and Elias went to work as a rural mailman and managed to buy a small orange grove. Then a war scare swept the country. Overwhelmed with patriotism, he enlisted in the militia. The crisis soon dissolved, and Elias saw no sense in remaining in the militia, not when he had a wife and baby son and an orange grove to care for. So he walked out of the army camp and went home. Military police arrived at his house to arrest him as a deserter. "I didn't desert; there isn't any war," he reasoned. The army men could find no answer to his logic. "At least you must give back the uniform," one insisted. "No, sir, I didn't get paid, so I'm going to keep the uniform," Elias replied.

A frost destroyed the orange crop and Elias was stricken with malaria. He decided, as he often did when his luck turned sour, that his life would improve if he moved on. He chose Chicago.

Seventy years before, Chicago had been a collection of huts on the shore of Lake Michigan. By 1889, when Elias and Flora Disney arrived with their infant son, it was a brawny city of 1,200,000 citizens, the railroad hub sending wheat and beef to the East, and cloth and threshers to the West. After a lifetime in small towns, Elias Disney was bewildered by the city's clamor, but he was determined to succeed after his failure in Florida. First, he needed shelter for his young family. He decided to build his own house, applying the carpentry he had learned on the Union Pacific. Flora said she would design it for him. "There's nothing mysterious about drawing up plans for a house," she argued, "and a woman ought to know more about making it livable." Following her plans, he built a square, trim, neat little house at 1249 Tripp Avenue, one of the two paved roads in the northwestern part of Chicago.

Elias painted the house white with blue trim, and visitors admired its clean lines and economy. He bought the adjoining lot and constructed another house, which he offered for sale. He began building homes in other parts of Chicago, and he developed relationships with bankers, who provided loans for prospective buyers. Flora drew up the plans, bought the building materials, did the bookkeeping, and even furnished the new house if the buyer so desired. In 1893, when building was in a slump, Elias took a job as a carpenter for the World's Columbian Exposition, working seven days a week at a dollar a day.

The family was growing. Raymond Arnold Disney was born on December 30, 1890, and Roy Oliver Disney on June 24, 1893. Elias and his wife and sons worshipped at St. Paul Congregational Church, and he became a close friend of the preacher, Walter Parr. Elias volunteered to build a new church for the congregation, and he put up a plain, serviceable structure with a tall, sloping roof. Flora played the organ in the new church, and Elias preached the sermon when the preacher was on vacation. When both their wives became pregnant in 1901, Elias made a proposal to the preacher: "If I get a boy baby, I'll name him after you; if your baby is a boy, you name him after me." Walter Parr agreed.

A fourth son was born to Elias and Flora Disney in the upper bedroom of the Tripp Avenue house on Sunday, December 5, 1901. Keeping his bargain with the preacher, Elias named the boy Walter Elias Disney. The Parr baby was also a boy, and he was named Elias. It had been eight and a half years since her last son had been born, and Flora Disney lavished attention on young Walter. He was a sweet-natured baby, handsomer than the other boys, who had their father's strong Roman nose. The mother liked to dress Walter in frilly clothes. Roy uncomplainingly pushed his little brother in a baby carriage up and down Tripp Avenue, and even bought Walter toys out of his own earnings— a gesture which might be considered prophetic.

Two years and a day after Walter's arrival, the first daughter was born to the Disneys, and she was named Ruth Flora. By this time Elias had grown concerned about rearing his children in the big city. The neighborhood was filling up with Poles and Irish and Swedes, most of them hard-working, God-fearing people. But the old-world family ties were unraveling, and some of the children ran wild while their parents scraped for a living. Not far away from the Disney neighborhood was Cicero, later the headquarters of Al Capone and other notorious criminals.

Elias Disney's concern grew each time he passed the streetcorner with its three saloons. His mind was made up when two neighborhood boys were arrested for killing a policeman in a carbarn robbery. One was sentenced to Joliet Prison for twenty years, the other to life imprisonment. "Flora, those two boys are no older than Herb and Ray!" Elias said to his wife. "We've got to get out of this cesspool of a city."

Flora agreed with her husband's proposal to move the family to the rural atmosphere they had known in their early lives. Elias visited communities in Colorado and Alabama where he had heard of opportunities, but none seemed suitable. Then he went to Marceline, Missouri, where his brother Robert owned property. The country was fertile, with green, rolling hills, a pleasant little town where supplies could be bought, and enough industry—there were coal mines and oil wells—for economic stability. Marceline, Elias Disney decided, would be the place where he could earn a good living and rear his five children in a wholesome Christian atmosphere.

2

WALT DISNEY remembered nothing of his early years in Chicago, but the memories of Marceline stayed with him throughout his lifetime. He recalled the place where he lived: "It was a beautiful farm, with a wide front lawn. Big weeping willow trees. It had two orchards, one called the old, one called the new. One variety was called Wolf River apples, and they were so big that people came from miles around to see them."

Marceline was one of a multitude of towns that owed their existence to the railroad. The Atchison, Topeka & Santa Fe was spreading through Missouri in 1888, and a new village grew up beside its tracks in Lynn County near the center of the state, 120 miles from Kansas City. The first settlers decided to call the place after the name of the railroad superintendent's daughter, Marceline.

By April of 1906, when the Disney family arrived to take over the Crane farm, Marceline had become a community of five thousand people. They were hard workers. Some were employed in the nearby Coal Mine No. 1, some in the oil and natural-gas fields. Merchants sold their wares in the red-brick and sandstone stores along Main Street. Most of the population lived on farms, growing fruit, vegetables, wheat, and barley and raising beef and pork for the big-city markets.

Flora Disney arrived first, bringing her three youngest children—Roy, Walt and Ruth. Elias Disney and the two older sons, Herb and Ray, came a few days later in a boxcar loaded with the family belongings, including a pair of horses Elias had bought in the Chicago stockyards. The family settled into the neat, square, one-storied whitewashed house built by a Civil War veteran, William Crane, recently deceased. Elias had purchased the house and forty-five acres at a price of $125 an acre, promising installment payments with money he was to receive for Chicago houses he had built.

Elias and the three older sons went to work immediately, plowing the spring fields and planting large areas of corn and sorghum, lesser amounts of wheat and barley. Elias bought cows for milking, and pigs, chickens and pigeons to feed the family. Flora Disney worked constantly, preparing huge meals, washing and mending the men's shirts and coveralls, hoeing the vegetable garden, churning butter to trade for provisions at the grocery store. Her butter was so sweet and pure that the groceryman gave it special position on his counter.

Walt, a wiry, towheaded boy with searching eyes, tagged after his mother to help with her chores, and he was followed by little Ruth. The farm and its surroundings were an endless source of wonderment to the boy. He played in the mud under a bridge near the house, waving shyly to farmer neighbors as they passed by in their buggies. He herded the pigs to new grubbing places, and they permitted him to ride on their backs, a feat that Elias Disney showed off to visitors. Walt gave special attention to a runty piglet he named Skinny. He nourished Skinny with a baby bottle, and the pig followed him around the farm like a pet dog.

As one season blended into the next, Walt learned to anticipate and enjoy the cycles of farm life. During the sorghum harvest, his father and brothers cut the cane and fed it into a horse-powered squeezer. Walt led the horse around in a circle until the cane was mashed. The molasses was stored in big vats and poured on breakfast pancakes or baked in cakes and gingerbread. If the crop had been bountiful, the excess was siphoned into brown earthen jugs and bartered at the grocery store in Marceline.

Harvesting time brought the big, puffing steam thresher to the farm, the neighbors' wagons hitched behind it. While the men worked in the fields, the women filled the kitchen with gossip and the aromas of fried chicken, corn bread and chocolate cake. At noontime the men came to the house and ate huge meals, exchanging views about the size and worth of the harvest. Then they stretched out on the lawn under the willow tree and slept for an hour before returning to the fields.

Hog-killing time brought neighbors back to the farm, and they helped Elias slaughter the animals and dip the carcasses into huge boiling kettles. The bristles were scraped off, and well-honed knives sliced the remains for ham, bacon, sausage, and headcheese.

As Walt grew older, he wandered farther from the Disney farm, sometimes with his brother Roy. Nearby were woods overgrown with walnut, hickory nut, hazelnut, persimmon, wild grape and chokeberry, all in their seasons offering food for passersby. Walt learned to watch for animals that lived in the woods—rabbits, foxes, squirrels, 'possums and raccoons. And he scanned the trees for birds—bobwhite, crow, hawk, woodpecker, meadowlark, cardinal, wren, swallow and wild dove. On hot summer days, Walt and Roy walked the few miles to Yellow Creek and cooled themselves in the slow-moving water.

The Santa Fe railroad tracks ran through the countryside a short distance from the Disney farm, and Walt would put his ear to the rail to hear the train coming. He always hoped that the engineer would be his uncle

Mike Martin, who worked the route between Fort
Madison and Marceline and often stayed with the Disneys overnight, bringing a striped bag of candy for the
children. Another diversion for Walt was watching the
horseless carriages chug by on the County Pike Road
in front of the farm. They had just begun to appear in
Marceline.

Things happened to young Walt that he could remember with absolute clarity in his mature years. He
wandered through an orchard on a summer Sunday and
saw an owl on the branch of an apple tree. He reached
up to pet the bird, but it flew away. Walt pursued,
found the owl perched within reach, and put his hands
over it. The owl screeched and clawed. Instinctively
Walt threw the owl to the ground and stomped on it.
The boy was overcome by remorse to find the owl
dead, and he buried it in a small grave. For months
afterward, the owl returned in Walt's dreams.

The most persistent family legend about Walt's boyhood on the farm was always described as his first
attempt at art. The incident was recalled by his sister
Ruth in an interview almost seventy years afterward:
"My folks had gone to town, and Walt and I were left
there alone. We spied a big barrel of tar and opened
it up. As we were looking at it, Walt said, 'Oh this
would be real good to paint with.' He added, 'Let's
paint on the house.' I wondered if it would come off,
and he said, 'Oh, sure.' So we went to work on the
long side of the white house, the side that faced the
main road. He drew houses, I remember, with smoke
coming out of them, and I drew zigzags. Two rows of
them. We dipped big sticks into the tar, and I can
remember the awful feeling when we realized a little
bit later that the tar wouldn't budge. My father was
so angry that he just left it there. It was still there on
the side of the house when we moved."

His mother taught Walt how to read. Elias Disney
decreed that it was more convenient for the boy to wait
until Ruth was old enough for school, and Walt was
almost seven before he was enrolled at the Park School,

a two-story red-brick building with two hundred students in grade and high school. Walt read the standard text, the McGuffey Eclectic Reader, and studied arithmetic, writing, geography and spelling. His grades were only fair, because he was always finding things that interested him more than schoolwork. One of his new discoveries was the movie house that had just opened in Marceline. One day after school he persuaded Ruth to accompany him to the theater, and on the bedsheet screen they saw an enactment of the crucifixion and resurrection of Christ. It was dark when they emerged, and they hurried home fearful of what would happen to them for staying out so late. Nothing did, because their parents were so relieved that the two children were safe.

The years in Marceline provided Walt Disney with a gallery of memorable characters. Warm-hearted Aunt Margaret, who came from Kansas City with crayons and pads to encourage Walt's drawing. Grandma Disney, full of mischief in her seventies, urging her grandson to fetch her turnips from a neighbor's farm. Uncle Robert Disney, an elegant figure who kept a cigar in his mouth even when his Vandyke beard was being trimmed in the barbershop. Uncle Ed, considered dim-witted by outsiders, but by his family simply a boy who never grew up. Walt found him a perfect companion, a grown-up who liked to do boyish things. They wandered the countryside together, and when Uncle Ed wanted to go to town, he simply flagged down the train and climbed aboard. Walt visited the nearby farm of Erastus Taylor and listened to the Civil War veteran recount the battles of Shiloh and Bull Run. The boy rode into town with Doc Sherwood, in black Prince Albert frock coat and beardless, having pulled out his whiskers one by one. The eccentric retired physician commissioned a portrait of himself and his prize stallion Rupert, and paid Walt a shiny new quarter for his drawing.

At first, Elias Disney was viewed with suspicion by his farming neighbors. He came, after all, from the big city, full of socialistic ideas. Some of the farmers, angered by having food processors and the railroad dictate terms, listened with sympathy to Elias's proposals to join the American Society of Equity. One night in 1907, he hired the Knights of Pythias meeting hall and invited farmers and their wives to a dinner. He had bought five gallons of oysters from Ed Hayden's grocery, and the diners admitted that they had never tasted such good oyster soup. But they were less receptive to Elias's arguments, and his hope for a union of farmers in Marceline proved a failure.

Despite his radical ideas, Elias Disney came to be well liked in Marceline. He was industrious and serious-minded, yet there was one note of frivolity in his nature. On Sundays he hitched his buckskin mare to the buggy and rode to the house of Grandpa Taylor. For an hour or two, Elias and Will Rensimer played on their fiddles to the piano accompaniment of the Taylors' daughter. Walt sat on a straight-backed chair throughout the concert, enthralled by the music and astonished by this unexpected aspect of his father.

At most other times, Elias Disney was sober, even dour. The task of supporting a wife and five children on a prairie farm had proved more of a burden than he had anticipated, and he brooded over the possibility of failure. He demanded more of his older sons, and only Flora's quick humor forestalled open rebellion.

By planting acreage Elias had rented from Robert Disney, Herb and Ray earned $175, and they bought themselves gold watches and chains for $20 apiece. Their father accused them of profligacy and asked what they planned to do with the rest of the money.

"We thought we might buy a heifer and a colt," Herb replied.

"No," Elias said firmly. "I've got a lot of debts on this farm, and that money should help pay them off."

For Herb and Ray it was the final tyranny. At noon the next day Herb rode a horse into town and withdrew his and Ray's money from the bank. After dinner the two sons said they were tired from their day's work, and they went to their room early. Later they slipped out the window and carried their bags to the Santa Fe station, boarding the nine-thirty train to Chicago.

The loss of his two sons was a blow to Elias Disney and his hopes of developing his forty-five acres into a prosperous farm. His efforts had been hampered by his own hidebound notions about farming. "Putting fertilizer on plants is like giving whiskey to a man," he expounded. "He'll feel better for a while, but afterward he'll be worse off than he was before." He was convinced otherwise when his neighbors persuaded him to fertilize a single patch of corn and observe the difference.

The well went dry in a Missouri drought. Elias dug others, but the yield was scant. His apples ripened when the market price was low. He buried the apples in layers of straw, as his father had done in Canada. When winter came, the apples remained fresh, and the family peddled them door to door. Flora sold her butter to local residents, and Elias declared it could not be wasted at home. In a rare act of disloyalty, Flora buttered her home-baked bread and passed it butter side down to her children.

The worst of Elias Disney's bad luck came in the winter of 1909. He contracted typhoid fever, then pneumonia. Roy assumed the burden of running the farm, but it was too much for a sixteen-year-old boy. Flora argued that the farm had to be sold, and Elias finally agreed. After four years of bone-wearying labor, he would get back only what he had paid for the farm.

Roy hitched up the wagon, and he and his little brother rode through the bitter prairie chill to tack up notices on telegraph poles and fences advertising the coming auction at the Disney farm. The two boys watched sorrowfully as their favorite animals were auctioned to other farmers. They had special affection for a six-month-old colt that they had known from birth. The auctioneer sold the colt to a farmer, and both boys cried as they saw it tied to the back of a buggy and led off down the County Pike Road.

Later that day Roy and Walt took the wagon into town to buy some provisions. As they were walking into the hardware store, they heard a persistent whinny. They gazed across the street and saw their colt, tied to the back of the farmer's buggy. The colt had recognized them, and the boys raced across the street to hug it and cry some more.

Elias had made plans to move on to Kansas City, but he and Flora agreed that the children shouldn't be taken out of school in midyear. They rented a house in town at 508 North Kansas Avenue, and when school was out in the spring of 1910, the family left Marceline. Walt Disney had lived there barely four years, yet that period left more of an impression than any other time in his life. Forty years later, when he built a barn for a workshop on his estate in California, it was an exact replica of the one he had known in Marceline.

3

ALL HIS remembered years had been spent amid the calm fields and country lanes of a farming town. Now the boy saw broad boulevards filled with trolleys and automobiles. The buildings climbed eight and ten stories, and the theaters glittered with a thousand electric bulbs. Noise was everywhere—the call of street vendors, the rumble of beer drays, fire wagons clanging down cobbled streets. The city was unsettling in its strangeness, but the eight-year-old Walt Disney found it exciting as well. Among his vivid early memories of the city was Fairmont Park, a place of amusement two blocks from his first Kansas City home. To a boy of eight, it seemed like a pleasure palace with its gleaming white buildings and its sounds of music and excitement. But Walt never got past the whitewashed fence. There was no money to lavish on such frivolity.

The Disneys first lived at 2706 East 31st Street in a house with cramped rooms and a privy in the back yard. Elias Disney's health precluded the hard labor he had known most of his life. He bought a distributorship for the morning *Times* and evening and Sunday *Star* newspapers, paying $3 apiece for seven hundred subscribers. Walt and his sister Ruth were enrolled at Benton Grammar School, and soon Walt joined Roy as delivery boy for his father. Walt arose at three-thirty and claimed the newspapers from the delivery truck at four-thirty. The *Star* and *Times* had been reluctant to give a franchise to Elias Disney because of his age —fifty-one—and he felt he had to prove himself. He wouldn't allow his boys to deliver from bicycles, throwing the newspapers on porches. He insisted that they lay the papers on the doorstep, making sure that the wind would not carry them away. During the wintertime, the papers had to be placed behind the storm doors.

For six years, Walt delivered the newspapers morning and night, missing only four weeks because of illness. In the beginning he carried the papers in a sling over his shoulder; later his father supplied a pushcart. The pushcart wasn't big enough to accommodate all of the Sunday papers, and after his first delivery Walt returned to the distribution point for another load. The newspapers had to be distributed in rainstorms and blizzards; many times young Walt fell up to his neck in snowdrifts. During storms he welcomed the end of his route, when he visited apartment houses. Then he would make his deliveries from floor to floor in the steam-heated hallways. The warmth was so alluring that he sometimes sat down in a vestibule to take a brief nap. He always awoke in panic, puzzling over whether he had finished his deliveries in the building, fearing that he would be late for school. Until late in his life, Walt Disney had a recurring dream in which he suffered torment because he had failed to deliver some newspapers along his route.

The other newsboys were paid for their deliveries, but not Roy and Walt. Their father gave them small allowances but nothing for carrying the newspaper. "Your pay is the board and room that I provide for you," he declared. Both boys considered that unfair; they believed that a day's work deserved a day's pay, even if the boss was their father. Roy, who was nineteen and had graduated from high school, could no longer tolerate his father's domination and his frequent outbreaks of temper. "He still treats me like a little boy," Roy complained to Walt. Roy decided to follow the course of his two older brothers and run away from home. One summer night in 1912, he told Walt he was leaving to help with the harvest at their Uncle Will's farm in Kansas. "Don't worry, kid; everything will be all right here," Roy said assuringly. In the morning he was gone.

Roy's departure placed more responsibility on Walt. When other boys proved unreliable, it was Walt who had to substitute for them or make a special delivery for a lost paper. When Elias added a new kitchen, a bedroom and a bath to the Disney home, he insisted that Walt help him. Elias had his own ways of working, and he grew impatient with Walt. "No, you don't saw the board that way, you saw it like this!" the father would say angrily, and slap the back of the boy's pants with the side of the saw. On such occasions Elias struck out with whatever was in his hand—a length of board, the handle of a hammer. Walt learned to run when he saw such outbursts coming. His mother intervened, telling Elias: "How do you expect Walt to know those things? He's only a boy."

Walt discovered his own amusements. When the circus came to the city, he followed the parade from beginning to end, his sister Ruth striving hard to keep up with him. He devised his own circus parade, enlisting Ruth and the neighborhood children to help decorate floats atop play wagons. When Ruth became ill with the measles, he amused her with drawings, including a series of figures that seemed to move when papers were flipped; at nine he had made his first attempts at animation.

Walt took a boyish delight in playing tricks on his parents. He was fascinated with magic tricks and one day brought home a small rubber bladder that could be inflated through a long tube to make a plate rise. He tried it first on his mother's pots in the kitchen. She was startled, then delighted, and she tried the stunt on her husband at dinner that night. Elias was too occupied to notice, but Flora was so convulsed that she had to leave the room. One day Flora answered the front door to find a nicely dressed woman. Flora began to converse with her until she recognized some of her own clothes. The visitor was Walt in his mother's clothes, a wig and makeup.

Flora Disney brought a note of gaiety to what was often a gloomy household. Elias had been perplexed by the defections of his three older sons and disheartened by the repeated failures of his enterprises. His thrift was extraordinary—he would walk miles rather than pay a nickel for the trolley—yet he continued with his unpromising investments. He could convince himself that a mining stock or a new invention could lead to riches.

He was always thinking up new ways to make money. Remembering the sweet butter on the farm, he arranged for a Marceline dairy to send him a regular supply. Flora Disney loaded the butter into a cart and sold it door to door; Walt accompanied her, but she insisted on pushing the cart herself. Their route took them into the well-to-do district, where some of Walt's classmates lived. The embarrassment was something the boy did not soon forget.

Most of Walt's school years were spent at Benton Grammar School, and they provided lifelong memories. He reminisced in a 1940 letter to a onetime teacher, Daisy A. Beck: "I often think of you and the days I spent at Benton. I can plainly see you and [school

principal J. M.] Cottingham coaching the athletic teams
for the annual track meet. I don't know whether you
remember or not but I participated in several events
and even won a medal one year on the championship
80-pound relay team. I was kept rather busy with my
paper route and didn't have much time to train, but I
did manage to get in on a few events. . . . Do you
remember the time I brought the live mouse into the
classroom and you smacked me on the cheek? Boy!
What a wallop you had! But I loved you all the more
for it. And I can still plainly see the kids marching,
single file, into the classrooms to the rhythm of the
piano in the hall with you and Miss [Catherine] Shrews-
bury standing over the radiators while the heat bil-
lowed out your skirts. It looked very comfortable to
me on those cold mornings—and sometimes I wished
that I might have worn skirts myself. I remember how
Cottingham would break in on any classes if he had a
new story and all work would cease until he had his
fun. He had his faults, but I still think of him as a
swell fellow."

Walt's record at Benton Grammar School was undis-
tinguished, despite his mother's coaching with his homework. Teachers complained that the boy's attention
wandered, that he failed to follow the normal curriculum. Part of this may have been due to exhaustion
from the early-morning regimen of newspaper deliveries.
But Walt seemed unwilling to conform to the ordinary
methods of learning. His reading of the classroom
assignments was perfunctory, although he made good
use of the public library. He read everything of Mark
Twain, whose Missouri childhood had been similar to
his own. He was engrossed by the success stories of
Horatio Alger and the adventures of Tom Swift. The
storytelling of Robert Louis Stevenson, Sir Walter Scott
and Charles Dickens also intrigued him.

Walt's abiding interest was drawing, but even in that
field he could not please his teachers. When his fourth-
grade teacher, Artena Olson, instructed the class to
sketch a bowl of flowers on her desk, she strolled

around the room and stopped at Walt's desk. He had drawn human faces on the flowers with arms where the leaves were supposed to be. The teacher chastised him for not following the assignment.

He continued to draw things the way he saw them. His earliest efforts duplicated the political cartoons he found in *Appeal to Reason,* the socialist tract his father subscribed to. Walt became accomplished at portraying the top-hatted capitalist with gold watch across his bloated belly, the oppressed laboring man in work clothes and square paper hat. He developed an ease for caricature, and one day he drew impressions of the patrons at Bert Hudson's barbershop. The barber liked them so much he asked Walt to draw a new caricature every week. His work was framed on the barbershop wall, and Hudson cut Walt's hair for nothing.

His drawing skill helped cement a friendship with a schoolmate at Benton, Walter Pfeiffer. The two boys had become acquainted at school. One day when Walt went to call on his new friend, he was told that he had the mumps. Since Walt had already had them—on both sides—he was allowed to visit his friend. He brought along paper and charcoal, and he showed Walter how to draw.

Walt became a steady visitor at the Pfeiffer house. Mr. Pfeiffer, a jolly German whose laughter filled the house, was an official of the United Leatherworkers Union. His daughter Kitty played the piano, and he liked to have the whole family join in song. Mr. Pfeiffer adored the theater, especially the Dutch-dialect comedy of Weber and Fields, and he rattled off the jokes with gusto. After the austerity of his own home, Walt was overwhelmed by the warmth and gaiety of the Pfeiffers. He began spending more time at their house than he did at his own.

Through the Pfeiffer family, Walt Disney was introduced to an enticing new world of vaudeville shows and motion pictures. Elias Disney had always considered such entertainments to be frivolous and time-wasting, so when Walt and Walter Pfeiffer started going to the theaters, Walt was careful not to let his father know.

Around the piano at the Pfeiffer house, Walt and Walter re-created the jokes and songs they had heard in the vaudeville houses and imitated the pantomime of the movie comics. With Mr. Pfeiffer's coaching, the two boys devised routines to perform at Benton School. Walt induced other students to wear funny costumes and repeat the jokes he had copied from the vaudeville comics. His most popular performance was "Fun in the Photograph Gallery." Walt portrayed an antic photographer, posing his fellow students, then dousing them with a jet of water from the camera. The audience was delighted when Walt produced the "photograph" —his own caricature of the student who had been squirted.

On Lincoln's Birthday when he was in the fifth grade, Walt converted his father's derby into a stovepipe hat with cardboard and shoe polish, borrowed his father's church-deacon coat with swallowtail, added crepe hair to his chin and a wart to his cheek. Principal Cottingham was so pleased with the impersonation that he took Walt into each class for a recitation of the Gettysburg Address, a ritual that continued until Walt graduated.

Walt and Walter Pfeiffer entered amateur night at a local theater with "Charlie Chaplin and the Count," Walt playing Chaplin in his father's derby, pants and work shoes and a lampblack mustache. They won fourth prize of twenty-five cents. Rehearsing as Walt delivered newspapers, the two boys developed other acts —"The Two Walts," "The Boys from Benton School," "Hans and Mike." Walt sneaked out his bedroom window for the performances, realizing that his father would not approve. One night Elias and Flora took their daughter for a rare visit to the neighborhood vaudeville house. A performer announced he would stack three chairs over his head and balance a boy on top. The Disney parents were startled to discover that the boy atop the stack was their son Walter.

In addition to his newspaper routes, Walt delivered

prescriptions for a drugstore and sold newspapers on streetcorners. During the noon recess he swept out the candy store across from school in return for a hot meal. Work became a constant, numbing routine. Sometimes as he dressed before dawn, he fell asleep while tying his shoelaces. Small diversions gave him pleasure, like playing with a miniature train left on a customer's porch during the summer or taking a few minutes from his deliveries for football or hockey with friends.

Walt looked forward to the times when his brother Roy returned home. Roy had twice gone to work on his Uncle William's farm in Ellis, Kansas, walking part of the way and hitching rides on freight trains. Later he was hired as teller at the First National Bank in Kansas City. Despite the difference in their ages, the two brothers maintained the same closeness they had known on the Marceline farm, and Roy provided counsel from his worldly experience.

One day Elias upbraided Walt for not handing him a tool fast enough. Walt's temper was as hot as his father's, and he replied sharply. Elias accused him of impertinence and ordered him to the basement for a thrashing. Roy overheard the exchange and confided to his brother, "Look, kid, he's got no reason for hitting you. You're fourteen years old. Don't take it any more." When Walt reached the basement, his father was still in a rage, and he swung a hammer handle. Walt grabbed it away. Elias raised his hand to strike the boy. Walt held him by both wrists, and his father could not escape. Tears began to appear in Elias's eyes. Walt loosened his grip and climbed the stairs. His father never tried to thrash him again.

Accustomed to his father's frugality, Walt rarely asked anything for himself. But he longed for a pair of high leather boots with metal toes and decorated leather strips over the laces, arguing that the boots would be practical for delivering newspapers through the slush and rain. Flora Disney persuaded her husband to buy the boots, and at Christmas in 1916 Walt found them under the tree. He wore the boots every day as he trudged through his morning and afternoon deliveries. One early spring evening, Walt was finishing the *Star* route at 31st Street and Indiana, where he usually joined his friends for a soda at the drugstore. As he crossed the street, he kicked a piece of ice, then yelped in pain. A horseshoe nail had pierced the boot and jammed into his big toe. His foot was frozen fast to the ice.

"Help! I'm stuck!" he yelled, but a trolley muffled his shouts. For twenty minutes he endured excruciating pain, and no one offered assistance. Finally a wagon driver chipped the ice loose and took Walt to a doctor's office. "Kid, I've got nothing to give you for the pain," the doctor said. "You'll just have to hang on." He assigned two men to hold Walt's leg, then he pulled out the nail with a pliers. Walt sweated in pain as the doctor removed the boot, opened the wound, and administered a tetanus inoculation.

Two weeks free from the ordeal of delivering the *Times* every morning gave Walt time to think about his future life. He discarded notions of being a doctor or lawyer; he realized he had been an indifferent student, and besides, none of the Disney sons had been afforded the luxury of a college education. The show world intrigued him—he had known no greater pleasure than performing before audiences—but he lacked the confidence to compete in big-time vaudeville. Cartooning interested him most. His drawings had evoked chuckles from the patrons of Bert Hudson's barbershop and his fellow students at Benton School. He enjoyed the children's art classes at the Kansas City Art Institute more than his regular schoolwork. By the time Walt's foot healed and he returned to his newspaper routes, he had decided to become a cartoonist.

By 1917, Elias Disney had been in Kansas City seven years and was growing restless. The newspaper distributorship had not grown as he had hoped, and it was hard to find reliable delivery boys. A new business enterprise beckoned. For $16,000, Elias could acquire an interest in the O-Zell jelly factory in Chicago, as well as the position of head of plant construction. He invested his entire savings, as well as $20 belonging to his son Walter.

Walt, who had graduated from Benton School on June 8, 1917, remained in Kansas City for the summer to help the new distributor with the newspaper route. Herbert Disney, who now had a wife and daughter, moved into the family house, and Walt and Roy continued living there. Roy suggested that Walt get a job on the railroad; Roy himself had worked two summers as news butcher for the Santa Fe, selling newspapers, cold drinks, fruit and candy to the travelers. Walt applied for a summer job with the Van Noyes Interstate News Company, claiming to be sixteen although he was a year younger. The job required a $15 bond, which Roy supplied from his earnings at the bank.

Walt was outfitted with a blue serge uniform with a badge on the lapel and gold buttons marked "Van Noyes Interstate." At the Van Noyes office in the Kansas City railroad station he picked up hampers packed with fruit, popcorn, peanuts, candy bars and soda pop. His first run was an eight-hour trip from Kansas City to Jefferson City, Missouri, and Walt placed the hampers in the news butcher's position on the two front seats of the smoking car. As the train pulled out of the station, Walt stood on the steps behind the conductor, hoping the youngsters on the platform would admire his uniform.

It was a hot summer day, and Walt found many customers for soda pop in the commuter cars. Instead of walking back to the smoker, he placed the empty bottles in a box at the end of the train. After a couple of hours he returned to collect the bottles. He was dismayed to find the commuter cars had vanished. "Those cars are always detached at Lee's Summit," the conductor explained. Loss of the empty bottles wiped out Walt's first-day profit.

Roy chided his brother for allowing the company to stock his hampers with overripe fruit. Walt sometimes left the hampers unguarded and returned to find candy and cigars missing. Once he sold soda pop to soldiers who filled a tourist car. They amused themselves by hurling the empty bottles from the train. Walt complained to the brakeman, "Those guys threw my bottles out the window!" The brakeman told the top sergeant, who made the soldiers pay for the lost bottles.

The romance of railroading was overwhelming for a fifteen-year-old whose only journeys had been from Chicago to Marceline, and Marceline to Kansas City. He rode the Missouri Pacific, the Kansas City, Southern & Missouri, and the Kansas & Texas lines to towns and cities in a half-dozen states. One of his favorite runs was from Kansas City to Downs, Kansas, a slow, six-hour trip during which the train stopped at every station, sometimes pushing boxcars onto sidings to clear the track. Walt went forward to supply baggagemen with cigars and chewing tobacco, then climbed over the tender to the cab, where the engineer and firemen allowed him to ride for part of the journey. During long stopovers, Walt explored the towns and cities. One day in Downs, where the train turned around and refueled, Walt was strolling past the stores when a policeman accosted him. The boy was accused of surveying the town for a robbery. The officer was unconvinced by Walt's claim of innocence until the train crew verified that the boy was a news butcher.

After all-day runs, Walt stayed overnight in railroad hotels or boarding houses, returning to Kansas City the following day. During a visit to Pueblo, Colorado, he recalled that a friendly salesman had recommended a place to stay. Walt located the address and he was greeted warmly by a motherly woman in a green velvet robe. She asked where he was from and offered to get him a beer. While she was gone, Walt admired the elegant furnishings and gold piano and wondered if the place were priced beyond his means. He heard laughter at the top of the red-carpeted stairs, and a young cowboy and a pretty girl strolled down, arm in arm. Walt suddenly realized he was not in the normal kind of boarding house, and he made a swift exit.

The summer travels had brought a new maturity to Walt, but no profit. The overripe fruit attracted flies, and the conductor made him throw it off the train. The empty bottles continued to disappear, and pilferage from the hampers added to the daily losses. Finally Roy advised, "You'd better give it up, kid. You're not going to get ahead of the game, so you might as well just take your loss." Walt reluctantly agreed. Summer would soon be over, and he would be joining his parents in Chicago to begin high school. Roy took the loss. Walt forfeited to Van Noyes the $15 deposit that his brother had lent him.

4

FROM THE October 1917 issue of *The Voice,* magazine of McKinley High School, Chicago:

> The freshmen are determined to make a great success this year, and from the early results, we may conclude that their boasts and determination have not been asserted in vain. They are already taking part in the vim and excitement of high school life.
>
> Walter Disney, one of the newcomers, has displayed unusual artistic talent, and has become a *Voice* cartoonist. . . .

Walt at last was getting his cartoons published. They were facile and humorous and reflected his own impatience to join the war effort. Roy had enlisted in the Navy, and Walt was envious when his older brother came home from the Great Lakes Naval Training Sta-

tion in his sailor's uniform. Walt had grown as tall as
Roy, but he was still too young to enlist. He inscribed
his cartoons for *The Voice* with such slogans as "Your
Summer Vacation—Work or Fight," and "Buy War
Saving Stamps—Save and Serve." One of his cartoons
showed two slackers scoffing at a doughboy ("Wounded,
hey? Well, that is too bad") while a pair of policemen
threatened, "We'll nab those two loafers when the
soldier leaves 'em." Walt also served as photographer
for *The Voice,* and he studied anatomy, pen technique
and cartooning three nights a week at the Chicago
Institute of Art. Among his teachers were Carey Orr,
cartoonist for the Chicago *Tribune,* and Leroy Gossitt,
of the *Herald,* and Walt was permitted to visit them
at the newspaper offices. He worked long hours over
drawings in his room, never revealing a project until
he completed it.

He began assembling a gag file. He sat for hours in
vaudeville houses, scribbling down jokes for cartoons.
He also copied gags from burlesque comedians at the
Haymarket and the Star and Garter—this was a time
when burlesque offered family entertainment, not the
bawdiness of a later era. Walt compiled the jokes and
tried out the best ones on his father. Elias listened to
them without a smile. Two days later, he would remark
straight-faced to his son, "You know, I've been thinking
about that joke you told me, Walter. It's funny, very
funny."

Elias Disney could not understand his son's fascination with the entertainment world, nor did he sympa-
thize with Walt's ambition to be a cartoonist. But he
agreed to pay for the boy's correspondence courses in
art—as long as Walt contributed to the family income.
Walt worked as handyman in the jelly factory, washing
jars and capping them, mashing apples for pectin, nail-
ing up boxes. One night he served as night watchman,
patrolling the factory with .38-caliber revolver and
flashlight. He turned on all the lights and kept the gun
in his hand so burglars would know he was armed.

The jelly factory paid him only $7 a week, and Walt

quit to work as a guard and gateman on the Wilson Avenue elevated railway line at forty cents an hour. Each afternoon Walt donned his cap and badge and rode the elevated to the terminus in Chicago. If too many gatemen appeared for work, Walt returned home. Usually he was assigned to the rear gate, where he loaded a car with commuters, then rang the bell twice to signal the motorman to leave the station.

When Walt finished his freshman year at McKinley High School in the spring of 1918, he and a friend applied for summer jobs at the post office. The friend lied about his age and was hired, but Walt admitted that he was sixteen and was turned away. He went home and penciled a few lines on his face, borrowed his father's suit and hat, and returned to the same employment window, declaring he was eighteen. He was hired.

Walt worked from twelve to fourteen hours a day, sorting the mail and making special deliveries throughout the city, riding free on streetcars and elevateds. One day the supervisor asked if Walt could drive a truck. "Sure," he replied; he had once driven a two-cylinder Buick in Kansas City. He was assigned to a White truck with four speeds forward and four reverse. Walt lurched through the Chicago streets on his deliveries, but by the time he returned to the garage he had mastered the truck. On Sundays he rode the streetcar to the end of the Grand Avenue pier and collected the mail, mostly postcards from vacationers to the folks back home. Then he took the streetcar to the post-office stables, harnessed a horse, hitched it to a mail wagon, and set out to pick up letters at boxes in front of the downtown hotels. The supervisor warned him: "Now, kid, leave that horse alone. He knows every box, and he knows his way back to the barn. Just keep your hands off the reins."

It was hard to avoid the reins, especially when automobiles sped past the wagon. But the horse seemed to know what to do. At the Rush Street bridge, which rose to allow boats to pass on the river, the horse came to a stop with its chest touching the chain; it waited stolidly for the bridge to lower, then proceeded across. Walt didn't need a route list. The horse halted beside every mailbox, and Walt jumped down to gather up the letters. As soon as he slammed the tailgate of the wagon, the horse began walking forward, and Walt had to run to catch up, stepping on the wheel hub to climb aboard. He realized that the slam was the horse's signal to start, so he learned to ease the tailgate shut, then climb on the wagon and say, "Go on."

The system worked perfectly until Walt reached a big hotel in the downtown Loop. He went inside the lobby to collect the letters, and when he returned to the street, the horse was gone. Walt was in a panic. A horse with a wagonful of mail had disappeared in the busy downtown streets, and he was responsible. He ran to the corners and peered down each block, but there was no sign of the horse. He returned disconsolately to the hotel entrance, then looked through the passageway to the next street. The horse was waiting patiently on the other side. Its routine was to proceed around the block and wait for the mailman to pass through to the other side of the hotel.

One day Walt was sorting letters with his fellow mailmen and joking about how the postal inspectors spied through holes in the wall. He noticed that the other men fell silent, and he turned around to find two uniformed inspectors standing behind him. "Disney, come with us," one of them said. He followed the two inspectors down a long corridor as hundreds of mail sorters watched. The two men took Walt to an office and began their interrogation.

"Two Sundays ago, you picked up a bag of mail at the Grand Avenue pier. What did you do with it?"

"I took it to the post office and put it down the chute."

"No, you didn't. The mail never reached the post office. Tell us what you did with it."

Walt was certain that he had deposited the mail as usual. Finally one of the inspectors said, "We'll tell you what you did with the mail. You hung it on a peg at the stable, and it's been there for two weeks. Now be more careful. And get back to work."

The summer of 1918 was the best that Walt had known. His hours for the post office were long, but there was no drudgery to the work, and he was outdoors most of the time. At night he took girls from McKinley High School to movies and vaudeville shows.

For the first time in his life, Walt had enough money to indulge himself, and he contemplated buying a movie camera or a canoe. A girl friend urged him to buy a canoe, but he decided on the camera. He mounted it on a tripod in an alley and photographed himself in imitations of Charlie Chaplin. To please his friend, he joined another boy in buying an inexpensive canoe; it was so small and unwieldy that he and the girl were swept out into the lake on a windy Sunday.

By late summer, the Allies had stopped the Germans in the second battle of the Marne, and Marshal Foch had ordered a counterattack. Walt grew more impatient to get in uniform, telling his parents, "I don't want my grandchildren asking me, 'Why weren't you in the war? Were you a slacker?'" The Navy had transferred Roy to Charleston, South Carolina, then assigned him to voyages between New York and France. Ray Disney had joined the Army. Walt wanted to take part in the same adventure; he couldn't conceive of returning to high school for another year. A friend at the post office, Russell Maas, shared his feelings. They decided to cross the border and enlist in the Canadian Army, which accepted younger recruits. Their plot was thwarted when Russell's mother discovered his packed suitcase; her son admitted the plan and she warned Flora Disney. One day Russell arrived at the post office and told Walt excitedly, "There's something forming here that you and I can get into. It's a volunteer group called the American Ambulance Corps, part of the Red Cross. They need drivers, and they're not fussy about how old you are."

At noon, the two young men hurried to the headquarters of the American Red Cross. They learned the age limit for ambulance-unit volunteers was seventeen. Both were sixteen, but they falsified their ages and signed up as the St. John brothers, Russell and Walter. The ruse succeeded until the applications for passports, which required their parents' signatures. Walt was forced to disclose his plan to his parents. "I will not sign any permission," Elias Disney declared. "It's signing a death warrant for my son."

Flora Disney argued that three of their sons had left the family home by stealth and she didn't want Walter to go the same way. "The boy is determined," she said. "I would rather sign this and know where he is than have him run off."

"Well, you can sign it for me—I won't!" Elias replied, and he stalked from the room. Flora forged his name on the passport application, and Walt altered his birthdate to read "1900." He and Russell Maas returned to the Red Cross, and their applications were accepted. The two boys received uniforms and reported to a tent encampment at a burned-down amusement park near the University of Chicago. Mechanics from the Yellow Cab Company taught them how to repair motors and drive cars over rough terrain.

An influenza epidemic struck Chicago, and Walt became so sick that he was ordered to a hospital. The ambulance driver asked him, "You live in Chicago, kid?" When Walt said that he did, the driver suggested, "We better take you home. With this flu going on, you'd never come out of a hospital alive." Walt took the advice. Two of his close friends had been taken to the hospital, and they had died the next day.

Flora Disney nursed her son through days of high fever and delirium, giving him poultices and heavy doses of quinine. Because his bedroom had no heat, Walt occupied his parents' room; when little Ruth became ill, her bed was placed beside the kitchen stove. Flora herself caught the influenza, which was killing Chicagoans by the hundreds, but she continued caring for her two children. Finally the fevers broke. Walt regained strength and returned to the Ambulance Corps. He was dismayed to learn that his outfit, including Russell Maas, had shipped out. Walt was assigned to a new unit and sent to Sound Beach, Connecticut, to await passage to France.

November 11, 1918, brought jubilation to the country, but the Red Cross volunteers at Sound Beach greeted the Armistice with ambivalent feelings. The reason for their volunteering had gone and they faced the future as peacetime chauffeurs. They called themselves Coxey's Army, after the ragtag band of unemployed who marched on Washington in 1894, and they grumbled about camp discipline, complaining that they were treated like draftees. Homesickness became endemic. Walt missed his mother's cooking, and he longed to see the girl who had promised to wait for his return.

Early one morning, lights flashed on in the barracks and the awakening volunteers heard a voice shout: "Up everybody! Up everybody! Fifty guys going to France!" A bunkmate shook Walt and said, "Hey, Diz, wake up; they're shipping out fifty guys." Walt replied groggily, "They won't pick me," and he returned to sleep. The fiftieth name called was Walter E. Disney. His companions rolled him out of bed and within an hour he was on the train to Hoboken. That night, November 18, he embarked for France aboard a rusting cattle ship, the *Vaubin*.

The disappointment over the end of the war was now forgotten in the new adventure of crossing the Atlantic on a ship laden with ammunition. Although there was no reason to fear German U-boats, the ship had to pass through waters that had been heavily mined. Disregarding the danger, Walt slept directly over the magazine hatch. As the ship approached France, minesweepers came alongside to provide an escort through the hazardous English Channel. The Red Cross volunteers lined the railing to watch the minesweepers, long booms on each side, patrol the waters, their gun crews scanning the surface for mines. At Cherbourg, huge anti-submarine nets parted to allow the *Vaubin* to enter the port. The ship didn't land, but continued on to Le Havre, arriving December 4. Walt disembarked with his shipmates, and the young Midwesterners toured the waterfront streets wonderingly. Few had been away from their own cities, and they were overwhelmed by the sights of the French seaport. They were astonished by the streetcorner urinals, and none could summon the nerve to use them. But after a day of sightseeing, one of the Americans could wait no longer. He stepped cautiously up to the *pissoir,* and his companions followed.

Members of the American Ambulance Corps trooped to the railroad station for the trip to Paris. Walt was fascinated to see how small the French engines seemed in comparison to those he had known in his summer as a news butcher. He stared out the window on the journey through the French countryside, noticing the high hedges and the groves of poplars that separated the small farms.

Paris still looked like a city at war. As he rode a taxi down the Champs Élysées, he saw the sidewalks filled with men in uniform. Sandbags still protected the monuments of the Étoile, and gun carts rattled through the streets. Walt had only a brief tour of the city before reporting to the American Ambulance Corps headquarters at St. Cyr, site of the French military academy. St. Cyr was a disappointment after the enticements of Paris. The volunteers were billeted in a chateau so dank and chill that Walt wrapped himself in newspapers before going to sleep on his cot. The food was dismal—mostly pork and beans. When December 5 arrived, Walt faced a grim seventeenth birthday.

Late in the afternoon he stopped by the canteen and found only one friend there. "Come on over to the bistro and I'll buy you a grenadine," the friend said. The pair walked to the nearby café and discovered it was deserted. As soon as they closed the door, Walt's friends emerged from under tables and behind counters shouting "Happy birthday, Diz!' All crowded to the bar and ordered grenadine, wine and cognac. They slapped Walt on the back and downed their drinks, leaving him to pay the bill. He emptied his money belt, but that was not enough. Walt had to sell his extra pair of Red Cross shoes for 30 francs.

Walt was transferred from St. Cyr to Evacuation Hospital 5 in Paris. First he drove five-ton trucks and ambulances converted into small cars by cutting off the back end. Then he was assigned to the motor pool— in reality, a taxi service for Army officers. He soon learned the geography of Paris, driving majors and colonels to various headquarters, hospitals, legations and, on occasion, bordellos.

Headquarters assigned Walt to drive a white truck loaded with beans and sugar to the devastated area of Soissons. He selected an assistant and set off through the Paris suburbs and into the French countryside. After he had passed through a village, the motor started to clank. The noise grew louder, and the chassis vibrated with the pounding of the engine. Finally, with a great rattling sound, the engine halted, and Walt coasted around a corner, parking off the road near a railway watchman's shack. Walt suspected that the truck had thrown a rod; no amount of tinkering would induce it to start again. He remembered the Red Cross driver's credo: Never leave your vehicle. So he dispatched the assistant back to the village to ride a train to Paris to bring help. Walt resigned himself to a long wait in the February cold.

He stayed in the cab for a few hours, but as night fell his feet grew numb from the cold. In his hesitant French he asked the railroad watchman if he could share the tiny shack. The watchman agreed, welcoming the young American's offer of the truck's emergency rations—bread, cheese, tinned beef and chocolate. Walt dozed through the night in the four-feet-square shack, enjoying the warmth of a tiny stove, to which the watchman added a lump of coal every half-hour. The next day brought no help from Paris, and Walt spent another night before the small stove. On the third day he was so hungry and so numbingly tired that he walked to the village inn and ordered a meal and a bed. When the meal arrived, there was a cockroach among the lamb chops and peas; Walt merely pushed it off the plate, swallowed the food and fell asleep on the bed.

He awoke in a panic, discovering that he had slept for twenty-four hours. He raced back to the railroad crossing and discovered to his horror that his truck was gone. He trudged back to the village, dreading the consequences when he returned to Paris. A freight train arrived, and the trainman allowed him to ride in the cupola on one of the cars. When Walt arrived at headquarters, he discovered what had happened. His assistant had enjoyed a two-day drunk before reporting the breakdown. The disabled truck was towed back to Paris, its cargo intact. Disney faced serious charges of abandoning his truck. A friendly sergeant from Evacuation Hospital 5 appeared before a board of officers and argued that the young driver had done all that was physically possible by remaining near his truck for two nights. The board agreed, and no discipline was imposed. The errant assistant landed in the guardhouse.

Americans continued leaving France in the postwar months, and little work remained for the Red Cross motor pool. Disney was reassigned to a canteen at Neufchateau, near Nancy. During long hours of idleness, Walt got out his pad and pencil and began cartooning. He mailed cartoons to *Life* and *Judge,* America's two leading humor magazines; all were returned with polite, printed notes of rejection. Composing a letter to his high school magazine, he illustrated it with a self-portrait and impressions of soldiers and prisoners-of-war he had seen. He drew posters for the canteen and caricatures for the soldiers to send home, and he decorated the canvas top of his ambulance with an alluring female. Borrowing a Croix de Guerre from a French officer, he painted a replica of the medal on his jacket; others at the canteen admired it and paid him to do the same on their jackets. He teamed up with an enterprising Georgian who had established a souvenir industry. The Georgian realized the desire of homeward-bound doughboys to collect mementoes of the war—especially those soldiers who had seen no combat. When the troop trains stopped at Neufchateau to change engines, he went down the aisles selling German helmets he had collected on battlefields. One day he noticed that Walt had painted his footlocker in camouflage colors. "Hey, Diz, can you paint me a sniper's helmet?" asked the entrepreneur. Walt obliged, and he aged the helmets with quick-drying shellac, earning five francs apiece. The Georgian rubbed the helmets in the dirt, shot holes in them, attached hair to the jagged edges, and sold them on the troop trains at inflated prices.

Walt mailed the profits from his enterprise to his mother, along with half of his monthly salary of $52. One day he entered a barracks crap game and emerged with $300. He hurried to the American Express office and dispatched the money to his mother with instructions to buy his sister Ruth a watch and bank the rest.

A dozen years later, Walt reminisced about the days at Neufchateau in a letter to Alice Howell, a Nebraska woman who operated the Red Cross canteen:

. . . Just in case you can't place me, I will try to give you a brief outline of the work I did. I was the chauffeur of the canteen car. It was my duty to hang around the canteen all day and run errands. I used to drive the girls back and forth from the canteen to their quarters, take them into the country to buy eggs, drive them to the Army commissary for supplies and occasionally on picnics. My main hangout was the little shanty attached to the canteen where the bread was cut. . . .

You will perhaps remember the time that General Pershing sent [his son] Warren down to spend the day with you and we all got into the little car I drove and went up to Domrimi [Domrémy], Joan of Arc's birthplace, and had a wonderful

picnic with fried chicken and all sorts of good
things to eat. And boy! how good that fried chicken
tasted!

I remember some of the boys from the Second
Cavalry who used to be around the canteen, and
I also remember the squad of German prisoners
who worked in the shower rooms. I especially
remember one of the prisoners whom I liked real
well, I believe his name was Rupert. I remember
how they used to play tricks on me to get me to
buy things for them.

One day Rupert came to me with an empty
wine bottle in his hand and gave me some money
saying that Miss Howell wanted me to buy her
some wine. Unsuspectingly I carried out his orders,
although all the time wondering how it happened
Miss Howell wanted me to buy her wine. When I
returned Rupert was waiting for me and insisted
that he take the wine to you. I did not think any
more about it until about half an hour later when I
went in the shower rooms. I found all the German
prisoners having a great time on that bottle of
wine. That was only one of the pranks Rupert
and his gang played on me. . . .

When the prisoners went on work crews, Walt and
Rupert sat in the canteen car and talked about the war
and the future of Germany. They became good friends
and helped each other in finding ways to relieve the daily
tedium. One day they drove to the outskirts of a village,
where the prisoners loaded cordwood onto trucks.
Schoolchildren strolled by on their way from school.
They had never seen German soldiers before, and they
started throwing rocks. Walt told Rupert, who spoke
fluent French, to order the children to stop. They
persisted, and on Walt's suggestion, the prisoners filled
their pockets with rocks. When the schoolchildren
ignored a second order to stop, Walt called, "Rupert,
charge!" The prisoners loosed a fusillade of rocks and
chased the children into the village.

Walt was assigned to chauffeur two dignitaries on a tour of the Rhine country, and before leaving he consulted the village priest on what to see. He gained a reputation as an expert guide, and he drove other visitors through France and Germany. On one trip he arrived in Strasbourg on July 14, 1919, to witness the first Bastille Day celebration in fifty years for the recaptured city.

In August the Neufchateau canteen was disbanded, and Walt was transferred to Paris. He found the city changed. The uniforms were disappearing, and the tempo and attitudes of Parisians were returning to normal. Walt found that the American Ambulance Corps headquarters at St. Cyr had been shut down, and his friends in the organization had departed. The Red Cross issued a call for ambulance drivers for a war in Albania, and Walt was tempted by the salary of $150 a month, more than he had ever earned. Then he encountered Russell Maas, the Chicago boy with whom he had joined the Red Cross. They talked of home, and over French coffee and cognac they concocted a scheme to build a raft and float down the Mississippi like a pair of Huck Finns. Both had bought German shepherd puppies, and they agreed the dogs would join them on the voyage. Russell was returning to America immediately, and Walt paid $75 for his dog to go with Russell.

The two young men from Chicago visited a photographic studio in Paris and posed for postcards to send to their friends and family back home. The two photographs afford a character study of the seventeen-year-old Walt Disney. In one, he appears in overseas cap, khaki uniform with jodhpurs and leggings, his heavy overcoat draped casually over his arm. He is bemused and proud. Then he posed in battle helmet, looking like the doughboy he had wanted to be. He is grimly serious, dedicated, a traveler of the world. There can be no doubt what Walt intended the photographs to accomplish: to let those at home know that he had grown to manhood in France.

On September 3, 1919, General Pershing and his staff departed from Paris, and other American units followed. The American Ambulance Corps was finally disbanded, and the remaining volunteers were dispatched to Marseilles for passage home. When Walt Disney and his companions reached the dock, they found their ship floating high in the harbor; a dock strike prevented loading. The unit was ordered to Nice until the strike was solved, and for three weeks, Walt lived a splendid life at a Riviera resort. Then the strike ended, and Walt boarded the ship at Marseilles for the voyage back to America and the start of his career.

5

A YEAR in France had been a heady experience for a Midwesterner not yet eighteen, and Walt Disney landed in New York brimming with hope and optimism. He was stimulated by the size and energy of Manhattan, and he wandered the streets with unabashed awe of the high buildings. Among the delights he found in New York were two new comedies of Charlie Chaplin. Walt hurried home to Chicago, and like many other young men returning from overseas, he saw his hopes turn to ashes. He had brought French laces and perfume to the girl who had promised to wait for him; but she had married three months before. When Walt visited Russell Maas to claim his German shepherd, he learned the dog had died of distemper. Russell had acquired a job and a girl friend and had lost all interest in a voyage down the Mississippi.

Elias and Flora Disney were astonished at the change in their youngest son. He had grown to five feet ten inches, and he was broad-shouldered and husky at 165 pounds. He had matured in other ways. His outlook was worldly—too much so for his father's taste. But Walt could still be boyishly playful, as when he described to his believing mother the huge Prudential Insurance sign he had seen atop Gibraltar as his ship passed through the strait. He showed her a small box which he said contained a battlefield souvenir. She shrieked when he opened it. Inside was a bloody human thumb, in reality Walt's own, painted with iodine and stuck through the back of the box.

A return to high school was unthinkable after Walt's European experiences. Nor would he consider a job his father offered at the jelly factory for the handsome salary of $25 a week. "Dad, I don't want that kind of job," Walt insisted. Elias reminded him that thousands of unemployed veterans would welcome such a position, but Walt remained firm.

"Then what do you want to do, Walter?" the father asked.

"I want to be an artist," Walt replied.

"And how do you expect to make a living as an artist?" Elias asked.

"I don't know," Walt admitted.

He knew that he didn't want to remain in Chicago; the city seemed noisy and dirty and unappealing. He decided to return to Kansas City. Roy had gone there after his discharge from the Navy at Seattle in February 1919. Walt wanted to see his boyhood friends, and he was convinced that the Kansas City *Star* would hire him as a political cartoonist. Against his father's wishes, Walt packed all his belongings, including the Red Cross uniform, and boarded a train for Kansas City.

Walt and Roy Disney had a joyful reunion at the Disney house on Bellefontaine Street, and the brothers talked until early morning about their adventures overseas. Roy was working as a teller for the First National Bank of Kansas City at a salary of $90 a month. He was hoping for an advancement so he could marry

Edna Francis, sister of Mitchell Francis, who had gone
into the Navy with Roy and worked in the same bank.
Walt told Roy of his plans to become a political cartoonist, and he displayed drawings he had done in
France.

He packed up the drawings and went to the offices
of the *Star,* where he was curtly informed that there
were no openings for a cartoonist. Walt decided he
would work his way up through the ranks, and he
answered an advertisement for a copy boy at the *Star,*
wearing his Red Cross uniform to lend him maturity.
It worked too well, and he was told he was too old
for the job. Walt protested that he was only eighteen,
but the employment man was unhearing. He cited Walt's
experience as a Red Cross driver and suggested that
he apply for work in the transportation department. "I
want to be a cartoonist, not a driver," Walt replied.
He took his cartoon samples to the Kansas City
Journal and drew a favorable reaction from the editor,
Lawrence Dickey. But the *Journal* had no immediate
need for another cartoonist.

Walt reported his disappointments to Roy, who tried
to persuade his brother to seek more practical employment. Roy mentioned his brother's plight to another
bank worker, who told him of two commercial artists
who were seeking an apprentice. Roy telephoned his
brother and told him to apply at the Pesmen-Rubin
Commercial Art Studio in the Gray Advertising Building. Walt hurried downtown and met Louis Pesmen and
Bill Rubin, who were impressed with the young man's
eager manner. They asked him to return with samples
of his art work, and he showed them his sketches of
Parisian streets. Pesmen and Rubin told him to report
for work the following day, the salary to be determined later.

The new employee was assigned to create rough
drawings of advertisements and letterheads for farm
equipment and supply companies. The first job was
for a firm that sold egg-laying mash, and Walt sketched
hens on nests, eggs overflowing nests, hens hatching

dollar signs. Lou Pesmen, who taught night school at
the Fine Arts Institute, had noted that most young
artists resented criticism. Not Disney. One day he was
working on a layout for the Carey Salt Company,
drawing cows licking salt blocks. Pesmen looked over
his shoulder, erased some lines, added others, and
Walt welcomed the changes. At the end of the week,
the two partners announced that their new assistant
would be paid $50 a month. "That'll do fine," said
Walt, not looking up from his work. When he reported
the news to Roy, he admitted he would have accepted
half that amount.

Walt was eager to please his new employers. Pesmen
designed covers for the weekly program of the Newman
Theater, and he instructed Walt to finish the art work
on the front cover. It was a job that normally would
have required a day, but Walt finished both the front
and back covers in three hours, adding original touches
of his own. He was assigned to the art work for the
Newman Theater newspaper advertisements, and years
later in an advertising conference at his Burbank studio,
he recalled one of his contributions: "The Newman
was playing a Cecil B. DeMille picture, *Male and
Female,* and all I had to work with was a standing
photo of the stars, Gloria Swanson and Thomas
Meighan. Well, I thought it would make a better ad if
they were lying down, and that's how I drew them."

A co-worker at Pesmen-Rubin was a stolid young
Dutchman with the curious name of Ubbe Iwwerks.
The son of a Dutch immigrant, he was the same age
as Walt; like Walt, Ubbe had left high school before
graduating. Ubbe had worked for a bank-note company
and on a farm, then was hired by Pesmen-Rubin in
the fall of 1919 to do lettering and airbrush work.
When Walt Disney arrived a month later, the two
eighteen-year-olds became friends. Walt showed Ubbe
the lettering samples he had executed when he was
hired. Most applicants lettered the alphabet, but Walt
had written variations of his own name: "Walter Disney, W. E. Disney, Walt Disney, Walter Elias Disney."

He asked Ubbe which one seemed best. "Walt Disney," said Ubbe, and Walt agreed.

Both young men turned out a large volume of art work for farm catalogues and Christmas ads for department stores and theaters. Then the pre-holiday rush ended, and both Walt and Ubbe were let go. Walt applied for work with the post office, and he delivered mail until after New Year's.

Walt and Ubbe Iwwerks (he later shortened his name to Ub Iwerks) discussed going into business for themselves. Walt Pfeiffer, Walt's boyhood pal and co-performer, persuaded his father to hire the two artists to design lettering for the United Leatherworkers' *Journal*. Walt searched for other business, and he called on a former neighbor, Al Carder, who edited a trade publication, the *Restaurant News*. Carder said he didn't have enough work to keep the two young artists busy, but he offered them a couple of desks in his office in return for an occasional design. Walt saw this as a chance to begin his and Ub's enterprise. He wrote his mother to send him the $500 he had earned as a Red Cross worker and sometime crap-shooter in France. His mother insisted on knowing why he wanted the money. He replied that he was going into business, adding that it was his savings and he could do what he wanted with it. After more exchanges of letters, she sent him half the amount.

The partners intended to call their enterprise "Disney-Iwerks." But when they put up the listing in the lobby of the Railroad Exchange Building, they discovered it sounded too much like an optical firm. So it became Iwerks-Disney Commercial Artists. Iwerks did the straight drawing and lettering; Disney was the cartoonist and salesman. He hustled around to print shops, theaters, stores and oil companies in search of work. The first month's business netted $135, more than they had been receiving at Pesmen-Rubin.

The Iwerks-Disney firm lasted only a month. On January 29, 1920, Ub spotted an advertisement in the Kansas City *Star:*

ARTIST
CARTOON AND WASH DRAWINGS
FIRST CLASS MAN WANTED
Steady, Kansas City Slide Company
1015 Central

Ub discussed the ad with Walt, and both agreed that Walt should apply for the job. He reported for an interview with the head of the Kansas City Slide Company, A. Vern Cauger, at the firm's office on Central Street. Cauger was impressed with the young man's cartoons and offered him a position at $40 a week. Walt was overwhelmed by the salary, but he had hoped to work part-time while he and Ub continued their new enterprise. Cauger insisted he wanted a full-time cartoonist. Walt discussed the matter with his partner, and Ub urged him to take the job. "I can manage the business," Ub assured him. But he was not outgoing enough to be a salesman, and the business quickly dwindled. In March 1920, Walt persuaded Cauger to hire Ub, and Iwerks-Disney went into limbo.

After Walt had been working a few weeks at the slide company—which had moved to 2449 Charlotte with the new name of Kansas City Film Ad Company —he received a call from Lawrence Dickey of the *Journal*. The newspaper needed a cartoonist, and Walt could have the job. If the offer had come earlier, the course of his career might have proved far different. But Walt had been introduced to something that intrigued him more than newspaper cartooning. He declined the *Journal*'s offer.

Now he was making cartoons that moved. Kansas City Film Ad produced one-minute advertising films to appear in motion-picture theaters. The animation was primitive: human and animal figures were cut out of paper and pinned to a sheet; the joints of the figures were moved and photographed, creating the illusion of movement. The artists made their cutouts and gave them to the cameraman with an outline of the action;

each department was jealous of its own secrets and declined to share them. But Walt was curious to learn how things worked. He made friends with the cameraman, Jimmy Lowerre, who showed the young cartoonist how the paper figures were photographed in stopmotion to provide the illusion of animation. Soon Lowerre permitted Walt to operate the camera himself.

Walt wasn't satisfied with such a crude method of animation. He noted how the New York–made movie cartoons like the Mutt and Jeff and Koko the Klown series moved with greater realism. They were created with drawings, not cut-outs, and Walt was determined to learn how. He found two books in the Kansas City public library, one a simple handbook by Carl Lutz on the essentials of animation, the other Eadweard Muybridge's classic study of human and animal motion. Walt pored over Muybridge's photographs of running horses and athletes in movement, then had the pages copied by a photostat firm. He returned the book to the library and kept the stack of photostats beside his desk as a guide for his drawing. His employers were delighted with the improved realism of the drawn cartoons, and he and Ub began turning them out for Film Ad.

Walt was dissatisfied with the material given to him by the Film Ad copywriters, and he began injecting gags of his own. In an ad for a bank, he depicted a man floating down a river on a raft with the catchline "You can't drift through your life." For another bank he drew a locomotive chasing a cow—"You'll never get anywhere until you get on the right savings track." For a maker of canvas car covers he showed an automobile with a sparkling top. The dialogue between owner and friend: "Hi, old top—new car?" "No, old car—new top."

The Film Ad company made live-action movies as well as cartoons, and Walt portrayed paint salesmen or garage mechanics in the films. When an automobile careened down a nearby hill and crashed onto its side in front of the Film Ad office, a resourceful film maker grabbed a camera and shouted, "Come on, Diz, follow me!" Walt hurried outside and climbed into the over-turned car. The cameraman spun the wheel and threw some dust in the air as the dazed young man emerged from the accident. The film became an ad for an insurance company.

Walt and Roy Disney were living with their brother Herbert and his wife in the house their parents still owned at 3028 Bellefontaine. Both young men often visited the home of Roy's sweetheart, Edna Francis, arriving conveniently at mealtime. During the meal, and often into the night, Walt talked about his work at Film Ad and his plans to advance beyond advertising films into something more rewarding.

The young artist was developing a style. While his vocabulary was unpolished and he sometimes used barracks language, he could express himself surprisingly well, especially when he was relating a fable or gag sequence he planned to draw. Now that he was earning a steady salary, he could afford to dress with a flair. Photographs show him as a young man in jaunty tweed cap, trim double-breasted dark suit with gray vest, his four-in-hand neatly tied. He is swinging a golf club in a city park, and clowning in a statue pose atop a giant urn, a cigar clamped in the side of his mouth. Then he appears at the Kansas City Artists Ball in full Western regalia, looking as handsome as a Hollywood cowboy. He was full-grown at almost six feet and had no trouble getting dates with the girls who worked for Film Ad.

Walt's ingenuity distinguished his work at Film Ad —and sometimes covered up his lack of draftsmanship. Assigned to a theater commercial for a hat company, he realized that he couldn't draw the handsome faces ordinarily seen in hat ads. Instead he drew comic faces under the hats, and they delighted Cauger, and theater audiences as well. Walt wanted to do his own experi-menting, and he asked Cauger for the loan of one of the company's stop-action cameras. Cauger resisted at first, but Walt continued asking him, and he gave in. Walt enlisted Roy to help rig a makeshift studio in the family garage. Working past midnight every night, Walt experimented with incandescent lights, called "inkies," until he achieved the best exposure for his drawings.

He needed a subject that would capture local attention, and he decided to exploit the anger of Kansas City citizens over the poor repair of city streets. In the hyperbolic style that marked his early cartooning, he depicted drivers' losing their teeth when striking ruts, trucks disappearing into gaping holes. He wanted to photograph his own hand making the drawings, in the manner of the Out of the Inkwell cartoons. But he couldn't fit his hand under the camera. So he made a photograph of his hand and moved the photograph under the camera to create the illusion that he was drawing.

Walt completed three hundred feet of cartoon and took the film to the Newman Theater Company, which owned three movie houses in Kansas City. "I like it, kid," said the manager, Milton Feld. "I can use one every week. How much do they cost?" Walt calculated his expenses and replied, "Thirty cents a foot." Feld agreed to pay that amount, and Walt left the office elated—until he realized that the thirty-cent figure did not provide any margin for profit.

Walt worked all day at Film Ad, then spent hours each night in his garage studio. Feld gave him suggestions for new cartoons—a theater anniversary, a political campaign, a Christmas program. Feld asked Walt's help with a bothersome problem for theaters —patrons who bothered their neighbors by reading aloud the titles for the silent movies. Walt created a comical professor who slammed a mallet on the head of title readers, or released a trapdoor that chuted them to the street.

Walt named the films Newman Laugh-O-Grams. A few of them have survived, and they show surprising skill in an artist so new to animation. The cartoonist's hand skims over the paper, seeming to make the droll drawings in lightning speed. As his knowledge of cartooning grew, Walt introduced real animation. "Kansas City's Spring Cleanup," obviously based on one of the city's periodic police scandals, shows a parade of policemen marching into headquarters. Signs of a struggle come from within, then bodies fly out. A man exits from the building to hang a sign: "Cops Wanted." There can be no doubt that the scandal-weary Kansas City audience reacted with applause.

The Newman Laugh-O-Grams began making a minor celebrity of Walt Disney. When he met friends from Benton School, they remarked about seeing his films. His boss at Film Ad was proud of Walt's achievements and always introduced the young man to important visitors. Cauger asked to borrow the Laugh-O-Grams to show his company's offices in other cities what could be done with cartoons for theaters. Walt had been urging Cauger to buy sheets of celluloid so the staff could copy the methods of the New York cartoon studios. Walt ordered a hundred new celluloids. The purchasing agent changed the order to cheap discards, and they arrived scratched and ink-stained, but Walt and his fellow workers cleaned each one with solvent and soft cloths. For Walt it was a thrill finally to make cartoons on celluloid, as all the important New York cartoonists did. His vision grew. "Why don't we make a series of cartoon shorts to sell to theaters?" he proposed to Cauger. The company owner rejected the suggestion. Film Ad had a thriving business of selling advertising movies to theaters throughout the Midwest; he saw no reason to attempt something new and risky.

Roy Disney had proved himself a steady, conscientious worker at the First National Bank, and his salary had increased enough to allow him and Edna Francis to talk seriously about getting married. During 1920, Roy suffered two serious attacks of influenza, and his doctor recommended removal of his tonsils. His brother Herb suggested a surgeon who would perform the oper-

ation during Roy's lunch hour at the bank. Roy had
the surgery done one noon and returned to his job.
His throat hemorrhaged, and Mitchell Francis rushed
him home. Afterward, X rays detected a spot on Roy's
lungs; it was tuberculosis. The Veterans Administration assigned him to a hospital at Santa Fe, New
Mexico. It was a tearful parting for Roy and Edna.
Five years would pass before they could marry.

Again Elias Disney failed. His investment in the
jelly factory disappeared in bankruptcy, and the company president was imprisoned for fraud. Again Elias
sought to improve his fortune by moving on. He and
Flora returned to Kansas City, where he sought work as
a carpenter. Elias found the garage of the Bellefontaine house taken over by Walt's contraptions. Elias
didn't understand why his son wasted his time on such
things, but he allowed Walt to continue using the
garage, for a rental of $5 a month.

Elias found little work in a housing industry hit by
the postwar slump. He helped one of Flora's relatives
build a house in Glendale, California, but decided
against moving there because the country was too arid.
The postal service had transferred Herb to Portland,
Oregon, and he urged his parents to join him. Elias
decided they would, and in November 1921, he and
Flora and Ruth left Kansas City by train. Walt went
to the station for their departure, and Ruth noticed
tears forming in his eyes. He said his goodbyes and
left abruptly.

New owners moved into the Bellefontaine house, and
Walt shifted his belongings to a rooming house. His
enterprise had outgrown the garage, and he now rented
a small shop. He could no longer do all the work himself, and he advertised for boys who wanted to learn the
cartoon business. Three applied, and Walt conducted
night school in the tiny shop, teaching the elements
of cartooning. He told the boys he couldn't afford to
pay them, but he promised they would share in future
profits of the enterprise, for which he confidently predicted success.

To achieve that sucess, Laugh-O-Grams needed to progress beyond the one-minute program filler. The next step would be cartoon shorts like those produced by the New York studios. He devised plans for a series of cartoons based on traditional fairy tales, modernized and sprinkled with gags. For six months Walt and his youthful film makers worked at night on their first production, *Little Red Riding Hood.*

Walt was so pleased with the cartoon that he quit his position at Film Ad, where he had been earning an impressive $60 a week. On May 23, 1922, he incorporated Laugh-O-Gram Films with $15,000 from local investors who contributed from $250 to $500 apiece. The new firm's capital equipment included three inker's and tracer's tables, seven chairs, three animating booths, one cabinet, superintendent's desk, projector, winder, electric fan, eight hundred feet of positive film, one still camera, movie camera and stand, lighting equipment and copying stand.

Walt persuaded Ub Iwerks to leave Film Ad, and Laugh-O-Gram Films took over the remaining assets of Iwerks-Disney Commercial Artists. They were joined by five other young animators—Hugh Harman, Rudolf Ising, Carman Maxwell, Lorey Tague, Otto Walliman —as well as a business manager, a girl who inked and painted the celluloids, a salesman and a secretary. All worked in a five-room suite on the second floor of the McConahay Building at 31st Street and Forest.

Laugh-O-Gram started production of a series of fairy-tale films following the pattern of *Little Red Riding Hood.* The salesman went to New York to hunt for buyers, and he made a releasing deal with a non-theatrical distribution company, Pictorial Clubs. The company sent a check for $100 and a note promising $11,000 for six cartoons. The workers at Laugh-O-Gram were jubilant, and Walt put five additional subjects into production—*The Four Musicians of Bremen, Jack and the Beanstalk, Goldilocks and the Three Bears, Puss in Boots,* and *Cinderella.*

The Laugh-O-Gram office was an exhilarating place

to work. The president of the company was twenty
years old, and he declined to act the role of executive.
He did some of the animation, operated the cameras,
washed the celluloid sheets—"cels"—for reuse. Many
of his employees were still in their teens, and they
shared his zest for the cartoon medium, often working
past midnight. They were unconcerned when they received only half of their salaries on weeks when the
company treasury was low. On Sundays they joined
Walt in Swope Park on the roof of their office building
and acted out the charade of filming a melodrama.

Walt had bought a Universal camera for $300 and
it saw multiple duty. On weekends, Walt mounted it
on the rear seat of a touring car and rode through the
downtown Kansas City streets cranking the camera, his
cap turned backward like a Hollywood cameraman. A
sign on the car read: "These pictures will be shown at
the Isis Theater tomorrow night." Walt contracted with
the Jenkins Music Company to make a film illustrating
the song "Martha," and he took three girls from the
office to a nearby woods to film a sequence. He delighted in playing the director, complete with mega-
phone.

He used the camera as Kansas City correspondent for
Selznick, Pathé and Universal newsreels. When the
New York offices telegraphed Disney with special assignments, cartoon filming ceased. Walt removed the
camera from the cartoon stand, picked up a tripod and
hurried out to photograph a news event. He rode the
streetcar to an automobile lot, rented a Ford motoring
car and placed a press sticker on the windshield. He
received an important assignment to cover the American Legion convention, which was being attended by
Vice President Coolidge, Marshal Foch and General
Pershing. The father of a schoolfriend owned the
building across the street from the reviewing stand, and
Walt carried his camera to the roof. It was a perfect
vantage point to film the dignitaries and the parade.
Payment for such assignments was $1 for a foot of
film—usually one hundred feet ordered. If the news-

reel did not use the film, the equivalent amount in unexposed negatives was returned to him.

Walt was convinced he could sell newsreel footage of airplane acrobatics, and he persuaded a couple of barnstorming pilots to perform for him. Walt consulted a cameraman friend on how to photograph in the air. He was told to "stop down all you can—limit the exposure to the barest minimum." Walt took his camera up in one of the planes and photographed some daring stunts. When his film was developed, it was totally dark except for a white doughnut caused by the whirring propeller. He had "stopped down" too far.

The camera was also used in taking baby pictures for proud Kansas City parents. That part of the enterprise resulted in publicity from the newspaper that Walt had once delivered, the Kansas City *Star:*

> The Laugh-O-Gram Films Company, Inc., 1127 East Thirty-First Street, has added the feature of photographing youngsters to its regular business of making animated cartoons. An admiring parent wishing to preserve the native graces of his progeny's actions notifies "Walt" Disney, president of the corporation and head cartoonist for the animated cartoons. The company furnishes a projector service with its filming, which provides that a private showing be made in the home— three showings for each hundred feet of film.

By the autumn of 1922, it was becoming more and more difficult for the youthful film makers to maintain their exuberance. The fairy-tale cartoons were being shipped off to Pictorial Clubs, but no money returned. Under the contract no payment was required until six months after signing, and by that time Pictorial Clubs had gone bankrupt. For producing the half-dozen seven-minute cartoons, Laugh-O-Grams had been paid only the deposit—$100.

With salary checks growing thinner, Laugh-O-Gram employees began to drop out. Ub Iwerks left the company to return to Film Ad. In late November, Walt persuaded his principal backer, Dr. Cowles, to supply an additional $2,500 to satisfy the company's major creditors. Walt found himself unable to pay his rooming bill, and for a couple of weeks he roomed with Ub Iwerks. Then Walt took up lodging in the Laugh-O-Gram offices—the rent had been paid in advance. Like others in the office, he ate on credit at the Forest Inn Cafe downstairs, operated by a pair of Greeks, Jerry Raggos and Louis Katsis. Since the offices had no bath, Walt made a weekly journey to the railroad station, where he bought a warm tub, a towel and a bar of soap for a dime. After the bath he stood on the platform where he had seen his parents, his sister and Roy depart for the West. He couldn't avoid tears as he watched the passengers leaving for other towns and cities. "It was so lonesome," he recalled in later years.

One day in December a local dentist, Thomas B. McCrum, paid a call to the Laugh-O-Gram office to inquire about a film to promote dental health. He was surprised to find that young Disney was the only person in the office, but they discussed the film and agreed on a fee of $500. In later years Walt liked to tell the story of how Dr. McCrum telephoned one evening and asked Walt to come to his house to complete the deal. Walt said that he couldn't. He confessed that his only pair of shoes was at the cobbler and he didn't have the $1.50 to redeem them. The dentist came to the office and gave him money for the shoes and an agreement for the dental-health film.

Walt hired back some of his Laugh-O-Gram workers for *Tommy Tucker's Tooth,* and the unexpected revenue recharged his ambition. He searched for another subject to put Laugh-O-Gram back in business. He had admired the Out of the Inkwell cartoons produced by Max Fleischer, in which cartoon figures animated on the drawing boards of artists. Why not reverse the technique and put a human figure in a cartoon world? He devised the idea of *Alice's Wonderland,* in which a real girl would act out adventures amid cartoon figures. He hired Virginia Davis, a winsome six-year-old model with Mary Pickford curls, and photographed her against a plain backdrop, devising a storyline that would be drawn later. He sent off enthusiastic letters to distributors in New York. One letter, dated May 14, 1923, went to a woman named M. J. Winkler who distributed Out of the Inkwell and other cartoons:

> We have just discovered something new and clever in animated cartoons!
>
> The first subject of this distinctly different series is now in production, and will require a few weeks more for completion. It is a new idea that will appeal to all classes, and is bound to be a winner, because it is a clever combination of live characters and cartoons, not like *Out of the Inkwell* or Earl Hurd's but of an entirely different nature, using a cast of live child actors who carry on their action on cartoon scenes with cartoon characters.
>
> These new subjects will be a full reel in length, and can be released at regular intervals of two weeks or a month. . . .

Disney suggested that Miss Winkler see Laugh-O-Gram's previous cartoons for Pictorial Clubs as an example of the company's work. She replied with an encouraging letter, and Walt began production. But his resources dwindled further. Dr. Cowles advanced him an occasional $10. Roy, who had moved from Santa Fe to another hospital in Tucson, sent Walt a blank check with instructions to fill it out in any amount up to $30. Walt wrote it for $30.

The money soon disappeared, and Walt's bill at the Greek restaurant continued to mount. When it reached $60 Jerry said his partner wouldn't allow him to extend any more credit. Two days later, Jerry went up to the Laugh-O-Gram office and found Walt sitting on a box and eating beans out of a can. "Oh, Walter," said the Greek, "I don't care what my partner says. You go downstairs and get something to eat."

With *Alice's Wonderland* half finished, Walt found himself completely out of funds. Walt went to his early

investors and asked them to help keep Laugh-O-Gram
in business; but they had already resigned themselves to
losing their money and saw no reason to throw away
more. On June 18, Walt dispatched a brave letter to
Miss Winkler:

> Owing to numerous delays and backsets we have
> encountered in moving into our new office, we will
> not be able to complete the first picture of our new
> series by the time we expected.
>
> However, it will be finished very soon, and the
> writer expects to be in New York about the first
> of July with a print of the same, and an outline
> for our future program. . . .

Unable to pay the rent at the McConahay Building,
Walt moved to smaller quarters. But there was no way
to continue. He described his situation in a letter to
Roy, who had moved to a veterans' hospital at Sawtelle,
west of Los Angeles. Roy replied, "Kid, I think you
should get out of there. I don't think you can do any
more for it." Walt resigned himself to bankruptcy.
When settlement was made years later, the creditors
received 45 percent of their claims. A modest income
had been received from the successors to the Pictorial
Clubs.

Another cartoon maker in Kansas City offered Walt
a job. But he wanted to leave the scene of his failure,
and to leave the cartoon business as well. Instead of
heading for New York, where the cartoon studios were
centered, he was going to Hollywood, where he planned
to become a director. His only problem was raising the
railroad fare. He went door to door photographing
babies, then sold his camera and bought a one-way
ticket to California.

He left Kansas City in July, wearing a checkered coat
and unmatching pants. He had $40 in cash, and his
imitation-leather suitcase contained only a shirt, two
undershorts, two pairs of socks and some drawing
materials. But when he paid his fare for the trip to
California, he bought a first-class ticket.

II

THE
CARTOON
MAKER

1923-1934

6

BY 1923, when Walt Disney arrived with his half-filled suitcase, Hollywood had become a company town. It had been scarcely a decade since movie makers started arriving in California, and now films were approaching the status of an industry. Mammoth studios had risen from the lemon groves of Hollywood, and others had grown up in Culver City and over the Cahuenga Pass in the San Fernando Valley. Walt set up residence with his uncle, Robert Disney, who had retired to Los Angeles, and began exploring the new, sunswept world.

Near his uncle's house was Edendale, where Mack Sennett filmed his Keystone Comedies. Not far away were the crumbling remains of Babylon, the gigantic set D. W. Griffith built for *Intolerance*. Walt rode the big red trolley of the Pacific Electric to Culver City and gazed in awe at the mammoth Circus Maximus of *Ben-Hur*. He walked along LaBrea Avenue in Hollywood, past the English bungalows of the Chaplin studio, hoping that he might glimpse the comedian he had idolized.

Walt wanted to be on the inside of the studios, directing movies. He ordered business cards proclaiming himself as Kansas City representative of Universal and Selznick Newsreels. He presented the card to the receptionist at Universal and announced that he wanted a pass to the studio. He seemed so self-assured that he was allowed to enter, and for hours Walt roamed the glassed-in stages and outdoor sets, watching film makers at work. Returning to the employment office the following day, he cited his experience in Kansas

City and asked for work as a director. He was turned away.

He drew the same reaction when he applied for work at other studios. No one was impressed by the raw kid from Kansas City. Walt said he was willing to accept any kind of work, just to be inside a studio. "No openings," he was told.

Walt ran out of money and had to borrow from Roy to pay Uncle Robert $5 a week for room and board. Walt visited his brother at the veterans' hospital in West Los Angeles and told him of his frustration. Roy suggested that Walt should return to the cartoon business. "No, I'm too late," Walt said. "I should have started six years ago. I don't see how I can top those New York boys now."

Yet the animated cartoon had made little progress in the ten years since it had become a movie attraction. Early attempts at cartoons had been made by J. Stuart Blackton's *Humorous Phases of Funny Faces* in 1906 and Winsor McCay's *Little Nemo* in 1911. McCay, a newspaper cartoonist, also toured in vaudeville with his *Gertie, the Trained Dinosaur,* which responded on the screen to his commands. Not until John R. Bray's *The Artist's Dream* in 1913 were the commercial possibilities of the cartoon realized. In the following year Bray introduced the first popular series, Col. Heeza Liar. Production of cartoon movies became practical with the 1914 innovation by Earl Hurd of using celluloid for action drawings and laying it over backgrounds. Thereafter series proliferated—Hurd's Bobby Bumps, Max Fleischer's Koko the Klown and Out of the Inkwell, Pat Sullivan's Felix the Cat, Paul Terry's Farmer Al Falfa, Bud Fisher's Mutt and Jeff, and others based on newspaper comic strips such as The Katzenjammer Kids, Krazy Kat, Bringing Up Father and Happy Hooligan. The cartoons were rarely more than comic strips that moved. Characters were two-dimensional, and they hurtled from one gag to another with no concern for plot.

It was rare for Walt Disney to be wanting in confidence, but he didn't believe he could compete with the professionalism of the New York cartoon studios. Besides, there were no cartoonists to help him in Hollywood; the animation business was entirely centered in New York. He continued seeking work at the studios. One day he encountered a Kansas City friend who was equally movie-struck.

"I got a job in a picture called *The Light That Failed*," the friend announced. "They need more extras. You can ride a horse, can't you, Diz?" "Of course," said Walt, although his riding days had ended in Marceline. The studio hired him for a cavalry charge, and Walt reconsidered his earlier ambition to become an actor. Then rain postponed filming, and the cavalry was cast with new extras.

Uncle Robert nagged Walt about his unemployment and his lack of prospects. Finally Walt concluded that the only way he could break into the movie business was with cartoons. He would have to start as he had before—by selling joke reels to movie theaters. He rigged up a cartoon stand in Uncle Robert's garage, using dry-goods boxes and spare lumber. He needed a patron, and he paid a call to the offices of Alexander Pantages, who operated a chain of movie and vaudeville theaters. Walt outlined his idea to an assistant, who replied, "Mr. Pantages wouldn't be interested." A voice answered, "How do you know I wouldn't?" Pantages himself appeared, and Walt outlined his plan. "You make me up one of those, and if it's what you describe, I will be very interested," said Pantages.

Walt returned to Uncle Robert's garage and started work on a scenario for the Pantages reel. The crude equipment would not allow anything complicated, so Walt decided to employ stick figures against simple backgrounds; the comedy would derive from gags in balloons over the characters' heads.

He pursued another possibility. He believed that *Alice's Wonderland,* which he had made in Kansas City, might still provide his entrée into the cartoon business. He printed some stationery with the letterhead "Walt Disney, Cartoonist" and he sent off a letter to Margaret Winkler, the cartoon distributor in New York:

This is to inform you that I am no longer connected with the Laugh-O-Gram Films, Inc., of Kansas City, Mo. and that I am establishing a studio in Los Angeles for the purpose of producing the new and novel series of cartoons I have previously written you about.

The making of these new cartoons necessitates being located in a production center that I may engage trained talent for my casts, and be within reach of the right facilities for producing.

I am taking with me a select number of my former staff and will in a very short time be producing at regular intervals. It is my intention of securing working space with one of the studios, that I may better study technical detail and comedy situations and combine these with my cartoons. . . .

Walt's Kansas City creditors agreed to release *Alice's Wonderland* for Miss Winkler to review. On October 15, a telegram arrived for Walt Disney from M. J. Winkler:

BELIEVE SERIES CAN BE PUT OVER BUT PHOTOGRAPHY OF ALICE SHOULD SHOW MORE DETAIL AND BE STEADIER THIS BEING NEW PRODUCT MUST SPEND LARGE AMOUNT ON EXPLOITATION AND ADVERTISING THEREFORE NEED YOUR COOPERATION WILL PAY FIFTEEN HUNDRED EACH NEGATIVE FOR FIRST SIX AND TO SHOW MY GOOD FAITH WILL PAY FULL AMOUNT ON EACH OF THESE SIX IMMEDIATELY ON DELIVERY OF NEGATIVE. . . .

It was late evening when Walt received the telegram. He rode the bus to Sawtelle and found the porch ward where Roy was sleeping. Roy awoke with a start and saw his brother standing over him with a wide smile, waving a piece of paper in his hand. "What's the matter?" Roy whispered.

"We're in! It's a deal!" Walt exclaimed. The other patients in the ward began to stir, and Roy shushed his brother and asked him to explain quietly. Walt told him the contents of the telegram. This, finally, was his chance to get started in the animation business in a big way. But he needed help—Roy's help. "Let's go, Roy," Walt pleaded. The older brother viewed the prospect calmly. Could Walt deliver the films on schedule? Walt assured him he could. Was it possible to make a profit? Walt had calculated that the reels could be produced for $750; that meant a 100 percent profit. "Okay, Walt, let's go," said Roy. Walt beamed, patted his brother on the shoulder, and stole out of the darkened ward.

Roy left the veteran's hospital the next morning and never returned; the spot on his lung had healed, and he was never again troubled with tuberculosis. He had saved $200 from his $80 monthly pension, and the money went into the new enterprise. Roy applied for loans at local banks and was told that movie cartoons were too risky an investment. Roy concluded that Uncle Robert was the only prospect as a backer. "Walter doesn't pay his debts," said the old man, citing Ray Disney's complaint that Walt had failed to return Ray's $60 investment in Laugh-O-Grams. Roy was persuasive, and Uncle Robert finally agreed to lend $500 for his nephews' new enterprise.

On October 16, 1923, Walt and Roy Disney signed a contract with M. J. Winkler for distribution of six Alice Comedies for a price of $1,500 apiece, and six more at $1,800 apiece, with an option for two more series. Walt told the distributor: "The first of this series, the title of which has been changed from *Alice's Sea Story* to *Alice's Day at Sea,* is now in production and in all probability I will have this subject to you by December 15th. But on account of the many details attached to the starting of a series of this nature it may require a week longer."

Among the many details was Alice herself. Miss Winkler had specified in her original telegram that Alice had to be played by the same little girl in the unfinished reel. Virginia's father agreed to leave his job in Kansas City and move his family to California. Walt promised to pay his star $100 a month.

Walt inquired about office rentals at a real-estate office, declaring he could pay $10 a month. The only place at that price was a room at the back of the real-estate office. "I'll take it," Walt said. He bought a secondhand camera for $200 and taught Roy how to operate it. Two girls were hired at $15 a week to ink and paint the celluloids, and Walt himself did all the animation. The first reel was finished on schedule, and on the day after Christmas came the joyous telegram from M. J. Winkler:

DAY AT SEA RECEIVED TODAY SATISFACTORY MAILING TODAY DRAFT ON LOS ANGELES BANK WITH DETAILED LETTER. . . .

The arrival of the first check cheered the Disney brothers, and Walt launched production on the second reel, *Alice Hunting in Africa*. For $10 a month, he rented a vacant lot at Hollywood Boulevard and Rodney Drive, three blocks away, where he could photograph live action with Virginia Davis and neighborhood kids whom Walt enlisted at fifty cents apiece. Alice's dog was portrayed by Uncle Robert's German shepherd, Peggy. In February of 1924, Walt hired his first animator, Rollin (Ham) Hamilton, and moved into a small store at 4649 Kingswell at a rental of $35, plus $7 for a garage which Walt converted into an office. The store window bore the letters: "DISNEY BROS. STUDIO."

Walt shipped *Alice Hunting in Africa* to Miss Winkler with the notation: "I sincerely believe I have made a great deal of improvement on this subject in the line of humorous situations and I assure you that I will make it a point to inject as many funny gags and comical situations into future productions as possible." The distributor replied that the timing of the films was greatly improved but the comedy still was lacking. Her customers had found the Alice cartoons "nice and clean" but felt they needed more laughs.

With the delivery of *Alice's Spooky Adventure* in February, Walt wrote: "I am trying to comply with your instructions by injecting as much humor as possible and believe I have done better on this production. I have had professional critics at all previews and have been informed that we are making big improvements on each one. However, they seemed to be well pleased with all of them at that. It is my desire to be a little different from the usual run of slapstick and hold them more to a dignified line of comedy."

Margaret Winkler was pleased with *Alice's Spooky Adventure* and used it to sell the series to distributors in southern New Jersey, eastern Pennsylvania, Delaware, Maryland and the District of Columbia. "I am very optimistic about the future and believe we have something here of which we will all be proud," the distributor wrote. The first Alice Comedy reached the theaters in March 1924.

Walt spent more money on each new comedy, and the margin of profit narrowed and sometimes disappeared. The tiny studio needed more financing, and Walt urged Roy to ask his Kansas City sweetheart, Edna Francis, for a loan. "Absolutely not," Roy replied. Walt himsef wrote to Edna, asking her not to tell Roy about the plea for cash. Edna had saved some money from her salary at an insurance company, and she sent Walt a check for $25. Roy was incensed when he found out. Walt importuned Carl Stalling, the organist at the Isis Theater in Kansas City who had once ordered a song reel from Laugh-O-Gram. Stalling contributed $275 to the Disney Brothers Studio.

Walt completed the first series of six Alice Comedies in late May 1924. He had done most of the animation, and it was hard, exacting work. He felt the company would progress faster if he could devote more time to the scenarios. Although he was facile with gags, he realized he didn't have the draftsmanship to be a top-notch animator. He decided to send for Ub Iwerks.

Ub was understandably reluctant to leave Kansas City. The last time he had joined forces with Walt Disney, he had ended with $1,000 in unpaid salary (he later received $450 in the bankruptcy settlement). Ub was earning $50 a week at Film Ad, and it seemed foolhardy to leave his position with an established firm for the nebulous future of Disney Brothers Studio in Hollywood. But Walt was a young man with rare powers of persuasion, and Ub wrote his one-time partner that he would come to California.

Walt's reply on June 1, 1924, was enthusiastic: "Everything is going fine with us and I am glad you made up your mind to come out. Boy, you will never regret it—this is the place for you—a real country to work and play in. . . . I can give you a job as artist-cartoonist and etc. with the Disney Productions, most of the work would be cartooning. Answer at once and let me know what you want to start. . . . At present time I have one fellow helping me on the animation and three girls that do the inking, etc. while Roy handles the business end."

Walt and Ub agreed on a salary of $40 a week, and Ub came to California in late June, driving the car of Virginia Davis's father. Now Walt could devote full time to gags and stories. His career as an animator was over.

With Ub on the payroll, there was little money left over for the two partners. Walt and Roy had moved out of Uncle Robert's house and were sharing a single room in a rooming house, with a bathroom down the hall. They ate their meals in the room or dined at a nearby cafeteria. The brothers devised a technique to stretch their dinner money. As they went down the cafeteria line, Walt ordered the meat course and Roy took the vegetable. When they got to the table, each portion was split in half, and they shared with each other.

The addition of Ub Iwerks as animator gave the Alice Comedy series an added boost, both in the quality of the drawing and the speed with which they were produced. But the money flow did not improve, and a note of desperation entered Walt's letters to the distributor. After her marriage to Charles Mintz, Margaret Winkler had retired. Mintz took over the company, and the relationship between producer and distributor was not as cordial as before. Mintz began sending half-payments for the films.

"We need money," Walt wrote to Mintz on August 29, 1924. "We have been spending as much as you have been paying us for [the films] in order to improve and make them as good as possible, and now that we are receiving only $900.00, it puts us in a ' 'ell of a 'ole.' I am not kicking about that, however, I am perfectly willing to sacrifice a profit on this series, in order to put out something good, but I expect you to show your appreciation by helping us out. As you know, we haven't had the money to spend on them, we will have to skimp, and at this time, it would not be best to do that. So please, for our sake as well as your own, give this more consideration and instead of sending us $900.00, make it the full amount excepting a fair discount which will enable us to pull through this period."

Mintz replied that his own company was short of money and he could not accelerate the payments. He reported that he had been able to book *Alice Gets in Dutch* into the new Piccadilly Theater in New York, but that the manager had complained that Alice appeared too light and her actions were too jumpy. Walt replied that he could improve both conditions, but a certain amount of jumpiness was inevitable because of double printing of the animation on the live action. Mintz continued to press for more comedy, and Walt wrote him that in *Alice Cans the Cannibals* "we have endeavored to have nothing but gags, and the whole story is one gag after another."

As the comedy improved in the Alice Comedies, public and critical acceptance grew. *Motion Picture News* remarked of *Alice's Wild West Show:* "Walt Disney, the cartoonist, produced a novel combination of an actual acting cast and cartoons in this single reeler and it is highly amusing and wholly entertaining." The *Kinematographic Weekly* of London commented of *Alice and the Three Bears:* "The artist's work and the living player are capitally united." *The Moving Picture World* said of *Alice Cans the Cannibals:* "Each one of these Walt Disney cartoons . . . appears to be more imaginative and clever than the preceding, and this one is a corker."

In December 1924, Mintz offered a contract for eighteen more Alices at $1,800 per picture, plus a share of the profits from rentals to theaters. At last the Disney Brothers Studio was on steady footing. Walt invited two more of the Laugh-O-Gram alumni, Hugh Harman and Rudy Ising, to leave Kansas City and join him.

Living together in one room had proved a strain on both Walt and Roy. They grew irritable and snappish, particularly over meals. Roy was the cook, since he spent more time in the room; on doctor's orders, he had to take an afternoon nap and quit work early. One night Walt claimed the dinner was unfit to eat, and Roy exploded, "All right, to hell with you! If you don't like my cooking, let's quit this arrangement." He sent off a telegram to Edna Francis asking her to come to California and marry him.

Edna arrived with her mother on April 7, 1925, and the wedding took place four days later at the home of Robert Disney. Elias and Flora Disney came to Los Angeles from Portland, accompanied by Herb. Walt served as Roy's best man, and the maid of honor was Lillian Bounds, a pretty girl who had been working as an inker and painter at the studio.

She had been born into a pioneering Idaho family and in 1923 had left business school in Lewiston to visit her married sister in Los Angeles. Lillian met a girl who worked at the Disney Brothers Studio, applying ink and paint to the cartoon celluloids. The girl said another job was open, and Lillian applied for it. Walt and Roy found her attractive and efficient, and she had the added advantage of living nearby, so they wouldn't have to pay her carfare. She was hired at a salary of $15 a week.

Walt was too immersed in his work to pay much attention to the new ink-and-paint girl. But after he had bought a little Ford runabout for the studio's errands, he sometimes drove the girls home from work. One evening as he dropped Lillian at her sister's house, he remarked, "I'm going to buy a new suit. When I get it, would it be all right if I called on you?" Lillian said it would be.

A check had just arrived from M. J. Winkler, and Walt convinced Roy that they should celebrate by purchasing suits. They went to the Foreman and Clark store in downtown Los Angeles, and Walt picked out a two-pants outfit while Roy settled for a one-pants suit. Walt's was gray-green, double-breasted and stylish. He arrived that night at Lillian's house and after meeting her sister and brother-in-law, he asked eagerly, "How do you like my new suit?"

Walt became a steady caller, often having dinner at Lillian's house, sometimes taking her out to a tearoom on Hollywood Boulevard. Walt acquired a new car, a secondhand Moon, dark-gray with a light on the radiator, and on weekends he and Lillian motored to Pomona, Riverside, and other Southern California cities. At night he and Lillian drove to theaters in Glendale or Hollywood. A dog he had bought Lillian kept her company in the car while Walt watched a rival's cartoon. Afterward Walt expounded on the merits or deficiencies of what he had seen.

Walt had often proclaimed that he would never marry until he reached twenty-five and had saved $10,000. He fell short on both counts. After Roy had married Edna, Walt suggested to Lilly that they should marry, too. Roy took Walt to a cut-rate jeweler, who displayed a three-quarter-carat diamond surrounded by tiny blue sapphires, priced at $75, and others at $35. Walt selected the $75 ring. On July 13, 1925, he placed it on Lillian's finger in the living room of her uncle, the fire chief of Lewiston, Idaho. The newlyweds honeymooned at Mount Rainier and Seattle, then returned to a $40-a-month kitchenette apartment in Los Angeles. Thereafter Lillian worked at the studio only in times of emergency.

Marriage brought added pressure on the Disney brothers to make their young enterprise succeed. Roy continued overseeing the financial affairs, entering expenses into the company ledger with a meticulous hand: a hat for Virginia, $4.95; salary for a teacher, two days, $20; tips for the projectionist and organist at a preview, $2; salary for Roy Disney, $50. On July 6, 1925, the Disneys made a $400 down payment on a lot at 2719 Hyperion Avenue, where they planned to build a larger studio.

Robert Disney had been repaid his original $500, but his nephews had to submerge their pride and ask their uncle for an additional $100 when their cash ran low. Roy contributed his $80-a-month pension. The studio's financial health depended largely on money from M. J. Winkler after delivery of each new cartoon. The checks were now being brought in person by Charles Mintz's brother-in-law and Hollywood representative, George Winkler, but the money did not arrive promptly enough for Walt. He complained to Mintz, who responded that Alices were being delivered too frequently. This started an angry exchange of letters.

Disney to Mintz, October 2, 1925: "First, let me say that it is my intention to live up to the contract and I expect you to do the same. . . . I intend to continue shipping pictures to you as fast as completed, which is about every sixteen days. I will expect you to take them as delivered and remit immediately. Your failure to do so will constitute a breach of contract and will force me to seek other distributors. . . ."

Mintz to Disney, October 6, 1925: ". . . Haven't

you a single spark of appreciativeness in your whole soul or are we going to face the same situation which we faced after having put a certain other short subject on the market only to have it proved a boomerang to us? . . . Now let me tell you something else. The first seven pictures were an absolute total loss to us and you can further take my word for it when I tell you that we have not made one single dollar on any picture that we have gotten from you. . . . you should whole-heartedly be ashamed of yourself. . . ."

Disney to Mintz, October 15, 1925: "Our contract calls for *final delivery* by January 5, 1926, with your option calling for twenty-six pictures the following year. I have built up my organization to where I can complete my deliveries of every two weeks, the following year, should you choose to exercise your option. With my present payroll, on a three weeks schedule I would absolutely be losing money, and to cut down my force is out of the question. You well know, yourself, how hard it is to get men trained in this line of work. My artists are all experienced, capable men, difficult to replace at any salary. How can I afford the loss which a delayed schedule would mean? . . ."

Mintz to Disney, November 17, 1925: "In the first place, I think you will agree with me when I tell you that we lost a lot of money on the first series of 'Alice Comedies.' I think you will also believe me when I tell you that, so far, on the second series, we are a great distance from breaking even. I think you will also agree with me when I tell you that to continue in that way, would not be plausible. If you have been reading the trade papers and if you have been mingling with film people, you have undoubtedly seen the handwriting on the wall. It is actually a fact that the Independent market has gone to smash. . . ."

The twenty-three-year-old film maker Walt Disney was receiving his education in the movie business. Creators of movie entertainment, unless they controlled their own releasing companies, were at the mercy of the distributor. It wasn't enough to be an original and creative artist, Disney learned; survival in the film business required a jungle toughness.

Despite Mintz's pleas of poverty, he proposed a new contract at $1,500 per Alice, plus a fifty-fifty share of the profits after he had received $3,000 in film rentals. Mintz wrote to Walt: "This may seem a little hard to you, but before making any definite decision, I would advise you to digest this letter thoroughly, talk it over with Roy and your uncle or with whomever you wish, and don't make any hasty decisions."

Negotiations continued by mail and telegram for the next two months, with the letters from each side skirting the edge of acrimony. "If you think this is a fair agreement, you have another think coming," declared Mintz. Disney answered by telegram:

MY OFFER IS THE LIMIT I CAN GO STOP YOUR PROPOSITIONS ARE ALL UNACCEPTABLE TO ME STOP THEREFORE UPON THE DELIVERY OF THE NEXT SUBJECT THE FINAL ONE OF THE NINETEEN TWENTY FIVE SERIES I WILL CONSIDER MY CONTRACTUAL OBLIGATIONS FULFILLED.

On February 8, 1926, after more counter-offers, Walt telegraphed a proposal which Mintz accepted. It was a variation on the terms they had discussed but it contained stipulations which were to be basic elements for the Disney operation of the future. Walt agreed to "make each picture in a high-class manner" and insisted that "all matters regarding the nature of the comedies are to be left to me." He also stated that "should the idea, or name of *Alice Comedies* be exploited in any way, other than motion pictures, such as toys, novelties, newspaper strips, etc., it is agreed that we shall share equally in profits derived therefrom." Most importantly, Walt's proposition was "subject to my ownership of all trademarks and copyrights on *Alice Comedies* excepting only rights relating to the series which you purchased under past contracts."

The new contract coincided with the move into the

new studio on Hyperion Avenue in the Silver Lake district, a few miles from downtown Los Angeles. It was a one-story white stucco building on a sixty-by-forty-foot lot, with a partition between the offices of Walt and Roy and the rest open space occupied by animators and inkers and painters. Walt reasoned that a single name could have more box-office appeal and identification, and so the Disney Brothers Studio became the Walt Disney Studio.

Something else was added. Walt had worried that his youthful appearance was a drawback in his dealings with the movie world. When he and his fellow animators grew mustaches on a bet, he was pleased with his new look of maturity. The mustache remained.

7

A 1926 photograph of the Disney production team posing in front of the new Hyperion studio gives a picture of the spirit of the enterprise. All but one are transplanted Kansas Cityans, and they appear imbued with the atmosphere of their new land. All but Roy Disney are in their mid-twenties; four still have the mustaches they grew on the office bet, and they seem more mature—although Disney's mustache gaves him the look of a sober Charlie Chase. The young men are posing with their precocious star, Margie Gay (Virginia Davis's parents had withdrawn her from the series to seek a dramatic career, with scant success). Margie stands on an upturned box topped with a stack of books. The men stand in a row, legs crossed like chorines posing. And in the Hollywood vogue of the Twenties, all wear knickers—or perhaps seem to, by tucking their trousers under long stockings. Their smiles are fixed and determined, revealing the righteousness of their cause.

They were indeed dedicated to their work of creating comedy cartoons. Having failed in Kansas City, Walt Disney was determined to make the Hollywood venture an ever-growing success, and he was almost messianic in his leadership of his staff. The others responded by devoting most of their waking hours to the studio. Yet Walt realized that drawing animated cartoons was tedious, wearying work, and he encouraged his artists to refresh themselves. A noontime baseball game was instituted in the vacant lot across from the studio. Some days Walt joined for an inning or two, although playing baseball was not one of his skills.

After two years of the Alice Comedies, Walt realized that the series was running down. The novelty of combining the playful little girl with cartoon figures had long before worn off, and it became increasingly difficult to integrate her into the cartoon action. Because Alice was not a basically comic figure, the bulk of the comedy had been assumed by Julius the cat.

Charlie Mintz wrote Disney on February 13, 1926: "*Alice's Mysterious Mystery* . . . is just another picture and has nothing in it whatever that is outstanding. It is short both on live action and on the entire footage. . . . as long as we are to do business together in the future, I think you will concede that I probably know a little more about what the market wants than you do. . . ."

Disney to Mintz, March 1, 1926: "I agree with you in regard to the live action and will assure you that I will do everything I can to work for the betterment of the pictures. Wherever it is possible, I will bring the girl closer to the camera and try to insert more closeups when possible, without making the picture draggy or sacrificing funny business. I am only too glad to have you offer criticism on the pictures and anything you suggest will be given careful consideration. However, I want you to understand that it is almost a physical impossibility to make each picture a knockout, and I only hope that you will be fair enough to let me know when I have a good picture, as well as to tell me about the poor ones."

Mintz to Disney, May 20, 1926: "You asked me some time ago to be fair with you and tell you when you made a good picture. Now, I will tell you that I think *Alice the Fire Fighter* is as good as anything you have turned out and perhaps a little better. I will also be fair with you a little more when I tell you that making good pictures as you are, you are your own worst enemy by either taking unqualified advice or refusing to take advice with a certain amount of past performances and sincerity behind it."

Disney to Mintz, June 15, 1926: "I want to thank you for the compliment on *Alice the Fire Fighter,* and want to say right here that I will not be satisfied until I am able to make them all as good, or better. I am putting every effort toward this end and hope that in a very short time our average will be above them all. (Including Krazy Kat.)"

By the end of 1926 it was apparent that the Alice Comedies had run their course. Carl Laemmle, the aggressive founder of Universal Pictures, had told Mintz that he wanted a cartoon series starring a rabbit. Margaret Winkler Mintz suggested to her husband that Walt Disney might make such a series to replace Alice. Walt was enthusiastic about the idea, and he sent off rough pencil sketches of rabbit characters. "If these sketches are not what you want," he wrote Mintz, "let me know more about it and I will try again."

Universal approved the sketches, and the Disney company was authorized to make the first cartoon in the series, which Mintz named Oswald the Lucky Rabbit. In early April of 1927, Walt and his staff devised a plot of an overproductive rabbit and turned out the first cartoon, *Poor Papa,* on a rush schedule. The reviewing committee at Universal Film Exchanges in New York expressed disappointment, pointing out the faults:

"(1) Approximately 100 feet of the opening is jerky in action due to poor animation. (2) There is too much repetition of action. Scenes are dragged out to such an extent that the cartoon is materially slowed down. (3) The Oswald shown in this picture is far from being a funny character. He has no outstanding trait. Nothing would eventually become characteristic insofar as Oswald is concerned. (4) The picture is merely a succession of unrelated gags, there being not even a thread of story throughout its length." The committee observed that with the exception of Charlie Chaplin, important movie comedians were "neat and dapper chaps." Oswald should have been young and romantic; instead, he was elderly, sloppy and fat.

In his reply, Walt admitted his disappointment with Oswald but defended the animation of Ub Iwerks, "whom I am willing to put alongside any man in the business today." Walt denied repeat-action paddings; the repeats had been used for comic effect. He conceded that Oswald could be made "a younger character, peppy, alert, saucy and venturesome, keeping him also neat and trim." But Walt cautioned against too much plot, because "by the time you have a story really started it is time to iris out, and you have failed to make the audience laugh."

Oswald the Lucky Rabbit, Walt Disney's first venture into the all-cartoon medium, provided an important lesson for the young film maker. He realized what he had known instinctively: that a strong, attractive central character was essential; and that a good storyline was needed, but too much plot could destroy laughter. He also learned that film-company committees could throttle creativity.

Walt and Ub worked late every night to transform Oswald into a more appealing cartoon figure. Walt admitted to Mintz upon delivery of the second Oswald, "This picture is far from being what I am working for in the future. I want to make Oswald have more personality and really create a likable character, and I believe that with a little time and patience on the part of you and Universal, that we will be able to develop a knockout series. We are changing the rabbit still more from the way he looks in this picture. We have eliminated the suspenders and changed his face considerably in the third one. I am also installing a new motor-drive on the camera to eliminate a certain unevenness in the photography that has been noticeable in the past. I believe this will give much cleaner and better stuff in the future."

With the third Oswald, Walt was still pleading with Mintz to remain patient "and give us a chance to get started." Oswald the Lucky Rabbit soon began to fulfill Walt's hopes. The rabbit became softer, more appealing, and the situations were funnier. Walt stinted on nothing. He refused to employ cycles—the repeat action which could save hours of work at the animation table. He insisted on photographing the rough animation and viewing it in a projection room. If it seemed to work, then Walt authorized the production process to continue. If not, the sequence went back to the animator. Such meticulousness was expensive, and the cost of the Oswald cartoons climbed. But the added quality paid off.

Reviews in the trade press helped draw the attention of film exhibitors. *Film Daily* wrote of *Trolley Troubles,* first of the cartoons to be released: ". . . As conductor on a 'Toonerville' trolley, Oswald is a riot. This and the two following in the series you can book on pure faith, and our solemn word that they have the goods." *Motion Picture News* found *Great Guns* "chock full of humor" and predicted, "This series is bound to be popular in all types of houses if the present standard is maintained." Said *Moving Picture World:* "In addition to striking a new note in cartoon characters by featuring a rabbit, these Disney creations are bright, speedy and genuinely amusing. . . . The animation is good and the clever way in which Disney makes his creations simulate the gestures and expressions of human beings adds to the enjoyment. They should prove worthwhile attractions in any type of house." Movie audiences responded to Oswald from the beginning of the series. Oswald was also attracting a specialized audience: the cartoon animators of New York City. They had watched the Alice Comedies with interest. They were overwhelmed by the original humor and fluid style of the Oswalds.

The growing popularity of Oswald prompted offers for use of the character on merchandise. Oswald first appeared on a chocolate-coated marshmallow candy bar made by the Vogan Candy Corporation of Portland, Oregon, the wrapper bearing the message: "Watch for OSWALD in Universal Pictures." The Philadelphia Badge Company issued a button with Oswald's likeness, and the Universal Tag and Novelty Company offered an Oswald Stencil Set. The Disney company received no royalty for the reproduction of Oswald, which Walt considered good publicity for the cartoon series.

Walt hired more artists, and Ub and his fellow animators began turning out an Oswald cartoon every two weeks. Universal and Mintz were obviously happy with the results; checks for $2,250 came promptly after the delivery of each new cartoon. Walt and Roy felt so encouraged by their prospects that they bought adjoining lots on Lyric Avenue and built identical prefabricated houses for $7,000 apiece.

The Oswald contract was scheduled to conclude in February of 1928. Walt treated Lilly and himself to a train trip to New York for the renewal negotiations with Mintz and Universal. Before leaving Los Angeles, Walt received a hint of impending trouble from Ub Iwerks. There were indications, Ub suggested, that Mintz's brother-in-law was doing more on his fortnightly visits to the Disney studio than merely collecting the completed Oswald and the lobby poster which Ub created for each new chapter. Ub had become suspicious of the confidential talks that George Winkler had been having with the other animators at the studio. Walt was inclined to dismiss Ub's suspicions, and he went off to New York with an air of optimism.

Mintz greeted Walt and Lilly cordially, and they were joined at lunch in the Hotel Astor by Margaret Winkler Mintz, who had started Walt's career by distributing the Alice Comedies. The conversation was warm, but Walt detected a hollow note in Mintz's geniality. Jack Alicoate, editor of *Film Daily,* stopped at the table, and Mintz introduced him to the young producer of the Oswald cartoons. "Oswald—oh, yes," said Alicoate. "I've heard nice things about them, especially the nice grosses." Walt was pleased, but he noticed that Mintz seemed disturbed by the remark.

Negotiations for the new Oswald contract were held in Mintz's office on 42nd Street. Walt began by suggesting that in view of the unquestioned success of Oswald, the price per cartoon should be raised from $2,250 to $2,500. "I'll give you eighteen hundred," Mintz replied.

Eighteen hundred dollars for each cartoon would mean a loss for the Disney studio. Walt asked for an explanation. "Either you come with me at my price, or I'll take your organization away from you," Mintz announced. "I have your key men signed up."

Walt couldn't believe it. Had Mintz actually plotted to steal away the Disney animators? And would his "boys," to whom he had taught the cartooning trade in Kansas City, desert him to work for Mintz? Walt told Mintz he needed time to consider the ultimatum. Walt hurried back to the hotel and telephoned Roy the news of Mintz's bombshell. Roy made an investigation and discovered that virtually all of the animators except Ub Iwerks had committed themselves to Mintz.

Mintz pressed for a decision, and Walt tried to stall. He found an ally in Alicoate, and the trade-paper editor arranged interviews at Fox and Metro-Goldwyn-Mayer. But neither company expressed interest in releasing Oswald. Now Mintz played his trump card: by contract, Oswald was the property of Universal Pictures, not Walt Disney. Walt was disheartened. All of his hard work and creative effort had created a valuable property which he didn't own. When he told Lilly the sorrowful news, he vowed, "Never again will I work for somebody else."

Charlie Mintz made another offer: He would pay for

the costs of producing each cartoon, providing liberal salaries for the studio employees, and sharing 50 percent of the profits. Walt had no intention of accepting the offer, but he asked for time to consider it. He hoped he could persuade Universal executives to intervene. "Give us a decent break," he pleaded, but Universal sided with Charlie Mintz.

"Well, we are still hanging around this Hell Hole waiting for something to happen," Walt wrote his brother on March 7. "Before you get this letter I hope you will have had a wire containing good news. I can't rush things any faster—just have to do the best I can. BUT I WILL FIGHT IT OUT ON THIS LINE IF IT TAKES ALL SUMMER. It sure looks like a fight to the finish —Charlie is very determined to get absolute control of everything and will do everything in his power to gain his end. But unknown to him we have a stronger power on our side."

Walt told Roy of waiting in the hotel room for a telephone call from Universal with the hope that "they will take advantage of the situation and give Charlie the air and deal direct with us. But I guess that is hoping for too much. But don't worry. I really do feel that everything will turn out all right. Anyways I believe that whatever does happen is FOR THE BEST."

Walt retained his calm attitude in messages to Roy, adding requests to turn off the water heater and make sure that his female dog did not become pregnant. "Keep your chin up," Walt advised his older brother. "We will be able to laugh last—that's the best laugh of all."

Finally there was nothing to do but concede defeat. Walt paid a last visit to the office of Charlie Mintz to say he could not accept the offered terms; Mintz could have Oswald. Surprisingly, Walt evidenced no rancor. He offered the older man advice: "Protect yourself, Charlie. If my artists did it to me, they'll do it to you." The triumphant Charlie Mintz refused to believe that Oswald could ever be wrested away from him. But that was what later happened.

Walt and Lilly packed their bags for the melancholy trip home. Walt sent a final telegram to Roy:

LEAVING TONIGHT STOPPING OVER KC ARRIVE HOME SUNDAY MORNING SEVEN THIRTY DON'T WORRY EVERYTHING OK WILL GIVE DETAILS WHEN ARRIVE —WALT.

8

THE BIRTH of Mickey Mouse is obscured in legend, much of it created by Walt Disney himself. He enjoyed telling the tale of how he dreamed up the mouse character on the train trip back from the Oswald disaster and how Lilly objected to the name of Mortimer Mouse and so he made it Mickey Mouse instead. He also hinted that the character originated with a pet mouse that played around his drawing board in Kansas City. Both stories had basis in fact, but the real genesis of Mickey Mouse appears to have been an inspired collaboration between Walt Disney, who supplied the zestful personality and the voice for Mickey, and Ub Iwerks, who gave Mickey form and movement.

When Walt and Lilly arrived at the Santa Fe station on a March Sunday morning in 1928, he gave no hint to Roy of the catastrophe that had befallen their enterprise in New York. Not until they arrived at their twin homes did Roy finally inquire: "Tell me about it, kid —what kind of a deal did you make?" Walt admitted cheerfully, "We haven't got a deal," and he related the events leading up to the final break with Mintz. But before Roy could become depressed, Walt quickly added: "We're going to start a new series."

Walt and Roy agreed on the new venture; now they faced the problem of how to get it started. Three more Oswalds had to be completed and delivered to Mintz, and the defecting cartoonists would not be leaving until June. Walt and Ub concocted a storyline to capitalize on the recent transatlantic flight of Charles Lindbergh, and Ub began the animation behind a locked door. If someone knocked, he quickly buried the new drawings and substituted Oswald. Ub drew the new cartoon, titled *Plane Crazy,* at a phenomenal rate—seven hundred drawings a day, breaking Bill Nolan's record of six hundred a day for Krazy Kat.

The rest of the animation process was not easy to hide within the studio, so Walt built a makeshift workshop in his garage on Lyric Avenue. Lilly, Edna and Walt's sister-in-law, Hazel Sewell, did the inking and painting of Ub's animation. Walt took the completed "cels" to the studio at night, and a loyal employee, Mike Marcus, operated the camera. Each morning before the animators arrived, all evidence of *Plane Crazy* was removed.

The cartoon was completed and scheduled for a preview at a Sunset Boulevard movie house on May 15, 1928. As was his custom at previews, Walt handed the theater organist a dollar so the cartoon gags would be punched over with music. The reception was good, though not overwhelming, and Walt was encouraged to begin production on a second picture, *Gallopin' Gaucho.* Now he was able to make the cartoon without the cloak-and-dagger secrecy; the Oswald renegades had left. Their departure had perplexed a newcomer at the studio, Wilfred Jackson. During his first week, the former art student noted that the animators laughed and chatted over their work, but on Saturday they took their seat cushions, visors and oher personal things with them. "They're a strange bunch," Jackson mused; "they have fun together all week, but they don't trust each other enough to leave their personal belongings at the studio." On the following Monday he learned what had happened when only Ub, Les Clark, Johnny

Cannon, three of the women inkers and the janitor
returned to work.

Walt sought a distributor for Mickey Mouse. He
showed *Plane Crazy* to executives at MGM; they con-
gratulated him but made no offer. Realizing that the
series would have to be sold in New York, where the
major companies maintained their business offices, Walt
engaged a New York film dealer, E. J. Denison, to
find a distributor.

"I feel that I can make good cartoons and that they
can be placed with a good distributor if the matter is
handled right," Walt wrote Denison. "But the time is
short and there would be no second chance this year
if we get off on the wrong foot." Walt wanted an
advance of $3,000 per cartoon and was willing to grant
one- or two-year options for twenty-six cartoons annually at a minimum length of five hundred feet. He
concluded: "It is our intention to carry on an advertising and exploitation campaign that should, in a very
short time, along with good pictures and a good release,
make the name of 'Mickey Mouse' as well known as
any cartoon on the market."

Denison tried to interest major distributors in Mickey
Mouse, but the results were discouraging. Denison
withdrew, and Walt was faced with an unsold series
and mounting costs. Meanwhile the revolution of sound
had commenced.

Except for a few abortive experiments, the motion
picture had been mute throughout its history. On
October 6, 1927, with the premiere of *The Jazz Singer*
at the Warners' Theater in New York City, the motion-
picture medium was changed forever, although most of
the film moguls were slow to realize it. Not Walt Disney. He recognized sound as an inevitable addition to
the art of animation. Even though the first two Mickey
Mouse cartoons had not found a buyer, he planned a
third, this one to be synchronized to sound.

Walt and Ub borrowed from a successful Buster
Keaton comedy for the third Mickey Mouse, *Steamboat Willie*. The action in the first part of the cartoon

was to be syncopated to an old vaudeville tune, "Steamboat Bill," the last half to "Turkey in the Straw."

"But how the hell do we match the sound to the action of a cartoon?" Walt pondered. He himself had only a passing acquaintance with music. Wilfred Jackson, whose mother was a music teacher, brought a metronome to the studio, and he and Walt devised a way to time music to the flow of the film through a sound camera—twenty-four frames per second. While Jackson played on his harmonica, Walt calculated on a blank music sheet how many frames of cartoon would be required to match the tune.

The mechanics had been solved. But would audiences accept dialogue and song from cartoon characters? For a quarter-century Krazy Kat, Koko, Oswald and all the other animated figures had spoken not a word, and cartoon producers feared the tenuous illusion of reality might be destroyed when the characters opened their mouths to speak.

On a warm July night, Walt invited his workers to bring their wives to the studio. Roy operated the projector outside a window—to lessen the noise of film running through sprockets. Walt, Wilfred Jackson, Johnny Cannon and Ub stood behind the bedsheet-screen in front of a microphone. As Mickey and the villain, Pegleg Pete, appeared on the screen, Jackson played "Steamboat Bill' on his harmonica. Ub accompanied him with washboard and sliding whistles, Cannon punctuated the action with sound effects, and Walt delivered the minimal dialogue. Each man in turn went out in front of the bedsheet to observe the illusion as the reel was replayed, and each concluded that the device would work. The wives, Walt noted, were more concerned with discussions of babies and recipes. *Steamboat Willie* was completed as a silent, with music and sound effects cued by marks on the film.

Talkies had created chaos in Hollywood, with the major companies monopolizing sound equipment and thwarting efforts of independent producers to convert their films to sound. The Disney brothers concluded that Walt should use their remaining resources to journey alone to New York, where sound systems were more readily available.

Walt stopped in Kansas City to confer with his old friend Carl Stalling, the theater organist who had advanced the brothers $275 when they needed it badly. Walt persuaded him to perform another service, and Stalling hastily composed a musical score for *Steamboat Willie,* timing it to the beats that Ub had marked on the film.

With the can of film under his arm and the musical score in his suitcase, Walt arrived confidently in New York on the day after Labor Day, 1928. He found the film industry in a state resembling Paris of 1789. The sound revolution had brought disarray to all the film companies, with producers scrambling to find recording systems that were efficient and cheap. Walt called on Jack Alicoate, the tradepaper editor, who referred him to experts in sound recording. Some of them advised Walt to record on phonograph records, as several of the big companies were doing. Walt was unconvinced. A record could get lost or broken, he reasoned; and the projectionist could start the record in the wrong groove. With sound and action out of synchronization, the illusion would be destroyed. Walt was convinced that the sound had to be recorded on the film itself.

He began making the rounds. Fox was too busy taking orders for its Movietone system to bother with a small cartoon maker from the Coast. RCA brusquely agreed to take on the assignment; Walt insisted on seeing what the company could do. He was shown an experiment in recording an Aesop's Fables cartoon. Walt wrote his reaction to Roy and Ub: "MY GOSH— TERRIBLE—A lot of racket and nothing else. I was terribly disappointed. I really expected to see something half-way decent. BUT HONESTLY—it was nothing but one of the rottenest fables I believe that I ever saw, and I should know because I have seen almost all of them. It merely had an orchestra playing and adding some noises. The talking part does not mean a thing. It doesn't even match. We sure have nothing to worry about from these quarters."

RCA said it would accept the recording of *Steamboat Willie* for $600, plus the cost of an orchestra, a $1,000 royalty charge, a "music tax" to be paid to a publisher, etc. "They are not anywhere within our reach; I have dropped them from my mind entirely," Walt wrote to California.

As Walt continued his dealings with the New York film world, he became more convinced of the future of sound. He wrote to Roy and Ub that talkies were still a mystery to most of the movie executives—"None of them are positive how it is all going to turn out, but I have come to this definite conclusion: Sound effects and talking pictures are more than a mere novelty. They are here to stay and in time will develop into a wonderful thing. The ones that get in on the ground floor are the ones that will more likely profit by its future development. That is, providing they work for quality and not quantity and quick money. Also, I am convinced that the sound on film is the only logical thing for the future. At the present it is necessary to have both in order to cover the field one hundred per cent."

The merchant of sound who most impressed Walt was P. A. (Pat) Powers, who owned an independent system called Cinephone.

"He is a dandy," Walt enthused in his letter home, relating an entire afternoon spent with the expansive movie executive. Powers introduced the young man from Hollywood to a movie actor, George Walsh, whom Walt described as "a fine fellow; he was telling me how to play polo and about what a great sport it was." Walt also met Carl Edouarde, conductor of the pit orchestra at the Strand Theater—"a dandy fellow—big salary, but he knows his stuff." Edouarde expressed eagerness to record the cartoon and said he could do it with five or six pieces and a couple of sound-effects men. Powers proposed a charge of $1,000 including a royalty on the Disney films, and he offered to use his connections to help arrange a releasing company. "I have made up my mind to score it with Powers," Walt wrote to Roy.

Later Walt was to learn that Pat Powers was known to the film trade as one of the great New York City slickers, his shenanigans in the early days of movies having become legend. An Irish blacksmith from Buffalo, Powers shouldered his way into the infant business by bootlegging cameras from the Patents Company, which owned the rights to film eqquipment. In 1912 Powers battled with Carl Laemmle for control of Universal. One day Powers and a gang of strong-arm men claimed the props and furniture at Universal and carried them away in vans. During a board meeting at 1600 Broadway, Powers declined to turn over the company's financial records to Laemmle; instead he threw them out the third-floor window. Laemmle eventually bought out his antagonist, and Powers continued his dealings in the industry. By 1928 he had returned to his beginnings—using pirated equipment. His Cinephone system was based on other people's patents.

The twenty-six-year-old cartoon maker from California was overwhelmed by Powers' Irish charm. Walt wrote home: "Powers is a very big and influential guy. . . . He is all wrapped up in his work. . . . He is personally taking care of me. . . . He is big enough that if he wants Adolph Zukor [head of Paramount] to look at it he simply calls him and says, 'Come on over, Adolph, and give it a look.' "

Walt gave Powers a deposit of $500, telling Roy to "be sure and have enough money in the account to meet the check." Walt had been in New York only a week, but already he was wearying of big-city life, and even *Steamboat Willie* itself.

"Personally I am sick of this picture *Steamboat Willie*. Every time I see it the lousy print spoils everything. Maybe it will be a different looking picture with sound. I sure hope so. I am very nervous and upset and I guess that has a lot to do with my attitude in the matter. This DAMN TOWN is enough to give anybody the HEEBIE JEEBIES. I sure wish I was home. I sure wouldn't make a good traveling salesman. I can't mix with strangers and enjoy myself like some people. This is not affecting my attitude toward the matter I came here for. That is the only thing that is on my mind. But I have so much time to kill at night that I almost go nuts." But in the letter he quickly recovered from depression and urged Ub to go forward with the fourth Mickey Mouse cartoon, *The Barn Dance*.

When the time came for the recording session, Walt learned that seventeen musicians would be required, plus three trap drummers and sound-effects men. "I argued till I was blue in the face for a very small orchestra," Walt wrote Roy, offering the consolation: "This is our first picture. It has got to be a wow. On the strength of it we are going to sell the entire series."

After the recording session on September 17, Walt telegraphed Roy:

> TONE VALUE PERFECT BUT RESULTS ARE NOT SATISFACTORY STOP ALL CONCERNED DESIRE BEST RESULTS OBTAINABLE THEREFORE ARE REMAKING IT USING DIFFERENT EFFECTS MEN I AM VERY OPTIMISTIC ABOUT RESULTS AND OUR FUTURE LOOKS BRIGHT STOP GAVE POWERS CHECK ONE THOUSAND BE SURE IT IS OK.

Walt had tried to hide his own crushing disappointment over the expensive failure. Conductor Edouarde had disregarded Walt's system of synchronizing music to film, declaring he could match the action by watching the screen. But the cartoon moved too fast for the musicians to follow. In California, Roy was struggling to find money for another recording session. Walt contributed what to him was an extreme sacrifice: Roy was given permission to sell Walt's beloved Moon roadster.

"I am figuring on a good release," Walt assured Roy and Ub. "I don't think we will have any trouble getting it; this may mean the making of a big organization out of our little Dump. Why should we let a few dollars jeopardize our chances? I think this is Old Man Opportunity rapping at our door. Let's don't let the jingle of a few pennies drown out his knock. See my point? So slap as big a mortgage on everything we got and let's go after this thing in the right manner."

Walt sat at midnight in his lonely room at the Hotel Knickerbocker and typed four-page, single-spaced letters about his New York experiences. Sometimes his desperation showed through: "Well, fellows, I have told you all I know, and then some. It is very hard to put the entire situation on paper. Try and read between the lines. If you knew the entire situation as I do I feel sure you wouldn't be able to Sleep or Eat. I can't." But in most of the letters he retained his native optimism, as when he ended his October 1 message: "All together now—'Are we downhearted?' HELL NO." The HELL NO was typed in red.

For the second recording session, Walt drew marks on the frames of the film to indicate the musical beats. He persuaded Edouarde to cut down the size of the orchestra and hire only two special-effects men. Walt himself supplied Mickey's squeaks, Minnie Mouse's shouts and the voice of a parrot calling "Man overboard! Man overboard!" This time Edouarde followed the beat marks on the screen, and the orchestra finished in perfect synchronization with the film. At last *Steamboat Willie* had sound. Now all Walt had to do was sell it.

Pat Powers arranged for showings at the offices of the major distributors, and Walt went from one to another with the same result. He appeared before the receptionist and said, "I'm Walt Disney and I have a cartoon to show." He was directed to a company official who told him, "Just put it in the projection room and we'll get to it as soon as we can." Walt sometimes waited at the projection room for hours as the movie men watched their own product. Finally, one of them said, "Oh, that cartoon thing that fellow brought over —put it on." Finally Mickey Mouse and Pegleg Pete

appeared on the screen, and Walt listened carefully
to determine if their antics got laughs. They did, but
when Walt asked for an opinion, the executives replied,
"We'll call you about it" or "We'll be in touch with
Pat Powers." But no one come up with an offer.

Walt's dealings with the film crowd brought both
disillusion and wariness. "I have certainly learned a
lot about this game already," he wrote Lilly on October
20. "It is the damnedest mixed-up affair I have ever
heard of. It sure demands a shrewd and thoroughly
trained mind to properly handle it. There are so
damned many angles that continually come up that if
a person hasn't the experience, etc. it would certainly
lick one. They are all a bunch of schemers and just
full of tricks that would fool a greenhorn. I am sure
glad I got someone to fall back on for advice. I would
be like a sheep amongst a pack of wolves. I have
utmost confidence and faith in Powers and believe that
if we don't try to rush things too fast that we will get
a good deal out of this. We will all just have to have
patience and confidence. I am very optimistic about
everything and want you all to feel the same way. I
really think our big chance is here."

Walt was convinced that *Steamboat Willie* was a
winner, and he couldn't understand why the companies
weren't flocking to sign up a series of Mickey Mouse
cartoons. It was explained to him by a show-business
veteran, Harry Reichenbach: "Those guys don't know
what's good until the public tells them."

Reichenbach was a colorful promoter-publicist who
was operating the Colony Theater in New York for
Universal Pictures. He had seen *Steamboat Willie* during one of the projection-room screenings and thought
it would create a sensation. "I want to put that cartoon
in the Colony," he said.

"Gee, I don't know," Walt replied. "I'm afraid that
if I run it at a Broadway house, it'll take the edge off
my chances to sell it to a distributor."

"No, it won't," said the persuasive Reichenbach.
"You can chase that cartoon all over town and those

companies won't buy. Not until the public tells 'em it's good. Let me run it for two weeks so the press can see it. You'll get good reviews, and the people will come in droves. I'll give you five hundred dollars a week." Walt was immediately convinced. That was more money than anyone had ever paid to play a cartoon in a single theater. The $1,000 was desperately needed to shore up the Disney finances.

Steamboat Willie opened at the Colony Theater on November 18, 1928, and it was the sensation that Walt had dreamed it would be. The bill featured a talking movie, *Gang War,* starring Olive Borden and Jack Pickford, and a stage show headed by Ben Bernie and his orchestra. But the patrons left the theater talking about *Steamboat Willie,* billed as "the FIRST animated cartoon with SOUND." *Variety* reported: "It's a peach of a synchronization job all the way, bright, snappy and fitting the situation perfectly. . . . With most of the animated cartoons qualifying as a pain in the neck, it's a signal tribute to this particular one. . . . Recommended unreservedly for all wired houses." *Weekly Film Review:* "It kept the audience laughing and chuckling from the moment the lead titles came on the screen, and it left them applauding." *Exhibitor's Herald:* "It is impossible to describe this riot of mirth, but it knocked me out of my seat."

Even the New York *Times* took note of the first sound cartoon by Walter Disney, described as the creator of Oswald the Rabbit and now of "a new cartoon character henceforth to be known as 'Mickey Mouse.' " The *Times* critic conceded that the film was "an ingenious piece of work with a good deal of fun. It growls, whines, squeaks and makes various other sounds that add to its mirthful quality."

Night after night Walt stood at the back of the theater and listened to the warm, fresh waves of laughter that greeted the cartoon images on the screen. Reichenbach had been right; at last the film companies were calling Walt Disney to come in and discuss a deal. Walt was so encouraged by the prospects that he sent for Carl Stalling to join him and start writing the scores for *Plane Crazy* and *Gallopin' Gaucho.*

Walt's homesickness showed in his letters to California. He began one to Lilly: "Dear Little Sweetheart: I have just returned from a little shopping tour. I bought me a pair of pigskin gloves (something like the ones I used to have). It is so cold here now that I really needed them. It is now about six o'clock and I haven't had anything to eat since about nine o'clock this morning. Carl developed a headache about two o'clock and had to go to bed. He is just sort of upset over the trip. . . . I am as hungry as the Devil right now, but will wait until he is ready. By that time I will sure be good and hungry. I wish I could sit down to one of my Mama's meals???"

The talks with film distributors followed the same pattern. They asked how much he wanted to be paid each week for producing Mickey Mouse. He replied that he didn't want to be paid by the week, that he had his own studio and wanted to remain independent. They answered that they would either hire him by the week or buy the cartoons outright. No, said Walt, he had to own the cartoons himself. No deal, said the distributors.

The only company that gave Walt encouragement was Universal, for whom he had created Oswald. When Walt reported to the Universal offices for a conference, he was startled to find Charles Mintz waiting in the reception room. Walt did not believe in bearing grudges, and he gave a cordial greeting to the man who had taken away Oswald and most of the Disney staff. Inside, the Universal bosses said they wanted Mickey Mouse and would give Walt a contract assuring a healthy profit. But Universal would retain control. The offer was tempting, but Walt still said no.

"I agree with you," said Pat Powers. "You should remain independent, and I am willing to help you. I want to promote Cinephone. That's my only interest: promoting Cinephone. Your Mickey Mouse can do it for me. I'll make you a better deal than any of the majors. I'll sell rights to the cartoons in each state, and I'll pay for the salesmen and all the expenses. I'll advance you the money you need to make the cartoons, and I'll take only ten percent of the gross."

The offer seemed far more attractive than any from the major companies, and Walt agreed to it. He and Carl Stalling added sound to *Plane Crazy, Gallopin' Gaucho* and the newly completed *The Barn Dance.* Walt's New York ordeal was over at last, and he could return to Lilly in triumph. He came home with a brand-new contract and $2,500 in cash—more money than he had ever seen before.

Roy considered the Powers contract far from triumphant. For the first time since they had entered business together, the two brothers had a stormy argument. Shaking the contract at Walt, Roy exploded, "Did you read this? Do you know what you promised?" He read the provisions for Disney to pay $26,000 a year for ten years' use of the Cinephone equipment. "What the hell," Walt replied, "I needed the equipment."

Powers shipped the sound system to the Hyperion studio, and Walt began producing Mickey Mouse sound cartoons. His animation staff was expanding, as the result of his recruitment of cartoonists in New York. Ben Sharpsteen and Burt Gillett joined him in the spring of 1929, and Jack King and Norm Ferguson arrived a few months later. The spark plug of the staff remained Ub Iwerks, who turned out a prodigious number of drawings every day. He timed the action to a musical beat, since the Mickeys were scored by Carl Stalling with songs. The timing was recorded on an exposure sheet, which Ub kept by his animation table. The exposure sheets caused the first squabble between Walt and Ub. Nearly every night, Walt returned to the studio to attend to business matters and to review the cartoon work that had been done that day; Lilly often accompanied him and fell asleep on the couch while he worked until early morning. Walt studied Ub's drawings and prepared exposure sheets for them. Ub seldom displayed emotion, but he was upset by this invasion of his artistic function. Walt's timing was not what he had planned, Ub snapped, and he wanted no such interference. Walt agreed to let Ub make his own exposure sheets.

On his next visit to New York, Walt witnessed the growing popularity of Mickey Mouse. He wrote Lilly that *The Barn Dance* "went over very well" at the Strand Theater on Broadway, and he added: "The Strand has a big cutout of Mickey in the lobby and gives it as much space as any of their other sound shorts. I am enclosing a programme—this shows how much prominence they give it. Mickey Mouse is getting to be a very familiar character on Broadway—he is what is known as a 'HIT.' The exchange men that buy them all give lots of praise for their cleverness—they all claim they are the cleverest sound shorts on the market. All the salesmen consider it their best asset in approaching customers—I am thankful for all the nice things that are said about them and I hope we will be able to prove to them that it is not an accident but a consistent standard."

Walt was immensely pleased with Mickey's ascendancy, but he had vague misgivings. Prosperity would permit him to build his organization and heighten the quality of the cartoons, but the studio would be forced to produce shorts, one after another, starring the same character. Walt had gone through that with Alice and Oswald, and he found it stultifying.

During a New York recording session, Carl Stalling suggested a different kind of cartoon, a graveyard frolic to be animated to Grieg's "March of the Dwarfs." When Walt returned to the studio, he and Ub devised a storyline with skeletons floating out of graves and dancing a bony gavotte. Les Clark contributed some of the animation, but most of it was done by Ub, working with more than his usual industry. He insisted on animating every frame of his sequences, and his stubbornness led to arguments with Walt, who reasoned that it was wasteful for the studio's best animator to make drawings that the in-betweeners could readily accomplish. The incident brought further friction between Walt and Ub.

But Walt, in a February 9, 1929, letter, when he returned to New York, sent encouragement to his chief collaborator: "I am glad the spook dance is progressing so nicely—give her Hell, Ubbe—make it funny and I am sure we will be able to place it in a good way. I have them all worked up and raring to see it—so we can't disappoint them—we have a wonderful score to it. The music sounds like a little symphony. I feel positive everything will fit the picture properly. . . ."

On the following day he wrote to Lilly: "I feel positive the 'Spook Dance' will make a real hit when shown. Everyone praises Ubbe's art work and jokes at his funny name. The oddness of Ubbe's name is an asset in a way—it makes people look twice when they see it. Tell Ubbe that the New York animators take off their hats to his animation and all of them know who we are."

Walt planned to release *The Skeleton Dance* as the first of a new series of cartoons to be called Silly Symphonies, each a new subject without continuing characters. The series would permit him and his animators to experiment with new story material and new techniques. He dispatched a print of *The Skeleton Dance* to Pat Powers, suggesting that he screen it for potential customers. Powers replied: "They don't want this. MORE MICE."

Walt was certain Powers was wrong, and he arranged to show *The Skeleton Dance* one morning at a downtown Los Angeles theater. Walt sensed the smaller audience's enjoyment of the cartoon, but the manager declared, "Can't recommend it. Too gruesome."

Walt sought a film salesman of his acquaintance, locating him in a pool hall. Walt said he was convinced *The Skeleton Dance* could be booked at the prestigious Carthay Circle Theater, if the owner, Fred Miller, could be induced to look at it. "All right, leave the

print; I'll get in touch with you," said the salesman,
returning to his game.

Miller saw *The Skeleton Dance,* liked it, and booked
the cartoon into the Carthay Circle. The response was
overwhelming, and Walt sent the reviews to Pat Powers
with the suggestion that Samuel L. (Roxy) Rothafel,
the famed Broadway showman, might be convinced
to play the cartoon at his giant Roxy Theater. His hunch
proved right, and the engagement at the Roxy provided
the impetus to launch the Silly Symphonies.

Mickey Mouse flourished into a national craze in
1929. Mickey Mouse Clubs sprang up all over the
country, and the cry of the anguished moviegoer, "What
—no Mickey Mouse?" became a catch phrase. (It
originated in a cartoon in the old *Life* magazine.) The
seeming prosperity of the Disney enterprise was illusory.
Walt insisted on greater quality in the Mickeys and
Symphonies, and the cost per cartoon climbed to
$5,000. Walt expected the added expense to be bal-
anced by receipts from Pat Powers. But weeks passed
without any checks from New York. Roy Disney went
to New York in an attempt to straighten out finances
with Powers. Roy was treated to Powers Irish charm
and fiscal obfuscation, and he returned with his suspicions confirmed. "That's guy's a crook," Roy told his
brother. "Go back there and see for yourself."

The brothers agreed that they needed legal assistance,
and they hired a colorful attorney named Gunther
Lessing, who had advised Pancho Villa during the
Mexican revolutionary's heyday. Walt reasoned, "If he
could help Pancho Villa, he's just the man we need."

In January 1930, Walt, Lilly and Gunther Lessing
departed for New York and the confrontation with Pat
Powers. Walt went alone to the first meeting, which
began with Powers' insistence that he was still only
interested in promoting Cinephone; the success of
Mickey Mouse had been merely a happy side-effect.
He was off-handed about the cartoon series, but in
reality he was desperate to sign again with Disney when
the one-year contract expired. Powers pressed for a

continuation of the contract, but Walt insisted first on an accounting of Powers' receipts from the cartoons. Shrugging off the demand, the Irishman said he had news that would convince the Disneys to sign again with Pat Powers. He handed over a telegram. It was a message from Powers' henchman on the West Coast that Ub Iwerks had been signed to a contract with Powers to create a new cartoon series at a salary of $300 a week.

Walt was stunned. Walt and Ub had grown up together in the animation business. They worked side by side for long nights to make successes of Alice, of Oswald and Mickey. Ub had invested part of his salary in the company, and Walt and Roy had made him a 20-percent owner and an officer of the firm.

"I can't believe it," Walt muttered.

"It's true," Powers said with a smile. "Pick up the phone and call your brother. He knows about it. Go ahead—call." Walt was too shaken to telephone Roy.

"Don't get upset," Powers continued. "You haven't lost Ub Iwerks. You can still have him—if you sign with me."

Walt shook his head. "No. I wouldn't want him. If he feels that way, I couldn't work with him."

"Look" Powers said, "you and your brother need money. I'll make you a deal that will relieve you of the concern about money matters. I'll pay you a weekly salary. I'm willing to go as high as twenty-five hundred dollars a week."

Powers was surprised that his munificent offer failed to impress the young cartoon maker—Walt was still trying to grasp the news that Ub had left him.

Roy confirmed it by telephone when Walt returned to his room at the Algonquin Hotel. Ub had come to Roy that day and said he wanted to be released from the partnership. Ub said that artistic differences had developed between him and Walt. He made no mention of the Powers contract. Gunther Lessing later negotiated an agreement that dissolved Ub's contract with Disney and paid him $2,920 for his one-fifth interest. (Hypothetically, if Iwerks had retained his share in the company, its market value would have reached $750,000,000.)

Walt contemplated his situation. By January of 1930 he had delivered twelve Mickey Mouse cartoons of the first series, three of the second series, and six Silly Symphonies. The cost of the cartoons had been $116,500, or $5,500 per picture. He knew that Powers had been collecting big rentals for the cartoons—almost $17,000 apiece. But by the time Powers took his 35 percent as distributor, plus costs for prints, processing, advertising, censorship fees, licensing, insurance, music rights, recording fees, print royalties and foreign dubbing, there was little left for the Disneys. Walt remembered Roy's instructions: "Don't break with Powers until we get some dough." When they met again, Walt told Powers that his brother had insisted that they needed more money at the studio. "Certainly," said Powers magnanimously. "Will five thousand dollars be all right?" Walt agreed that it would, and he immediately dispatched the check to Roy in California.

Walt and Gunther Lessing conferred about their next move. Both agreed that Walt should demand to see Powers' accounts of receipts from the Disney films. Powers proposed his counter-offer: "Make a deal with me and I'll show you the books." The alternative, he indicated, was to take him to court, a process which would require time and money that the Disney brothers could ill afford.

Walt and Roy discussed whether to provoke a fight with Powers and try to recover the revenue they deserved, or simply walk away from the shifty promoter and begin anew. They decided to walk away.

Walt broke off the negotiations with Powers and began talking to other distributors about a release. Unlike his experience of a year before, he was now welcomed into the home offices of the major companies as father of the famous Mickey Mouse. Felix Feist, sales manager of Metro-Goldwyn-Mayer, strongly recommended a contract for the Mickey Mouse and Silly Symphony series, but after four days of deliberations the MGM attorneys decided against it. The ubiquitous Pat Powers had issued threats to sue any company that signed a contract for the Disney cartoons.

Columbia Pictures was not so timid. The company's belligerent founder, Harry Cohn, was then bulling his way into the ranks of the important producers, and his director, Frank Capra, advised him to make a deal with the brilliant young cartoon maker. Cohn offered $7,000 advance for each cartoon. Importantly, Columbia established a war fund of $25,000 to combat Pat Powers if he tried to contest the new contract.

Powers was enough of a realist to recognize his defeat. He suggested a settlement by which he would relinquish the twenty-one Disney cartoons in return for a cash settlement. The figure he mentioned was more than $100,000. Walt wanted to be rid of Powers and to regain control of his films. He agreed to pay Powers the tribute, even though he believed that the old pirate owed him much more. Walt arranged a $50,000 loan from Columbia to conclude the deal.

Walt telegraphed the news to Roy on February 7, 1930:

HAVE DEFINITELY BROKE WITH POWERS STOP WILL DELIVER NO MORE PICTURES STOP PLAN TO TEMPORARILY SUSPEND PRODUCTION MICKEYS AND CONCENTRATE ON SYMPHONIES WHICH WE WILL DELIVER TO COLUMBIA.

Walt returned to California with the hope that a new distributorship would afford enough financial independence so he could devote full energies to improving the quality of the cartoons. But once more that independence was to prove elusive.

Walt's almost total immersion in his work contributed to his nervous breakdown in late 1931.

He had been pushing himself and his animators hard, seeking greater quality in the cartoons instead of coasting on his already substantial reputation. There were inevitable disappointments. Some of his artists met the challenges he gave them; others did not. Each failure was a personal defeat to Walt.

The financial troubles returned. For all the euphoria that marked the beginning of the Columbia contract, Walt and Roy found themselves in the same fiscal squeeze that they had known with Pat Powers. With each new cartoon the brothers seemed to slip deeper in debt. Walt kept adding to his payroll, and he instructed his animators to take more care with their drawings. That always meant more expense.

Animation was an anomaly in the motion-picture business. The normal movie could be made cheaply or expensively, according to the cost of the talent and the production values. A cartoon was handcrafted—fifteen thousand pictures drawn, inked and painted for each seven-minute film. A cartoon could not be made with less tedium, and any refinement of the technique inexorably pushed costs higher. Animation as practiced by Walt Disney would always be a perilous enterprise, with prosperous times when the product succeeded and the threat of insolvency when it didn't.

Money worries and the stress of leading a crew of volatile, talented artists through uncharted territory began to wear on Walt. He became more irritable with his employees, snapping at them for minor offenses. A sudden disappointment could plunge him into a crying spell. He spent sleepless hours in bed at night, staring at the ceiling as he reviewed the day's events and planned the future. In story sessions his mind went blank and he couldn't recall what was being discussed. He consulted a doctor, who advised him to leave the studio and seek a complete rest. Walt and Lilly decided to take their first non-business trip since their honeymoon, five years before. Roy took charge of the studio, and Walt and Lilly left to fulfill his ambition on his return from France: to voyage down the Mississippi River. But when they visited the St. Louis waterfront, they discovered that only barges floated down the Mississippi; the Depression had wiped out the passenger trade.

The Disneys boarded a train for their first trip to Washington, D.C. When they registered at the Mayflower Hotel, the publicity man recognized the famous guest from Hollywood and asked if he could make any arrangements. "Yes, I'd like to meet General Pershing," Walt replied. "When I was driving a canteen car in France, I drove his son, and I heard the general give his farewell speech in Paris on the back of a truck. He was my hero, and I'd sure like to meet him."

"Well, that's pretty hard to arrange," the publicity man said. "Would you like to see President Hoover instead?"

"No, the President's too busy," Walt replied, "and I wouldn't know what to talk to him about. But I would like to see General Pershing." An appointment proved impossible, but Pershing sent an autographed copy of his memoirs. Walt took Lilly to see the Washington Monument, Mount Vernon, the Lincoln Memorial and the Capitol.

Then they traveled by train down the Atlantic Coast to Key West and boarded a ship for Cuba. They spent a week of sightseeing in Havana, then cruised through the Panama Canal and up the West Coast to Los Angeles. Walt and Lilly agreed that was the best part of the trip. He strolled around the deck, became acquainted with other passengers on the cruise, spent hours staring at the ship's wake. By the time the ship docked at San Pedro, he was totally relaxed.

When Walt returned to work, he remembered the doctor's advice to vary his studio routine with exercise. He went to the Hollywood Athletic Club two or three times a week for boxing, calisthenics and swimming. Then he took up golf, rising at five-thirty and playing nine holes on the Griffith Park course, returning home for a big breakfast before reporting to the studio. He often left work early so he and Lilly could ride horse-back in the hills behind their home. This was part of the regimen suggested by her doctor. He advised a physical buildup for both Lilly and Walt as a possible solution for their inability to have a child.

9

By 1931, the Mickey Mouse Club had a million mem-bers, and Mickey was known in every civilized country of the world. Douglas Fairbanks, Sr., ingratiated him-self to Polynesian natives by showing them Mickey Mouse cartoons, and Mary Pickford declared Mickey her favorite star. In London, Madame Tussaud's mu-seum enshrined Mickey in wax. Mrs. Franklin D. Roosevelt wrote to Walt from the White House: "My husband is one of the devotées of Mickey Mouse. . . . Please believe that we are all of us most grateful to you for many delightful evenings." A rare discordant note was heard from German censors who banned a Mickey Mouse cartoon because "the wearing of Ger-man military helmets by an army of cats which oppose a militia of mice is offensive to national dignity."

The craze for Mickey Mouse brought a new and important source of income to the Disney enterprise. Use of Oswald's likeness had been granted to a few manufacturers, largely for the publicity value. Walt first realized the financial possibilities of licensing when he was in New York for negotiations with Pat Powers in late 1929. He recalled later that a man called at his hotel and offered $300 in cash for permission to imprint Mickey Mouse on school writing tablets. "As usual, Roy and I needed money, so I took the three hundred," Walt said.

More offers arrived. On February 3, 1930, Roy signed the first contract for merchandising, granting the George Borgfeldt Company of New York the right to manufacture and sell "figures and toys of various materials, embodying design of comic Mice known as Minnie and Mickey Mouse, appearing in copyrighted motion pictures." Disney would receive 2½ percent royalty on items selling for fifty cents or less, 5 percent for more expensive products. The first license made by Borgfeldt went to a Swiss firm for the manufacture of Mickey and Minnie handkerchiefs.

After Mickey Mouse began to capture the nation's affection, Walt assigned the prolific Ub Iwerks to devise a comic strip for newspapers. While Ub was at work on the strip, an offer for syndication came from the Hearst agency, King features. Ub prepared several specimens until Walt was satisfied, and the Mickey Mouse comic strip made its appearance on January 13, 1930. Ub's assistant, Win Smith, drew the Mickey Mouse comic for three months, then it was taken over by Floyd Gottfredson, who continued with the strip until 1975. Walt reviewed Gottfredson's work for the first year and a half, then lost interest. Sometimes on trips he mailed Gottfredson copies from newspapers with a comment such as "There's too damn much junk in this strip," prompting the cartoonist to remove the clutter. The Mickey Mouse strip proved a big seller for King Features, which began syndicating Mickey and Silly Symphony comics in color for Sunday supplements on January 10, 1932.

In 1932, an energetic Kansas City advertising man named Herman (Kay) Kamen telephoned Walt with proposals about how to merchandise Mickey Mouse and the other Disney characters. Walt and Roy had been dissatisfied with their New York and London agents, and they invited Kamen to California for a discussion of his ideas. The Disneys were impressed, especially with Kamen's emphasis on the quality of the merchandise to bear the Disney imprint, and on July 1, 1932, Kamen signed a contract to represent the company. One of his first deals was with a baking concern for ten million Mickey Mouse ice-cream cones.

The salesmanship of Mickey Mouse produced seemingly miraculous results. Kamen licensed the Lionel Corporation, pioneer in manufacture of toy electric trains, for the merchandising of a Mickey and Minnie wind-up handcar with a circle of track for the price of $1. Lionel had been hit hard by the Depression and had filed for bankruptcy. Within four months, 253,000 of the handcars had been sold, and the association with Disney was credited by a bankruptcy judge as a major factor in returning Lionel to solvency.

The Ingersoll-Waterbury Company, makers of timepieces since 1856, had been pushed close to bankruptcy in the early Thirties, when Kamen licensed the firm to manufacture Mickey Mouse watches. Within weeks, demand for the watches caused the company to raise the number of employees at its Waterbury, Connecticut, plant from three hundred to three thousand. Two and a half million Mickey Mouse watches were sold within two years.

Highbrow critics tried to analyze Mickey's popularity in terms of mass psychology. Walt Disney was amused but unimpressed by such intellectualizing. He offered his own explanation: "Mickey's a nice fellow who never does anybody any harm, who gets in scrapes through no fault of his own but always manages to come up grinning." He was quick to give credit for much of Mickey's nature to Charlie Chaplin: "We thought of a tiny bit of a mouse that would have something of the wistfulness of Chaplin—a little fellow trying to do the best he could."

What emerged in Mickey Mouse was more Walt Disney than Charlie Chaplin. The most obvious connection was the voice. The nervous, flustery falsetto—a line of dialogue was often preceded with a shy "heh-heh-heh"—was just right for Mickey. It was no easy matter to get color into such an unnatural, limited voice, but Walt managed. No one else could capture the gulping, ingenuous, half-brave quality. But the similarity didn't end with the voice. Both Walt and Mickey had an adventurous spirit, a sense of rectitude, an admitted lack of sophistication, a boyish ambition to excel. Both were unashamedly devoted to the ideals of Horatio Alger. Both clung to the old-fashioned notion of remaining steadfast to one sweetheart.

The Disney animators recognized this unstated similarity, and when drawing the Mouse often kept in mind—subconsciously, at least—the characteristics of Walt. In describing his concept of how the cartoon should appear, Walt called upon his considerable histrionics, acting out each role and each line of dialogue. His depiction of Mickey was so accurate, so inspired, that animators wished they could capture the Disney facial expressions and movements. Once they managed to do so.

In one of the cartoons, Mickey had a line the animators couldn't fit a drawing to: "I'm Mickey Mouse; you've heard of me, I hope?" One of the animators asked if Walt would allow himself to be photographed while he recorded the line. "Oh, gosh, you don't want that, do you?" he replied. They assured him the film would be helpful. "Well," Walt replied, "if you put the camera in the control booth seventy-five feet away and don't bother me while I record the line—okay." The resulting film helped solve the animator's problem.

Walt was the devoted guardian of Mickey's integrity. Many times he said in story conferences, "Mickey wouldn't do that." He had an unerring sense of detecting when the gag men were going too far, when they were reaching for comedy business which would perhaps draw bellylaughs but would be at variance with the naturalness of Mickey's character. That is why Mickey Mouse captured the world's affection as had no other cartoon character: he remained himself, an enormously likable figure.

The success of Mickey Mouse was bringing many changes to the Hyperion studio. The physical plant underwent the first of its many mutations, with additions to the front, side and rear of the original building in 1929 and 1930. New offices were constructed in 1930, and the following year brought the completion of a new two-storied Animation Building and a sound stage. Walt, who had sometimes answered the studio telephone himself in the early years, now had a second-floor office with an oriental rug over planked flooring, stained-glass windows and a handsome wood desk.

Studio personnel was expanding rapidly. Veteran animators and story men left the New York cartoon studios to join the exciting things that were happening at Disney's. Among them were Dave Hand, Rudy Zamora, Tom Palmer, Ted Sears, Burt Gillett, Jack King, Webb Smith. Bert Lewis took over the music department after Carl Stalling left for another cartoon studio. Frank Churchill joined the studio as a pianist-composer. The infusion of new talent prompted Walt to set increasingly higher standards for the Mickey Mouse cartoons and the Silly Symphonies.

As each new cartoon approached, Walt issued hortatory memos to the staff. A July 20, 1931, message called for suggestions for the eighteenth Mickey, *The Barnyard Broadcast*. By this time Mickey and Minnie had been joined by other cast regulars, Pluto the Pup, Horace Horsecollar and Clarabelle Cow. Walt announced a forthcoming meeting to discuss the cartoon and outlined the plot:

Story to be built around a Barnyard Broadcasting idea. Action will center on the efforts of Mickey and his gang trying to broadcast. Probably work in piano playing, quartet in goofy numbers, the "Swiss Yodelers." Mickey could do a solo number on his banjo and Minnie could play a solo on the harp. The barnyard birds come in and sing, whistle and chirp while Minnie is playing the harp. Possible to use the little canary singing all through the broadcast or use the little barn swallows instead.

Clarabelle and Horsecollar could do a dance together or individually. Possibly use Pluto in the story, carrying him in his characteristic dumb style. Could cut back to all the barnyard animals listening in on their respective radio sets. The chickens in their chicken coops, hens laying eggs to the radio reception, pigs in their pens dancing, etc., sheep in the pasture, birds in the trees with their little nests fixed up like homes, all listening in on their sets.

Mickey could be the announcer. Could work up a hillbilly act with Clarabelle, Horsecollar, Mickey and Minnie as the hillbillies.

I expect everyone to contribute some ideas to this Gag Meeting. The ideas must be built around the group of characters as suggested above, and in such a way as to tie them in with the ideas as outlined. Any ideas that you work up to submit at the meeting should be accompanied by small sketches to illustrate the gags. Kindly have such material prepared and ready to hand in at the beginning of the meeting. Supply yourself with a pad and pencil for the purpose of making notes or sketching out any ideas that might present themselves during the course of the meeting.

Everyone give this some deep thought and see if we can't come up with a good peppy meeting.

Walt and his artists were developing new techniques for the animation industry. The drawback to cartoon making had always been that the animator could not judge the effectiveness of his work until it was completed and on the screen. In their eagerness to please Walt, his animators developed a process which would permit a preliminary view of what the action would be. As the animator completed key poses, his assistant, or in-betweener, photographed the drawings, developing the print himself and drying it on a revolving drum. When enough of the drawings had been completed, the film was spliced onto a loop. Then the animator could get a visual impression of how his character would move. The films were projected in a small, unven-

tilated closet, and thus the place for preliminary review of animation was dubbed "the sweatbox."

Another important new technique was the storyboard.

Animators had long been hampered in story sessions
by the necessity of verbalizing what was essentially a
visual medium. They brought sketches or created them
on the spot, but there was no way to present the complete continuity of what would appear on the screen.
The storyboard provided that. It was simplicity itself:
a large fiber board four feet by eight, on which sketches
were pinned. Thus Walt could see at a glance how the
action would progress. If scenes were eliminated, they
could be unpinned and discarded. New scenes could be
added. When the final sequence was decided upon,
Walt and his animators could visualize the cartoon
from beginning to end.

With his staff expanding, Walt Disney began to establish the attitudes and modes of operation that would
continue throughout his professional career. Not yet
thirty, he had been in the animation business a dozen
years, and his maturity belied his years. Some of his
underlings had worked longer in New York cartoons,
but all viewed Walt Disney as a leader to be followed,
and obeyed. Away from the studio he could indulge in
horseplay and be "one of the boys." But during work
hours his attitude precluded casual intimacy. He was
incapable of small talk. His employees learned not to
engage him in the banter that animators used as relief
from the tedium of drawing. His mind was too involved with the problems of the moment—a storyline
that defied solution; a cartoon that failed to evoke
laughs at the preview; an overdue check from Columbia
Pictures that threatened next week's payroll. His workers learned not to be offended if he passed them in the
hallway without a word; they knew that he was preoc-
cupied with a studio problem.

Walt was developing one of his most valuable traits:
the ability to recognize a man's creative potential and
force him to achieve it.

Wilfred Jackson was a rawboned student from Otis Art Institute when he applied for a job at the Disney studio in 1928. He was so eager to learn animation that he offered to work for nothing—or even pay tuition. He was assigned to help the janitor wash paint off cels. Soon he was animating, drawing a cycle of Minnie running along the riverbank in *Steamboat Willie*. Each time he proved himself in a new challenge, Walt promoted him to a job of greater responsibility. To Jackson it seemed that he was being pushed beyond his capacities; but he was so anxious to prove himself to Walt that he tried ever harder. One day he remarked to Walt: "I'd sure like it if you would let me handle a whole picture myself."

Jackson meant that he wanted to animate an entire cartoon; Walt had other ideas. He told Jackson: "You know, I've got a lot of loose ends that have been cut out of the Mickeys. Why don't you work up some kind of story that would tie all of them together?" Jackson didn't like being handed bits and pieces of other animators' work instead of creating his own subject. But he concocted a story with Mickey being stranded on a desert island with a piano—one of the film fragments conveniently had a piano sequence—and dreaming of previous episodes in his life. The result was an entertaining cartoon, *The Castaway*. Jackson had proved to Walt that he could be a director, which was not what he intended to be. But he recognized later, as Walt had already concluded, that he could not compete with the accomplished animators from New York. He proved to be an expert director, and he remained one for more than thirty years.

Ben Sharpsteen had worked for Max Fleischer on Happy Hooligan and Out of the Inkwell before coming to work for Walt in 1929. After the New York invasion began in full force, Sharpsteen grew discouraged over his ability to keep up with the new animators. Walt recognized Sharpsteen's capacity for working with young talent, and he suggested, "We've got to teach these new boys all about animation; you do it." Sharpsteen found himself in charge of training the fledgling artists, laying the groundwork for an educational expansion in the mid-Thirties. After Sharpsteen had the program in motion, Walt needed another director. He chose Ben Sharpsteen.

Walt's work was all-consuming. He seemed to think and talk about nothing else. One evening Sharpsteen met Walt and Lilly at a drugstore near the studio. Walt had been thinking about another barnyard adventure for Mickey, and he unburdened himself of the entire plot, enacting in the doorway of the drugstore the roles of cats, pigs, goats and Mickey himself.

No source of story material was overlooked. When Walt received a traffic ticket for speeding, he related the incident to those he met in the studio hallways. With each recounting, the encounter with the law became more embellished, until the story proved too good for private telling. It became the basis for the next Mickey Mouse cartoon, *Traffic Troubles*.

The releasing contract with Columbia Pictures had proved unsatisfactory. Walt and Roy had no quarrel with Harry Cohn, the Hollywood autocrat of Columbia's fortunes, but they felt they were being mistreated by the distribution office in New York. Columbia exacted 35 percent of all revenue from the cartoons, and deducted the costs of prints, transportation, insurance, advertising, etc. The contract provided for Columbia and Disney to take equal shares of the remainder, minus the $7,000 Columbia advanced for each cartoon. But nothing ever remained. In two years Columbia released fifty Disney films and all were charged with a deficit because of the original $50,000 that Columbia had advanced to pay off Powers.

With income restricted and costs constantly mounting, Roy Disney sometimes found it difficult to meet the payroll. On one payday each worker found only a $10 goldpiece in his envelope. When Roy complained to his brother about their limited resources, Walt replied, "Don't worry." Even when the nation's banks were closed by President Roosevelt in 1933, Walt refused to share Roy's concern. "Why should money be so important?" Walt reasoned. "Maybe potatoes will become the medium of exchange, and we can pay the boys in potatoes."

Walt realized the studio could not produce cartoons at a perpetual loss. The Disneys asked Columbia to increase the advance on each cartoon to $15,000. Columbia declined.

The veteran producer Sol Lesser had become a friend of the Disneys, and he mentioned their distribution problems to Joseph Schenck, president of United Artists. Schenck told the Disneys, "You are producers; we are a company of producers. We will sell your cartoons on their own. We don't sell any other shorts, so your product won't be released with a bunch of others in block-booking. We'll give you fifteen thousand dollars advance on each cartoon. We also have a close connection with the Bank of America, and we can help you get financing."

The proposal was extremely attractive to Walt, not merely because of the terms. United Artists represented the Tiffany's of the movie business; its partners were Mary Pickford, Douglas Fairbanks, Charlie Chaplin and Samuel Goldwyn. Walt was especially thrilled at the prospect of being associated with the great Chaplin. The comedian proved to be as much of a fan of the Disney cartoons as Walt had been of Chaplin's comedies. "You're going to develop more; you're getting ahold of your medium," Chaplin told Walt. "But to protect your independence, you've got to do as I have done—own every picture you make." Walt agreed with the advice.

With the association with United Artists agreed upon, Walt determined to add a new element to animation: color.

For years Walt had been intrigued with the notion of adding color to his cartoons. He had told his technicians to experiment with nitrates and other elements that might provide color on the screen. But nothing proved practical, except for the primitive technique of using blue film stock for night scenes, green for underwater, and red for fire. Then in the early 1930s, Technicolor developed a method of combining three negatives of the primary colors. By 1932 the process had not been perfected for live-action photography, but it could be applied to cartoons. Technicolor showed a test reel to Walt Disney, and he was convinced. Roy wasn't.

"We'd be crazy to take on the expense of color just after we've made a deal with United Artists," Roy argued. "They won't advance us any more money for color."

"Yes, but don't you see, Roy?" Walt replied. "Maybe United Artists won't give us any more dough, but the pictures will create so much excitement that we'll get longer playdates and bigger rentals. That'll bring the money back eventually."

"Eventually! It'll be years before we see that money, with all the advances that are charged against us already. We can't do it."

Roy added his fears that the colors might not stick to the celluloid or would chip off. Walt's answer: "Then we'll develop paints that *will* stick and *won't* chip." Roy remained unconvinced. He asked others in the studio to dissuade his brother from his disastrous course. Walt heard their arguments and became more certain that color would raise animation to new levels of creativity. He saw color as a means of establishing the Silly Symphonies. From the beginning, they had been a kind of stepsister to the enormously popular Mickey Mouse series. United Artists had been reluctant to take on the Symphonies and did so only when Walt agreed to borrow on his star's name with the billing "Mickey Mouse Presents a Walt Disney Silly Symphony."

Walt used his brother's reluctance to evoke a concession from Technicolor. "Roy says color is going to cost us a lot of money that we'll never get back," Walt argued. "So if we take a chance on it, you've got to assure us that every other cartoon producer isn't going to rush into the theaters with Technicolor." The com-

pany agreed to grant Disney two years' exclusive use
of the three-color process. Roy grumblingly consented
to a contract.

Production had been half completed on a Silly Symphony called *Flowers and Trees,* an idyll in which plants
animated to the music of Mendelssohn and Schubert.
Walt ordered the black-and-white backgrounds re-
painted and all of the action restaged in color. A special camera stand was constructed to photograph the
colored cels. Roy's fears were confirmed: the dried
paint did chip off the celluloid and colors faded under
the hot lights. Walt worked night and day with his
laboratory technicians until they developed an adhering
paint of stable colors.

After the first few scenes had been completed, Walt
showed them to a friend, Rob Wagner, publisher of a
literary magazine in Beverly Hills. Wagner was so impressed that he invited Sid Grauman, impresario of
Grauman's Chinese Theater, to see the film. The film
lasted only a minute, but Grauman said he wanted
Flowers and Trees to open with his next attraction,
Strange Interlude, starring Norma Shearer and Clark
Gable. Walt worked his animators overtime to finish
ahead of schedule, and Technicolor speeded the pro-
cessing. When *Flowers and Trees* appeared at the
Chinese, in July 1932, it created the sensation that
Walt had hoped for. No longer was the Silly Symphony
the neglected half of the Disney product; *Flowers and
Trees* got as many bookings as the hottest Mickey
Mouse cartoon. Walt decreed that all future Symphonies
would be in color.

The staff continued to grow, but Walt realized that
simply adding more animators and background artists
and story men would not achieve the quality he sought.
The veteran animators from New York were good for
the slambang Mickey Mouse action, but they didn't
understand what Walt wanted in Silly Symphonies.

A new kind of artist was coming to the Disney
studio. Unlike the self-made cartoonist from New
York, the newcomers were college men or graduates of

art schools, drawn to the creative ferment of the Disney studio. Many came to Disney because jobs for artists and architects were as scarce as Cadillacs in Depression America. Walt often remarked that the Depression was his greatest ally in assembling a staff of top-flight talent.

In 1931, Walt arranged with Chouinard Art Institute in Los Angeles for his artists to attend night classes, with the studio paying the tuition. Since many of the young employees couldn't afford cars, Walt himself drove them downtown to the school, returned to the studio for an evening's work, then picked up the students when the classes were over. When the United Artists contract assured a greater flow of funds into the studio, Walt decided to establish a school at the studio. He asked a Chouinard teacher, Don Graham, to conduct classes two nights a week on the studio sound stage. The first class of the Disney Art School was held on the night of November 15, 1932, with twenty-five artists in attendance. The number of students grew, especially when others learned that Graham demonstrated motion with the aid of a nude female model.

Graham was admittedly unschooled in animation, and some of his students resisted his instruction. Scornful cartoons appeared on the studio bulletin board, depicting Mickey Mouse with an anatomically detailed pelvis. But as time went on, each side learned from the other. Graham and the other teachers realized the animator's peculiar problem of creating characters that were both convincing and entertaining. The animators discovered that their instructors could be helpful in providing keys to the movement of human beings and animals. The art school began to fulfill the function that Walt had designed for it: to develop the talent that would carry animation to heights that only he then envisioned.

Animation—and Walt Disney Productions—took a great step forward with *The Three Little Pigs* in 1933.

It began merely as the thirty-sixth Silly Symphony, a variation of the old fable. As Walt pointed out in his initial memo, the original tale could not be followed exactly; in it the wolf ate the two pigs who made their houses of straw and sticks, then the industrious pig feasted on the wolf after it fell into boiling water. Walt outlined the basic elements of the story and added:

> These little pig characters look as if they would work up very cute and we should be able to develop quite a bit of personality in them. Use cute voices that could work into harmony and chorus effects when they talk together. . . . The building of the houses holds chances for a lot of good gags. All this action would be set within rhythm and should work out very effectively. . . . Pull quite a few gags of the wolf trying to get into the little houses, and the pigs' attempts to get rid of him. Chance for funny ways in which the little pigs attack him, the different household props they would use. . . . The idea of the three pigs having musical instruments gives us a chance to work in the singing and dancing angles for the finish of the story. . . . Might try to stress the angle of the little pig who worked the hardest, received the reward, or some little story that would teach a moral. Someone might have some angles on how we could bring this moral out in a direct way without having to go into too much detail. This angle might be given some careful consideration, for things of this sort woven into a story give it depth and feeling.
>
> It is not our intention to make a straight story out of this, we want to gag it in every way we can and make it as funny as possible. These little pigs will be dressed in clothes. They will also have household implements, props, etc., to work with, and not be kept in the natural state. They will be more like human characters.

ALL GAGS MUST BE HANDED IN BY FRIDAY DE-
CEMBER 30TH AT 4 P.M. I EXPECT A BIG TURNOUT
ON THIS STORY IN SPITE OF THE CHRISTMAS.

Walt's choice of men to work on *The Three Little Pigs* was inspired. To draw the pigs themselves he selected Fred Moore, a brilliant, intuitive animator who had arrived at the Disney Studio in 1930 with a set of sketches on shirt-laundry cardboards. He was only eighteen, but soon he was animating alongside the veterans. Moore invested each pig with a distinct personality and drew them with a rounded solidity that made them seem like authentic porkers. Norman Ferguson, who had come west from the New York studios, created the wolf and made him a sly, slobbering masterpiece of a villain. Walt stressed the need for a song to tie all the elements together, and that was the responsibility of Frank Churchill. He had dropped out of UCLA to play honky-tonk piano in Tijuana and Juarez bars, and became a radio and movie studio musician before being hired by Disney to arrange cartoon scores. For *The Three Little Pigs* he composed a jingle along the pattern of "Happy Birthday to You," and story man Ted Sears provided some couplets: "I build my house of straw . . . and I build my house of sticks . . ." The chorus came naturally: "Who's afraid of the big bad wolf?" There seemed to be no way to end the chorus until Pinto Colvig, who had portrayed many of the voices in the cartoons, played a phrase on the ocarina.

The Three Little Pigs breezed through production and was previewed with excellent results. Walt was elated, and he sent a message to his brother Roy in New York: "At last we have achieved true personality in a whole picture!" Roy conveyed Walt's enthusiasm to the United Artists salesmen. When a print of *The Three Little Pigs* arrived in New York, Roy arranged a screening in a projection room at the United Artists office. The hardboiled salesmen remained silent during the cartoon, and one of them afterward said, "This is kind of a cheater, don't you think?" Roy asked what he meant. "The last cartoon Walt sent us was *Father Noah's Ark*, with dozens of animals," said the salesman. "Now he gives us only four."

The United Artists publicity man, Hal Horne, laughed and assured Roy, "This is the greatest picture Walt's ever made."

The salesman's glum comment seemed to have been borne out when *The Three Little Pigs* opened at the Radio City Music Hall. Audiences found the cartoon amusing, but the personalities of the pigs and the wolf failed to register on the Music Hall's mammoth screen. Only when *The Three Little Pigs* started playing neighborhood theaters in New York did the explosion begin.

Audiences everywhere were captivated by the pigs and joined in loathing the wolf. He, after all, was the symbol of the Depression that had crimped everyone's life. The song "Who's Afraid of the Big Bad Wolf?" became a national rallying cry.

The Disney organization was unprepared for the sudden success. The company had never had a song hit, and no contract had been made to publish "Who's Afraid of the Big Bad Wolf?" Orchestra leaders all over the country sent their arrangers to theaters to copy the tune and lyrics so the song could be played for audiences. Irving Berlin's music company sought permission to publish the song, and Roy entered into a contract.

The success of *The Three Little Pigs* was unparalleled in cartoon history. Theater marquees all over the country billed it above the feature movies. First-run houses changed their feature attractions but kept offering *The Three Little Pigs* week after week. One New York theater played it so long that the manager drew beards on the pigs in the lobby poster; as the run extended, the beards grew longer.

The United Artists salesmen responded characteristically; their message to Walt was "Send us more pigs!" He refused, never wanting to repeat himself. But Roy convinced him that bringing back the pigs

would be good for business. Walt made three more—
The Big Bad Wolf, Three Little Wolves, and *The Practical Pig.* None approached the sensation of the original, and Walt made a comment he repeated for years afterward: "You can't top pigs with pigs."

On November 18, 1932, the Academy of Motion Picture Arts and Sciences gave its first award for a cartoon to Walt Disney for *Flowers and Trees;* he was also presented a special award for the creation of Mickey Mouse. His status as a maker of film entertainment had been officially acknowledged, and Walt was beginning to make a modest venture into Hollywood society, through polo.

He had taken up the sport with his usual thoroughness. Encountering Jack Cutting in the studio hallway, Walt remarked, "I understand you're a good horseman. Would you like to play polo?" Cutting said he would. Walt also enlisted Norm Ferguson, Les Clark, Dick Lundy, Gunther Lessing and Bill Cottrell, and he even persuaded Roy to join. All were summoned to the conference room at the Hyperion studio, where they found pads and pencils and copies of the text, Cameron's *As to Polo.* Walt had hired a polo expert, Gil Proctor, who lectured about maneuvers, plotting them on the blackboard. When the rudiments had been learned, the eight poloists began practice sessions at a riding academy in the San Fernando Valley. Practice started at six in the morning and was completed in time for all of the players to report to the studio by eight. Walt erected a polo cage at the studio; on the lunch hour or during work breaks, the players could sit on a wooden mount and practice hitting the wooden ball. When their coach considered them well enough trained, they began competing in matches at Victor McLaglen's stadium on Riverside Drive. Walt and Roy later played at the Riviera Club with such figures as Will Rogers, Darryl F. Zanuck, Spencer Tracy, James Gleason, Big Boy Williams and Frank Borzage. Walt was not the best of the players, but he was a hard-riding competitor, making up with aggressiveness for what he lacked in skill.

In 1933 Walt and Lilly moved into a new home they had built in the Los Feliz district a few miles from the studio. It was a handsome house with a swimming pool dug out of the hard mountainside rock. Soon there would be a new arrival, as Walt wrote in a letter to his mother in Portland:

. . . The doctor says Lilly is in perfect condition and everything is okay, and within a week or so everything will be over—except the crying!

The spare bedroom, where you and Dad stayed, is all fixed up like a nursery. We have a bassinette and baby things all over the place. On the dresser, bed and everywhere else are all kinds of pink and blue "tinies" that I don't know anything about. Really, it's quite a strange atmosphere to me—I can't conceive of it belonging to us. It seems all right for somebody else to have those things around, but not for us. I presume I'll have to get used to it, and I suppose I'll be as bad a parent as anyone else. I've made a lot of vows that my kid won't be spoiled, but I doubt it—it may turn out to be the most spoiled brat in the country.

I bought my baby a present last week. I found a nice half-thoroughbred mare, which I thought would make a wonderful present for my baby. Of course, I figured I could make use of it until the baby got old enough to use it. I will stable it and use it for polo until the youngster grows up and is able to take it over. Don't fall over dead when I tell you I have six polo ponies now. But after all, it's my only sin—I don't gamble or go out and spend my money on other men's wives or anything like that, so I guess it's okay. Anyway, the wife approves of it. . . .

The baby girl arrived on December 18, 1933, thirteen days after Walt's thirty-second birthday. She was named Diane Marie Disney.

III
TOWARD A
NEW ART
1934–1945

10

By 1934 Walt was employing a dozen story and gag men, forty animators, forty-five assistant animators, thirty inkers and painters, and a twenty-four-piece orchestra, plus camera operators, electricians, sound men and other technicians. In the six years since the loss of Oswald the Rabbit, the Disney staff had grown from six to 187.

The turnover in creative personnel was high. Because Burt Gillett was credited as director of *The Three Little Pigs,* he was quickly hired away by another cartoon studio. The major studios recognized from the Disney example that gold could be mined from short cartoons, and they began making their own. One cartoon producer made a habit of luring away Disney artists after each Disney success. "Let Disney win the awards and train the artists," said the rival; "I'll hire them away and make the money." It was a logical plot, but it somehow failed in execution. The rival's cartoons could never match the Disney quality.

The nation still hadn't escaped the Depression, and new young artists were easy to find. Within the space of two or three years, Walt hired the animators who, along with Les Clark, were to form his basic crew for decades to come: Milt Kahl, Frank Thomas, Marc Davis, Woolie Reitherman, Eric Larson, John Lounsbery, Ward Kimball, Ollie Johnston.

All came to Disney with little or no knowledge of animation. Walt wanted to shorten the apprentice period and prepare the newcomers—and the studio veterans who were willing to learn—for the challenges he was envisioning. In 1934 he converted the Disney Art School to a full-time basis, instead of a limited schedule of night classes. He put Don Graham on the payroll to work three days at the studio and two nights in classes. Graham sat for hours with Walt in sweatboxes as they reviewed the photographed pencil sketches of the new animators. Twice a week Graham took groups of artists to the Griffith Park zoo to sketch animals. At the studio, the artists spent half a day drawing in life classes, half a day studying production methods. Night school was expanded to five nights a week, with 150 students attending classes in animation, character drawing, layouts and backgrounds.

Early in 1935, Walt's plans for the future were taking shape, and he instructed Don Graham: "I need three hundred artists—find them." A massive talent search was launched through want ads in newspapers from California to New York. Graham opened an office in the RCA Building in Manhattan and interviewed applicants and reviewed their portfolios.

In a long, insightful memo to Don Graham in 1935, Walt articulated better than he ever had before his beliefs about animation, drawn from his sixteen years in the medium.

He began by saying that he wanted to talk with Graham about establishing "a very systematic training course for our young animators . . . and a plan of approach for our older animators." He had been encouraged by the results of the school thus far; after lectures by such veterans as Norman Ferguson, Fred Moore, Ham Luske and Fred Spencer the quality of animation at the studio increased measurably.

Walt listed the qualities of a good animator:

1. Good draftsmanship.
2. Knowledge of caricature, of action as well as features.
3. Knowledge and appreciation of acting.
4. Ability to think up gags and put over gags.
5. Knowledge of story construction and audience values.

6. Knowledge and understanding of all the mechanical and detailed routine involved in his work, in order that he may be able to apply his other abilities without becoming tied in a knot by lack of technique along these lines.

Walt was convinced that a scientific approach to the art of animation could be achieved. Then he discoursed on his own conclusions about animation:

> The first duty of the cartoon is not to picture or duplicate real action or things as they actually happen—but to give a caricature of life and action —to picture on the screen things that have run through the imagination of the audience—to bring to life dream-fantasies and imaginative fancies that we have all thought of during our lives or have had pictured to us in various forms during our lives. Also to caricature things of life as it is today—or make fantasies of things we think of today. . . .
>
> A good many of the men misinterpret the idea of studying the actual motion. They think it is our purpose merely to duplicate these things. This misconception should be cleared up for all. I definitely feel we cannot do the fantastic things, based on the real, unless we first know the real. This point should be brought out very clearly to all new men, and even the older men.
>
> Comedy, to be appreciated, must have contact with the audience. This we all know, but sometimes forget. By contact, I mean that there must be a familiar, sub-conscious association. Somewhere, or at some time, the audience has felt, or met with, or seen, or dreamt, the situation pictured. A study of the best gags and audience reaction we have had, will prove that the action or situation is something based on an imaginative experience or a direct life connection. This is what I mean by contact with the audience. When the ac-

tion or the business loses its contact, it becomes silly and meaningless to the audience.

Therefore, the true interpretation of caricature is the exaggeration of an illusion of the actual, possible or probable. That idea, behind the things I just mentioned above, can be incorporated in every stage of instruction—from the life drawing clear on through to the planning and staging of the work.

I have often wondered why, in your life drawing class you don't have your men look at the model and draw a caricature of the model, rather than an actual sketch, but instruct them to draw the caricature in good form, basing it on the actual model. I noticed a little caricature of one of the models in the life class made by Ward Kimball, and it struck me that there was an approach to the work that we should give consideration. I don't see why using this method, you can't give the class all the fundamentals of drawing they need and still combine the work with the development of a sense of caricature. . . .

During the few brief years since *Steamboat Willie,* a creative pattern had evolved at the Disney studio. At the top, of course, was Walt, who supervised the entire process in a total and comprehensive way. Then came the directors, who were responsible for assembling the creative efforts and carrying out Walt's dictates in terms of character and action. The Story Department, with Walt in constant collaboration, provided plots and gags. The animators made the drawings that gave life to the cartoon. They were aided by assistants and in-betweeners, who relieved the animators of the tedium of multiple drawings. Finally came the women who copied the drawings on celluloid with ink and applied the colors.

Of all the contributors to the creative process, Walt had greatest respect for the animators.

Throughout his career, Walt maintained a curious

relationship with the animating breed. He kidded them, abused them, praised and berated them, but above all he recognized their indispensable contribution to the art of animation. It was something he could not do himself. His early attempts at animation were admittedly primitive; his work was fast but it seldom rose above the level of comic strip humor along the lines of George McManus and Bringing Up Father.

His relationship with animators formed an abiding pattern. The cough was an important part of it. The Disney cough, aggravated by his heavy smoking of cigarettes, was prevailing and individualistic. It could be heard down the corridors of the Hyperion studio—and later at Burbank—and it announced his presence, passing or imminent. For the lazy, the cough could inspire terror; others, surer of their accomplishments, found it reassuring—it meant that their work might be reviewed and perhaps approved. The cough, his animators were sure, was a courtesy to them. It sounded Walt's impending arrival, and, although he ran the studio and paid their salaries, he respected their privacy and would not barge into their offices unannounced.

But Walt didn't mean the cough to summon his workers to attention for his arrival. He was irritated when he entered an office to find the artists had hurried to their desks after hearing him. "I don't care if you're loafing," he said angrily. "Everybody gets tired. If you feel stale, get some fresh air. But don't let me catch you jumping back to your desks."

Another Disney pattern: the drumming fingers.

Walt's fingers were expressive and forever moving. He made eloquent use of his hands while he was describing a cartoon plot to an animator, or even a casual acquaintance. He had an artist's fingers, narrow and pliant, and hence he was good at making things. His animators learned that the fingers acted as a device to reveal his degree of approval or annoyance. If Walt was engrossed with the action on the screen in a sweatbox, his fingers would be motionless. If his interest started to drift, he began to drum on the arm of his chair. Animators listened for the sound, and if the drumming became a tattoo, they knew they would be sent back to their drawing boards.

There could be no doubt that Walt Disney was the boss. He enjoyed the position, and he enforced it. But he could be tolerant of the foibles of his artists. A Disney favorite was Roy Williams, a zany, roly-poly gag man who had arrived at the studio in 1930. One day Williams found that his salary had been reduced by a director because of tardiness. Williams rigged a bucket on a door, and the director was splashed with water. The director stormed into Walt's office and demanded that Williams be fired. "That's personal business between you and Roy," Walt replied. "Now get the hell out of here; you're getting my carpet all wet."

Another Disney favorite was Norman Ferguson. He was an animating natural, an artist whose knack of capturing character comedy helped make Pluto one of the most durable of the Disney stars. Walt feared that Ferguson's genius would be blurred in the copying of the drawings by his assistant, Nick George; to prevent that, Walt turned over a wastebasket and sat on it next to George's desk. "Now don't get it too polished, Nick," Walt instructed as George did his copying. "Keep that rough quality of Fergie's."

Ferguson could turn out up to forty feet of animation a day—the average was ten to fifteen—and he knew his worth. He asked Walt to pay him $300 a week. "But that's as much as *I'm* getting, Fergie," Walt protested. But he agreed to pay Ferguson $300 a week.

Walt seldom surveyed his animators' work while they were creating. He understood the fragile nature of the creative process, and he wouldn't intrude. But there was nothing to stop him after the animator had left for the day. Walt's nighttime visits to the offices became legendary, and animators often left their best work on the drawing table overnight, anticipating that

Walt would inspect it. But sometimes they arrived in the morning to find crumpled sheets of paper rescued from wastebaskets and pinned on a storyboard with the notation in the unmistakable Disney script: "Quit throwing the good stuff away!"

11

WALT DISNEY realized that the creative energies of his young artists could not be satisfied by the grinding out of eight-minute, gag-packed cartoons, nor was he content with the repetition of well-worn formulas for familiar characters. Besides, the economic basis for cartoon shorts was deteriorating, despite the continuing popularity of Mickey Mouse and the emergence of new Disney stars: Pluto, the ingenuous hound, who first appeared in a Mickey Mouse, *The Chain Gang,* in 1930; the affable, dim-witted Goofy, who started in *Mickey's Revue* in 1932; and the explosive Donald Duck, who made his debut in a 1934 Silly Symphony, *The Wise Little Hen.* The Depression had forced theaters to offer more and more entertainment to lure customers, and exhibitors had adopted the double feature—two full-length films on one bill. That meant there was little left in each theater's budget or running time for short subjects. Despite the fact that Walt Disney cartoons drew more people to the movies than many features, bookings for the cartoons became more difficult. At the same time, the cost of the cartoons continued to climb.

Walt had long recognized the inevitability of the cartoon feature. All of his planning had aimed in that direction: developing greater drawing skill with the art school; experimenting with color and photographic innovations; using the Silly Symphonies as proving ground for new techniques and themes. In 1934 he decided it was time to move ahead on the feature. His decision was unilateral. Roy was acutely aware of the narrowing gap between the cost of cartoons and the fiscal returns, and he was alarmed by Walt's plan to spend perhaps $500,000 on a feature. Lilly was apprehensive too. But Walt could not be dissuaded.

He could never explain why he had chosen *Snow White and the Seven Dwarfs* for the first feature. He liked to recall how he, along with other Kansas City newsboys, had been invited in 1915 to the silent version of *Snow White,* starring Marguerite Clark, at the Convention Hall. The movie was projected on four screens in the huge auditorium, and from where he was sitting, Walt could watch two of them. It had been his most vivid early memory of attending the movies. But his choice of *Snow White* was more pragmatic than sentimental. He recognized it as a splendid tale for animation, containing all the necessary ingredients: an appealing heroine and hero; a villainess of classic proportions; the Dwarfs for sympathy and comic relief; a folklore plot that touched the hearts of human beings everywhere.

Disney animators first learned of the project one evening when several of them returned from dinner at a café across Hyperion Avenue. They found Walt waiting for them, and he said, "C'mon in the sound stage; I've got something to tell you." They followed him onto the bare stage, lighted by a single naked bulb, and they took chairs in a semicircle before him. He began to tell them the story of *Snow White and the Seven Dwarfs* as it might be animated on the screen. He acted out each part, his eyebrows ascending as he mixed dread potions as the evil Queen, his face beaming when he depicted the merry Dwarfs. The performance took two hours, and at the end, when the Prince's kiss awakened the sleeping Snow White, there were tears in the eyes of his listeners. "That's going to be our first feature," Walt announced.

He began by installing a small unit of story men and

artists in an office adjoining his. By late 1934, Walt's original story had been transferred into an outline of the characters and a suggested plot. Snow White was described in terms of Janet Gaynor, fourteen years old; the Prince an eighteen-year-old Douglas Fairbanks, Jr. The Queen received the most detailed description: "A mixture of Lady Macbeth and the Big Bad Wolf. Her beauty is sinister, mature, plenty of curves. She becomes ugly and menacing when scheming and mixing her poisons. Magic fluids transform her into an old witchlike hag. Her dialogue and action are over-melodramatic, verging on the ridiculous."

Walt recognized from the outset the difficulty of establishing Seven Dwarfs, each with a recognizable and endearing quality. The solution was to name them for their most recognizable characteristics. The outline listed them, with tentative names for all but one:

HAPPY—A glad boy. Sentimental, addicted to happy proverbs. His jaw slips out of its socket when he talks, thus producing a goofy speech mannerism.

SLEEPY—Sterling Holloway. Always going to sleep. Always swatting at a fly on the end of his nose.

DOC—The leader and spokesman of the Dwarfs. Pompous, wordy, great dignity. Feels his superiority, but is more or less of a windbag.

BASHFUL—Has a high peaked skull which makes him ashamed to take off his hat. Blushing, hesitating, squirmy, giggly.

JUMPY—Joe Twerp. Like a chap in constant fear of being goosed. Nervous, excited. His words and sentences mixed up.

GRUMPY—Typical dyspeptic and grouch. Pessimist, woman-hater. The last to make friends with Snow White.

SEVENTH—Deaf, always listening intently, happy. Quick movements. Spry.

*　　*　　*

Walt worked with the *Snow White* unit through 1935, while maintaining his supervision of the short cartoons. His seemingly limitless energies again faltered, and he complained of the same lack of concentration that had presaged his nervous breakdown in 1931. A doctor gave him injections for thyroid deficiency, and the treatment seemed to increase his nervousness. Roy perceived the danger signs in his brother, and he suggested, "Why don't we take the girls to Europe for a vacation? It's the tenth wedding anniversary for both of us, and I think Lilly and Edna deserve it for putting up with us." Walt agreed, and the four Disneys embarked for a tour of England, France, Switzerland, Italy and Holland.

Walt in later years wrote to a friend about an incident on the trip: "My brother Roy and I were in London prior to going to Paris to receive a medal from the League of Nations for Mickey Mouse. Under much protest, being strictly the sports clothes type myself, we were persuaded to have morning suits made. We were told that other attire would be inappropriate since it was to be an important occasion with ambassadors and other dignitaries in attendance. The fitting itself was a panic, with Roy's coat on me and mine on him, my pants on Roy and someone else's pants on me. The place was in a turmoil. Anyway, we went to the affair in Paris properly attired only to find that everyone there had wanted the boys from Hollywood to feel at home, so they came in casual clothes! I haven't had the thing on since!"

Walt enjoyed driving through the places he had known as a Red Cross driver, including Strasbourg, where he was again fascinated by the mechanical figures that appeared at the striking of the town clock. He tried to gain entrance to the workings of the clock so he could see how it operated, but the local officials wouldn't allow it.

Everywhere the Disneys went in Europe they saw evidence of the appeal of the Disney cartoons. Crowds greeted them at railway stations; reporters came to the hotels for interviews. In Rome, the Disneys were received by Benito Mussolini in his huge office. For Walt, the most significant part of his European trip was seeing a theater in Paris that played six of his cartoons and nothing else. That convinced him more than ever that audiences would accept and welcome a cartoon the length of a live-action feature.

After eleven weeks abroad, Walt returned to the studio with renewed energy. When the doctor telephoned to remind him of his thyroid injections, Walt told his secretary: "Tell him I'm cured. He can shoot those things in his own butt from now on."

Walt was bristling with ideas after his European trip. He brought with him children's books with illustrations of little people, bees and small insects, and he told his staff in a memo: "This quaint atmosphere fascinates me and I was trying to think of how we could build some little story that would incorporate all of these cute little characters." In a long memo to Ted Sears and the Story Department on the day before Christmas 1935, Walt outlined a score of ideas for future cartoon subjects. Most of them were for Silly Symphonies, which afforded greater freedom in the choice of story material, but he also had ideas for Mickey Mouse, including "a burlesque on Tarzan, with Mickey as the ape man and have him live in the jungle with the wild animals for his friends."

Having for the first time seen the cartoons in foreign lands, Walt observed: "The more pictures we can make without dialogue, the better it will be for our foreign market. We have to depend on the foreign market very strongly now on account of the necessity of having larger grosses. However, I wouldn't let this stand in the way of any good plot or idea that had dialogue in it."

Walt concluded the memo by urging improvement of the Story Department:

Let's not take any Tom, Dick or Harry that shows up. Let's be very discriminating about it. See if we can't really find someone who has the qualifications. How about this fellow in Portland who sent in the Lion and Mouse story? Have you heard any more about him? Let's try to make arrangements with the people; get them in here and let's try them out.

I honestly feel that the heart of our organization is the Story Department. We must have good stories—we must have them well worked out— we must have people in there who can not only think up ideas but who can carry them through and sell them to the people who have to do with the completion of the thing. The only way we can develop this Story Department is by starting in and trying to find these people—then we must get them in and try them out—we must try to develop them. If they don't prove up, we must get rid of them before it is too late. We don't want to get the place cluttered up with a lot of people who are only so-so. I also feel that the Story Department is one of our weakest spots today when it should be one of our strongest. I think you should make a drive to get more gagmen like [Harry] Reeves and [Roy] Williams—men who can really produce something. Only, if it is possible, we must get gagmen who have a little more feeling for situation gags, for personality gags and who have a little showmanship in their system. They might develop into men who will be capable of carrying a story through to completion.

Walt started to grapple with the technical problems of the feature he envisioned. Only the most caricatured of human figures had been portrayed in the Disney cartoons; more realistic drawing would be needed to establish the credibility of Snow White and the Prince. An attempt had been made in a 1934 Silly Symphony, *The Goddess of Spring,* to portray Persephone as a realistic girl, a prototype for Snow White. The result was unconvincing, but Walt was not discouraged.

'We'll get it next time," he assured the animators. The solution, he decided, was to photograph a girl in actions such as would be needed in the film. A young Los Angeles dancer, Marjorie Belcher—known later as Marge Champion—was hired to walk and spin and dance before the camera, and her movements provided keys for the animators to follow.

Another problem was the essential flatness of the animated film. Audiences would accept the cavortings of two-dimensional pigs and wolves against painted backgrounds for an eight-minute span, but eighty minutes would emphasize the artifice of the animation process.

The answer was the multiplane camera. It developed into a towering device with a camera pointed downward through four or five layers of paintings. The various levels depicted planes of vision, and the lens focus could be moved through the planes, creating the same effect of a moving camera in live action. Again, Walt used the Silly Symphony as testing ground for the multiplane camera. It was first employed in *The Old Mill*. Walt described the short as "just a poetic thing, nothing but music. No dialogue or anything. The setting of an old mill at sunset. The cows going home. And then what happens at the old mill at night. The spider coming out and weaving its web. The birds nesting, and then the storm coming up and the old mill going on a rampage. And with the morning the cows come back, the spider web was all shattered, and all that. It was just a poetic thing."

The Old Mill was an exceptional success, winning critical praise and an Academy Award. It showed the Disney artists what could be accomplished in terms of mood and visual imagery.

The work on characters and story for *Snow White* continued. Jumpy was renamed Sneezy, and the unnamed Dwarf became a dim-witted mute. His was the last name to evolve. Walt advocated Dopey, but others objected that it sounded too modern and connoted narcotic addiction. Walt discovered that the word had appeared in Shakespeare, and he decreed that the seventh Dwarf would be called Dopey.

His clarity of vision can be seen by his comments in story conferences during the preparation of *Snow White* (Walt had prudently begun the practice of having a secretary make verbatim transcripts of the conferences):

> *Snow White is visited in the cottage by the Queen in her witch's disguise:*
> . . . At the time the menace comes in, Snow White should be doing something that shows she is happy and that she is trying to do something nice for these little men. That's the time the menace should strike. It's most powerful when it strikes when people are most happy. It's dramatic. . . .
>
> She's taken aback when she first sees the Queen. She doesn't suspect the Queen, but there's a lunatic around somewhere and he approaches you; you have that funny feeling. It's nothing you can put your finger on. You wouldn't have the police come, but you'd be on your guard.
>
> That's the point we ought to bring out with the animals. They are dumb but they have a certain sense like a dog who knows that somebody is not a friend. When the birds see that old witch they know that everything is not right and they're alarmed and back out of the way, retreat quietly. It has just dampened everything.
>
> But when the birds see the vultures that have followed her, that tells them something that even a human won't recognize. . . .
>
> *Conclusion:*
> . . . Fade in on her in the glass coffin, maybe shaded by a big tree. It's built on sort of a little pedestal, torches are burning, two dwarfs on either side with things like guards would have, others are coming up and putting flowers on the coffin. It's all decked with flowers. The birds fly up and drop

flowers. Shots of the birds; show them sad. Snow White is beautiful in the coffin.

Then you hear the Prince. The birds, dwarfs, everyone hear him offscreen. As they turn to look, here he is silhouetted against the hill with his horse. As he walks down the hill singing the song, cut to Snow White in the coffin. As he approaches, everyone sort of steps back as if he had a right there. He goes up to the coffin and finishes the song. As he finishes the song, he lifts the glass lid of the coffin and maybe there's a hesitation, then he kisses her. From the kiss he drops down and buries his head in his hands in a sad position, and all the dwarfs see it and every dwarf drops his head.

All the animals are sad, but then Snow White begins to wake up like she's coming out of a sleep and begins to sit up. Nobody notices at first. One dwarf looks up and sees it, takes it, then several of them take it maybe. She sits up. The Prince comes back and sees it. He springs to his feet. The music begins to pick up, the birds take it and go crazy, the dwarfs go crazy, hug each other. As he carries her along, they are all happy, following along. The music gets bright. The birds and animals are cutting capers. . . .

Story men and animators made contributions at the conferences, but it was always Walt's voice that dominated, suggesting camera angles, indicating moods, and, most valuable of all, acting out his concept of the dialogue and action. Sometimes he made contributions from his own experience. In 1936 he was invited to the annual encampment of the Bohemian Club, a San Francisco organization of artists and civic figures. The ritual consisted of wining, feasting and camping out in a redwood grove north of San Francisco Bay. When Walt returned to the studio, he complained of being unable to sleep because of the symphony of snores in nearby tents. He described and reproduced each of the snores to the hilarity of his story men. The result was the snoring sequence in the Dwarfs' cottage.

As always, Walt paid close attention to the music. Except for an abortive attempt at learning the violin as a boy, he had had no real experience with music. Yet he had an uncanny knack for picking music that would appeal to the public. He liked melody, and he preferred music that wasn't too loud or too high-pitched (composers and arrangers learned not to use piccolos in Disney scores).

Early attempts at *Snow White* songs did not please him. He complained that they followed the pattern of Hollywood musicals, which introduced songs and dances at regular intervals without regard to the progression of the story. "We should set a new pattern, a new way to use music," he argued. "Weave it into the story so somebody just doesn't burst into song."

Nor was Walt satisfied with the voices that he auditioned for the role of Snow White. His office was connected to the sound stage by wire so he could listen to auditioning singers. None possessed the childlike quality Walt was seeking. One day his talent man assured him that the next candidate would be perfect; she was a fourteen-year-old with a bell-like soprano. Walt listened and commented: "She's too mature; she sounds between twenty and thirty." The girl was Deanna Durbin. Finally Walt heard a voice that made him say, "That's the girl! That's Snow White." She was eighteen-year-old Adriana Caselotti, who had been family-trained in Italian opera.

The small unit working next to Walt's office was joined by other animators and background artists until by the spring of 1936, the feature cartoon occupied the talents of virtually everyone in the studio. Making of the shorts continued, since they sustained the flow of much-needed cash. But the real sense of pioneering excitement centered on *Snow White,* and each breakthrough in technique and character delineation was greeted like a new weapon in a holy war.

*   *   *

Walt was selecting his animators with the same thoughtful care that another film producer would exercise in choosing human actors for an all-star movie. Freddy Moore, Bill Tytla, Fred Spencer and newcomer Frank Thomas proved to be the animators who could instill humor and individual characteristics in the Dwarfs. Norm Ferguson superbly limned the menace of the Witch. Ham Luske accepted the formidable challenge of making Snow White move with human grace. Grim Natwick also contributed to Snow White and animated the Prince, the least successful of the human figures. Snow White's animal friends were entrusted to three young artists, Milt Kahl, Eric Larson and Jim Algar. All of the animators and the background artists, too, drew inspiration from the preliminary sketches of Albert Hurter and Gustaf Tenggren, whose European origins and training helped provide the flavor and mood of a fairy tale.

The controlling hand of Walt Disney followed every phase of production. He realized the need to test each sequence as it was developed, and the story sketches were filmed on a "Leica reel," as the rough sequences had come to be called, so it could be judged before being committed to the final process of animation. These were viewed in the sweatbox by Walt, by supervising director Dave Hand, and by the individual sequence directors—Bill Cottrell, Wilfred Jackson, Ben Sharpsteen, Larry Morey and Perce Pearce. Walt also looked at reels of rough animation, know as "pencil tests." He screened preliminary footage for many of the creative workers, and they were asked to respond to such questions as: Does any section seem too long or too short? Did any of the business strike you as being objectionable? Were there any spots where the audience would laugh at the wrong time? Do you recall any gags where you thought the point was missed? Is the personality of each character consistent?

As each sequence was approved for production, new ones were being prepared. Almost every working day through the last half of 1936 and into 1937, Walt held story conferences with members of his staff. A storyboard meeting on November 24, 1936, concerned the scene of the Witch preparing the poisoned apple:

WALT: The thought just struck me on the buildup of the music to where she says, "Now turn red, etc." that where it starts you might go into innocent, sweet music while she is saying something about how innocent it looks. The music changes as the apple changes and could stay that way until she says, "Have a bite." It would be a good contrast.

HAND: You mean the innocence of the apple or of Snow White?

WALT: The apple. You have seen the poison seeping into it and the buildup on the hocus-pocus around it. Then some innocent little theme there, coming back to the heavy music after she says, "Have a bite."

RICHARD CREEDON: Admiring the apple as if she'd like to eat it herself—"Pink as a maiden's blush."

WALT: Something to show how tempting the apple is, how tempting it would be to anybody she offered it to.

BILL COTTRELL: Wouldn't you want that when you are back on her? She even goes sweet herself. She'd change her personality into the peddler woman. Then look over at the raven for, "Have a bite?"

WALT: It would be part of her sales talk here. The apple has just changed from this terrible thing in blowfly colors and the skull to a beautiful red. There wouldn't be too much of it; just enough for contrast. . . .

FERGUSON: Would it be too much of a burlesque on her if when she said, "I'll be the fairest in the land," she started to pretty up, fixing her hair?

WALT: Why not? She's clowning. Take that at-
    titude with her in it.

Walt's initial estimate of $500,000 for *Snow White*
proved absurdly low; it was going to cost three times
that amount. United Artists executives exhibited little
enthusiasm for the project, and influential figures
throughout the film industry doubted the wisdom of
the Disney experiment with a feature cartoon. Walt
learned that it was being called "Disney's Folly," and
there were predictions that *Snow White* would sink
him into bankruptcy. He expressed his concern about
the negative publicity to Hal Horne, the exploitation
manager of United Artists who had first recognized the
worth of *The Three Little Pigs*. Horne had become a
good friend of the Disney studio, and Walt often sought
his advice. "What should I do about all the bad talk
about the feature?" Walt asked.

"Nothing," Horne replied. "Keep them wondering.
Let 'em call it 'Disney's Folly' or any other damn
thing, as long as they keep talking about it. That picture is going to pay off, and the more suspense you
build up, the more it'll pay off."

Not all of the important people in the film industry
lacked faith in *Snow White*. W. G. Van Schmus, who
managed the nation's largest movie theater, the Radio
City Music Hall, had long been friendly with the
Disneys and paid the highest rental for the Mickeys
and the Symphonies. Whenever he came to Hollywood,
he paid a call to the Disney studio. Walt showed him
the work in progress on *Snow White,* and Van Schmus
was impressed. "Walter, it'll be a success," he said.
"I'll book it for the Music Hall."

Encouragement also came from Walter Wanger, a
distinguished producer who played polo with Walt and
Roy. Wanger assured Joseph Rosenberg, the Bank of
America executive who supervised loans to Walt Disney Productions: "Joe, if Walt does as well on the
feature as he has done with everything else he's made,
the public will buy it."

Still, Rosenberg retained a banker's normal caution. When Roy asked for more money to complete *Snow White,* Rosenberg was reluctant. Roy advised Walt, "You've got to show Joe what you've done on the picture so far."

"I can't do that," Walt insisted. "All I've got is bits and pieces. You know I never like to show anybody a picture when it's all cut up. It's too dangerous."

"Walt, you'll have to," Roy replied. "The only way we're going to get more money is to show them what they're lending money for."

Walt grudgingly agreed. He ordered his staff to work overtime to prepare a presentation that contained the essential elements of *Snow White.* Since only a few of the sequences had been completed, the action had to be bridged by pencil sketches and rough layout. Finally enough film was collected to provide a rough impression of *Snow White,* and Walt arranged to show it to Rosenberg at the studio on a Saturday afternoon.

Only the two men were present in the projection room. The room darkened and on the screen came the scene of a fairy-tale book opening. What followed was a jumble of fully animated sequences in color alternating with long stretches of penciled sketches of static figures. The sound track was fragmentary, and Walt filled in the gaps with his own recital of the dialogue and action. Despite Walt's energetic performance, Rosenberg's response was only an occasional, "Yes, yes."

Finally the showing ended with Snow White and the Prince living happily ever after. The lights came on in the projection room, and Walt searched the banker's face for a sign of approval. There was none.

Walt followed him out the door, down the studio street and into the alley where Rosenberg's car was parked. Rosenberg talked about Roy, the weather, anything except what he had just seen in the projection room. He climbed in the car, started the motor and said, "Thanks—goodbye." Then he added: "That thing is going to make a hatful of money."

With financing assured, production on *Snow White* accelerated. Artists worked uncomplainingly on Saturdays and Sundays, and at night, too; all were imbued with the crusadelike mission to make the first feature cartoon a success. Only one negative note appeared. Among the written responses to a showing of partly finished film was an anonymous "Stick to shorts." Walt was upset for days. Years afterward whenever an employee responded negatively to a Disney idea, he pointed a finger and exclaimed: "I'll bet you're the guy who wrote 'Stick to shorts'!"

As *Snow White* was being completed, the Disneys came to the end of their association with United Artists. They had been dissatisfied with the distributor's terms, and the proposals for a new contract offered little improvement. United Artists insisted on the television rights to the Disney cartoons, and Walt refused to part with them. "I don't know what television is, and I'm not going to sign away anything I don't know about," he reasoned. RKO offered much more favorable terms, and the Disneys signed a releasing agreement for the shorts and for *Snow White*.

The studio was racing for a Christmas release of *Snow White,* but when Walt reviewed a nearly completed version of the film, he noticed something disturbing: When the Prince leaned over to kiss Snow White in her glass coffin, he shimmied. Something had gone wrong in the camera work or the animation. "I want to make it over," Walt announced to Roy. "How much will it cost?" Roy asked. Walt replied that it would require several thousand dollars. "Forget it," said Roy, who had borrowed all he could. "Let the Prince shimmy." And ever afterward he did.

The sales force of RKO began discussions on how to sell the film. One of the distribution executives told Walt: "We've got to play down the fairy-tale angle." When Walt asked why, the man replied: "Because audiences don't buy fairy tales. We've got to sell it as a romance between the Prince and Snow White and play down the Dwarfs. We can call it simply *Snow White*."

"No, it's *Snow White and the Seven Dwarfs*," Walt insisted. "It's a fairy tale. That's what I put a million and a half into, and that's the way it's going to be sold."

Finally on December 21, 1937, *Snow White and the Seven Dwarfs* was seen by the public in a glittering premiere at the Carthay Circle Theater in Los Angeles. The great names of Hollywood and the leaders of the film industry stepped out of their limousines to praise Walt Disney on the radio. Inside the Carthay Circle they laughed at the floppy antics of Dopey and some cried when the Dwarfs found Snow White in a deathlike sleep. When the movie ended, the audience stood and cheered.

Many years later, Walt reminisced in wonderment: "All the Hollywood brass turned out for my cartoon! That was the thing. And it went way back to when I first came out here and I went to my first premiere. I'd never seen one in my life. I saw all these Hollywood celebrities comin' in and I just had a funny feeling. I just hoped that some day they'd be going in to a premiere of a cartoon. Because people would depreciate the cartoon. You know, they'd kind of look down.

"I met a guy on the train when I was comin' out. It was one of those things that kind of made you mad. I was out on the back platform—I was in my pants and coat that didn't match but I was riding first class. I was making conversation with a guy who asked me, 'Goin' to California?' 'Yeah, I'm goin' out there.' 'What business you in?' I said, 'The motion-picture business.' Then all of a sudden, 'Oh, is that right? Well, I know somebody in the picture business. What do you do?' I said, 'I make animated cartoons.' 'Oh.' It was like saying, 'I sweep up the latrines.'

"Sometimes people make you mad, and you want to prove something to them even though they mean nothing to you. I thought of that guy on the back platform when we had the premiere of *Snow White*. And the darn thing went out and grossed eight million dollars around the world."

12

THE TWO million drawings that made up *Snow White and the Seven Dwarfs* had been combined to produce eighty-three minutes of superlative motion-picture entertainment. Critics were unanimously enthusiastic, audiences were enthralled. All attendance records were broken in an unprecedented three-week run at the Radio City Music Hall; the attraction could have run longer, but the Disney brothers believed it should play the New York neighborhoods while the public interest was still high. The Seven Dwarfs, especially Dopey, became immediate folk figures, and the film's songs, particularly "Heigh Ho, It's Off to Work We Go" and "Whistle While You Work," were heard from every radio. Walt and Roy Disney enjoyed the unique experience of watching money pour into their corporation. Within six months after the release of *Snow White,* they had paid off all their bank loans. The $8,000,000 that the film earned in its first release was a phenomenal sum, considering that the average price for theater admission in the United States in 1938 was twenty-three cents—and a heavy percentage of those seeing *Snow White* were children admitted for a dime.

Walt was euphoric. To see "Disney's Folly" turn out so magnificently well was dreamlike. The experience erased all the bitter happenings of his early career: the bankruptcy of Laugh-O-Grams; the loss of Oswald; the defections of the animators he had brought into the business; the chicanery of Pat Powers.

He was enormously proud of his artists. They had worked long hours at salaries that were modest compared to similar work in other industries, although higher than those paid in other cartoon studios. Some of the Disney animators were so eager for *Snow White* to succeed that they tacked up advertising posters on fences and telephone poles when the movie opened in Los Angeles.

The Disneys had instituted a system of bonus payments to employees when the studio fortunes were prospering, and with the *Snow White* success, surprise amounts appeared in paychecks. Walt also wanted a dramatic way to show his appreciation for his workers' efforts, and he announced a festive weekend for the entire studio staff at the Lake Norconian resort, east of Los Angeles. It was a mistake. The latent bohemianism of the Disney artists sprang forth fullblown. Legends of the riotous happenings were repeated for years. The event was not.

Snow White and the Seven Dwarfs indicated the direction in which the Disney organization had to go. Short cartoons would continue to be the staple product, providing a steady income and permitting Walt to train new animators and develop fresh techniques. But the shorts were sold to theaters in blocks, and even the exceptionally good ones earned very little more than average cartoons. (Walt sometimes mused over how much more money *The Three Little Pigs* might have amassed if it had been feature-length.)

Features had to become the creative thrust of the studio. Walt realized that the company could expand only by producing full-length movies to compete for theater rentals with the topflight attractions of the major studios. He began devoting his major attention to features, paying less heed to the shorts. Thus began the pattern of his creative life: As he discovered each new, unexplored medium, his interest dwindled in the one that he had previously conquered.

Again Walt pressed for expansion. He hired more and more artists, looking ahead to the time when the studio would be producing several cartoon features simultaneously. Obviously the Hyperion Avenue plant could no longer accommodate his ambitious program. It had grown chaotically, spilling to adjoining lots and across the street. In 1937 and early 1938, the studio had added a feature building, three film vaults, part of a sound stage, test camera bungalow, camera building, projection booth, electric shop, sound shop, paint lab and inking building, as well as several nearby bungalows which were used for various purposes. Air conditioning was nonexistent, and work on cels had to be suspended during the summer's hottest days because the artists' sweat dripped on the ink and paint.

Walt and Roy agreed that they needed to build a new studio. They found fifty-one acres for sale on Buena Vista Street in Burbank, just over the hills of Griffith Park. On August 31, 1938, they put a deposit of $10,000 on the property, the purchase price to be $100,000.

Walt and Lilly now had a second daughter, Sharon Mae, born on New Year's Eve, 1936. The Disneys did some entertaining at home, mostly for relatives and close friends at the studio. Walt and Lilly went to the studio at night to play badminton with other husbands and wives. Although Walt was now accepted as one of Hollywood's most successful and creative film makers, he rarely mingled with Hollywood society. He went each year to the Academy Awards banquet and usually came home with an Oscar. For *Snow White and the Seven Dwarfs* he received a special one, consisting of one full-size and seven dwarf Oscars mounted in a stair-step arrangement. Such appearances before his peers caused an uncommon lack of ease. The ten-year-old Shirley Temple, noticing his demeanor when she presented him with the *Snow White* Oscars, commented, "Don't be nervous, Mr. Disney."

The Oscars brought new fame to Walt Disney, and he found himself being recognized when he appeared in public. He was not entirely pleased. "I never have time to ponder over the fact that I may be what they call 'a celebrity,'" he wrote in response to an inquiry from Arnold Herrmann of Elmhurst College, Illinois.

"And if I am one it has never helped me make a better picture, nor has it ever bettered my polo game, which I certainly wish it would! Here's once when it happened, though—it did get me a good seat to one of the football games last winter. But then, what about the mob that pounced on me for autographs after the game! No, being a celebrity doesn't mean so much!"

Walt had to give up polo. Roy had urged him to do so, arguing that the man on whom their enterprise relied for its creative direction should not risk his health in such a dangerous sport. Walt resisted until he played in two matches in which horsemen suffered fatal injuries. Then he himself was involved in an accident and crushed four of his cervical vertebrae. The injury might have healed if he had been placed in a cast. But he consulted a chiropractor, who manipulated the broken bones and contributed to an arthritic condition that pained Walt Disney until the end of his life.

Both Walt and Roy became increasingly concerned about their parents, who were living in Portland and, despite the advance of their years, were working as hard on the small apartment houses they owned as they had on the Marceline farm. When Flora Disney's health broke down, Roy flew to Portland to convince his parents that they could no longer exert themselves. Walt wrote his mother: ". . . We have been worried for some time for fear you and Dad have been attempting too much and jeopardizing your health. I was glad that Roy was able to sit down and talk things over with you and reason things out. I think you should keep in mind that your health is worth far more than any money that might be derived by trying to do too much with your own hands. After all, money is no good to us if we do not have good health to enjoy it. I would a lot rather be poor and healthy than rich and have ill health. Anyway, I want you to know that we have been praying and hoping that everything would turn out for the best, and it is a big relief to us to

know that you are getting along so well. . . . I hope
Dad will listen to reason and stop doing the heavy
work that he has been doing. It might lead to com-
plications with his rupture. I can't understand why he
won't take things easier and behave himself. It may
be that the trouble you had will be a warning to
him . . ."

The elder Disneys continued to live in Portland until
1938, when Roy and Walt convinced their parents that
the Southern California climate would be better for
them.

The sons paid $8,300 for a comfortable bungalow
in North Hollywood, a short distance from the house
of Roy and Edna and their son Roy Edward, who was
eight years old.

New Year's Day of 1938 was a joyous celebration
for the whole Disney family; it was the golden wedding
anniversary of Flora and Elias. All of their sons gathered for the event. Herb now lived in Los Angeles
with his wife and daughter; he still worked for the
post office. Ray had moved west from Kansas City and
was running an insurance business. Ruth remained in
Portland, where she had married Theodore Beecher
and had a son. At the anniversary celebration Walt
recorded a mock interview with his parents, and it
demonstrates the raillery within the family.

WALT: Well, you folks are almost ready to cele-
  brate your fiftieth wedding anniversary.
FLORA: We're not a-gonna celebrate.
WALT: Why not?
FLORA: Oh, what's the use?
WALT: Well, Dad likes to celebrate. He's always
  enjoyed a good time.
FLORA: We've been celebratin' for fifty years.
  Gettin' tired of it.
WALT: What about you, Dad? Don't you want to
  make whoopee on your golden wedding anni-
  versary?

ELIAS: Oh, we don't want to go to any extremes a-tall.

WALT: Well, I hoped you wouldn't go to any extremes if you're whoopeeing it up.

FLORA: He don't know how to make whoopee.

WALT: Mother, how was it to live with a guy for fifty years? That's an awful long time.

FLORA: Well, it was a long time, but—

WALT: I think he was kind of ornery at times, wasn't he, huh?

FLORA: Sure, he was ornery. You know a little bit about that yourself, don't you? Do you remember the time you painted the whole side of the house when we went to town?

WALT: Me?

FLORA AND ELIAS: Yes, you!

WALT: Oh, that was Roy or somebody. I wouldn't do a thing like that.

FLORA: No, it was you.

WALT: Well, it must have been Roy, because I couldn't think of myself doing a thing like that.

Home movies of the Disney family were taken during the 1930s, and they afford a revealing portrait of the elder Disneys in their late years. Flora Disney appears better-looking than in still photographs, which accent the deep, hollow eyes. She has a twinkle in the movies, especially when she is teased by Walt. Elias seems different, too, not the somber person of the photographs. Posing for the cameraman on a lawn swing, he tries to force a kiss on Flora, but she objects and places a pillow between them. He seems unmarked by his lifetime of disappointments. Indeed, he retained his socialist idealism to the end of his life. Walt, who had supported Franklin Roosevelt but was growing more conservative, once asked, "Dad, how do you feel about having voted fifty years for candidates who never won anything?"

"Walter, I feel fine," Elias replied. "We have won. We've won a lot. I've found out that things don't always come about in the form you have advocated. But you keep fighting and they come about in some way or another. Today, everything I fought for in those early days has been absorbed into the platforms of both the major parties. Now I feel pretty good about that."

Elias Disney was in his seventies when he discovered that he had been voting illegally all his life. His voting status was challenged, and it was discovered that he was an alien in the eyes of the law. When the family had moved from Canada to Kansas, his father had taken out naturalization papers; when he achieved his citizenship, his minor children became citizens, too. But Elias had come of age before the process had been completed, and he remained a Canadian citizen. Although born in Ohio, Flora Disney was also an alien because of marriage.

"I raised my family here; this country has been good to me," Elias announced. "I'm going to die an American citizen." And so he and Flora spent long hours re-studying the Constitution and American history for their citizenship examinations. When they appeared in court, the judge remarked, "Mr. Disney, you won't have to go through this," and Elias and Flora were declared naturalized.

The elder Disneys had been in their new home less than a month when tragedy struck. A defective furnace caused Flora's death by asphyxiation on the night of November 26, 1938. Walt and Roy were devastated, blaming themselves because their mother's death had happened in the house they had bought. Walt was sensitive about the tragedy until the end of his life. Twenty years later, one of his secretaries casually mentioned his mother's death. "I don't want that ever brought up in this office again," Walt said sternly, and he hurried out of the room.

The cry of distributors and exhibitors after *Snow White and the Seven Dwarfs* was the same that greeted the hit of *The Three Little Pigs:* "More pigs!" Now the movie men implored: "Give us more Dwarfs!" Walt Disney refused to repeat himself. He embarked on three new animated features that were totally different in content and style.

Pinocchio came first. The picaresque tale, written by Carlo Lorenzini under the pen name of Carlo Collodi in 1880, seemed like an ideal subject for a feature cartoon, and Walt pursued the new project almost demonically. He was determined to make it even greater than *Snow White*. During a story meeting on March 15, 1938, he was exploding with ideas for the sequence in which Pinocchio was swallowed by the whale:

> Pinocchio should use every ounce of force he has in his swimming to escape the whale. This should be built to terrific suspense. It should be the equivalent of the storm and the chase of the Queen in *Snow White*. . . .
>
> The old man [Geppetto, already swallowed by the whale] should get excited when the whale starts after the fish. When the fish start coming in, he could look toward the whale's mouth and say, "Tuna!" Pinocchio could be swimming with the fish, and the whale swallows them all. As the old man is fishing inside the whale, he pulls out one fish after another, and finally pulls out Pinocchio, without realizing it. The cat sees Pinocchio, gets excited and meows at the old man, but the old man goes right on fishing. Finally Pinocchio calls, "Father!" The old man realizes who it is and shouts, "Pinocchio! My son!"
>
> We can get comedy out of the whale sneezing with Pinocchio and Geppetto inside. They should react in a certain way—it would be the equivalent to the hiccups in the giant's mouth. The whale would quiver before the sneeze and shake them around, throwing them off their feet onto the floor. They would be shouting over the noise of the whale. When he sneezed, it would slosh the water all around, and up on the sides, and it would drop down on Geppetto and Pinocchio like a shower.

The sneeze stirs the water up so when they escape, the water is already rough and stormy.

They get ready, and the sneeze blows them out. Then as the whale comes into another sneeze and the inhale starts drawing them back, they have to paddle hard against it. . . .

The underwater stuff is a swell place for the multiplane, diffusing and putting haze in between, with shafts of light coming down. I would like to see a lot of multiplane on this.

Because of what Walt and his staff had learned on *Snow White,* they should have had an easier time with *Pinocchio.* But they didn't. The story had splendid elements of adventure, but *Pinocchio* lacked the appealing characters of *Snow White.* Pinocchio himself was a nettling problem. He was a puppet come to life, and he could not be animated as a normal boy would be; his moves had to be simple and unsophisticated, as though he had known no previous history. His face was expressionless, and he lacked the boyish qualities that could make such a character engaging. After six months, Walt called a halt in production. He realized that new elements had to be added before *Pinocchio* could come to life.

The answer was to surround Pinocchio with intriguing, flamboyant characters. The most important was Jiminy Cricket. In the book, the cricket had played a brief role as admonisher of the errant puppet, only to be rewarded by being crushed under Pinocchio's foot. For the film, the cricket was installed as the boy's conscience, trying to guide him away from evil companions and the pitfalls of pleasure-seeking. But how could an ugly insect be converted into a likable character? And how could he be large enough to play in scenes with human figures?

Several artists attempted concepts of the cricket, complete with antennae. Walt rejected them all. He sent for one of the younger animators, Ward Kimball. When Kimball entered the boss's office, he had every intention of resigning. His work for *Snow White* had been on the bed-building and soup-eating scenes, and both had been cut from the final version. Kimball tried to express despair, but Walt started one of his spellbinding narratives, describing the adventures of Pinocchio and his voice of conscience, Jiminy Cricket. By the end of the recital, Kimball had forgotten his resolve to quit. He accepted Walt's assignment to produce a workable cricket, and Kimball's Jiminy was appealing and uncricketlike. The problem of size was resolved by skillful use of camera angles. Jiminy Cricket's success was assured with the addition of two hit songs for him to sing, "When You Wish Upon a Star" and "Give a Little Whistle." They were composed by Leigh Harline, with lyrics by Ned Washington, and sung by Cliff Edwards.

The sticklike figure of Pinocchio became more rounded and boylike, and he was presented as a boy who was easily swayed by bad influences, rather than a determined delinquent. The interplay between him and Jiminy worked perfectly, although no one ever solved the fundamental problem of a hero with no will of his own. Pinocchio was literally a puppet who was alternately drawn between good and evil; hence he could never match the human appeal of Snow White.

With *Pinocchio* at last on the right track, Walt ordered the film into full production, and his staff shared Walt's resolve to make the second feature greater than the first. If anything, there was an over-abundance of zeal, with the directorial units competing to make their sequences the most important and effective in the movie. Walt had to maintain control, lest *Pinocchio* end up three times its desired length. He indulged his artists in the use of special effects and the multiplane camera for visual images that far exceeded those of *Snow White*. The results were highly effective artistically—and expensive. When *Pinocchio* was finally completed, it had cost a stunning $2,600,000.

* * *

Fantasia came into being because of Walt Disney's concern for the career of Mickey Mouse. Walt retained his almost mystical attachment to Mickey; to him the Mouse was not merely a revenue-producing cartoon character nor even a good-luck talisman. Walt was Mickey's voice, his alter ego, and it troubled Walt to see the Mickey Mouse career decline. It had been inevitable. Mickey had been an international attraction for a decade, and few movie stars could sustain their careers for that long a time.

In the beginning, Mickey Mouse could do anything. He was drawn with a series of circles of varying sizes, and he moved with what animators call the "rubber-hose technique"—action with little relation to human or animal movement. As cartoons became more sophisticated, so did Mickey. Freddy Moore was the first to apply the "squash-and-stretch technique" to the animation of Mickey, making him more human and appealing. Moore gave the face more character and definition; for the first time, Mickey had a cheek when his teeth went together.

Even with a more pliable face and figure, Mickey presented problems. He was cuter, but he lacked the primitive vitality of the early cartoons. With his shy manner, he was essentially a latent character, not the instigator of comic happenings. That function befell the broader characters who supported Mickey in the cartoons. Inevitably, they became stars of their own series—Donald Duck and Pluto in 1937, Goofy in 1939. The sizes of all three made them easy to work with; Donald was the height of a duck, and Pluto and Goofy could be portrayed dog-size. But the Mickey story men and animators were faced with the recurrent problem: "What can you do with a four-foot mouse?"

In 1938, Walt decided to star Mickey Mouse in a cartoon presentation of *The Sorcerer's Apprentice,* an old fairy tale which had been interpreted as a poem by Goethe and a concert piece by the French composer Paul Dukas. Mickey was cast as the apprentice whose misuse of the sorcerer's powers wreaks disaster. The entire action would be done in pantomime to the Dukas music. Walt seemed pleased that no dialogue would be required; he suspected that Mickey's (Walt's) hesitant falsetto contributed to the character's difficulty in playing varied roles.

Walt planned to release *The Sorcerer's Apprentice* as a two-reeler, but that changed after a chance meeting with Leopold Stokowski, the distinguished conductor of the Philadelphia Orchestra. During a conversation at a party, Walt mentioned that he was starring Mickey Mouse in *The Sorcerer's Apprentice*. Stokowski, a devoted follower of the Disney cartoons, volunteered to conduct the Dukas music for Walt.

Stokowski visited the studio and was overwhelmed by everything he saw. He was especially fascinated with the recording of sound and the ability of technicians to alter and combine various tracks of music. When Stokowski began the score, he recorded each section at a time—woodwinds, brass, percussion, etc. He spent hours at the mixing board, combining the sections in varying degrees of volume. "This is the ultimate in conducting," he said delightedly.

Stokowski suggested other musical works which could be interpreted in animation. Walt listened to the recordings and his imagination soared. He announced that *The Sorcerer's Apprentice* would not be released as a two-reeler, but would be part of a full-length film that would feature other works of serious music as well. The new project was given the working title of *The Concert Feature*.

One of Stokowski's suggestions was the Toccata and Fugue in D Minor by Bach. Walt did some reading about Bach and discovered that the composer had been a church organist who had often improvised his works in flights of creativity. Why not illustrate the Toccata and Fugue, he suggested, in the same free manner? He tested his theory by listening to the Bach composition again and again, and he and Stokowski discussed their reactions. A loud crescendo seemed to Walt "like coming out of a dark tunnel and a big splash of light

coming in on you." A passage suggested orange to
Walt. "Oh, no, I see it as purple," said Stokowski. A
woodwind portion gave Walt the image of a hot kettle
with spaghetti floating in it. Walt was amused later
when highbrow critics professed to see profundities
in the abstractions created for the Toccata and Fugue.

He wasn't aiming at anything highbrow. Nor was
he trying to bring classical music to the mass audience.
He was simply trying to use serious music as another
tool for animation. Always he stressed the visual. "I
remember when I used to go to a concert when I was
a kid," he told his artists. "I can still see the orchestra
tuning up, and then the conductor coming out and
starting the music, and the violin bows going up and
down in unison." It had been a visual experience for
him—the images of the players on the stage, and the
mental pictures that the music had inspired.

In most cases, the music for The Concert Feature
was selected first, and the visual image applied afterward. For one sequence, it was the reverse. Walt wanted
to depict the creation and evolution of Earth, and he
instructed Dick Huemer to find a suitable piece of
music. Huemer had been assigned to The Concert
Feature because of his taste for classical music—Walt
often introduced him: "Meet Dick Huemer; he goes
to operas." Huemer could locate only a second-class
work called Creation, and Walt explained his problem
to Stokowski. "Why don't we do the Sacre?" the conductor exclaimed.

" 'Socker'? What's that?" Walt asked.

"Sacre du Printemps—Rite of Spring, by Stravinsky,"
said Stokowski. He told how Stravinsky had depicted
the primitive people of the Russian steppes with weird
dissonances; the music could easily portray the earth's
paroxysms during its birth and early history, Stokowski
declared. Walt listened to a recording of the composition, and he immediately agreed.

Walt hired Deems Taylor, the noted music com-
mentator, to advise on The Concert Feature and later
to perform the narration. Like Stokowski, Taylor was

enchanted by the inner workings of the Disney studio. One day when Walt complained that sometimes he believed his artists had never grown up, Taylor replied: "How can you grow up in this atmosphere, for God's sake? It's like living in Santa Claus's workshop."

Taylor and Stokowski joined Walt and his story personnel in conferences about the selection and treatment of the music. On September 30, 1938, they were discussing the Arcadian sequence to accompany Beethoven's *Pastoral Symphony* in the film:

STOKOWSKI: In listening to this music, it seemed to come in three large masses: The first is the faun school, and so forth; the second is the little feminine one; the third is very excited, where something is all jumbled up together. That's the general plan of the music—if you keep it in three big masses.

WALT: There's a theme that comes in with the dancing—the flute—then the dancing lesson. Then the beauty, or love, or water and swimming, and then comes what I would call the chase excitement. It really is four.

STOKOWSKI: I think beauty, love, excitement is part of the chase. It's in the music—and part of the chase. So it's the flute playing; the fauns dancing with or around the girls and the excitement.

WALT: There would be a lot of comedy in that chase if you had a group of little fauns. It would be better than only one, because he would be awfully busy. You would have an awful lot to show. You could show two or three little guys try to bulldog him and everything. You can accomplish more with half a dozen.

TAYLOR: If Oscar sneaked up on the sleeping Pegasus on the ground, and it went up in the air with him on his back—

WALT: Yes, he might sneak up on what he thinks is the rear end of a horse, lasso it, and it flies

up. And here's Oscar hanging on to it, and it
dumps him in a pool. The whole last end of
four minutes can be full of life. If we get stuck,
we can ignore that part that is supposed to be
love. The flying horse comes down, maybe to
help the girls, and it flies down like a humming-
bird. It can fly around and kick in the air while
still flying.

TAYLOR: Show Oscar terrified, going up and up
and up and he sees what's down below—something that is a reproduction of Greece in the
history books. . . .

Walt felt dissatisfied that the playback of recordings
could not duplicate the full, rich orchestral sound he
heard in the recording studio. He assigned his Sound
Department to develop a new system of multi-aural
sound which could reproduce the actual performance
in a concert hall—and then some. For Schubert's *Ave
Maria,* he wanted the voices of the choristers to sound
as if they were in procession down the aisle of the
theater.

The result of the research was Fantasound, which
recorded music with several microphones and reproduced it on an equal number of loudspeakers, creating
a stereophonic effect. To get the best possible quality,
Walt had Stokowski record the entire score at the
Philadelphia Academy of Music, which was noted
for its superb acoustics. The music bill alone for *Fantasia* amounted to more than $400,000, and when the
long production ended, the total cost was $2,280,000.

The third project Walt Disney chose to follow *Snow
White and the Seven Dwarfs* was *Bambi.* Although it
was started at the same time as the other two, it was
the last to be released.

The Felix Salten book of a deer's coming of age in
the forest provided a natural vehicle for a cartoon
feature; only through animation could the story be
adequately told. But *Bambi* was different from anything

Disney had ever attempted. It was far more serious than *Snow White* and *Pinocchio,* and the characters were all animals. Walt realized that to carry such a storyline, his animators would need to create characters that were realistic; the deer would have to be deerlike, the rabbits rabbitlike. Could his artists meet such a challenge and still create a film that would be entertaining?

He determined to give them all the tools they needed. He hired a noted painter of animals, Rico LeBrun, to lecture on the structure of animals and how they moved. He sent a cameraman, Maurice Day, to Maine to photograph thousands of feet of forests, snowfall, rainstorms, spider webs, changes of light and seasons. The Maine Development Commission provided two live fauns for the Disney studio, and they were sketched and photographed as they grew. Rabbits, ducks, skunks, owls and other species were added until the studio resembled a small zoo. A local naturalist contributed hundreds of photographs of animals in action.

During one of the first story conferences on *Bambi,* Walt outlined some of his ideas for the production:

When it comes to the animation, we can do a lot with the rabbit. He has a certain mannerism that can be drawn. We might get him to twitch his nose. . . . I don't like to have us get off the track too much to show his life. Everything should be done through Bambi. . . . The owl ought to be a stupid, silly thing. He is always trying to scare people. I like his crazy screech as it is described in the book. He might be a sort of Hugh Herbert [an eccentric movie comic] type. . . . I would hate to see any of the characters too straight. You would want that in Bambi's mother. You would want Bambi more or less straight in a way. The comedy would come from him as a kid through his questions and his curiosity. The rest of the characters I would like to see come out of life. . . . I would like the Old Stag to say what he has to say in a direct way, and in such a voice that Bambi is unable to answer him. What he says will be sort of final. That can be put over through the voice. . . . I like Faline's character in the book. She is clever and she understands things. Bambi asks a lot of questions which she can answer. If we build her that way, we will be able to get a lot of stuff over when she and Bambi get together. . . . Let us start moving on the thing and not drag it out too long. After we get our characters set, we should write all our business for the characters and build the first half. Then we should record it and get our sketches. We will shoot the sketches and make a music track all of which will make our story pretty tight. Our sound track will be a dummy track composed of a cello, a violin, a piano and an organ, which will be enough to give us an idea of the music. When we do that, we will have a chance to preview the thing before we go into layout and animation. That would include the first part of the picture, up to the end of the first winter.

Walt tried to push ahead in a deliberate way, but *Bambi* simply would not be managed. Once again, he and his artists were pioneering. Even such a matter as the spots on the faun's skin provided complication. The best of animators had to spend forty-five minutes on each drawing; daily output would be eight drawings, half a foot of film, compared to a normal rate of ten feet per day. Less experienced animators required an hour and a half to draw the faun.

The storyline continued to present problems, and Walt realized that he could not maintain the same production pace as with *Pinocchio* and *Fantasia*. He formed a small unit of young animators—Frank Thomas, Milt Kahl, Eric Larson and Ollie Johnston—to concentrate on *Bambi*. "Don't show me anything until you're satisfied with it," Walt instructed.

Thomas went to work on the scene in which a butterfly lands on the tail of the young Bambi. Kahl drew a sequence of the faun leaping over a log and falling in a tangle on top of Thumper. When the rough animation on both scenes was completed, Walt saw the result in a sweatbox. Tears filled his eyes. "Fellas, this is pure gold," he remarked to Thomas and Kahl. He had at last seen what he wanted *Bambi* to be.

With three features and the regular program of shorts in production, the Hyperion studio was filled to overflowing. The *Bambi* unit moved to a rented building at 861 North Seward Street in Hollywood. The story-research, promotion, engineering, comic-strip and training departments occupied the second floor of a building at 1717 North Vine Street. Walt was anxiously looking forward to the time when he could have all of the studio departments at the new headquarters in Burbank.

Planning the new studio was a fresh and immensely stimulating experience for Walt. For a dozen years he had endured the chaotically makeshift studio on Hyperion Avenue, where animators worked in cluttered, poorly lighted rooms through the chill of winter and the summer's heat. He was determined to build a new studio where he and his fellow workers could create in an atmosphere of comfort and congeniality.

Walt involved himself with every aspect of planning, conferring with architects, draftsmen, furniture designers, interior decorators, landscapers, acoustic experts, carpenters and plumbers. One day Otto Englander burst into Walt's office with an idea for ending the first movement of the *Pastoral Symphony* in *Fantasia*. Englander found Walt seated on the floor of his office amid a clutter of chromium tubes and blue leatherette cushions. Walt explained sheepishly that he was considering a new design for an animator's chair, and he was taking it apart to see how it was constructed. Walt listened as Englander explained his idea (having two cupids draw a curtain before the audience), approved it, and returned to his dissection of the chair.

The new studio, Walt insisted, would need to be big enough to accommodate his maximum production. That meant the regular program of eighteen to twenty short cartoons, plus the features. If he released one feature a year, he would need facilities for three features, since they seemed to require three years to produce. If he increased his output to two a year, then six features would be in production at one time.

The center of the production process would be the Animation Building, where the various phases of animation could flow smoothly from one to the other in a movie-making assembly line. It would house the Story Department, directors, layout men, animators, assistant animators and in-betweeners. When the animation had been completed, the work would move through an underground tunnel to the Inking and Painting Building, then to the Camera Building and beyond to the Cutting Building. Three stages would be built, one for recording music, the other two for dialogue and sound effects. There would also be a theater, a process laboratory for experimenting with film methods and a restaurant.

A key element in the planning was air conditioning. At the Hyperion Avenue studio, Walt had often grumbled because dust on cels and lenses interfered with production. Variation in humidity was also a problem, since the water paints cracked and chipped off celluloid in dry weather and smeared when it was humid. Walt also realized that the summer weather was much hotter in the San Fernando Valley, and he wanted his employees to work in comfort the year round. Walt invited engineers of General Electric to confer with architects and structural engineers during the planning stages, rather than try to install air conditioning after the buildings had been erected. A system was devised to pipe fresh, cool air to every office.

"But what if someone opens a window—that'll destroy the whole system," Walt reasoned. The solution: remove the window cranks.

The extent of the planning presaged Disneyland and

Walt Disney World. Water for the air-conditioning system, as well as the Process Laboratory, lawn sprinkling, toilets and other uses, came from two wells sunk three hundred feet into the earth. Not only were the major buildings connected by tunnels; the utilities were placed underground as well. The studio would become a miniature city, with its own streets, storm drains, sewage system, fire hydrants, telephone exchange and electric distribution system. The sizes of the streets, conduits and pipes were all calculated to provide for future expansion without interfering with studio production.

Walt lavished his most concentrated planning on the Animation Building. It was designed as a three-story structure with eight wings connected to a central corridor. The wings would be on a true east-west axis, each office with an outside view. The plan provided a maximum of rooms with north light; those facing the sun would be shielded with venetian blinds that could be adjusted to lessen the glare. Because Burbank was close to earth faults, the building would be constructed in ten separate units which would move independently in case of earthquake.

Everything was designed for the comfort of the Disney animators. Each piece of furniture was planned to combine function with graceful modern appearance. The animation desk was redesigned to eliminate waste time and motion, and carpets and drapes in harmonizing pastel colors would help provide a restful, quiet atmosphere. The sweatbox would be abolished, although the cognomen remained; animators would be able to review their work in comfortable projection rooms.

Walt aimed to make the Burbank studio a worker's paradise. The buildings would be surrounded by broad lawns, where the employees could play baseball, badminton and volleyball during their lunch hours. They would be able to eat in a modern restaurant where the appetizing meals would be served at prices below the studio's cost. If an animator felt the need for a malted milk or a cup of coffee during the day, he would

need only to call the snack shop on the first floor and
it would be delivered to him. The penthouse of the
Animation Building would be the equivalent of a
gentleman's club, where the animators and executives
could make use of a lounge, soda fountain, sun deck,
gymnasium and showers. Except for after-work parties,
no liquor was served. Walt himself never drank until
after the workday was over, and he disapproved of
those who took long lunch breaks at nearby bars.

Walt and Roy asked their father to supervise the
carpentry in the building of the new studio, hoping the
work would help alleviate the despondency he had
felt since the death of Flora. Although he was eighty,
Elias Disney donned work clothes and spent a full
day overseeing the carpenters and pounding nails himself. As he watched the construction grow, he expressed
his concern to his youngest son: "Walter, how on earth
are you going to support this big place with those
cartoons of yours? Aren't you afraid you'll go broke?"
Walt replied, "Well, if I do fail, Dad, I can get out
easy. You notice how this place is built, with rooms
along long corridors? If I go broke with my cartoons,
I can always sell it for a hospital." Elias Disney was
greatly relieved by the explanation.

Walt followed each phase of the planning and drove
to the Burbank property almost every day during the
excavation and construction. With his studio operation
now scattered from Hyperion to Hollywood, he was
anxious to have the new studio completed. The Camera
Building was finished first, and filming began there on
Pinocchio in August of 1939. When the lease on the
Seward property ran out in the fall, the *Bambi* unit
occupied part of the uncompleted Animation Building.
On the day after Christmas, the major part of the
studio began the move from Hyperion to Burbank, a
few of the departments following in the spring.

For his own office, Walt chose a suite on the third
floor in the far northeast corner of the Animation
Building. The suite contained an outer office, an office
for his secretary (Dolores Voght), Walt's own spacious

office, a conference room and a room where he could sleep if he had to remain overnight at the studio.

Such an occasion arose a month after he had moved into the new studio. He later related his experience: "I was all set to go to sleep about ten-thirty when all of a sudden the air conditioning shut off for the night. 'Whoooooooo'—it was like submerging in a submarine. There was plenty of air in the room, but I had this feeling that I was suffocating. I yelled, but there was nobody around. I ran over to the window and clawed and scratched, trying to get it open; all I did was cut up my fingers. Me—the guy who told them to take all the handles off the windows! I finally had to break the window so I could breathe."

13

THE NEWFOUND prosperity of Walt Disney Productions started to end in September of 1939 with the beginning of the Second World War. Forty-five percent of the company's income flowed from overseas; now such important markets as Germany, Italy, Austria, Poland and Czechoslovakia were closed to the Disney product, and income from England and France was frozen. The film market was changing at home, too. With Europe at war and America's young men being drafted into military service, the tempo of the nation was quickening, and movie audiences were less intrigued with the fairy tales of Walt Disney. When *Pinocchio* was released in February 1940, it was inevitably compared to *Snow White*. Walt was convinced that *Pinocchio* was a greater artistic achievement, but audiences did not warm to the characters as they had to

Snow White and the Dwarfs. Business was good, but far short of what was needed to offset the heavy cost of production.

Fantasia presented special problems. Moviegoers had known little experience with classical music in films, and they were not prepared for this new kind of Disney film. Walt insisted that *Fantasia* would be released under the best possible conditions. "We can do a better job than RKO," Walt said. RKO, which had little enthusiasm for selling a "longhair musical," readily agreed to relax its exclusive distribution contract. Walt set up a special unit headed by a young film salesman named Irving Ludwig. Walt instructed Ludwig to engage prestige theaters in the major cities and equip them with sound systems to accommodate the stereophonic Fantasound. The theaters were also outfitted with special lighting and curtain controls so that each sequence in the film would be presented as an individual unit. The theater staffs were hired and trained by Disney.

Fantasia opened November 13, 1940, at New York's Broadway Theater, the same place, then named the Colony, where Mickey Mouse had made his debut in *Steamboat Willie*. Movie critics generally hailed *Fantasia* for its imaginative innovation; classical-music critics looked down their noses. Audiences were responsive, both in New York and Los Angeles, where the film played the Carthay Circle. In San Francisco, a projection booth had to be built in the Geary Theater, which normally presented stage attractions. Walt was nervous at the opening in San Francisco, which was the headquarters for his creditor, the Bank of America. He remarked to Ludwig: "There will be a lot of bankers here tonight; be sure to tell them we're doing very well with this picture."

The film succeeded in its initial engagements; it also opened in Boston, Cleveland, Chicago and Detroit with full stereophonic sound. But except in New York, where *Fantasia* ran for a year, the engagements were not sustained. Parents balked at paying roadshow prices for their children; those who did complained that *Fantasia* was not the standard Disney film. Some claimed that their children were frightened by the *A Night on Bald Mountain* sequence.

Diminishing returns made it impractical to attempt more of the Fantasound installations, which cost $30,000 per unit; at any rate, electronic equipment was growing scarce because of the government's defense needs. RKO wanted to put *Fantasia* into general release in a shorter version. Walt fought for the uncut film, but he was forced to give in; he needed all the income he could find to keep the new studio going. Finding it too painful to cut the film into which he had poured his creative strength, he told the RKO executives: "You can get anybody you want to edit it—I can't do it."

Fantasia was reduced from two hours to eighty-one minutes and released on a double bill with a Western. *Fantasia,* which had cost $2,280,000, produced an even greater loss than *Pinocchio.*

In 1940, Walt realized that he would have to scale down his ambitions for feature films. While *Bambi* moved slowly through the production process, Walt began work on two features which could be made at more realistic costs. One was *The Reluctant Dragon,* the studio's first venture into live action. The humorist Robert Benchley portrayed a visitor to the Disney studio, and during the film he met Walt, learned how cartoons were made and how the studio operated. The device tied together three short cartoons, *Baby Weems, How to Ride a Horse,* starring Goofy, and *The Reluctant Dragon.* The film did not earn quite enough to recover its $600,000 cost.

Walt tried to prove with *Dumbo* that a cartoon feature could be produced on a modest budget in a reasonable span of time.

Based on a book by Helen Aberson and Harold Pearl, *Dumbo* was an engaging tale of a big-eared baby elephant who learns to fly. The simplicity of the story became evident to one of the Disney animators,

Ward Kimball, when he met Walt in the parking lot one day. Walt proceeded to tell him the entire plot of *Dumbo*. The recital took only three minutes, yet it was a practical, well-rounded, airtight vehicle for a cartoon.

Walt assigned economy-minded Ben Sharpsteen to be supervising director. Sharpsteen avoided the excesses that had skyrocketed the expense of the previous feature cartoons. Story work took six months, animation required only a year. The film was completed for $800,000, with a running time of sixty-four minutes. The RKO salesman argued that it was too short for a feature and asked Walt to add another ten minutes. Walt, who had originally planned *Dumbo* as a thirty-minute featurette, replied, "No, that's as far as I can stretch it. You can stretch a thing so far and then it won't hold. This picture is right as it is. And another ten minutes is liable to cost five hundred thousand dollars. I can't afford it." *Dumbo* proved to be one of the most endearing of the Disney feature cartoons, providing the Disney company with an $850,000 profit.

When Roy Disney asked Walt to visit his office one day in 1940, Walt realized that meant trouble. Over the years he had learned that when Roy came to Walt's office, he usually bore good tidings. When Walt was summoned to Roy's office, that meant bad news.

"Sit down, kid," Roy began, shutting the door behind Walt. Roy took his place behind his desk and said, "This is serious. I've got to talk to you."

Walt studied his brother's long face and asked, "What's the matter?"

Roy outlined the financial reverses of the past year: how the profits on *Snow White* had been eaten up by the costs of *Pinocchio, Fantasia* and *Bambi;* how the European war had caused a sharp decline in theater revenue; how the company now had a thousand employees in a brand-new studio built at a cost of $3,000,000.

"And now, Walt," Roy concluded, "we are in debt to the bank for four and a half million dollars!"

Roy expected his brother to be shocked and concerned. Instead, Walt began to grin, and then he burst out laughing.

"What the hell are you laughing at?" Roy demanded.

"I was just thinking back," Walt said between fits of laughter. "Do you remember when we couldn't borrow a thousand dollars?"

Roy, too, began to laugh. "Yeah, remember how hard it was to get that first twenty-thousand-dollar credit?" he recalled.

They regaled each other with memories of when they had to plead for loans to meet the weekly payroll. "And now we owe four and a half million dollars!" Walt remarked. "I think that's pretty damn good." When their amusement was over, Walt asked his brother, "What are we going to do?"

"I'm afraid we're going to need some outside capital," Roy replied. "We'll have to issue a preferred-stock issue."

Both Disneys had resisted the issuance of stock. Theirs was an extremely personal business, and Walt despised the idea of having outsiders share in the decisions that he had made by himself throughout the company history. The two brothers had operated as a partnership until Walt Disney Productions was incorporated in 1929, assuming the partnership's assets of $85,852 and liabilities of $32,813. The new company issued 10,000 shares of stock, 3,000 apiece to Walter and Lillian Disney and 4,000 to Roy. In 1938, Walt Disney Productions was reorganized to absorb three other companies that had been created in the early 1930s: Liled Realty and Investment Company, which took care of the Disneys' real estate; Walt Disney Enterprises, which dealt with licensing of the cartoon characters; and the Disney Film Recording Company. The new Walt Disney Productions in 1938 issued 150,000 shares of stock, with Walt and Lillian Disney receiving 45,000 apiece, and Roy and Edna 30,000 apiece.

Despite Walt's misgivings, Walt Disney Productions

made its first public offering of stock in April 1940, with 155,000 shares of 6-percent cumulative convertible preferred stock at $25 par value and 600,000 shares of common stock at $5. The prospectus for the sale listed Walter E. Disney as President and Executive Production Manager of the corporation, and Roy O. Disney Executive Vice President and Business Manager. Total assets of Walt Disney Productions at the end of 1939 were $7,000,758.

The stock offering quickly sold out, contributing $3,500,000 of much-needed capital to the Disney company. Financial troubles were assuaged for a time, at least, but other problems began to appear.

During the last half of the 1930s, the Hollywood movie studios, like many other industries in the country, were undergoing unionization. Emerging from the nightmare of the Depression, the nation's workers sought greater security in their jobs, as well as a larger share of the new prosperity. Franklin Roosevelt's New Deal gave them the apparatus for unionization with the National Labor Relations Board. The film industry was ripe for the unions. Jobs were often subject to the whims of the producers and the fluctuations of the movie market. Filming went on six days a week, and night shooting was common, without overtime. Studio workers recalled vividly the grim times when they were ordered to take 50-percent cuts in salary during financial crises, while the executives made no such sacrifice. By 1940, most of the salaried workers in the industry —actors, directors, writers, crew members—had been unionized. The Disney studio had closed-shop agreements with musicians, cameramen, electricians, costumers, restaurant workers, makeup artists, prop men and other set workers. Union organizers next went after the cartoonists.

The nature of the Disney enterprise had changed immensely in a brief span of years. The studio work force had grown from a handful of artists working in day-to-day collaboration with Walt to a factory-like operation of a thousand persons. A close personal relationship with Walt was no longer possible for the great majority of employees, and many of them felt overlooked in the creative process. The move to the new studio was traumatic for some. Hyperion had been cramped and chaotic, but it had created a feeling of group endeavor. The Burbank studio, for all its order and comfort, seemed to magnify the stratification between job functions. Those in the lower categories felt neglected, underpaid. Indeed, some of their salaries seemed low, though not unusually so by post-Depression standards.

The hints of discontent were exploited by a new element in the studio. Many of them had arrived from the East during the expansion before and after *Snow White,* their double-breasted tweed suits and homburg hats contrasting with the sport shirts of the Californians. The newcomers were products of the artistic ferment of Manhattan, and they rejected the paternalism of Walt Disney. They argued that the only protection the studio workers had was in a union. Some of their listeners agreed, especially as the European war plunged the company into financial problems. With their market shrinking, the Disneys obviously could not afford the inflated staff. Rumors of mass layoffs circulated through the studio.

Two unions sought to organize the Disney cartoonists: the unaffiliated Federation of Screen Cartoonists and the Screen Cartoonists Guild, affiliated with the A.F.L. Painters and Paperhangers Union. The leader of the Screen Cartoonists Guild was a tough leftwinger, Herbert Sorrell, whose strikes and jurisdictional battles brought turmoil to Hollywood labor. Sorrell's hard-fisted tactics infuriated Walt. Years later, Walt gave this version of a meeting with Sorrell in Walt's office:

Sorrell claimed he had a majority of the cartoonists in his union and demanded a contract. "You sign with me or I'll strike you," Sorrell threatened.

"I've got to live with those boys from now on,"

Walt replied. "I must have a vote. You've got to put it to a vote through the Labor Board, and whatever way it comes out, I'll go along with it. Then I'm keeping faith with them. I'm not signing with you on your say-so."

"All right, I'm warning you," Sorrell said. "I can make a dust bowl out of your place here, Disney. You don't know what you're doing. The strike will hurt you. I can pick up that telephone and I'll have you on unfair lists all over the country. I've got friends. I've got connections."

"That may be true," Walt said. "But I've got to live with myself. I can't sign these boys to you. I have no right to. They have come to me from the other union and claimed you don't have them. A vote will prove it."

Walt decided to take the matter directly to his employees. In February 1941, he addressed studio meetings about "the real crisis we are facing . . . a crisis that's going to vitally affect the future security of all of us." He warned his listeners: "Everything you are going to hear is entirely from me. There was no gag meeting or anything to write this thing. It's all me, and that will probably account for some of the poor grammatical construction and the numerous two-syllable words."

He began by telling of the storms he had weathered during twenty years of the cartoon business. He delivered his credo: "I have had a stubborn, blind confidence in the cartoon medium, a determination to show the skeptics that the animated cartoon was deserving of a better place; that it was more than a mere 'filler' on the program; that it was more than a novelty; that it could be one of the greatest mediums of fantasy and entertainment yet developed."

He told of his hungry years, how he and Roy sold their cars and mortgaged everything to meet the payroll in 1928, how they refused to join other producers in enforcing a 50-percent pay cut in 1933. Over seven years, almost $500,000 had been paid to Disney employees in bonuses and adjustments. He and Roy could have taken dividends worth $2,500,000; instead, they invested everything back into the company.

Walt outlined the hectic expansion following *Snow White,* the building of the new studio, the collapse of the foreign market and the financial crisis it brought. Three solutions were offered: salary cuts for everyone, which might have caused panic; abandonment of feature production, which would have laid off half the studio staff; selling a controlling interest to a major company or individual. Walt said he rejected all three, preferring to enforce economies that had helped to bring production costs down to more realistic levels.

He went on to blow down rumors that had been circulating and to deny that the new studio fostered a system of class distinction. One of the rumors was that girls were being trained to replace higher-priced male artists. Not so, said Walt. The girls were being trained to make them more versatile employees, to prepare for the future when men might be drafted, and to give women equal opportunities with men.

Walt also dealt with the much-asked questions: "Why can't Walt see more of the fellows? Why can't there be fewer supervisors and more Walt?"

He explained that the staff had grown too large for him to devote his attention to everyone, adding, "It's my nature to be democratic. I want to be just a guy working in this plant—which I am. When I meet people in the hall, I want to be able to speak to them, and have them speak to me, and say 'hello' with a smile. I can't work under any other conditions. However, I realized that it was very dangerous and unfair to the organization as a whole for me to get too close to everybody. This was especially true of new men. You all know that there are always those who try to polish the apple or to get their advancement by playing on sympathy. It is obvious that this is definitely unfair to the conscientious, hard-working individual who is not good at apple-polishing. I know and am well aware of the progress of all the men after they reach a certain spot in this organization. . . . And, fellows, I take my hat off to results only."

Walt concluded by citing the studio's heavy financial load—weekly operating expense of $90,000—$70,000 in salaries—and by pointing out the employees' advantages in vacations, holidays, sick leave, etc. The remainder combined pep talk ("The future of this business has never looked better . . . and I want you to know that I'm rarin' to go") and blunt realism ("It's the law of the universe that the strong shall survive and the weak must fall by the way, and I don't care what idealistic plan is cooked up, nothing can change that").

He closed by quoting his memorandum to the staff: "The Company recognizes the right of employees to organize and to join in any labor organization of their choosing, and the Company does not intend to interfere with this right. HOWEVER, the law clearly provides that matters of this sort should be done off the employer's premises and on the employees' own time, and in such a manner as not to interfere with production. . . ."

It had been a rare performance by Walt Disney, an exercise in self-revelation which had never happened before and never would again. That he would be so frank and open with his massed employees indicated how serious he considered the situation. Recent events had perplexed him—the descent of the company's fortunes, the disaffection of a portion of his workers, the threats from Sorrell. In the next months he often responded from raw emotion, saying and doing things he later realized were unwise. Some of his associates believed he was being ill served by advisers who considered a tough stance as the best policy.

On May 29, 1941, Walt was astonished to find a picket line in front of the studio. Herb Sorrell had called the Screen Cartoonists Guild out on strike, claiming support of a majority of the Disney cartoonists. Yet 60 percent remained on the job. Of the three hundred strikers, many were sincere believers in the principle of unionization. Some were concerned about the recent and impending changes at the Disney studio and were convinced that a union was the best protection for their jobs. Some were radicals who seemed more interested in the strike itself than in the results it might bring.

Walt at first took the strike lightly. On the second day, he stood inside the studio gate and shouted wry comments to those he recognized in the picket line. "Aw, they'll be back in a couple of days," he said.

But they weren't. Herb Sorrell directed the strike from a tent pitched in the vacant lot across from the studio entrance, and he stepped up his campaign. Unable to shut down Disney production when other unions refused to honor the picket line, Sorrell organized a secondary boycott of Technicolor, and he successfully stemmed the flow of film into the studio. Sorrell launched a propaganda campaign in union papers and leftist publications across the country, accusing Disney of being anti-union and operating a sweatshop. The anti-Sorrell Federation of Screen Cartoonists was branded as a company union.

Walt struck back with public statements and paid advertisements—almost with his fists. One day as Walt parked his car inside the gate, one of his striking animators announced over the loudspeaker: "There he is—the man who believes in brotherhood for everybody but himself." Walt started taking off his coat and was stalking toward the gate when studio police intercepted him.

He found it punishing to sit in negotiation meetings and listen to his own employees try to dictate conditions under which they wanted to work. In his public statements he said naive things that were damaging to his own cause. Finally, out of frustration and dismay, he walked away from the strike, accepting an offer for a goodwill and film-making tour of South America. Before he left, he poured out his feelings in a letter to a newspaper columnist:

To me, the entire situation is a catastrophe. The spirit that played such an important part in the building of the cartoon medium has been destroyed. From now on, I get my artists from the hiring hall of the Painters and Paperhangers Union. Out of the 700 artists and assistants coming under this jurisdiction, 293 were on strike and 417 remained at work.

The Union refused to use the ballot to give the people here the right to determine their choice. In turning down the ballot, they said, to use their own words: "We might lose that way. If we strike, we know we will win." . . .

I was willing to sacrifice everything I had and would have fought to the last ditch had it not been for the fact that a lot of innocent people might have been hurt. It didn't take long to see that there wasn't a fair, honest chance of winning; the cards were all stacked against me, so for the time being I have capitulated, but, believe me, I'm not licked—I'm incensed. . . .

The lies, the twisted half-truths that were placed in the public prints cannot be easily forgotten. I was called a rat, a yellow-dog employer and an exploiter of labor. They took the salaries of my messenger boys and claimed them to be the salaries of my artists. My plant and methods were compared to a sweatshop, and above all, I was accused of rolling in wealth. That hurt me most, when the fact is that every damned thing I have is tied up in this business. The thing that worries me is that people only read headlines and never take enough time to follow through and find out the truth.

I am convinced that this entire mess was Communistically inspired and led. The People's World, The League of Women's Shoppers, The American Peace Mobilization and every known Communistic outfit in the country were the first to put me on their unfair list. The legitimate American Federation of Labor unions were the last and they were reluctant to move. . . .

I am thoroughly disgusted and would gladly quit and try to establish myself in another business if it were not for the loyal guys who believe in me—so I guess I'm stuck with it.

This South American expedition is a godsend. I am not so hot for it but it gives me a chance to get away from this God-awful nightmare and to bring back some extra work into the plant. I have a case of the D.D.'s—disillusionment and discouragement. . . .

By the time he returned from South America, the strike had been settled—badly. The resolution brought even more problems, especially when the inevitable layoffs came with the slowing down of production. Strikers and nonstrikers had to be dismissed in a predetermined ratio, producing hardship and bitterness.

Walt was on his travels when he heard of the strike settlement. One of his companions from the studio muttered comments against the strikers. "Now, wait a minute," Walt interrupted. "For whatever reason they did what they did, they thought they were right. We've had our differences on a lot of things, but we're going to continue making pictures, and we're going to find a way to work together."

Afterward, he seemed to bear no bitterness toward most of the strikers, and some of them achieved important positions in the company in later years. But Walt could not forgive the animator who had mouthed inflammatory remarks through the loudspeaker. The government said the man had to be reinstated, but Walt refused to talk to him, and the striker left the studio after a couple of years.

The 1941 strike had a profound effect on Walt, shading his attitude toward politics and his relations with his employees. He was pushed further toward con-

servatism and anti-communism. And he suffered disillusion in his plan to make the Disney studio a worker's paradise. The noonday volleyball games continued,
but the snack shop in the Animation Building was
closed. Workers now had to sign in and out on a time-
clock. Never again would the studio's creative people
know the same free, intimate relationship with Walt
that had existed in the studio during its formative years.

The South American trip had been suggested by
John Hay (Jock) Whitney, director of the motion-
picture division for the Coordinator of Inter-American
Affairs, Nelson Rockefeller. Whitney had argued that
the government's Good Neighbor Policy could be fur-
thered if Walt Disney and his artists visited South
America to demonstrate the artistic side of the United
States culture. The need was urgent, said Whitney.
Many Germans and Italians had settled in South
America, and there was strong sentiment for the Axis
powers. Although the United States was not at war in
mid-1941, it supported the Allies and feared the spread
of Nazi and Fascist sentiment in countries of the western hemisphere.

"A goodwill tour?" said Walt. "I'm no good at that.
I can't do it."

"Then would you go down there and make some
pictures?" Whitney asked.

"Well, yes, I'd like to do that," Walt replied. "I'd
feel better about going to really do something, instead
of just shaking hands."

But the decision wasn't entirely his own. With the
Disney company's finances in straitened circumstances,
the Bank of America exercised a benevolent, super-
visory influence on major decisions. Starting in 1936,
the bank established a revolving line of credit with
Walt Disney Productions, lending money on need and
receiving in return all revenues from RKO's distribution
of the Disney films (all receipts from licensing of
cartoon characters went directly to the company). By

1940, Disney had borrowed $2,000,000 in 5-percent demand notes from the Bank of America. In 1941, the total had reached $3,400,00, hence the bankers were eyeing Walt's future projects with greater care.

"How do we know Walt can make anything out of South America?" asked one of the bankers. "How do we know that it might not turn out to be one of those propaganda things that won't make a dime in the theaters?"

The U.S. government made up for the bankers' reluctance. Jock Whitney reported to Walt that the government would underwrite the tour expenses up to $70,000 and would guarantee him $50,000 apiece for at least four, perhaps, five films based on the South American trip, the moneys to be returned if the films made a profit in theatrical release. With the studio strike dragging on into the summer of 1941, Walt decided to go.

He picked his traveling staff with care, asking each person individually and then assembling the entire group in his office and designating duties like a field general before battle. Norm Ferguson would be the producer-director. Webb Smith, Bill Cottrell and Ted Sears would develop stories. Jack Miller, Jimmy Bodrero and a married couple, Lee and Mary Blair, would help conceive the characters. Chuck Wolcott was in charge of music. Herb Ryman, an artist formerly with MGM, would study the landscapes, buildings, people. Larry and Janet Lansburgh would work on animals and characterizations. Frank Thomas would collaborate with Fergie on animation. Jack Cutting, who had traveled in South America, would check on authenticity and advise on the foreign-language versions. John Rose would handle administrative matters.

The expediton of seventeen—Bill Cottrell and Walt were accompanied by their wives—left Los Angeles on August 17, 1941. They flew across the country on a DC-3, which stopped for fuel and press conferences

in Fort Worth, Nashville and Jacksonville. The plane
lacked air conditioning, and at each stop cold air was
pumped into the cabin. It soon dissipated after takeoff,
and the passengers sweltered until the plane reached
a cooler altitude. The cross-country trip to Miami required twenty-four hours, and the company stopped
overnight at a resort hotel, then flew across the Caribbean in a Pan American Stratocruiser. The travelers
realized the closeness of the war when the plane landed
at British islands during nighttime; the cabin's curtains
had to be drawn, and the runways were unlighted.
Luggage was carefully examined at each airport.

The first stop on the South American continent was
Belém, at the mouth of the Amazon, where the group
visited a zoo and stayed overnight. Then on to Rio de
Janeiro, where the work began. Walt told the American
ambassador that he and his people were in Brazil to
work and he wanted to limit the social events.

Jock Whitney had arrived in Rio to help with the
arrangements, and the Disney group was entertained
by President Vargas at a lavish dinner. The days were
full, with visits to farms, zoos, schools, art galleries and
beaches to absorb the color and customs. Then to
night clubs and festivals to see the dancing and hear
the native music. After three weeks, the troupe moved
on to Buenos Aires, where Whitney again assisted in
relations with the government. Disney headquarters
were established in the Alvear Palace Hotel, and a
miniature studio was set up in the roof garden.

In Argentina as in Brazil, Walt Disney was lionized.
Mickey Mouse and Donald Duck were immensely
popular, and crowds followed Walt wherever he went.
He was invited to an *asado,* or barbecue, at a huge
estancia, and the guests were outfitted in gaucho costumes. With his black hair and mustache and olive
skin, Walt looked the perfect gaucho, and the Argen-
tines were delighted.

After a month in Buenos Aires, El Groupo, as the
travelers called themselves, flew over the Andes to

Chile. They spent a week there, then split up for the return home. Ryman, Miller and the Blairs flew on to visit Bolivia, Peru and Mexico; the rest took a fifteen-day boat trip back to the United States. The work of compiling the sketches, paintings, stories and music into storyboards was begun in a glassed-in section on the boat's deck. The liner made several stops, including one at a small Colombian town where Walt and others took a steamer ride thirty miles up a river and into a rain forest. That might have been the inspiration, his companions later suspected, for Walt's Jungle Cruise fifteen years later at Disneyland.

Walt and his party continued through the Panama Canal and landed at New York, arriving in time for the premiere of *Dumbo*. Then the Disneys flew home to Los Angeles for a joyful reunion with Diane and Sharon, whom they hadn't seen in twelve weeks. Walt's homecoming was also marked by sorrow. During his absence, Elias Disney had died. He was eighty-two years old, and he had never fully recovered from the loss of his beloved Flora. When he heard in South America the news of his father's passing, Walt commented to a companion, "I only wish that Roy and I could have had success sooner, so we could have done more for my mother and father."

On his return to the studio, Walt began work on the South American subjects, which were planned as a series of shorts. As the material developed, he realized that it could be developed into a feature. To the cartoons he added live-action footage of the troupe's travels, much of it photographed by Walt himself with a 16mm camera.

The trip had proved an enormous success. The South Americans, who had been subjected to the visits of speechmaking politicans and diplomats, now realized that the United States also had people who were young and creative and down-to-earth. The Latin Americans were further complimented by the two films that resulted from the trip, *Saludos Amigos* and *The Three Caballeros*. (Walt took a staff to Mexico to research

Mexican portions of the latter film.) A New York critic called *Saludos Amigos* "at once a potent piece of propaganda and a brilliant job of picture-making." The films were sucesses in both the Americas, and, as Walt pointed out later, "the government never lost a nickel on them—we paid for our own trip and the pictures, too."

14

ON THE afternoon of December 7, 1941, Walt Disney answered the telephone at his Los Feliz home. The studio manager told him, "Walt, the studio police just phoned me; the Army is moving in on us."

Still shocked by the news that the Japanese had bombed Pearl Harbor, Walt asked what he meant. "The Army—five hundred soldiers," said the manager. "They told me they're moving in."

"What did you tell them?" Walt asked.

"I said I'd have to call you."

"What did they say to that?"

"They said, 'Go ahead and call him—we're moving in, anyway.' "

The soldiers commandeered the Disney sound stage, ordered the film equipment removed, and installed gear for repairing trucks and anti-aircraft guns. An officer remarked that the stage was ideal because it could be used during a blackout. Next the Army claimed the employee parking sheds and used them for storing three million rounds of ammunition. Military police were posted at each gate, and all Disney workers, including Walt and Roy, were fingerprinted and given identification badges to wear at all times. Artists doubled up in rooms of the Animation Building so the soldiers would have places to sleep.

The Army unit, which supported anti-aircraft installations in the mountains around Los Angeles, remained at the studio for eight months. It moved out when fears of a Japanese attack on the mainland were over, but other military personnel moved in. The Disney studio had converted to war.

The studio had already been preparing for its wartime role before Pearl Harbor. Walt wanted to prove that he could make training films, and in March 1941 he enlisted the help of a project method engineer from nearby Lockheed Aircraft Corporation, George W. Papen. Working in his free time, Papen assisted in preparing a film, *Four Methods of Flush Riveting*. It was so effective that Lockheed used it to instruct the flood of new aircraft workers. Canadian officials studied it and were convinced that Disney could help their war effort. The studio was commissioned to supply four shorts to promote sales of war savings certificates and stamps and another to instruct recruits on use of the Boys' anti-tank gun.

Shortly after the United States entered the war, Walt received a telephone call from the Navy Bureau of Aeronautics in Washington. The officer said the Navy wanted twenty short films on aircraft identification, the first ones to be delivered in ninety days, the remainder within six months. "The budget is eighty thousand dollars," he said. "Can you do it?" Walt said he thought he could. "Okay, Mr. Disney, if you consider this a contract, we have a recording of this conversation. Go right ahead. We will send a man out in three weeks."

When Walt hung up the telephone, he realized that *he* had no recording of the conversation to give him evidence of the contract. But he went ahead with the project, gathering all the information he could find on aircraft identification. When the adviser arrived from Washington, he was surprised to see the studio had prepared exactly what was needed. The twenty films were completed at a cost of $72,000—$8,000 under the allotment, but not enough to take care of contingencies and to provide a profit.

More orders for films came to the Disney studio: from the Navy for *Aircraft Carrier Landing Signals;* from the Agriculture Department for *Food Will Win the War;* from the Army for a film to indoctrinate airplane spotters in the WEFT system (wings, engine, fusilage, tail). The studio produced *Chicken Little,* an anti-Nazi film showing the evils of mass hysteria; *Education for Death,* depicting how German youth were converted into Nazis; and *Defense Against Invasion,* promoting immunization against disease. The orders came in such volume that Walt and Roy were forced to reconsider the direction of the company. With the market for cartoon features at its lowest point and the studio staff facing depletion by the draft, it seemed prudent to cut back on features, except for *Bambi,* which was still making tedious progress. Walt abandoned preparations for *Alice in Wonderland* and *Peter Pan* and shut down animation on *Wind in the Willows.* A favorite studio legend concerns the animator who was assigned to *Wind in the Willows,* departed to serve in the Army, then returned four years later to resume animating the same sequence in the same film.

Walt was stimulated by the challenge of interpreting complex subjects in a compelling and enlightening way. He applied his skill to explaining bombsights and factory methods with the same zeal that he had to recounting the exploits of Mickey Mouse and Snow White. His technique was demonstrated in story-conference notes of May 24, 1942, for a subject to be called *The Winged Scourge.* The film was being made for the Coordinator of Inter-American Affairs, Nelson Rockefeller, and the storyboard showed a lecturer on malaria prevention being interrupted by the Seven Dwarfs.

The film is basically to tell people how to get rid of mosquitoes. The only reason to bring the dwarfs in is to add a little interest; when you get into gags and impossible things, you're not accomplishing the job we're supposed to do—show in a simple way how to get rid of mosquitoes.

The idea as I saw it was we'd talk the picture and after you've explained everything and emphasized the importance of getting rid of the mosquito—it's a serious thing—then, to get relief a bit, we'd go into the operation of the thing, pep up the ending by taking seven ordinary citizens. The narrator says, "It's not a difficult task—we're selecting seven people at random." Then we show them it's the dwarfs . . . we take each dwarf and he goes about his work, does it as it's supposed to be done. Maybe it's Dopey spreading the oil . . . let him be cute, but don't go into these gags.

Where you'd get your interest—we'd throw it to the music. Digging the ditch . . . with a scythe he's cutting the weeds. . . . Dopey's getting the crankcase oil, he goes up and gets this old oil and comes on off and sprays it over the thing, just doing the business, but he's doing it in rhythm. Nothing they'll laugh at to beat hell, but something to listen to. It's a serious problem, but we are showing how simple it is. Even Dopey can do it. . . .

The demand for war films continued, and the Disney studio, which had previously been averaging 30,000 feet of completed film a year, now was producing 300,000 feet a year. The greatly increased volume was accomplished by a smaller staff working longer hours. Walt wrote to a friend: "For some time now, the studio has been working on a six-day basis with two nights of overtime each week. However, I have learned that if this is continued over a certain period of time, the efficiency of the personnel is impaired, so we have set a limit of fifty-four hours per week. A mental fatigue results in this particular type of work and although we are doing our best to combat it, we must get our Government films out as needed."

The draft had taken one-third of Walt's artists, and he worried whether he could continue his output with a depleted staff. Navy and Army officers attached to the studio offered to make representations to draft boards. Walt suggested: "Let's bring the draft-board members over here. They think we're just making Mickey Mouse. We'll show them what else we're doing." When draft-board members discovered they had to be cleared by Army and Navy intelligence as well as the FBI, and then could not enter certain areas because of top-security work, their attitudes changed. So vital was the Disney war work that drafted employees were sent back to the studio in uniform to resume their work.

Some of the Disney workers chose to stay at the studio, others did not. One of those who left was Card Walker, who had come up through the ranks and in early 1942 was a unit manager in cost control on the short subjects. Walker visited Walt's office and told of his intention to join the Navy. At first Walt argued that the young man possessed valuable knowledge that was essential to the studio's war work. "Well, Walt," said Walker, "I feel very emotional about it; I just want to get into the war." Walt paused and admitted that he envied Walker. Walt reminisced about his own experience with the ambulance corps in France, and he concluded, "You're a lucky guy; I'd like to go myself."

It wasn't easy for Walt to adjust to sharing his studio with outsiders. Not only did the armed forces and federal officials have the run of the place; Lockheed Aircraft also occupied space for manufacturing. The wartime invasion extended even to Walt's private office. An admiral requested a rush project, a film about Rules of the Nautical Road. The admiral didn't have authorization as yet, but the film was urgently needed to instruct new navigators. The author of a book on navigation, a Navy commander, arrived at the Disney studio. Since the commander had no place to stay, Walt volunteered his own small bedroom off his studio office. The commander stayed for months, washing and hanging up his laundry in Walt's bathroom. The film was completed before the Navy came through with an appropriation.

Walt made frequent trips to Washington for dealings with the government. When he couldn't get a hotel reservation, he sat through several performances in a movie house in order to get some rest. During one of the Washington trips, he met with Frank Capra, the director who had convinced Harry Cohn that Columbia Pictures should release Mickey Mouse. Capra had joined the Army Signal Corps, and he complained to Walt, "I've got to get out of Washington. I can't make pictures here. Have you got any room at the studio?" Walt agreed to give him space, and Capra moved in, assembled a staff and borrowed artists and facilities from the studio to prepare the series called Why We Fight. The Capra unit was not funded until later.

Business relations between the Disney studio and the government were chaotic. At the beginning of the war, the Disney board of directors voted to donate the studio's services at cost, as its contribution to the war effort. Government bookkeepers could neither understand nor permit this, and they insisted on paying cost plus a small profit, thus permitting the government to question all expenditures. The accountants couldn't fathom the workings of the movie business. They demanded to know why a crew should be paid for standing by between projects. Walt tried to explain that he had to maintain his staff so he could undertake a new project when it appeared. Wrangles over financing continued more than two years after the war.

Some of the Disney war work was never paid for. Walt's artists designed more than 1,400 insignia for military units at an average cost of $25. "I had to do it," Walt said afterward. "Those kids grew up on Mickey Mouse. I owed it to 'em."

In December 1942, John L. Sullivan, a Treasury Department official, telephoned Walt. Henry Morgenthau, the Secretary of the Treasury, had an urgent special project he wanted to discuss. "Can you fly to Washington tonight?" Sullivan asked. Walt mentioned his daughter Diane's birthday; he had twice been away on her birthday, he didn't want to miss another one. "This is very important," Sullivan insisted, and Walt agreed to make the flight.

Walt presumed the project would be a campaign to sell war bonds. But when he arrived at Morgenthau's office, he learned of a different mission. "We want you to help us sell people on paying income tax," Morgenthau announced.

The suggestion puzzled Walt. "Wait a minute," he said. "You're the Treasury speaking. You're the United States government. Sell people on paying taxes? If they don't pay 'em, you put 'em in jail."

Guy T. Helvering, the Commissioner of Internal Revenue, spoke up. "That's my trouble. Under the new tax bill, we've got fifteen million new taxpayers next year. I can't prosecute fifteen million people. We've got to make them understand what taxes are and the part the taxes play in winning the war."

"I came back here all prepared to help you sell bonds," Walt remarked.

"That's the point," Helvering said. "People think when they buy a bond, that's going to pay for the war. But how are we going to pay off the bonds? By taxes. We don't want to prosecute those people. We want them to pay their taxes and be excited about paying their taxes as a patriotic thing."

Morgenthau said to Walt: "Now you've got the idea. See what you can do for us."

That evening Walt met over drinks with Sullivan and Helvering at Sullivan's house in Virginia. The two Treasury men outlined the points they sought to put across to the public, and Walt began devising an idea for the film. He called the studio and ordered a story crew to start work. Then he telephoned his daughter Diane to wish her a happy birthday.

Walt hurried back to California. It was late December, and Morgenthau wanted the film in the nation's theaters by February. The cartoon had to be completed and processed through Technicolor in less than six weeks. Walt dropped everything else to work on the film. He and his crew labored eighteen hours a day, sleeping on cots in the Animation Building. When the storyboards were completed, Walt flew to Washington to show them to Morgenthau.

Neither Sullivan nor Helvering was permitted in Morgenthau's office during the presentation. Only Morgenthau's secretary and an aide were present. Walt was warned beforehand: "Keep an eye on the secretary. She wields a lot of influence."

Walt set up the storyboards and went into one of his eloquent performances. He described how Donald Duck was patriotic in the extreme—except when it came to taxes. But when Donald was shown that paying taxes meant helping to win the war, his attitude changed. He refused calculators and headache pills, filled out the simplified tax form and hurried to the mailbox to file his return early. Red-white-and-blue flags in his eyes lighted up, and he raced from California to Washington to submit his tax in person.

Walt's audience of three sat expressionless through the entire recital, and they remained silent when Walt finished. Then the aide said tentatively, "Well, I, uh— I always visualized that you would create a little character who would be called Mr. Taxpayer." The secretary was more blunt: "I don't like Donald Duck."

Morgenthau said nothing, and Walt's Irish temper began to mount. "Well, you want to get this message over," he said. "I've given you Donald Duck. At our studio, that's the equivalent of giving you Clark Gable out of the MGM stable. Donald Duck is known by the American public. He'll open doors to the theaters. They won't be running a cartoon of Mr. Taxpayer; they'll be running a Donald Duck cartoon. By giving you this, I'll be losing money. Every theater that plays this short will knock off a Donald Duck cartoon that would have been booked. I did it because I want the thing to be successful. I felt it was the only way to tell the story: by using a character they know and putting him into a situation that they themselves will be in. If you don't like this, I'll have to throw away half the picture, because it's already in work."

The Secretary of the Treasury looked up from his desk and said resignedly, "I leave it to you."

Walt hurried back to California to finish the film, titled *The New Spirit,* and the Treasury ordered an unprecedented eleven hundred prints to saturate the nation before the March 15 deadline for tax payments. The Treasury Department estimated that the film was seen by sixty million people; a Gallup poll indicated that *The New Spirit* affected 37 percent of the taxpayers on their willingness to pay.

As Walt had predicted, many theaters that received the Treasury's film at no expense canceled their orders for Donald Duck cartoons. Only the Radio City Music Hall sent a check for the Disney cartoon it had ordered but didn't show.

When the bill for *The New Spirit* was presented to the Treasury, Morgenthau questioned it. The total was $80,000, and the Secretary complained to Walt: "You said you could make a cartoon for forty-three thousand." Walt explained that his own cost had been $47,000 because of the hurry to complete the project; the rest of the expense was caused by the huge order for Technicolor prints. Morgenthau said he would have to go to Congress for a deficiency appropriation. It was submitted at the same time the President's wife, Eleanor Roosevelt, had appointed an exotic dancer to a civil-defense post. Congressmen denounced employment of "a fan dancer and Donald Duck" as examples of boondoggling in civil defense. Walter Winchell defended Disney in his newspaper column and radio broadcast, but Walt received mail accusing him of being a war profiteer.

Donald Duck also starred in the most popular of the wartime Disney shorts, *Der Fuehrer's Face.* The storyline showed Donald having a nightmare in which he dreamed he was working in a German munitions factory. Oliver Wallace, the onetime movie-theater organist who became a prolific composer for the Disney studio, was assigned to write a song for Donald and his companions to sing in saluting Adolf Hitler. Wallace said he was riding a bicycle along the studio streets when the inspiration came to him and he nearly fell off. The idea: to punctuate the "Heils!" with over-ripe raspberries.

The contemptuous treatment of Hitler delighted audiences throughout America, and the song became one of the most popular during the war. *Der Fuehrer's Face* was translated into all European languages and smuggled into the Continent by the underground, infuriating the Nazi High Command.

Victory Through Air Power was a unique Disney venture. It was an advocacy film not sponsored by the government but produced by Walt Disney because he shared the beliefs of Alexander de Seversky.

Until his trip to South America, Walt's acquaintance with air travel had been an occasional cross-country flight. Then he flew over Amazon jungles and through Andean passes, saw Brazil, Argentina and Chile more thoroughly and faster than he could have any other way. Along the way he talked to pilots and ground crews, prowled through hangars and control towers, asking endless questions about how things worked. By the time he returned to Los Angeles, he had traveled twenty thousand miles, and he was a confirmed proponent of the airplane.

Walt was overwhelmed by the logic of the 1942 book *Victory Through Air Power,* written by Major Alexander P. de Seversky, once a commander of Russian air squadrons in the First World War, later an inventor of bombsights and navigation controls, a speed flier and advocate of air power to win World War II. A naturalized citizen, he convinced many of his fellow Americans with the arguments in his book. Historian Charles Beard called *Victory Through Air Power* "a more important book for Americans than all the other war books put together." The New York *Herald Tri-*

bune commented that the Seversky book "if read and heeded, might become a turning point in the war."

On May 4, 1942, Walt telegraphed his New York representative:

> AM ANXIOUS CONTACT MAJOR ALEXANDER DE SEVERSKY BY TELEPHONE AND MAIL. WILL YOU ENDEAVOR GET THIS INFORMATION TO ME EARLIEST POSSIBLE MOMENT BUT DEFINITELY ELIMINATE MY NAME FROM ALL INQUIRIES MADE.

Walt reached Seversky and said he wanted to make a film of *Victory Through Air Power*. Within a few weeks the project had started with the crew that had recently completed *Bambi* after five years of production. Because of the urgency of its theme and the changing world events, the new film had to be finished within months.

By July, preliminary storyboards had been prepared, and Seversky came to the studio to assist. He and Walt proved good collaborators, sparking ideas off each other:

WALT: Do you think there is anything in taking the people back forty years and showing the progress we have made? It would be a little reminiscent thing. Show how progress in this speeded up during the first war and then slowed down a bit in peacetime and then shot up again during this war.

SEVERSKY: Sure. And for this war the progress will still be faster. You could point out that when the Germans bombed Coventry they used five hundred airplanes and unloaded two hundred and fifty tons of bombs. And today at Rostov, fifty planes carried two hundred and fifty tons of bombs. In two years, a ratio of ten to one. . . .

WALT: We leave here to go back forty years ago to the historic Wright Brothers taking off and show this telegram and then that little item in the newspaper about their being home for Christmas. Then suppose we move along to the start of the last war and how everything advances in wartimes. Show how when the last war started they didn't even have enough guns in their planes, then go on up a few years when they have these dogfights and fancy maneuvers.

SEVERSKY: Yes, they had the Sikorsky bombers within three years.

WALT: And at the beginning of the war, range was practically nothing. But right after the war, they had this Navy plane nonstop flight to the Azores.

SEVERSKY: And then you could show how commercial aviation had developed wonderfully since then. Of course, we paid no attention to the military end, and the military planes did not develop as fast as the commercial. But since the beginning of the war we have advanced terrifically. . . .

WALT: What did you use in the war—a gun?

SEVERSKY: Well, back in 1915, all I had was a pistol. Then later we used automatic rifles and then we started using machine guns.

WALT: At first, you know, they used to wave to each other when they passed each other on their way to their destination. Then one Frenchman put some bricks in his plane; he didn't want to wave at the Germans, and the next time he passed, he threw a brick at a German. And from there it progressed to dogfighting.

SEVERSKY: Karsikoff was flying with a big heavy ball with a hook on it, and when he met another plane, he threw the ball out and the hook would catch on the enemy plane. This ball would have another ball attached to it, and the other ball would tear up the plane. He downed a couple of planes that way. . . .

* * *

Seversky was designated as technical adviser on *Victory Through Air Power,* but he became more than that. A draftsman and engineer, he created sketches which were used as guides by the Disney artists. He remained at the studio throughout the eight-month production period, changing elements of the script as events of the war substantiated his predictions. One sequence theorized on the use of air power to eliminate hydropower dams of the enemy. Before the film could be completed, the Royal Air Force bombed the Rhineland dams in almost the exact method proposed by Seversky.

When Walt was in Washington, he was invited to a meeting of high naval officers. They queried him about *Victory Through Air Power,* and one of the admirals complained, "Do you know what that's going to do our battleship program?" Walt replied, "Gee, you don't really believe in battleships, do you?" They did indeed, and they offered arguments. "I believe in air power," Walt insisted. "I just want to tell the story of air power." The Navy men persisted, and Walt later omitted portions of the film illustrating Seversky's bias against heavy ships.

Victory Through Air Power was released in July of 1943, only fourteen months after Walt had first talked to Seversky. The Disney selling force steadfastly avoided the term "propaganda," but that's what the film was. As such, it succeeded, exerting a vast influence on the thinking of both the public and policy-makers.

In his biography of advertising man Albert Lasker, *Taken at the Flood,* John Gunther wrote that Lasker had long tried to arrange a meeting between Seversky and President Roosevelt or to screen *Victory Through Air Power* at the White House. But Lasker had failed because of the watchfulness of Fleet Admiral William D. Leahy, "who thought that Seversky was a crackpot." Gunther added:

Meantime, the film received wide attention in theaters in England. Lasker, through a British friend, got a print to Winston Churchill, and the Prime Minister was much impressed by it.

Came the Quebec Conference between Roosevelt and Churchill in the summer of 1943. Critical military decisions, preparatory to the invasion of Europe the next year, had to be made, but the conference was deadlocked. F.D.R. and General Marshall wanted to set a definite date for the operation, but Churchill, the RAF, and General Arnold felt that this should not be done until certain conditions were met, such as the undisputed command of the air over the English Channel. In an effort to break through this impasse Churchill asked Roosevelt if he had ever seen *Victory Through Air Power*. F.D.R. said no, and a print was flown by fighter plane from New York to Quebec; the President and the Prime Minister saw it together that night privately, and Roosevelt was much excited by the way Disney's aircraft masterfully wiped ships off the seas. It was run again the next day, and then F.D.R. invited the Joint Chiefs to have a look at it. This played an important role in the decision, which was then taken, to give the D-Day invasion sufficient air power.

The film lost $436,000 for Walt Disney Productions and Walt admitted later, "It was a stupid thing to do as a business venture. It was just something that I believed in, and for no other reason than that, I did it."

Victory Through Air Power contributed to the downward trend of the Disney finances during the war. *Bambi,* released in August 1942, had earned a disappointing $1,200,000 in the United States, with foreign receipts at $2,190,000. *Saludos Amigos,* issued in February of 1943, drew $500,000 in the United States and $700,000 abroad, much of it from South America.

Since the film cost slightly under $300,000, it provided a profit.

As in the Depression, the Disney studio failed to share in the prosperity of the motion picture business. The other companies were grinding out war movies and musicals for an entertainment-hungry nation, and theaters were earning huge profits. But not with Disney pictures.

There was no *Snow White and the Seven Dwarfs* to rescue the Disney brothers from debt. The studio issued a dozen short cartoons annually during the war; returns on them were limited by the economics of the movie business. The training and propaganda films contracted by the government barely paid for maintaining the staff and studio. The indebtedness to the Bank of America climbed to more than $4,000,000, and some of the bank's board members expressed concern over the revolving line of credit extended to Disney.

One day Joe Rosenberg, the bank's Los Angeles liaison with the studio, telephoned Roy to request that he and Walt answer questions about their loan at the board of directors meeting in San Francisco. In later years Roy enjoyed recounting the story of how he and Walt traveled north in a state of gloom. They had never before been summoned to a command appearance before the board. With the war continuing to occupy the studio's major effort, they could offer little hope for an immediate upturn in the company's finances. Their gloom deepened when they were escorted into the Bank of America's dark-paneled board room and saw the twelve solemn-faced directors seated around the large table. Nothing could proceed until the arrival of A. P. Giannini, the founder and board chairman of Bank of America. After fifteen minutes he entered, leonine-faced and commanding in presence. He declined to take a chair, listening to the discussions as he walked around the table. As he passed the Disneys, he nudged them in the backs and muttered, "Don't look so downhearted; it isn't going to be that bad." Walt and Roy found reason for hope. A.P. had long been their champion; when traveling in Europe, he sometimes sent them postcards with the message, "I saw one of your pictures and it was pretty good."

The matter of the Disney loan came before the board, and Walt and Roy explained how war conditions had interrupted the studio's profitability. Giannini began interrogating the directors: "You've been lending the Disneys a lot of money—how many of their pictures have you seen? Which ones?" He demanded answers from each board member, and he discovered that several of them had seen none of the Disney movies.

"Well, I've seen them," Giannini remarked. "I've been watching the Disneys' pictures quite closely, because I knew we were lending them money far above the financial risk. But I realized that there's nothing about those pictures that will be changed by the war. They're good this year, they're good next year, and they're good the year after. Now there's a war on and the Disneys' markets are in trouble. Their money's frozen, or else they can't get in countries. You have to relax and give them time to market their product. This war isn't going to last forever."

He strode out of the room. Walt and Roy returned to Los Angeles with the assurance that they would be able to stay in business.

15

WALT DISNEY'S dealings with his employees followed patterns. Newcomers to the studio, and even some longtime employees, were perplexed by his manner and misread silence for disinterest, gruffness for disfavor. Others learned to understand the enigmatic nature of his creative gifts. None professed to understand the man himself, and he was not given to intimacy and self-revelation. But the patterns of his working life, firmly ingrained now that Disney had reached his forties, could be discerned by those who studied his day-to-day dealings with his staff.

He rarely issued direct praise for work that had been done well. He seemed to expect excellence and did not express gratitude when he received it. Commendation usually came in the form of a bonus check or a remark to a third person, with the realization that the praise would be handed on.

He commanded attention. Roy once remarked of his brother: "He had an eye that would grab yours when he was telling you something, and if you would waver and look around, he'd say, 'What's the matter —aren't you interested?' Oh, he wouldn't let go of your eyes. He was so intent on everything he did, and that was his way of looking into you. You couldn't lie to him and say you liked it if you didn't; it would show right in your eyes. People couldn't stand up to him if they weren't pretty right."

He did not like to be contradicted, either by his collaborators or by himself. In a story conference a director made the mistake of rebutting a Disney suggestion by saying, "But Walt, you said the opposite thing in our last story meeting. It says so in the conference notes." Walt viewed the observation coldly. What mattered was the viewpoint he offered at the moment, not one he had held a week before.

He disliked having his view of fantasy confronted with logic. A Brazilian artist, brought to the studio to work on the South American features, attended a story meeting for a sequence in which an Argentine horse played ragtime piano. "But horses don't play the piano!" the Brazilian protested. Walt immediately lost interest in him as a collaborator.

He could apply his own particular logic to win a point. In a story session for a jungle scene, dialogue was suggested for all the beasts, including a giraffe. Walt halted the discussion by declaring, "Giraffes don't talk; they have no vocal cords." The giraffe remained mute while the other animals spoke.

He listened to all ideas, but in the end he alone made the decision. When he suggested a switch in a *Pinocchio* sequence that Bill Cottrell had written, Cottrell said, "I like my way better." "Yes, but let's do it my way," Walt replied. "But if we don't try it my way, we'll never know whether or not it would have worked," Cottrell suggested. "No, we won't," Walt said with finality.

While he disliked opposition to his ideas, he would not tolerate yes-men. That was misunderstood by some of his underlings, including a director who was asked in a sweatbox session what he thought of an animation sequence. "I don't know; Walt isn't here," he replied. Walt had no respect for men who uncritically assented to his suggestions; he himself realized that not all of them had value. He could ascend in a flight of fancy to such heights that both he and his listeners realized that his ideas wouldn't work. The matter would not be mentioned again.

Some of Walt's creative people enjoyed a lively relationship with him. One of those was Bill Peet, who made important story contributions to the cartoon features. Walt once paid him a rare compliment: "If I were you, Bill, I wouldn't be working for me." Because of his respect for Peet, Walt tolerated Peet's heated arguments over story matters. Walt also endured the temperamental outbursts of Milt Kahl, whose talent as an animator was exceeded by no one's. Walt developed a system of dealing with Kahl's pique: "I just wait three days after Milt has asked to see me; by then he has forgotten what he was mad about."

One of Walt's most valued animators in the 1930s was a young man whose natural talent made him an instant success. If anything, animation came too easily to him, and, his fellow artists believe, the lack of challenge contributed to his alcoholism. As his drinking increased, his work output declined in volume and quality, and Walt shifted him to the position of supervisor, hoping the animator could impart his knowledge to others. But the added responsibility plunged him further into drink. Finally Walt discharged him, hoping that the shock would bring a turnabout. But it didn't, and he died at an early age.

His was a rare case. As long as drinking did not interfere with an employee's performance of his duties, Walt did not object. A supervisor once came to him to complain about a story man who kept a bottle in his desk drawer. Walt, who disliked informers, replied: "Find out what he's drinking; I want you to try some of the same."

Disney artists cherished a tale about a story man we shall call Al, a brilliant, inventive fellow who sometimes drank his lunch at a nearby restaurant. One day he returned to the studio and crawled behind a stack of storyboards leaning against his office wall. He quickly fell into a blissful, silent sleep. An hour later he awoke groggily in his confined quarters. Terror struck his heart as he heard the unmistakable cough of Walt Disney. A storyboard session was going on, and Walt was making comments as a story man described the action. "All right, let's see the next one," Walt remarked, and a storyboard was removed from the stack. Another cough by Walt made Al's throat start to tickle, and he clapped a hand over his mouth. The story man raced through the presentation, removing one board after another. Finally he was reaching the end of the sequence, and only one board remained. Al concluded that exposure was inevitable. It never came. In his muddled state he had failed to realize that the final storyboard would remain in place.

The story of Al's near-disaster circulated through the studio and finally reached Walt. "We ought to have a place at the studio where guys can sleep it off," he commented. He was also tolerant when an animator was arrested on a homosexual charge. "Let's give him a chance; we all make mistakes," Walt said. The animator continued at the studio for years afterward.

A group of story men once discovered that by sticking a pushpin in a lump of clay and balancing a ruler on the pinpoint, they could make the ruler spin indefinitely, like a propeller. It became the office toy, and they improved upon the device by counterbalancing chunks of art gum on the ruler. One early afternoon they were huddled over the spinning ruler when Walt's portentous cough was heard down the hallway. They quickly wheeled a storyboard in front of the ruler, hiding it as Walt entered. During the story session, two of the men stared fixedly at the whirling ruler. Finally Walt said, "What the hell are you looking at?" The men froze as Walt gazed around the storyboard and saw the object of their fascination. He studied it for a moment and said, "You've got too much friction there, with the pin sticking into the wood. What you need is some kind of a bearing. . . ." For weeks afterward, he inquired of the story men, "How are you doing with that gadget?"

When Walt entered a meeting, the men automatically rose to their feet as a matter of courtesy. The ritual was nothing that Walt asked for, and it was the only deviation from the consistent informality of the studio. Unlike other studios, where creative people worked behind closed doors, the office doors at Disney's were almost always open, and visiting between offices was approved.

Everyone at the studio, from Walt and Roy downward, used first names in addressing each other. New employees sometimes learned this from Walt. One day after the new studio had opened, Walt called the barbershop for a haircut appointment. Before his arrival, the new barber, Sal Silvestri, debated what to call the boss. When Walt walked in the shop, the barber said, "Good afternoon, Mr. Disney."

"What's your name?" Walt asked.

"Sal."

"Mine's Walt. The only Mister we have at the studio is our lawyer, Mr. Lessing." (A few others were called Mister in early years at the studio: Joseph Rogers, a white-haired carpenter; Emile Flohri, once a cover artist for the old *Life* magazine; A. G. Keener, a venerable paymaster.)

Walt rarely fired anyone. When an employee fell into disfavor, he was usually given a meaningless assignment and soon left the studio voluntarily. Walt employed a pair of writers who seemed to produce nothing of value. He admitted their incompetence and explained why they remained: "Because they always do a story the wrong way; once I've seen how they do it, I know the *right* way."

From all of his employees, Walt required a devotion to the collaborative effort, a sublimation of their own egos for the benefit of the studio product. The animated cartoon, as developed to an art by the Disney studio, required the efforts of many creative people. Those who were willing to contribute their work with selfless dedication remained and flourished. Some could not find gratification under such a system and left the studio to seek more individual achievement. Among the Disney alumni who achieved success elsewhere were Walt Kelly, Frank Tashlin, Virgil Partch, Hank Ketchum, George Baker, Sam Cobean, Chuck Jones and David Swift. Similarly, Disney's attempts to collaborate with well-known personalities usually ended in failure. Over the years such figures as Aldous Huxley, Thomas Hart Benton, Salvador Dali and Marc Connolly came to the studio to work on projects. Each time their efforts failed to reach the screen.

From the earliest years, when he changed the company from the Disney Brothers Studio to Walt Disney Studio, Walt had promoted his own name. Was this evidence of his ego drive? Possibly. But it was also shrewd business. Increasingly over the years, "Walt Disney Presents" became recognized throughout the world as a symbol of quality entertainment for the family.

Walt once expressed his feelings bluntly in a talk with a young animator, Ken Anderson. "I'm impressed with what you've been doing, Ken," Walt remarked. "You're new here, and I want you to understand one

WALT DISNEY

Ruth and Walt, 1913

Flora and Elias Disney
in Kansas City, 1913

Teen-age Walt
in Kansas City

In France, 1919

Laugh-O-Gram studio, 1922

Walt in back seat, 1922

Walt in Hollywood, 1923

*Lilly, Walt, Ruth, Roy, and Edna Disney
in front of the first studio, 1925*

Ub Iwerks, 1929

DISNEY CARTOONS
present
A
MICKEY MOUSE
SOUND CARTOON

STEAMBOAT
WILLIE

A WALT DISNEY COMIC
by UB IWERKS

RECORDED BY CINEPHONE SYSTEM

COPYRIGHT MCMXXIX

DISNEY CARTOONS
present
A
MICKEY MOUSE
SOUND CARTOON

STEAMBOAT
WILLIE

A WALT DISNEY COMIC
by UB IWERKS

Walt in front of Hyperion studio, 1931

Walt with Mickey Mouse merchandise, 1931

Walt and his brother Roy Disney pose with Mickey Mouse and Oscar (Special Award given by the Academy of Motion Picture Arts and Sciences for the creation of Mickey Mouse), 1932

Walt in his office at Hyperion studio

Walt with Leslie Howard

Walt receiving honorary Oscar
from Shirley Temple, February 23, 1939

*The elder Disneys' 50th wedding anniversary:
(seated) Herb, Flora, Elias, Walt; (standing) Ray, Roy*

George Balanchine, Igor Stravinsky and Walt with model for Fantasia, *December 1939*

Disney art class studies a deer for Bambi

The picket line, 1941

In South America, 1941

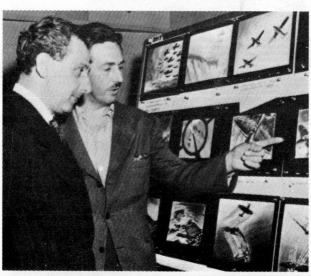

*Seversky and Walt studying storyboard
for* Victory Through Air Power, *July 1942*

Walt and daughter Diane

*Sharon, Lilly, Diane and Walt
en route to England, 1949*

Testing the Carolwood Pacific at the studio

Walt on the set of Treasure Island
with Robert Newton

At the Academy Awards, 1954

Escorting Diane to the church; Sharon at rear

Herb Ryman's sketch for Disneyland

The September 12, 1953, plan for Disneyland
drawn by Marvin A. Davis

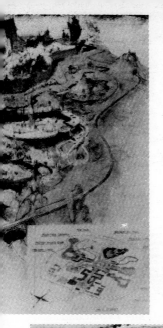

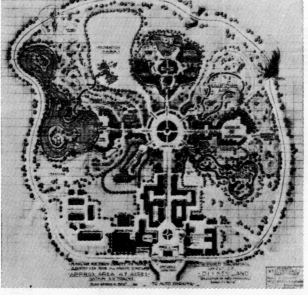

Greeting the first children to enter Disneyland

On the set of Mickey Mouse Club *with director Sidney Miller (left) and producer Bill Walsh (right)*

Under the sign with his father's name, Disneyland

Lilly and Walt in London

Former President Eisenhower presents Walt with Freedom Foundation Award, 1965

The Grauman's Chinese premiere of Mary Poppins:
Julie Andrews, Walt, Dick Van Dyke

The Millers, Disneys and Browns, 1961

*President Johnson presents
the Presidential Medal of Freedom to Walt, 1964*

*On the site of the Florida project
with Roy, Card Walker and Joe Fowler*

thing: there's just one thing we're selling here, and that's the name 'Walt Disney.' If you can buy that and be happy to work for it, you're my man. But if you've got any ideas of selling the name 'Ken Anderson,' it's best for you to leave right now."

Walt bore no rancor toward those who left him, and he welcomed many of them back. Among those who returned was Ub Iwerks. Walt's earliest collaborator had parted with the company in 1930 to found Ub Iwerks Studio in Hollywood. He produced the Flip the Frog series for MGM, and later tried other series, with medium success. Ub's real interest was the technical aspect of animation, and he returned to the Disney organization to pursue his research in 1940. After ten years apart, both Ub and Walt were reluctant to make the first move toward reconciliation. Ben Sharpsteen helped get the two old friends together. Neither Ub nor Walt was inclined to be demonstrative, but fellow workers thought they detected an unspoken affection between the two. Ub's contributions in new optical techniques proved to be as valuable in the studio's later history as had his animation of Oswald and Mickey Mouse in the early years.

"I take my hat off to talent," Walt said on many occasions. He sometimes grumbled to his animators, "I'd like to have a machine to replace you s.o.b.'s," but they never took him seriously. They realized that he was just as dependent on them for the creative impetus to the Disney product as they were on him for guidance and inspiration. No one could minimize the animator's work to Walt, not even animators themselves. As a part of the Disney Art School curriculum, Alexander Woollcott, Frank Lloyd Wright and other noted figures addressed the evening classes. One of the young animators commented to Walt: "We're lucky to be able to hear people like them." "Listen," Walt replied, "they're lucky, too. They can learn as much from you guys as you can from them."

While Walt was sometimes stern with his employees, he could also be compassionate, usually in a subtle way. During preparations for *Victory Through Air Power,* young Ken Anderson was demonstrating a storyboard about aerial tactics to Walt Disney, Alexander de Seversky and a group of visiting admirals. When Walt took out a cigarette, Anderson produced a brand-new lighter and sparked the flint. The lighter exploded in a blue flame, singeing Walt's mustache white and blistering his nose. "What the hell are you trying to do, burn me up?" he exclaimed, rushing out of the room. Anderson was devastated. Word of the incident spread through the studio, and he was shunned like a pariah. He wept that night, fearing that his career with Disney was over. In the morning he was surprised to hear Walt's jaunty voice on the telephone: "Hi, Ken, what are you doin' for lunch?" The two men lunched together in the studio restaurant in full view of other employees. Walt, who had shaved off his mustache, made no mention of the previous day's accident; he had a facility for ignoring disagreeable subjects. When Ken returned to his office that afternoon, his fellow workers no longer avoided him.

Walt Disney's personal life became more private as he grew older and became more famous. Although she appeared dutifully for public occasions, Lilly did not enjoy the glare of publicity. Walt's marriage to Lilly was one of mutual give-and-take. He discovered early that he had married no meek, acquiescent wife. Lilly listened to his dreams, but she did not respond with unquestioning support. When she thought he was wrong, she said so. She was especially chary about new and adventurous projects, often siding with Roy in opposing ambitious plans that might break the company. But, like Roy, she admitted her mistake when Walt proved himself right, and that made the triumph more pleasurable. "Lilly," he said admiringly, "you're the only person I can count on never to 'yes' me." Although she had been afraid that *Snow White* would cost too much, she loved the film itself. She also enjoyed *Fantasia* and *Bambi,* cared less for *Pinocchio.*

She didn't like Donald Duck at all, especially his voice. But she admitted that she adored Mickey Mouse—"because there's so much of Walt in him."

Lilly grew accustomed to having Walt impose his work on their home life. His enthusiasm was contagious, and she listened as he spouted his newest ambitions—he demanded the same attention from her as he did from those at the studio. As his studio responsibilities grew, he brought more work home. He often ran movies at home, both his own and those of other studios. Lilly watched them with Walt, but when he started showing rushes of live-action filming, she asked, "Do we have to see those scenes over and over again?" Thereafter he always watched rushes at the studio. Walt and Lilly rarely dined out. It was often seven or seven-thirty before he arrived home from the studio in the evening, and he didn't want to waste the time in going out to a restaurant.

His taste in clothes continued the dapper inclination of his youth. He liked to wear sport jackets of bold colors and designs, with sweaters of gray or blue underneath. He also had a passion for hats. Tyroleans, fedoras, panamas, the jauntier the better. He bought several at a time, and he always wore his hat at an angle he considered rakish. Lilly thought the angle made him look cocky. She hated the hats and had her revenge one day at a bullfight in Mexico City, where he and his staff were researching for *The Three Caballeros*. During an accolade for a bullfighter, Lilly removed Walt's hat and sailed it into the ring. Walt once bronzed a hat Lilly particularly disliked and presented it to her as a gift.

Walt considered himself religious, yet he never went to church. The heavy dose of religiosity in his childhood discouraged him; he especially disliked sanctimonious preachers. But he admired and respected every religion, and his belief in God never wavered. His theology was individual. Once the studio nurse, Hazel George, asked him if he believed in the Immaculate Conception. His reply: "I believe every con-

ception is immaculate, because a child is involved."
Unlike Cecil B. DeMille and other film makers, Walt
did not believe in mixing religion and entertainment.
He never made a religious film, and churchmen were
rarely portrayed in Disney movies. Walt and Lilly sent
their daughters to Sunday school, but made no attempt
to impose their own religious views on the girls. Walt's
attitude was expressed in an excerpt from a 1943 letter
to his sister Ruth: "Little Diane is going to a Catholic
school now which she seems to enjoy very much. She
is quite taken with the rituals and is studying cate-
chism. She hasn't quite made up her mind yet whether
she wants to be a Catholic or a Protestant. Some people worry about her interest in Catholicism, but I feel
differently about it. I think she is intelligent enough to
know what she wants to do and I feel that whatever
her decision may be is her privilege."

Walt drove Diane and Sharon to Sunday school and
afterward they often went to amusement parks in Los
Angeles. At Griffith Park near their Los Feliz home,
the girls rode the big merry-go-round again and again.
Their luck at grabbing the gold rings and winning another ride seemed uncanny. They didn't know that
their father was bribing the merry-go-round attendant.

On Christmas morning, a huge tree appeared in the
Disneys' two-story living room; Walt had spent much
of the night decorating it while Lilly filled the stockings
and laid out the multitude of gifts. Many of them were
toys of Mickey Mouse and other Disney characters
(aside from the children's toys, there was no evidence
of Walt's studio life in the Disney house). Walt strove
to maintain the Santa Claus myth as long as possible.
One Christmas morning when Diane was eight, she
awoke to find a beautiful playhouse on the back-yard
lawn. It looked like a fairy-tale house out of a Disney
cartoon, with tiny leaded-glass windows and a mush-
room chimney. It had running water and a fully
equipped kitchen, even a telephone. While Diane was
admiring the house, the telephone rang. A jolly voice
announced himself as Santa Claus—Diane suspected

later that he was their rotund butler—and asked how she liked the place. "I love it, Santa," she said. Later she was telling a neighbor boy how Santa Claus had brought her the lovely playhouse. "Santa Claus!" the boy said. "There were men from your dad's studio putting up that house all day." She refused to believe him.

While Walt did not overindulge his daughters, he delighted in finding them gifts. Hazel George chided him for giving them too much. "You're depriving Diane and Sharon by making life too easy for them," said the studio nurse. "There will be no challenges for them if you give them everything." Walt thought about it and replied, "Girls are different."

He lived surrounded by women. Besides Lilly and the two daughters and the cook, there was often a female relative living with the Disneys; Walt complained wryly that even the family pets were female. But his grumblings seemed half-hearted. He appreciated femininity, and he liked to play the role of father; he spent long hours in the swimming pool teaching Diane and Sharon to swim, though he himself was not a practiced swimmer. By the time each girl was three, he had taught them to ride horseback, and the family rode together during vacations in Palm Springs.

The Disney temper sometimes flared at home, as it did at the studio, and his wife and daughters learned to be wary of it. The outbursts quickly subsided, and he sometimes felt remorse afterward. More often he simply resumed normal relations, his flash of temper having cleared the air. Diane inherited the same temper and sometimes clashed with her father; Sharon, three years younger, grew up as "Daddy's girl."

During the 1930s and 1940s, the memory of the Lindbergh kidnapping haunted many famous parents, and Walt took steps to protect his daughters. He allowed no photographs of Diane and Sharon to be published, and he took them to no public events where photographers might be present. The window screens on the Los Feliz house were reinforced. The girls were so shielded from publicity that they scarcely knew of their father's fame during the early years. Diane was six when a school friend asked her, "Is your father really Walt Disney?" That night as he was reading the newspaper in his favorite chair and ottoman, she said to him with a degree of resentment: "You never told me you were Walt Disney!"

Walt and Lillian Disney would not allow others to supervise the upbringing of their children, as was the custom with famous Hollywood parents. Walt drove his daughters to dancing lessons and birthday parties. Each weekday morning he made a wide circuit, delivering Diane to Marlborough School in the Wilshire District, then taking Sharon to Westlake School in Westwood before going on to the studio in Burbank.

Diane and Sharon often accompanied their father to the studio on Sundays. The big empty place became another playground for them, and they ran around the baseball diamond outside the restaurant and learned to ride bicycles on the parking lot. They also accompanied Walt as he prowled through the offices looking at work his artists had done. As the girls became older, Walt taught them to drive a car in the parking lot.

He could be a stern father. He would not tolerate rudeness in children, and a flippant or discourteous remark brought swift discipline. When Sharon was seven, her father once chastised her, and she ran upstairs to her room inveighing against "that mean old man—that mean Daddy!" Walt followed her and administered a spanking. At the dinner table one night Diane made an impudent remark and received a slap on the face. Walt brooded about it the next day at the studio. Hazel George, an expert at reading Walt's moods, asked him what was the matter. "If you must know, I slapped Diane last night," he admitted.

"She must have done something bad," the nurse said.

"Damn right she did. She stood there, giving me that dirty Disney look."

IV
STRETCHING
THE HORIZON
1945–1961

16

"AFTER THE war was over, we were like a bear coming out of hibernation," Roy Disney once remarked. "We were skinny and gaunt and we had no fat on our bones. Those were lost years for us."

For the rest of the movie industry, the war had been a period of unparalleled prosperity, and the demand for film entertainment continued in the immediate postwar years. Walt and Roy Disney found themselves in the anomalous position of facing financial peril—it usually happened that the cyclical trends of the film business had little effect on the Disney company. After four years of devoting most of its energies to government work, Walt Disney Productions was out of tune with public tastes, financially depleted, confused about its own destiny. It was a bad time for Walt Disney. His artists were returning from military service, and he faced the challenge of rebuilding his staff and charging it with enthusiasm. But he had no great, innovative challenge, like a *Snow White* or a *Fantasia*.

By the end of the first postwar year, the company's indebtedness to the Bank of America had swollen to $4,300,000. The domestic market provided little income. *Pinocchio, Fantasia, Bambi* and *Dumbo* were now playing in the European markets which had been erased during the war, but the damaged economies of the countries would not allow export of the revenue. With the Disney debt mounting and the company's future unpromising, the Bank of America urged Roy to effect economies. Roy related the bank's concern to Walt. But Walt refused to cut down his staff or curtail production. His answer was the same as it had always been in beleaguered times: "We can lick 'em with product." That was his credo; when times were bad and the bankers were complaining, the studio needed to get its entertainment before the public.

Joe Rosenberg, who had helped arrange the money to finish *Snow White,* continued the bank's pressure. Finally Roy told him: "Look, Joe, don't keep beating me over the head about this thing. There is only so much I can do with Walt. You come out and talk to him. Maybe you can impress him with how serious this matter is."

Rosenberg made an appointment with Walt, arriving at the studio in a driving rainstorm. Roy accompanied him to Walt's office, and Rosenberg began expounding on the Disney financial condition. He explained that the bank had a responsibility to its depositors and had to invest its money prudently.

"Now you know that the Bank of America has always been friendly to the Disney company and has helped it in every way possible," said Rosenberg. "But no matter how friendly we feel, we must protect our investors."

"Are you finished?" Walt interrupted.

"No. Roy and I are agreed that you must cut down on your outgo drastically. Your expenses each week are entirely too high in light of the amount of income you are receiving. You've simply got to cut back."

"Is that all?" Walt asked.

"No, let me finish, let me finish." Rosenberg went on with his lecture, despite Walt's interruptions. Finally, Rosenberg said, "All right, I'm finished. What have you got to say?"

Walt gazed out at the rain falling in the studio streets. "You know, I'm disappointed in you, Joe," he began. "I thought you were a different kind of banker. But it turns out you're just a regular goddam banker. You'll loan a guy an umbrella on a sunshiny day, but when it rains you want it back. Okay. You can have it back. We'll take our business to another bank."

Rosenberg stared at Walt in open-mouthed amazement. He realized Walt actually believed he could borrow from another bank when he was already more than $4,000,000 in debt. Rosenberg leaned back his head and laughed loudly. "Walt, you take the cake!" he exclaimed.

It was the end of the meeting, but not the end of pressures from both the bank and Roy. The exchanges between the two brothers became more argumentive, with each refusing to give ground. Before, they had always been able to resolve their differences by compromise, usually with Roy agreeing to try to find the money to support Walt's projects. But now Roy was convinced that the money simply could not be found, and for Walt to expand production would be ruinous.

Their biggest quarrels came when Walt proposed embarking on the studio's first postwar cartoon feature. He wanted to start production on *Peter Pan* or *Alice in Wonderland,* which had been in story development before the war. Mindful of the financial debacle of *Pinocchio,* Roy insisted that the company could not undertake a lengthy, multi-million-dollar production. He claimed that neither *Peter Pan* nor *Alice* had public appeal. The two brothers argued until eight o'clock in Roy's office one evening. After a heated exchange, Roy snapped, "Look—you're letting this place drive you to the nuthouse. That's one place I'm not going with you!" Roy stalked out of the office.

Both brothers slept poorly that night. Roy arrived at his office early the next morning, feeling totally depressed. He heard Walt's cough down the hallway. Walt entered, his face as grim as Roy's. Walt seemed too emotional to speak. Then he said, "Isn't it amazing what a horse's ass a fellow can be sometimes?" Both brothers smiled, and the argument was over.

Walt postponed the start of his first postwar cartoon feature, agreeing the studio couldn't afford a costly project which would not reach the theaters for three or four years. By that time his company might be insolvent—or forced to amalgamate with a bigger corporation. The thought of subjecting himself to the control of a parent company was repugnant to Walt—"I would rather liquidate or sell out than do that."

Walt embarked on a series of brief cartoon subjects, based on musical themes. He did not choose the classics, as in *Fantasia;* he had once planned a sequel but abandoned it because of the commercial failure of *Fantasia.* This time he picked middlebrow or popular pieces, with stories based on legends such as the Martins and the Coys and Casey at the Bat. Dinah Shore, Benny Goodman, Jerry Colonna, Nelson Eddy and the Andrews Sisters were among the performers on the sound track. One modern classic was included—*Peter and the Wolf* by Sergei Prokofiev. The Russian composer offered the composition to Disney during a visit to the studio, declaring, "I have composed this with the hope that I would get to see you and that you would make a cartoon with my music."

The short cartoons were combined in a feature called *Make Mine Music,* released in August 1946 for a modest profit. Except for the *Peter and the Wolf* episode, Walt was not pleased with the film. He realized that his animators were capable of much better.

Walt resumed production on *Mickey and the Beanstalk,* which had been interrupted by the war. It was combined with a cartoon based on a Sinclair Lewis story, "Bongo," and released as *Fun and Fancy Free.* Donald Duck and Goofy, supposedly the supporting players, dominated *Mickey and the Beanstalk,* and it was the last important effort by Walt to revive Mickey's career in films. It was also the first time that someone else recorded Mickey's voice. Walt complained that his voice was getting too hoarse for the famous falsetto, and he said to the studio's sound-effects expert, Jim Macdonald, "Why don't you do it?" Macdonald delivered the voice of Mickey thereafter.

Song of the South derived from the Uncle Remus stories of Joel Chandler Harris, which Walt had enjoyed since childhood. He planned it as a cartoon feature, but to reduce costs he interspersed cartoons with a live-action story. *Song of the South* proved an important transitional film, pointing the new direction that Walt believed he had to take.

"I knew that I must diversify," he recalled later. "I knew the diversifying of the business would be the salvation of it. I tried that in the beginning, because I didn't want to be stuck with the Mouse. So I went into the Silly Symphonies. It did work out. The Symphonies led to the features; without the work I did on the Symphonies, I'd never have been prepared even to tackle *Snow White*. A lot of the things I did in the Symphonies led to what I did in *Fantasia*. I took care of talents I couldn't use any other way. Now I wanted to go beyond even that; I wanted to go beyond the cartoon. Because the cartoon had narrowed itself down. I could make them either seven or eight minutes long—or eighty minutes long. I tried the package things, where I put five or six together to make an eighty-minute feature. Now I needed to diversify further, and that meant live action."

Song of the South was 70 percent live action and 30 percent cartoon, with some sequences of both. Combining live action and cartoons was not the simple matter that it had been in the Alice Comedies. Now Walt was dealing with Technicolor film and sophisticated animation, and the technical matters required meticulous planning. The live action was photographed first. James Baskett, who was portraying Uncle Remus, performed before actual sets that were painted to seem like cartoon backgrounds. The live-action footage was edited to its precise length, then given to the animators, who added the cartoon figures.

The introduction to the first cartoon sequence presented a special problem. The action called for Baskett to explain to the boy, played by Bobby Driscoll: "The critters was closer to the folks, and the folks was closer to the critters, and it was better all around. It was one of those Zip-a-dee-doo-dah days. . . ." He was to begin the movie's feature song against a real-life scene projected onto a transparent backdrop, then walk into the cartoon set. Wilfred Jackson, who was directing the sequence, realized the problem of making the transition from rear-projection to the actual set. He tried it once and it didn't work. On the last day of the filming at Goldwyn studio, Walt arrived on the set, and Jackson admitted that he had no solution. At such times of crisis Walt became uncommonly gentle, and he gathered Jackson, cameraman Gregg Toland and other technicians into a circle for a discussion of the problem. None of the proposals seemed practical. Then Walt said, "Why don't we do this? We'll have Jim sitting in front of the fire, and we'll light his face but not the background. We'll be in tight, with a clear area of blue sky behind his head. We'll have the other lights covered with cardboard. When Jim says 'Zip' all the lights will come on, and he'll walk into the bright animation." His solution not only worked; it gave the scene additional value.

Song of the South had its premiere in Atlanta, where Joel Chandler Harris was still revered, and the film drew almost as warm a response as *Gone with the Wind*. The Academy of Motion Picture Arts and Sciences named "Zip-a-dee-doo-dah" the best movie song of 1946, and James Baskett won a special Oscar for his performance as Uncle Remus. Theater business for *Song of the South* was generally good, but the production cost had been high—$2,125,000—and the profit was only $226,000.

In his search for ways to sustain the studio during the postwar period, Walt considered the making of commercial and educational films. Such an activity seemed a natural outgrowth of the informational films the studio had made during the war, and it held the promise of much-needed revenue. Walt brought educators to the studio for conferences on how films could augment instruction in the schools. The educators offered a multitude of theories, and Walt listened to them all. Disney agents solicited contracts from big corporations for information films, and several firms sought the

Disney expertise. The studio made films on tire-making for Firestone and hand tools for General Motors.

Ben Sharpsteen, who had been in charge of the industrial films, one day showed Walt a storyboard for a film sponsored by a Midwestern electrical company. Walt remarked, "This isn't for Disney. We should be in the entertainment business. Let's stop all this."

"But what about the pictures that are being planned?" Sharpsteen asked.

"Cancel 'em."

"What about the money we've already received for them?"

"Give it back to 'em."

Walt came to the same conclusion about the educational films: "That's not for us. Let's stick to entertainment. We'll make educational films, but they'll be sugar-coated education." The genesis of his plan came soon afterward when he stopped Sharpsteen in the hallway of the Animation Building and asked, "Do we have any photographers in Alaska?"

"Not that I know of," said Sharpsteen.

"Well, we should. That's a fascinating place, Alaska. A lot of servicemen were stationed up there during the war, and they learned about it. Some of them are going back as homesteaders. That's our last frontier, the last undeveloped place in the United States. We should have some photographers up there. Look into it."

Sharpsteen prepared some storyboards about the folklore of Alaska. Walt wasn't interested. He pointed to photographs of seals and Eskimos in their winter and summer lives, and he said, "That's the sort of thing we should look for. Let's get going on this."

Alfred and Elma Milotte, a couple who had made travelogues and industrial and training films, were hired by Disney to spend a year in Alaska photographing all aspects of human and animal life, with special emphasis on the seasonal activities of the seals and the Eskimos. They began making regular shipments of film to the studio. Walt saw little in the footage to interest him, but he instructed Sharpsteen to have an editor classify the film by subject matter and keep a running file. The volume of film mounted; Roy Disney became concerned over growing costs. He asked Sharpsteen, "What is Walt going to do with all that Alaska stuff?" Sharpsteen suggested that Walt might make "some kind of glorified travelogue out of it."

Walt decided to see Alaska for himself. In August of 1947, he accepted the invitation of a friend, Russell Havenstrite, for a flying tour of Alaska. Lilly and Sharon were also invited, Diane being away at summer camp. Shortly before departure time, Lilly decided the trip would be too rugged for her, and so Walt went off with his ten-year-old Sharon. The party flew in Havenstrite's luxurious DC3, landing for fuel in Seattle, then proceeding to Juneau and Anchorage. Walt played both father and mother to Sharon, braiding her hair and washing out her underwear and rescuing her when she went sleepwalking. The trip continued beyond the Arctic Circle and to the base of Mount McKinley, and Walt took photographs everywhere. Near the end of the journey, a flight was scheduled from Nome to the Eskimo hamlet of Candle. Havenstrite had just received news that he had become a grandfather for the first time, and he and Walt began to celebrate during the flight. Soon the pilot announced that the radio had gone out, and there was no way to find a landing field through the dense clouds. The surrounding country was mountainous, and visibility was getting worse. The pilot could do nothing but continue circling and hope for a break in the clouds. Walt contemplated the fate of his old polo friend, Will Rogers. He took another drink.

The flight had been scheduled for a half-hour; after two hours, the plane was still circling, and gasoline was running low. The pilot could wait no longer, and he descended into the clouds. Finally the fog thinned out and the ground came in sight; the plane was directly over Candle! The travelers rejoiced as they landed, and when Walt stepped out of the small plane, he fell on his face. When he later related the adventure, he admitted, "I don't know whether I kissed the ground —or fell on it."

After his Alaska trip, Walt viewed the Milotte footage with greater interest. But he could see no theatrical value in the endless views of canneries, forests, glaciers and mountain peaks. One sequence intrigued him. The Milottes had spent two seasons in the Pribilof Islands, filming the habits of the vast herds of seals.

"Ben, I've been thinking about those Alaska films," Walt said to Sharpsteen. "Why don't we take what we have and build a story around the life cycle of the seals? Focus on them—don't show any humans at all. We'll plan this for a theatrical release, but don't worry about the length. Make it just as long as it needs to be so you can tell the story of the seals." The completed picture ran twenty-seven minutes.

Walt himself suggested the title: "Well, it's about seals on an island, so why don't we call it *Seal Island?*" He announced that *Seal Island* would be the first of a series to be called True-Life Adventures—even though he hadn't yet thought of other subjects to follow. The RKO salesmen declared it was impossible to sell a half-hour film and argued that it should be an hour and ten minutes. "I can't make it an hour and ten minutes," Walt replied. "I'd rather have the audience enjoy a half-hour than say the thing's too long."

He decided to prove the appeal of *Seal Island* as he had with *Steamboat Willie* and *The Skeleton Dance*: by going directly to the audience. In December 1948, Walt persuaded Albert Levoy, who operated the Crown Theater in Pasadena, to book *Seal Island* on a bill with a lengthy feature. Five thousand questionnaires were handed out to the theater's customers; most of them replied that they preferred to see a film like *Seal Island* than another feature. Because *Seal Island* appeared in the Los Angeles area during the calendar year, it qualified for the Academy Awards, and it won as best two-reel documentary. The film was booked into the Loew's State in New York on a bill with *The Barkleys of Broadway,* and it drew an excellent critical reaction.

RKO was finally convinced to push *Seal Island,* and the company learned it could make as much money from a half-hour featurette as it could from a second feature.

As his first venture into non-cartoon features, Walt planned a film *So Dear to My Heart,* based on a Sterling North novel about a Kansas farm family of the same period when Walt was growing up in Marceline. The RKO salesmen argued that it would be hard to sell a Disney picture without cartoons, and he grudgingly included animated sequences. The film starred Burl Ives, Beulah Bondi, Harry Carey and the two child performers from *Song of the South,* Bobby Driscoll and Luana Patten. The two youngsters were the Disney studio's first contract players since the Alice Comedies.

So Dear to My Heart continued the lackluster record of the postwar Disney films, and other "package" movies—*Melody Time,* another musical potpourri, and *The Adventures of Ichabod and Mr. Toad,* combining *The Wind in the Willows* and *The Legend of Sleepy Hollow*—also produced disappointing returns. The Disney product had failed to recapture its market, and now the entire film industry was beginning to undergo a convulsion which would shatter its foundations. Television had started to take its hold on the American public.

The Disney debt to the Bank of America mounted alarmingly, and the bankers were adamant: economies must be made. Walt reluctantly agreed, and he issued a communication to his staff requiring "a constructive attitude toward every dollar which goes into developing, producing and selling the scheduled pictures." He announced he was enforcing a 34-percent reduction in payroll accounts, payroll taxes and capital additions and listed his objectives for the future:

1. a production schedule that would be adhered to;
2. limitation of picture budgets to what had been projected;
3. thorough preparation of stories so there would be a minimum of change;

4. a continuing effort to sell and exploit the pictures;
5. policing of all departments to prevent unnecessary expenses.

Walt acknowledged the need for sound economic policies at the studio, but he emphasized to the bankers that slashing of production would be suicidal; the only way back to financial health, he was convinced, was to "lick 'em with product." But what kind of product? The "package" pictures were not the answer. Walt realized that he had to return to the full-length cartoon.

Three classics had been in development for several years—*Peter Pan, Alice in Wonderland* and *Cinderella.* Walt did not feel comfortable with either *Peter Pan* or *Alice,* finding the characters too cold. *Cinderella,* on the other hand, possessed the qualities of *Snow White and the Seven Dwarfs,* and he chose to go ahead with it. Walt assigned all of his top talent to the production. Ben Sharpsteen supervised production, with Wilfred Jackson, Ham Luske and Gerry Geronimi as directors. The story men were Bill Peet, Ted Sears, Homer Brightman, Ken Anderson, Ed Penner, Winston Hibler, Harry Reeves and Joe Rinaldi. Walt attended every story meeting, contributing his usual flood of ideas:

[The Fairy Godmother sequence] The carriage should be dainty. The wheels shouldn't be enough to hold the weight. We should feel that it's a fairy carriage. . . . Cut out all excess dialogue and work on some new dialogue for Cinderella in counter to the melody while she is crying. Have her run out and hit the spot, and as she is saying this, let the animals come up and get closer. Have them gather around in a sympathetic manner. They don't know whether they should approach her or not. . . . Have the miracle happen at the end of the song. "The dream that you wish will come true" is where we start to bring the Fairy Godmother in. She materializes because she is there to grant the wish. The voices come back at Cinderella. Her faith is being thrown back at her.

Everybody has gone through a "the hell with it" feeling. . . .

[The Fairy Godmother's Magic Song, "Bibbidi-Bobbidi-Boo"] We can get orchestral effects. The pumpkin can carry the beat. We might get the effect we want by having the music go up an octave. We should get something like a verse to come to, instead of returning to the chorus. . . . We can get personality into the song. It shouldn't be the Deanna Durbin type of thing. I don't see her as goofy or stupid, but rather as having a wonderful sense of humor. Edna May Oliver had sort of what I mean—dignity, humor, etc., although she was more on the sarcastic side. . . . I think the Fairy Godmother should be elderly—old enough to have wisdom. She should have a certain sincerity. She should have no identity, just be a type. . . .

[The warning scene] Have the Fairy Godmother warn Cinderella. Work out some little thing—the dress will become rags again, the coach will become a pumpkin—after the stroke of twelve everything will be just as it was before. The Fairy Godmother is apologetic about this, but she is giving Cinderella an opportunity and hopes that by twelve something will happen. . . . The Fairy Godmother could say, "Be on your way, child. Break hearts. Have fun. But don't forget on the stroke of twelve everything will be as it was before." The Fairy Godmother Union has set this up. If she performed miracles that lasted, she'd be out of business. . . .

The directing animators for *Cinderella* were the Disney reliables: Milt Kahl, Frank Thomas, Eric Larson, Ward Kimball, Ollie Johnston, Marc Davis, Les Clark, John Lounsbery, Woolie Reitherman and Norm Ferguson. Extensive live-action photography was done as a guide for the animation. While the live action was helpful for the directors, who could determine beforehand whether the action would prove effective as cartoon, it restricted the animators. One of them remarked later that the human characters of *Cinderella* "seemed to have muddy feet."

It had always been difficult to invent new mice in the studio that Mickey Mouse built, but Ward Kimball managed to make the *Cinderella* mice original and charming. Their nemesis, Lucifer the spoiled housecat, presented more of a problem. None of the character renderings pleased Walt. Then one day he was visiting Kimball's steam train at his San Gabriel home. Walt saw the Kimballs' housecat, a round, furry calico, and he exclaimed, "Hey—there's your model for Lucifer."

The economics of the postwar movie business provided the opportunity for Disney's first completely live-action feature. Like most war-damaged countries, England had frozen the payments due to American film companies, and Disney and RKO had amassed millions of dollars that could be spent only in the United Kingdom. RKO suggested that Walt use it to make films in England. He liked the idea and at first contemplated establishing a cartoon studio in England. But that would have meant training a complete staff of English animators, or else taking his own artists to England. He decided to use the frozen funds to make a live-action version of *Treasure Island*. He assigned a veteran Disney hand, Perce Pearce, as producer and another American, Byron Haskin, to direct. Lawrence Edward Watkin, whose novel *On Borrowed Time* Walt had admired, adapted the Robert Louis Stevenson novel, and Bobby Driscoll starred as Jim Hawkins. The rest of the cast and production staff were English.

Treasure Island gave Walt the opportunity to take Lilly, Diane and Sharon to England and leave behind the day-to-day concerns of the studio. He was stimulated by the challenges of live-action filming. When he returned to Burbank, he needled his animators: "Those actors over there in England, they're great. You give 'em the lines, and they rehearse it a couple of times, and you've got it on film—it's finished. You guys take six months to draw a scene."

The animators took his kidding good-naturedly, but they understood what was happening: Walt had found a new toy. Said one of the animators: "We realized that as soon as Walt rode on a camera crane, we were going to lose him."

17

EVERY DECEMBER over a twenty-five-year period, Walt Disney wrote a newsy letter to his sister, Ruth Beecher, in Portland, Oregon, detailing the family events and what was going on at the studio. On December 8, 1947, he wrote, "I bought myself a birthday-Christmas present—something I've wanted all my life—an electric train. Being a girl, you probably can't understand how much I wanted one when I was a kid, but I've got one now and what fun I'm having. I have it set up in one of the outer rooms adjoining my office so I can play with it in my spare moments. It's a freight train with a whistle, and real smoke comes out of the smokestack —there are switches, semaphores, station and everything. It's just wonderful!"

Trains held an almost mystical fascination for Walt Disney, dating back to his Missouri farm days when he waved to his engineer uncle. As an adult it gave him pleasure to visit the Southern Pacific station in Glendale, a few miles from his Los Feliz home, to feel the vibration of the tracks and then watch the passenger trains pass through on the route to San Francisco. He delighted in operating his electric train for visitors to his office. Among them were two Disney animators, Ward Kimball, who had a full-size railroad on his property, and Ollie Johnston, who was building a one-twelfth-scale steam train at his home. Johnston invited Walt to watch the laying of the track and to visit the machine shop in Santa Monica where the locomotive was being built. Johnston and Kimball took Walt to see a steam railroad operating at the Beverly Hills home of Richard Jackson. "By God, I want one of those for my own!" said Walt.

He borrowed books on railroading from Kimball, Jackson and Johnston, and he sought others from libraries and book dealers throughout the United States. The Southern Pacific Railroad supplied blueprints, which Walt pored over with Ed Sergeant, a mechanical draftsman at the studio. Walt began paying regular visits to the studio machine shop, where Roger Broggie taught him how to operate a lathe and use other tools. Ray Fox in the carpenter shop showed Walt how to work with wood. Soon Walt had a complete wood and metal workshop at his home.

One day in 1948, Walt said to Ward Kimball, "How would you like to go back to the Railroad Fair in Chicago?" Kimball readily agreed, and the two train buffs traveled by Santa Fe Super Chief to the fair, an immense pageant saluting the development of the railroad in America with full-size trains traveling across a mammoth stage. The most dramatic part of the program was a depiction of the Lincoln funeral train, with a Civil War locomotive slowly pulling the black-draped cars, including one from the original train. A Negro couple walked alongside the mournful procession while "The Battle Hymn of the Republic" was played and sung. Walt's eyes filled with tears every time he saw the Lincoln train cross the stage.

Disney and Kimball spent all of their days and evenings at the show. They climbed in and out of engine cabs, rode them across the stage during the show, talked endlessly to old-time engineers and firemen.

When Walt returned home, he told Lilly, "That was the most fun I ever had in my life."

He began laying plans for his own train. He assigned Ed Sergeant to draw up plans for a one-eighth-scale model of an old Central Pacific engine, Number 173. Patterns were made in the studio prop shop, and Roger Broggie supervised the castings and fittings in the machine shop. Walt himself learned to do sheet-metal work and laid out and fabricated the headlamp and smokestack. He made several parts in a milling machine, silver-soldered and brazed smaller fittings, and began constructing the wooden boxcars and cattle cars to carry passengers. Ollie Johnston was also building cars for his train, and one day Walt came to his office and said in a conspiratorial way: "Why don't you come out to the shop with me? I found out where they keep the hardwood."

While Lilly appreciated the peace of mind that Walt's railroad hobby had given him, she harbored some apprehensions about the miniature-train project. She and Walt had been looking for property to build a new house, and Walt made the proviso that the plot had to be large enough to accommodate his miniature railroad. Lilly was not certain that she wanted a train circling her new home. Walt anticipated her reluctance by having a legal agreement drawn up "between WALTER E. DISNEY (hereinafter called Walt), as first party; LILLIAN B. DISNEY (hereinafter called Lillian), as second party; and DIANE MARIE DISNEY and SHARON DISNEY, both minors (hereinafter called, respectively, Diane and Sharon), as third parties."

The agreement declared Walt as the owner of a parcel of land on which he proposed to build a residence "for the comfort, convenience, welfare and betterment of the Second and Third Parties (and incidentally, for himself)." It continued:

WHEREAS, Walt is or is about to become the sole proprietor and owner of a certain railroad company known as the Walt Disney R. R. Co., which

railroad company proposes to construct and operate a railroad in, on, upon and over the right of
way hereinafter described and delineated, in the
operation of which railroad Walt desires to have
and at all times to retain complete, full, undis-
turbed, unfettered and unrestricted control and
supervision, unhampered and unimpeded by the
other parties hereto or by any of them, they having
heretofore made known and asserted to Walt in
various sundry and devious ways their collective
intention to reign supreme within, and so far as
concerns, the aforesaid residence, and

WHEREAS, the Second and Third Parties, in the
future and notwithstanding Walt's ownership of
the fee title to the aforesaid parcel of land, and
notwithstanding their many enthusiastic assurances
verbally given to Walt in their present enthusiasm
over said new residence and their anticipated plea-
sures and happiness therein, may, and probably
will, seek to assert rights, privileges and authorities inconsistent with Walt's reserved and retained
control and supervision over said railroad company and the operation of said railroad company
upon the right of way herein referred to, all to the
detriment of said railroad and its efficient, profitable and pleasurable operation, and to the injury
of Walt's peace of mind (the presence and sound-
ness of which mind Second and Third Parties
hereby admit).

THAT WHEREAS, Walt and Lillian are husband
and wife and Diane and Sharon are their children,
in which family there presently exists an atmosphere of love, understanding and trust which all
parties hereto are intensely desirous of preserving;

NOW THEREFORE, in consideration of the promises and of other good and valuable considera-
tions the receipt of which is hereby acknowledged
by Lillian, Diane and Sharon, the said Lillian,
Diane and Sharon hereby jointly and severally
quit claim, transfer, assign and set over to Walt

all their right, title and interest in and to the right of way. . . .

After much looking, Walt and Lilly had found property that satisfied her desire for a roomy, comfortable house and his for enough space to run his railroad. They built the house on Carolwood Drive in Holmby Hills, a residential area between Beverly Hills and Bel Air, and after moving in, Walt expressed his delight in a letter to the wife of Jack Cutting, who represented Disney interests in Europe: "Jack probably told you about our soda fountain which seems to be supplying the whole neighborhood with sodas at my expense. But I'm happy to do it since it does keep our kids on the home ground and we know where they are. The girls like the new house very much and I think it is going to be the means of keeping them from going away from home to school, which will be all right with me. Then, too, the house with the railroad is a very enticing place for grandchildren—especially grandsons—if I'm lucky enough to have any!"

He called it the Carolwood-Pacific Railroad, and it was planned with customary thoroughness. Each car was individually designed, with special care devoted to the caboose. It was fashioned in exact scale—the bunks, clothes lockers, washstand, potbellied stove; Walt even had newspapers of the 1880 period reduced in size and placed in the newspaper rack. A three-hundred-foot test track was laid out on one of the studio stages, and studio workers were invited to take rides. The railroad passed its trials, and another track was tested outdoors.

Walt designed a half-mile run along the canyon side of his Carolwood property. He planned the site carefully, planting trees and keeping the elevation low so that his neighbors would not be disturbed. He also wanted no visual intrusions to distract his passengers; he paid to have power lines relocated so they would not be viewed from the train.

Walt named his engine the Lilly Belle as a conciliatory gesture to Mrs. Disney, who was unenthusiastic about the project and acquiesced only because of the obvious pleasure that the railroad gave Walt. She objected, however, when Walt wanted to make a six-foot cut in their slope to accommodate the track. Because of Lilly's opposition, he had to redesign the route with a ninety-foot tunnel. He planned it with an S-curve so the passengers would be in the dark for part of the ride; the element of mystery appealed to him. His foreman suggested, "Walt, it'd be a lot cheaper if you built the tunnel straight." "Hell," Walt replied, "it'd be cheaper not to do this at all." He gave his secretary strict instructions not to tell him how much the tunnel cost.

Walt delighted in donning his coveralls and engineer's cap and transporting his daughters' friends or guests at cocktail parties around the route of the Carolwood-Pacific. On weekends he spent hours alone with the train, making engine adjustments and keeping the cars in repair. One day he was experimenting with remote controls, sitting in the first car instead of the tender, and operating the throttle with wires. As he rounded a curve, the front wheel hit a rock and the jolt uncoupled the engine from the tender. Walt fell backward, pulling the wires and putting the engine in full throttle. It speeded off down the track alone.

Walt jumped off the car and raced after the engine, which was spewing steam high into the air. He couldn't catch it, so he ran to the spot where the engine would emerge from the tunnel. It came out, hit a curve, and tumbled off the track, breaking off the stack and cowcatcher. It lay on its side, hissing and belching steam like a dying dragon. Walt yelled to Lilly: "Come on out if you want to see a terrible sight." She hurried outside to find the broken locomotive and its crestfallen engineer. "Oh, Walt, that's too bad!" she said.

Walt later admitted that the train wreck had a good side. It was the first time that Lilly had ever expressed any sympathy for the Carolwood-Pacific Railroad.

None of Walt Disney's endeavors, not even his hobbies, was without a purpose, and the Carolwood-

Pacific formed part of his growing plan for a new kind of enterprise for Walt Disney Productions.

The idea had its inception, he later said, on the Sunday mornings when he took Diane and Sharon to amusement parks after Sunday school. As his daughters went on the rides, Walt studied the boredom of other parents, and he noted the squalor of the parks—paint cracking on carousel horses, the grounds dirty and littered, the ride operators cheerless and unfriendly.

Another element contributed to his thinking. He mentioned it in a remark to Ward Kimball: "You know, it's a shame people come to Hollywood and find there's nothing to see. They expect to see glamour and movie stars, and they go away disappointed. Even the people who come to this studio. What can they see? A bunch of guys bending over drawings. Wouldn't it be nice if people could come to Hollywood and *see* something?"

Walt began talking about building an amusement park on an eleven-acre triangle the studio owned across the street on Riverside Drive. He started formulating his plans for the amusement area, which he intended to call Mickey Mouse Park. He outlined his ideas in a memo on August 31, 1948:

The Main Village, which includes the Railroad Station, is built around a village green or informal park. In the park will be benches, a bandstand, drinking fountain, trees and shrubs. It will be a place for people to sit and rest; mothers and grandmothers can watch over small children at play. I want it to be very relaxing, cool and inviting.

Around the park will be built the town. At one end will be the Railroad Station; at the other end, the Town Hall. The Hall will be built to represent a Town Hall, but actually we will use it as our administration building. It will be the headquarters of the entire project.

Adjoining the Town Hall will be the Fire and

Police Stations. The Fire Station will contain practical fire apparatus, scaled down. The Police Station will also be put to practical use. Here the visitors will report all violations, lost articles, lost kids, etc. In it we could have a little jail where the kids could look in. We might even have some characters in it.

The memo listed other attractions: a drugstore with soda fountain; an opera house and movie theater, which could also be used for radio and television broadcasts; toy, doll, hobby and book shops; a toy repair shop and doll hospital; a candy store and factory that would sell old-fashioned candy; a magic shop and store for dollhouse furniture; a shop where Disney artists could sell their works; a music store and shop for children's clothing; a colorful hot dog and ice cream stand; a restaurant with rooms for birthday parties; a functioning post office.

Walt planned a horse-drawn streetcar that would take guests from the main entrance to the Western Village. The Village would have a general store selling cowboy items; a pony ring; a stagecoach; a donkey pack train; and perhaps a Western movie theater and and a frontier museum. Surreys and buckboards would be available to take people through an old-fashioned farm and into the Carnival Section. "This will be attached off the village and will be the regular concession type which will appeal to adults and kids alike. There will be roller coasters, merry-go-rounds . . . typical Midway stuff. (This will be worked out later.)"

Whenever Walt mentioned Mickey Mouse Park to Roy, Roy reminded his brother of the immense debt to the Bank of America and the continuing failure of the Disney postwar films to produce profits. Roy believed he had convinced Walt that undertaking an amusement park would be financial folly. In reply to an inquiry from a business friend, Roy wrote: "Walt does a lot of talking about the amusement park idea, but truthfully, I don't know how deep his interest really is. He is more interested, I think, in ideas that would be good in an amusement park than in running one himself, and because of the tax situation Walt doesn't have money of his own to put into these things."

18

THE DISNEY fortunes began to turn in 1950. The long hungry years ended with public acceptance of *Cinderella,* the first unqualified hit for the studio since *Snow White and the Seven Dwarfs. Treasure Island* was also well received, and the second of the True-Life Adventures, *Beaver Valley,* proved even more popular than *Seal Island.* By the end of 1950, the debt to the Bank of America had been reduced to $1,700,000.

The new, unaccustomed prosperity relieved Walt of the anxiety he had felt in the floundering postwar years. The worried scowl that studio workers had grown accustomed to now appeared less often. In April 1951, he wrote to his producer in England, Perce Pearce: "Everything is looking swell here at the plant. *Alice* is just about ready to be wrapped up and I think it is about as good as can be done with it. I think it is going to be an exciting show. While it does have the tempo of a three-ring circus, it still has plenty of entertainment and it should satisfy everyone except a certain handful who can never be satisfied."

He revealed his reservations about *Alice in Wonderland.* He had wrestled with the subject since 1933, when he contemplated a version with Mary Pickford as a live-action Alice. Years later he planned to put Ginger Rogers in a cartoon Wonderland. Aldous Hux-

ley at one time worked on a script. Walt abandoned
Alice in Wonderland again and again until finally he
scheduled it to follow *Cinderella.* He dropped the idea
of a live-action Alice. "Practically everyone who has
read and loved the book of necessity sees the Tenniel
Alice," he explained in a letter to a New Jersey fan,
"and no matter how closely we approximate her with
a living Alice, I feel the result would be a disappointment." Walt tried to alter the storyline to fit the cartoon needs, at one time expanding the role of the
White Knight as hero-rescuer. But he was intimidated
by the threats of Lewis Carroll purists, and he returned
to the original story. During storyboard sessions, Walt
tried to maintain his normal enthusiasm, but it was
difficult.

Animation was as tedious as the story development.
Walt kept asking his animators why the drawing was
taking so much time. The unspoken answer was that
the animators weren't enjoying it. The animators sometimes arrived at brilliant invention, but it was punishing work. Everyone felt relief when *Alice in
Wonderland* was finished. Especially Walt. He vowed
never again to undertake a tamper-proof classic.

He had hoped to keep faith with the traditionalists
while trying to please the millions who expected an
entertaining show from Walt Disney. He satisfied
neither. *Alice in Wonderland* had its premiere in Lewis
Carroll's home country, and London critics belabored
Disney for the liberties he took. American audiences
were also disappointed, and the film lost $1,000,000,
erasing the glow of prosperity that *Cinderella* had
brought to Walt Disney Productions. "Some day," Walt
sighed, "I would like to reach the position where this
company doesn't have to live from one picture to the
next."

Peter Pan was the next cartoon. Walt had bought the
rights to the James M. Barrie play in 1939 and had
spent years trying to fashion a cartoon story. As with
Alice in Wonderland, he found it difficult to bring
warmth to the characters, and *Peter Pan* was set aside

from time to time. Then in 1951 Walt put it into production. With the studio expanding into new fields, he could no longer lavish time on all aspects of the film. His comments in storyboard sessions seem more succinct, though no less incisive:

We don't have the right crocodile yet. . . . It's out of character. . . . Watch so as not to get Hook's teeth too big. . . . Rebuild the Tick Tock scene of Hook. Get expression of fear in his eyes. I don't like the hair raising. . . . Smee cries too much. . . . We want to make the music a little more important. I think music will tie it together. . . . Don't hesitate to reshoot anything you need. Anything you don't need, don't hesitate to throw it away after you have looked at it. . . . An overlap is never good. Cut close. On the last "See!" you need room for Smee to compose himself before he sticks out his tongue. Then, "Woom!" . . . I like the business of Hook getting all dolled up. It's good business. . . . You hear the creaking of the ship and the "Tick tock." Have a ray of light streaming out from the porthole and the crocodile would be swimming around in the water in the stream of light, and at a certain point we would see his eyes. . . . When we get the fight going on the ship and the croc finally comes in, it should be a nice surprise. . . . I was thinking of the fight —the tempo would pick up and the croc's tail would wave faster. Perhaps arrange a few places where Peter Pan might have Hook out over the water, and the croc is waiting—but don't slow it up.

Walt was planning a second English-made live-action feature, *The Story of Robin Hood,* for filming in the summer of 1951. His pre-production memos to his aides in England, Perce Pearce and Fred Leahy, indicate his concentration on details:

The final tests arrived the first part of the week and we looked at them. I think [Richard] Todd is wonderful, and I feel he will project a great deal of personality and do a lot for the role.

Joan Rice is beautiful and charming. I think, however, she will need some help on her dialogue. I thought, at times, she lacked sincerity, although one of her close-ups was very cute. I do not care much about her costumes in the first scenes. It seems that women of that period always have scarves up around their chins, but I think it does something to a woman's face. I'd like to see us avoid it, if possible, or get around it in some way or other—maybe use it in fewer scenes.

When we see Miss Rice disguised as a page, this costume seemed bulky and heavy. The blouse or tunic was too long and hung too far down over her hips—it didn't show enough of her and I thought distracted from her femininity. I do not believe the costume did much to set off her femininity. I think a slight showing of the hips would help a lot.

I liked Elton Hayes as Allan-a-Dale. He has a good voice with quite an appeal.

The last word I had from Larry [Watkin] was to the effect that he would be sending in a new and completed script very soon. I have been following his changes and the little thoughts I have are close to "lint-picking," which I feel he is smoothing out in his final script, so I won't bother about passing on my thoughts until I get his so-called final script. . . .

Television was also occupying Walt's thinking. The networks had been importuning him to provide entertainment for the new medium, and in 1950 Walt agreed to produce a Christmas show for the National Broadcasting Company. As producer he assigned Bill Walsh, a onetime publicist who began at the studio as a gag writer for the Mickey Mouse comic strips in 1943.

Walt acted as guide to the studio for ventriloquist Edgar Bergen and his dummies, Charlie McCarthy and Mortimer Snerd, and the Disney daughters also appeared on the show. It attracted a huge audience, impressing Walt with the value of television as a signboard for the studio's theatrical product. Another Christmas special was produced in 1951. Walt foresaw a future for educational films on television, and he reactivated the studio's educational division.

With his work at the studio intensifying, Walt found relaxation in his hobby of miniatures. He began by making his own small objects for the caboose of the Carolwood-Pacific train; he spent hours nightly fashioning tiny replicas of furniture in the red barn he used for a workshop. His long, slender, dextrous fingers allowed him to manipulate small objects with inordinate skill.

He was fascinated with small objects, and he collected them during his travels to Europe. When Lilly, Diane and Sharon returned from a shopping tour of Paris, they found Walt on the floor of their hotel suite, surrounded by small animated animals. He was particularly impressed with a caged bird which moved its tail and beak and issued an intermittent song. He brought the bird to the studio and instructed one of his technicians, Wathel Rogers: "Take this apart and find out how it works." Rogers performed an autopsy on the bird and discovered that it was operated by clockworks and a double bellows.

One day Walt said to Ken Anderson: "I'm tired of having everybody else around here do the drawing and painting; I'm going to do something creative myself. I'm going to put you on my personal payroll, and I want you to draw twenty-four scenes of life in an old Western town. Then I'll carve the figures and make the scenes in miniature. When we get enough of them made, we'll send them out as a traveling exhibit. We'll get an office here at the studio, and you and I will be the only ones who'll have keys." While Anderson started work on the sketches, Walt placed advertisements in newspapers and hobby magazines seeking vintage miniatures of all kinds.

He began work on the first of the scenes, which he called Granny Kincaid's cabin, based on a set of *So Dear to My Heart*. Everything was depicted in scale —the spinning wheel, rag rug on the plank floor, flint-lock rifle on the wall, guitar, washbowl and pitcher, family Bible on the center table. In the bedroom beyond the living room could be seen the feather-bed four-poster with crazy quilt. The kitchen was equipped with wood-burning stove and tiny pots and utensils. Walt attended to every detail. For the chimney he picked up pebbles at his vacation home in Palm Springs. To bend wood into the contour of chairs, he borrowed the pressure cooker from the family kitchen. He planned Granny Kincaid's cabin without human figures; viewers would hear the voice of Granny describing the scene, and Walt recorded a narration by Beulah Bondi, who had played Granny in *So Dear to My Heart*.

Even before he finished Granny Kincaid's cabin, Walt was planning a more ambitious scene. He wanted movement in the miniatures, and he devised a frontier music hall with an entertainer performing a dance. To provide a model for the figure, he hired Buddy Ebsen to demonstrate an old-time dance before the camera. Then Walt asked his machine-shop crew to analyze the action, frame by frame, and try to devise a way to animate a nine-inch figure with the same movements. Roger Broggie and the shop technicians invented a system of cables and cams to make the figure dance.

"That's good," said Walt as he watched the antic dance of the little man. "Now let's try something different." His new project was a miniature barbershop quartet that would not only move but sing "Sweet Adeline." The machine shop improved on the dancing-man mechanism and routined the quartet to a minute and a half of singing.

Walt began dropping by the shop every day to observe the progress on the models. Often he lost track of time and his secretary called frantically to inquire, "Is Walt still there? He's an hour late on his appointments." Walt's scheme for the traveling exhibit was to depict a series of interconnected small-town scenes—the general-store window could be seen from the barbershop, etc. But the project never got beyond early stages of the singing quartet. Walt realized that the small size of the exhibit would not allow enough volume of viewers to make it profitable. Besides, he wanted his craftsmen to devote their efforts to the amusement park he wanted to build.

Roy Disney continued his opposition to the park. He argued that with the failure of *Alice in Wonderland,* the company had fallen deeper into debt, and a venture as risky as an amusement park simply couldn't be financed. Walt responded by citing an incident of their childhood. It had happened in April 1906, when the Disney family was en route from Chicago to Marceline. During the visit to Flora's sister in Fort Madison, Walt had found a pocketknife in the street. "Give it to me; you'll cut yourself," said his older brother, appropriating the knife.

Forty-five years later, Walt taunted Roy, "Yeah, it's just like the time you took that knife away from me in Fort Madison. You've been taking things away from me all my life!"

When Walt Disney was a young man, a fortuneteller had predicted that he would die at the time of his birthday before he reached the age of thirty-five. Although he was not superstitious, the prediction had a profound effect on him, and he continued to brood about it long after it had been proved false. The sense of mortality weighed on him, and he seemed to be in a race against time to accomplish all the work he wanted to do. "I hate to see the weekend come," he remarked, complaining of the break in his usual pace. Similarly, he resented holidays. He enjoyed taking Lilly and their daughters to Europe and delighted in showing them the places he had known in the First World War. But

while he was away, he instructed his secretary to send
him daily reports of studio activities. "You don't know
how homesick I am when I'm away," he said.

Walt's devotion to work limited his social life. He
liked to watch the Hollywood Stars baseball team at
Gilmore Stadium and occasionally attended the horse
races at Santa Anita and Hollywood Park. On warm
summer evenings he and Lilly listened to the Symphonies Under the Stars at the Hollywood Bowl. They
dined out at Chasen's, Romanoff's or Trader Vic's, but
most of the time they ate at home. Their entertaining
was generally with small dinner parties, and they were
strictly social, not business.

Walt grew better-looking as he matured. By the
time he reached fifty, his five-foot-ten-inch frame had
filled out, and his face seemed more distinguished. His
hair remained as thick as ever, assuming an edge of
gray. The mustache, which had given him a dapper appearance in his earlier years, looked appropriate now.
(Oddly, he didn't like actors with mustaches in his
movies; he thought they looked like "city slickers.")
His taste in clothes grew more conservative; he no
longer wore the sporty outfits of his early Hollywood
days. He insisted that his clothes be comfortable, and
he rarely wore a necktie at the studio, preferring Western-style neckerchiefs with the Smoke Tree Ranch insignia, of which he had dozens. His wife and daughters
found it impossible to buy clothes for him, except for
sweaters and handkerchiefs. He preferred to choose his
own outfits, and every two years he went to Bullock's
Wilshire in Los Angeles and bought a supply. Whenever his jackets were sent to the cleaners, the pockets
had to be emptied of the crackers and nuts he carried
for snacks while he was working.

Walt dressed and undressed swiftly. One evening
Sharon commented that he hadn't changed his clothes
for a friend's party that was beginning in a few minutes. "It'll only take me a couple of minutes to dress,"
Walt replied. "Besides, it doesn't matter if I'm late. All
they do is stand around and drink."

The Disneys spent Easter, Thanksgiving and between Christmas and New Year's at Smoke Tree Ranch, a Palm Springs development where families maintained vacation houses, taking meals in a communal dining room. The girls were growing up. In 1951, Diane entered the University of Southern California, and Sharon was a sophomore at Westlake High School. Walt attended parents' night at Sharon's school—sometimes complaining about too much homework for his daughter—and went to the Dads' Dinner at Diane's sorority. He was convinced that Sharon, whose grades were sometimes mediocre, was the beauty of the family and Diane was the brain. He encouraged Diane to write, explaining that women had been successful in contributing scripts at the studio. He showed copies of her humorous poems to visitors to his office and sent her short stories to the Story Department for analysis.

He enjoyed watching his daughters mature, but he resented the passing of their childhood. Once when he was visiting friends, a little girl sat on his lap. Memories of the younger Diane and Sharon returned, and he told the girl, "I think you'd better get down, dear, or you're going to see your Uncle Walt cry." He cried easily, at his daughters' graduations, over scripts, sometimes at the same movie scene he saw over and over. Since he was stinting with praise, his animators considered it a triumph if Walt cried at a scene they had created.

He was growing more conservative. By 1940 he no longer supported Franklin Roosevelt, and he voted for Wendell Willkie. His politics remained Republican thereafter. In the late 1940s he took an active role in the Motion Picture Alliance for the Preservation of American Ideals, formed by industry leaders who were concerned about the Communist influence in Hollywood. Communist support of the strike against his studio remained a bitter memory for Walt Disney.

He had become disillusioned in his role as employer, explaining, "It went way back to the time when I had this little studio with kitchen chairs and old benches to sit on and the drawing boards that I had made myself. I used to sit in that chair all day long myself, and I knew how hard it could get. So I got some old cushions and pillows to sit on. We got all these ragtag pillows all around. Every guy'd have a different one. So one day we got a little money and I talked Roy into letting me buy some new rubber foam cushions. I gave each a cushion for his chair, and gosh, they were happy and grateful. One of the guys got his own cushion and now he had two cushions on his chair. The next thing I knew, all of these fellows were demanding two cushions. I said, 'Gosh, that's the limit. They were happy with no cushions; I gave 'em a cushion and they want two!' "

At times when Walt and Roy could not afford cash bonuses, they gave their workers payments in common stock. From a par value of $5 in 1945, the price climbed to $15 in 1946, then tumbled as the company underwent its postwar adjustment. Many employees sold their stock, and Walt considered it an act of disloyalty and lack of faith in the company.

Walt himself was convinced that the studio would revive, and he bought stock at its low ebb. The stock was his principal asset, and although he lived well, by Hollywood standards he was not a rich man. When a doctor friend asked to borrow $5,000 in 1951, Walt wrote him: "I know my answer to your request will sound funny but I haven't got the money. I am strapped myself and have borrowed to the hilt on my insurance and on personal notes—am close to fifty thousand dollars in debt, which is the limit of my personal borrowing ability. The new house cost much more than I anticipated and consequently I'm really up to my neck. So I can only say that I'm sorry that I'm unable to comply with your request."

He was unconcerned about amassing money for himself, but he worried about his family's future in the event of his death. He paid little heed to his personal bank account, which his secretary, Dolores Voght Scott, supervised. Roy often asked her: "How are

Walt's finances? Don't let him get involved in some crazy scheme."

Walt's daily routine began with meetings at eight and eight-thirty. He reviewed storyboards in other offices or held conferences around a low square table in his own office. When he had no visitors for lunch, he ate at his desk, his favorite meal being chili and beans. He was a connoisseur, preferring to combine a can of Gebhardt's, which had much meat and few beans, with a can of Dennison's, which had less meat and more beans. The dish was preceded by a glass of V-8 juice and accompanied by soda crackers. If visitors were coming to lunch, they were ushered into Walt's conference room at noon. He served them an apéritif of V-8 juice, a ritual that puzzled European visitors, who were accustomed to something stronger. Walt discoursed for half an hour and then led his visitors to the Coral Room of the commissary, where the table in the northeast corner was reserved for him. Walt often used the lunches for press interviews. He realized the value of publicity in the selling of motion pictures, and he made himself available for all requests that his publicity director, Joseph Reddy, considered to be of value. Walt seemed to enjoy interviews, not merely for the ego satisfaction. He liked to sum up the activities of his company, to reflect on its problems and triumphs, to try out a new story idea on an outsider. The Disney interview was an unstructured affair. Walt usually began expounding on the matters that had occupied him that morning. He continued talking about the many projects of the studio, responding occasionally to an interjected question.

After lunch, Walt liked to climb in a golf cart and show the visitor what was happening on the studio stages and in the shops. More meetings were scheduled in the afternoon, and he often left the office to inspect projects in the shops. At five in the afternoon, he quit work for his stretching exercise, a drink of Scotch and a rubdown.

By the end of the day Walt was in considerable pain

from the old polo injury to his neck. One day in 1951 he complained about it to Floyd Odlum, the industrialist who had long been promoting research in treatment of arthritis. Walt wrote Odlum about a specialist Odlum had recommended: " . . . He diagnosed my case as a form of arthritis, but not the usual variety. It seems I have a calcium deposit that continues building up in my neck which is probably caused by a polo injury I received some years ago when I took a spill from my horse. He thinks he can relieve this condition somewhat, but he has also convinced me that I will probably have to live with it the rest of my life. My heart and other vital organs, along with the history of my ancestry, all indicated that I am going to live a long life, so I am going to have to learn to live with this condition and make the best of it. . ."

Hazel George, the studio nurse, applied the treatment. It consisted of hot packs and intermittent traction. She tried a prone position which would allow the heat and traction to be applied at the same time. Walt declined because he couldn't sip his drink at the same time. "I'll give you a straw," Hazel suggested. The treatment was administered in a room next to Walt's office, and he called it his "laughing place," as in the Uncle Remus stories. It was where he could gain a perspective on the day's activities, exchange gossip with Hazel, confide his plans. Walt, who had received honorary degrees from Harvard, Yale and the University of California, once remarked to Hazel, "I'd trade all my degrees for your real one." She advised him it would be a bad idea—"It would ruin you; your work would lose its originality, its spontaneity."

One evening in a mellow mood, Walt reflected to Hazel: "You know, I finally found out who I am."

"Who are you?" Hazel asked.

"I'm the last of the benevolent monarchs."

She thought about it and replied: "That's good. Now I know what I am."

"What's that?"

"The last of the court jesters."

The conversations with Hazel sometimes grew philosophical, and once she and Walt were discussing various kinds of love—parents for children, human beings for pets, etc. As sometimes happened, Walt tired of the conversation and ended it with a summation: "Well, Hazel, let's face it—love is like everything else; if you don't have it, you can't give it."

The heat treatment and traction lasted forty-five minutes, and Walt felt relaxed and refreshed, eager to return to work. Hazel tried to discourage him, but she was not always successful. He sometimes called a story meeting that lasted into the evening. Dinner was kept waiting for him at home. He ate heartily and sometimes had to cut down his consumption when his weight pushed over 185 pounds. When research connected animal fats with the occurrence of heart disease, he asked a doctor, "Does that mean eating fats could make you old before your time?" He was told it did, and Walt went on a diet to cut down on fats.

But he wouldn't quit smoking. He admitted that he was wrong in smoking. One day he mused to Hazel: "You're right about one thing: Smoking and drinking are sins. Because you are one of God's creatures and if you don't take care of the body He gave you, you are committing a sin." He still smoked.

On rare occasions, Walt went out in the evening to banquets and civic dinners. He disliked such affairs, but he agreed to attend out of duty. When a formal speech was expected, he agonized over it. He detested the stilted speeches that were written for him—"I don't use all those big words; make it sound like me!" Walt was most effective when he had no written speech, but merely talked to the audience as he would in normal conversation. He could evoke as many laughs as a standup comedian.

Walt never told jokes, either before an audience or in conversation. Employees learned not to try to tell him jokes, since he hadn't the patience to listen to them. Telling a dirty joke to Walt could evoke a stony silence. Not that he was prudish. Like any farm boy, he had learned about sex at an early age. To him, sex was not a ludicrous subject, nor did it hold any great mystery. Above all, he believed that sex was a private matter, and that is the way he preferred to leave it.

He refused to be treated as a special person because of his position as head of an ever-growing enterprise. He allowed no one to light his cigarettes, help him on with his coat, or hold doors open for him. Sycophantic employees lasted a brief time around Walt. When he visited a movie set or walked down a hall, he didn't like to be accosted; his time was limited, and he wanted to choose the persons he talked to, whether it was a producer or a prop man. He especially disliked being burdened with others' personal problems. As the studio grew, it became more and more difficult for Walt to remember the names of his workers. To assist his memory, he made periodic visits to the personnel department to match names and photographs of those he encountered in his daily rounds.

Disney workers, even those with longtime service at the studio, were perplexed over how to react in casual encounters with the boss. They realized that he could be concentrating on an important company matter and would not want to be disturbed; but those who did not greet him were sometimes given a gruff "Whassa-matter, you mad at me?" A secretary faced the dilemma one afternoon as she found herself walking toward Walt in the long, lonely corridor of the Animation Building's third floor. He seemed to be immersed in thought, and she decided her best plan was to pass him without a greeting. As she did so, she heard a voice, almost disembodied, like a ventriloquist's say, "Hi, good-lookin'." She was puzzled. After she had gone ten paces, she turned to look at the retreating figure. At that moment Walt swung around, pointed a finger and exclaimed an impish "Hah!" Then he continued on his way.

19

AFTER A quarter-century as a producer of animated cartoons, Walt Disney in the early 1950s demonstrated his versatility with a wide variety of films. He applied the same principles he had used as a cartoon maker: Prepare the stories thoroughly. Create interesting characters. Above all, make it "read"—nothing ambiguous, nothing uncertain. Walt even carried over the methods of animation; all of the live-action films were prepared on storyboards, with each scene, each camera angle sketched on paper before anything was put on film. Thus Walt could perceive the pacing of the movie, juxtaposing action sequences with exposition to maintain audience interest while furthering the plot.

Walt's *modus operandi* had changed little from the days when he had only cartoon shorts to supervise. He once described his function in a homely story: "My role? I was stumped one day when a little boy asked, 'Do you draw Mickey Mouse?' I had to admit that I do not draw any more. 'Then do you think up all the jokes and ideas?' 'No,' I said, 'I don't do that.' Finally he looked at me and said, 'Mr. Disney, just what do you do?' 'Well,' I said, 'sometimes I think of myself as a little bee. I go from one area of the studio to another and gather pollen and sort of stimulate everybody. I guess that's the job I do.' "

He continued his phantom tours of the studio on weekends. "I go over and just float around at my leisure when I have no pressure on me," he said. "I sit down and look at story sketches and things. The boys know that I do that. And the boys pull all kinds of tricks to find out whether I've been there, you know. They arrange papers in a certain way on the chairs, and when they arrive in the morning, they say, 'Well, Walt wasn't in this weekend.' But they don't know that I put the papers right back where they were."

There was no waste motion in Walt's operations. He rarely indulged in small talk before a conference; when he strode into the room, discussion began immediately. When the meeting was over, he left as swiftly as he had entered, without goodbyes. Since he dealt so often with intangibles, his instructions in story meetings could be imprecise, and veteran studio hands endeavored to fathom Walt's thinking. Said Wilfred Jackson: "In a conference he'd make a passing remark about something, and I'd forget about it. Later, when he looked at the material in the sweatbox, he'd complain, 'Why wasn't that in? We discussed it, didn't we?' The big part of my career was to decide when Walt meant it and when he didn't mean it. I could never tell when he was just trying to get me to think. 'Don't do something just because I told you,' he'd say."

Once Walt had described a fight sequence for a Mickey Mouse short, acting out all the parts. Jackson was confident that he could capture what Walt wanted. But when Walt saw the animation, he complained, "You've got the tail all wrong. Look—Mickey's mad all over. His tail is tense, not a limp thing hanging there. What's the matter, Jack—didn't we talk this over?"

Walt's contributions to the live-action scripts took a different form. He no longer needed to propound the appearance and action of each character; the actors would supply their own appearances and actions. He concerned himself primarily with story construction, dialogue and the staging of scenes.

At the beginning of a story conference, producers and writers recognized they had failed when Walt handed over the script with the comment "Well, I've read this thing," then turned to another topic of conversation. More often he sat down at the low, square table in his conference room and began analyzing the script's merits and defects. He had usually done his homework the night before, marking changes and suggestions in a red or blue pencil. Sometimes his contributions were specific; he would compose two or three pages of dialogue to improve the timing and sense of a scene. Often he suggested general things: "This scene isn't playing; I believe in leaving something to the audience's imagination, but you're making them play every climax off-camera; the picture starts too slowly; jump to page four and begin there." His suggestions were not final; he was willing to listen to argument from the producer and writer. But there were two things he disliked: being interrupted when he was in the midst of interpreting a scene; and having someone argue a point that he had rejected at a previous meeting.

Walt had an instinct for recognizing when a film project was not going well. Sometimes there were stories that defied solution, and he simply dropped them. Months, perhaps years later, he picked up the project and started all over again. By this time, his creative subconscious may have provided a solution. *Alice in Wonderland* and *Peter Pan* were examples of films with long histories. A *Hiawatha* feature was another. It metamorphosed over a period of twenty years, and when a story man lacked an assignment, Walt instructed, "Put him on *Hiawatha*." But, despite all the efforts, *Hiawatha* was never produced.

Lady and the Tramp dated back to 1937, when Walt started work on a story about a sedate cocker spaniel. Then he read about a short story, "Happy Dan, the Whistling Dog," by Ward Greene, an editor for King Features, distributor for the Disney comic strips. Happy Dan was a free soul, a mutt with loyalty to no man. Walt told Greene, "Your dog and my dog have got to get together." Greene agreed, and in 1943 he wrote a story called "Happy Dan, the Whistling Dog, and Miss Patsy, the Beautiful Spaniel." Walt started developing a script, then dropped the project, reviving it almost a decade later. He insisted on calling it *Lady and the Tramp,* over the opposition of Greene and RKO salesmen. "That's what it's about—a lady and a tramp," Walt declared.

After the constrictions of dealing with two classics, *Alice in Wonderland* and *Peter Pan,* Walt felt comfortable with a subject that he could mold to his own patterns. He was at his dramatic best in a story meeting about the scene in which the Tramp kills a rat that is menacing the baby at Lady's house:

Lady's barking, trying to get Jim's attention, then you see the light coming, his shadow coming up —she's waiting when the door opens. She barks, starts up the stairs, he tries to grab her, says, "Girl, what's the matter?" Jim Dear chains Lady to a doghouse outside in the rain because of her barking. She has to get Tramp's attention instead.

She says, "A rat!" Tramp says, "Where?" She says, "Upstairs in the baby's room!" He says, "How do you get in?" She says, "The little door in the back." He runs right through the door in the back. . . .

It's quick, short things. He'd go right in there. We have this guy cautiously coming up the stairs —remember, he's an *intruder.* He doesn't know which door it is. Then he picks up the scent, and he comes in the room and there's the baby's crib. We get suspense for a moment. The baby's crib, and it's dark. He starts looking around the room, and suddenly he sees two eyes glowing over there. He begins to growl and his hair bristles. Then you see the form move, and he runs over there.

It has to be like a couple of guys fighting in the dark and not knowing where the other guy is. A hell of a realistic fight there. We can do it in the shadows from the window onto it—shadow forms against silhouette forms, against the light. Certain lighting effects will make it very effective. . . .

You actually want to put on a thing like he's a damn good ratter. The rat, of course, always faces him. When the rat moves, he goes—grabs him— gets him—throws him. A nervous thing—when the rat goes over here, he won't go after it. . . . One thing about a ratter, he'll never attack when a rat or a mole is on its back. He waits for the thing to get on its feet to go, and he grabs at the back of the neck. The dog that's not a ratter will just bite him in the stomach, and the rat will come up and go through his cheek with his teeth. The rat gets a death grip on the dog's cheek. . . .

Walt produced two more adventure films in England, *The Sword and the Rose* and *Rob Roy*. He contemplated two other projects to film at the studio: Jules Verne's classic adventure *20,000 Leagues Under the Sea* and *The Great Locomotive Chase,* based on an incident during the Civil War. Both had special appeal for Walt; the first for Verne's remarkable anticipation of submarines, atomic power and self-contained underwater suits; the second for its Civil War lore and the chance for him to play with full-sized trains. Harper Goff was assigned to create story sketches for both projects, and Walt presented them to a group of visiting executives. They decided in favor of *20,000 Leagues Under the Sea,* and their preference helped Walt decide to go forward with it.

The production would be expensive, Walt realized. It required construction of a new stage with a huge tank for underwater filming; important stars for the four leading roles; locations in the Caribbean, where water was clear enough for filming; costly effects photography with storms and a monstrous squid; expensive sets, including the submarine *Nautilus* itself.

Because of the cost, Walt was hesitant about mentioning the *20,000 Leagues* project to his brother. Later Walt commented about Roy's surprising reaction: "I first told him it was going to cost three million with all we had to do. It wasn't contested, and as time went

on, I went down to see him and I'd say, 'Looks like
that thing's going to run three million, three hundred
thousand.' He'd just nod and smile. And then as I kept
going along, we got to where it was three million, eight
hundred thousand. He still nodded and smiled. And
finally it got to four million, two hundred thousand,
and he was still smiling. It was the first time he ever
did that on a picture. For some reason, he believed in
it from the very start. I got worried then. I thought
there was something wrong with him. But he just had
faith and confidence in it."

A special kind of director was needed for *20,000
Leagues Under the Sea,* the studio's most ambitious
production. Walt and his staff viewed the movies of
numerous directors before the choice was narrowed to
three. Films of each were screened, and Walt asked
his staff members to vote on a selection. All selected
Richard Fleischer. "That's fine," Walt commented,
"because I've already picked him."

Fleischer came to the studio, and Walt made the
offer for *20,000 Leagues Under the Sea.* "Do you know
who my father is?" the director asked. Walt smiled
and said that he did.

"I cannot direct the picture unless he gives his permission," Fleischer said. "I know he will have strong
feelings about it, and I must abide by his decision."

"You're absolutely right," Walt said. "Go ahead and
ask him."

The director's father was Max Fleischer, the pioneering cartoon maker. During his youth, Richard Fleischer
had often heard his father inveigh against Walt Disney
for borrowing techniques and raiding the Fleischer
studio for animators (although Fleischer in turn lured
away Disney personnel when he opened an animation
studio in Florida). Max Fleischer had sought to make
the first sound cartoon, and later the first cartoon feature; both times his releasing company, Paramount,
refused approval, and Walt Disney accomplished the
innovations. When Richard Fleischer asked if he should
go to work for his father's arch-rival, Max Fleischer

replied, "Of course you should. And tell Walt that I think his judgment is very good."

For a year Walt worked with Fleischer and the screenwriter, Earl Felton, in developing the script for *20,000 Leagues Under the Sea*. Harper Goff designed a *Nautilus* to fit Jules Verne's description of a submarine disguised as a sea monster. The interior, devised by John Meehan, was decorated in lush Victorian style, with velvet-covered furniture and a pipe organ. For the first time, Disney hired important Hollywood stars: James Mason as Captain Nemo; Kirk Douglas as harpooner Ned Land; Paul Lukas as the gentle scientist, Professor Aronnax; Peter Lorre as his assistant, Conseil.

Filming began in the clear Caribbean waters near Nassau, then shifted to Jamaica for the cannibal-island sequence. The company returned to the studio to begin shooting the fight with a giant squid on the newly completed Stage 3 with its 90-by-165-foot tank. As Walt watched the rushes, he realized the scene wasn't working. It was being filmed on a flat sea at sunset. The studio technicians had constructed a realistic squid, but it became unwieldy when the kapok in its tentacles soaked up water. After a few days of shooting, Walt visited the set and told Fleischer, "I want you to start on the dramatic scenes and postpone the squid fight until later. This stuff is awful." The director agreed: "It's phony as a three-dollar bill; the wires are showing, and there's no illusion at all."

Production shifted to another stage for interior scenes with the principal actors. Walt put his technicians to work on a more maneuverable and convincing squid. They produced a two-ton beast with eight forty-foot tentacles and two feelers fifty feet long. Twenty-eight men were required to animate the squid with hydraulics, compressed air and electronics. With hideous yellow eyes and a snapping beak, it presented a fearsome menace for Nemo and his submariners. To add to the horror, the squid attack was filmed not in the pink calm of sunset, but in a howling storm. Tons of water hurtled down on the tank, wind machines whipped the spray, and arc lamps sent lightning flashes through the dark.

The sequence required eight days to film and added more than $250,000 to the budget. The increased cost strained Roy Disney's warm feelings toward *20,000 Leagues Under the Sea* and tried the bankers' patience with Walt's spending. He was required to show them the early footage from the film before they would agree to lend him more money. The added expense was a worthwhile investment; the squid fight proved to be the visual highlight of the film.

The success of the True-Life Adventure films prompted naturalists to submit movies to the Disney studio. One of the offerings was ten minutes of desert film made as part of a doctoral thesis by N. Paul Kenworthy, Jr., a student at the University of California at Los Angeles. He had painstakingly photographed a sequence in which a wasp stung a tarantula into paralysis and laid its eggs inside the spider's body; when the young wasps hatched, they fed upon the preserved body of the tarantula, then flew off.

"This is good stuff," Walt said enthusiastically when he reviewed the film. "Let's get hold of this young man and set him up out in the desert and see if he can come up with other good stories. We could build the whole thing around the desert."

Kenworthy and a colleague, Robert H. Crandall, spent months in the desert filming animal life, and the studio solicited film from other nature photographers. They produced exciting sequences—a family of peccaries treeing a bobcat; a kangaroo rat protecting its young by kicking sand at a sidewinder; a red-tailed hawk in a death battle with a rattlesnake. Walt viewed the footage and told his producer, Ben Sharpsteen: "This is a feature. This is where we can tell a real, sustained story for the first time in these nature pictures." Jim Algar directed *The Living Desert* and wrote the narration with Ted Sears and Winston Hibler, who had been the voice of the True-Life Adventures from the beginning. As with the other films, the talk was minimal. The Disney philosophy likened narration to rolling a hoop with a stick; if the film was well edited, the hoop needed only an occasional hit to keep it rolling.

Predictably, RKO salesmen were opposed to the idea of selling a full-length documentary to theaters, and their reluctance added to the Disneys' growing discontent with the distribution company. The sales force was tough and thorough, and the contract terms were favorable, but RKO began to decline in morale and efficiency after Howard Hughes bought control of the company in 1948. Hughes tired of running the film company and offered to give it outright to the Disneys, along with a $10,000,000 bank-credit line, but there was a catch: RKO had incurred heavy liabilities during its decline. After a meeting with Hughes to discuss the offer, Walt told Roy, "We've already got a studio—why do we need another one?"

With *The Living Desert* nearing completion, Roy realized that RKO had neither the enthusiasm nor the know-how to sell such an attraction. He established a small sales organization called Buena Vista, after the street where the studio was located. *The Living Desert* was first booked into the Sutton Theater in New York, along with a cartoon featurette, *Ben and Me*. It was an immediate success, and Buena Vista added more salesmen and released *The Living Desert* in a careful, deliberate way throughout the country. Proportionately, it became the biggest profit-maker in Disney history, earning $4,000,000 after a production cost of $300,000.

Howard Hughes' neglect of RKO had caused the company to deteriorate rapidly, and Roy decided to seek another distributor for the studio's product. He and Card Walker went to New York for discussions with the major film companies, and the results were discouraging. Although the companies were eager to have the prestige of the Disney name, their terms seemed excessive. Roy recognized the drawback of releasing through a major company; the distributor naturally favored its own studio's product, giving less favorable playdates to independent producers.

Roy summoned the key salesmen of Buena Vista and told them they had proved with *The Living Desert* that they could distribute a film successfully. Roy pointed out that the company had two attractions of great promise—*20,000 Leagues Under the Sea* and *Lady and the Tramp*. "Now if you have the guts and vision and are willing to work, do you want to go forward with our own distribution company?" Roy asked. The salesmen readily agreed, and thereafter all the Disney films were distributed by Buena Vista.

While *The Living Desert* proved an immense success with the public, some reviewers in intellectual journals criticized its anthropomorphism. This was part of a growing trend as the Disney product became more popular and more diverse. The same kind of critic who had embraced the Disney cartoons in the 1930s began to attack Disney films as sentimentalized and corny. Walt was at first perplexed, then hurt by the critiques, some of which seemed political in nature.

One evening as the studio nurse was applying the heat treatment to Walt's neck, he grumbled about a bad review *The New Yorker* had given a Disney film. Hazel George answered him, "Why should you care what those urban hicks say?"

"What did you call them?" Walt asked.

"Urban hicks."

Walt laughed with delight and said admiringly to Hazel, "That's what an education will do for you."

20

THE VISION of an amusement park grew in Walt Disney's mind. On each trip to Europe and during his travels through the United States, he attended outdoor attractions of all kinds. Zoos, especially. Before leaving on another journey to Europe, Lilly warned him, "Walt, if you're going to look at more zoos, I'm not going with you!"

He visited county fairs, state fairs, circuses, carnivals, national parks. He studied the attractions and what made them appealing, whether people seemed entertained or felt cheated. His most depressing experience was seeing Coney Island. It was so battered and tawdry and the ride operators were so hostile that Walt felt a momentary urge to abandon the idea of an amusement park. His spirit revived when he saw Tivoli Gardens in Copenhagen; it was spotless and brightly colored and priced within the reach of everyone. The gaiety of the music, the excellence of the food and drink, the warm courtesy of the employees —everything combined for a pleasurable experience. "Now *this* is what an amusement place should be!" Walt enthused to Lilly.

Walt realized that he would have to provide his own financing and planning for the park, since Roy maintained his opposition. To Lilly's dismay, he began borrowing on his life insurance; before he finished, he was $100,000 in debt. He started assembling a staff to help in planning. Among the first to be recruited was Harper Goff, an illustrator who played with Disney animators in the Dixieland band Firehouse Five Plus

Two, which had created a national sensation. Walt assigned Goff to create preliminary drawings of the park.

Walt continued collecting miniatures of all kinds, even animals. In Europe he became fascinated with tiny Sardinian donkeys and shipped four of them to the studio. Harper Goff told him about a Shetland-pony act in a horse show at the Pan Pacific Auditorium. Walt watched the ponies draw a wagon in intricate maneuvers, and he talked to the trainer, a retired welder named Owen Pope. Months later, Walt invited Pope and his wife Dolly to bring their ponies to the studio and start training other animals for an amusement park. In 1952, the Popes moved into a trailer under the water tower, becoming the studio's only residents. One day Roy came down to look at the ponies and chat with the Popes. Later Walt asked Pope, "What did you say to my brother?" Pope asked if he had offended Roy. "No, not at all," Walt said. "It's the first time I've seen him express the slightest interest in my park idea."

By this time Walt had decided on a name for the park: Disneyland. As his concepts grew, he realized that he needed an organization to help him create Disneyland, and in December of 1952, he founded Walt Disney, Incorporated, with himself as president and Bill Cottrell as vice president. Later, because Roy feared that company stockholders might object to use of the Walt Disney name, the title became WED Enterprises, the initials of Walt's name.

WED was a personal corporation for Walt's activities outside the studio. He bought the rights to the Zorro stories, which had provided film vehicles for Douglas Fairbanks, Sr., and Tyrone Power, and prepared fourteen scripts for a television series to be produced by WED. But when Walt made his presentation to the television networks, the answer was the same: "You'll have to make a pilot film."

"Look, I've been in the picture business for thirty

years," Walt replied. "Don't you think I know how to make a film?"

"But this is different; this is television," he was told. Walt argued that entertainment was the same in any medium, but network thinking was inelastic. No pilot, no series. Walt set aside the *Zorro* project. There was plenty for WED to do in the planning of Disneyland.

Richard Irvine was newly arrived at WED. He had been an art director on *Victory Through Air Power,* then moved to Twentieth Century-Fox when Disney production stalled during the war. Walt had invited Irvine back to help design *Zorro,* and later assigned him to Disneyland. One of Irvine's first duties was to act as liaison with the architectural firm of William Pereira and Charles Luckman, who were making preliminary studies of Disneyland. Walt dissolved the contract with Pereira and Luckman when their concepts failed to match his. Walt's close friend, architect Welton Becket, advised him, "Walt, no one can design Disneyland for you; you'll have to do it yourself."

Irvine was joined by another art director from Twentieth Century-Fox, Marvin Davis. They collaborated with Harper Goff in expanding the original drawings that Goff had conceived for Disneyland. They studied the Disney feature cartoons for ideas to use in amusement-park rides. They drew storyboards of the rides, and Walt contributed his storytelling talent. He described the entire Snow White ride as if it were a movie cartoon, visualizing all the park's attractions for the designers just as he had brought cartoons to life for his animators.

Walt and his planners drove to Pomona to watch how people at the Los Angeles County Fair responded to the attractions. They traveled to Knott's Berry Farm in Buena Park and measured the walkways and observed how the traffic flowed. Walt was particularly interested in the movement of people. He watched them as they walked freely from one attraction to another, then pointed out how they grew irritated when crowds jammed up.

The plans for Disneyland grew, even though Walt had not decided where it would be located. He had abandoned the idea of building it at the studio, not only because of the lack of cooperation from the City of Burbank but because his ideas had outgrown the Riverside Drive property. He continued to pour his creativity into Disneyland—and his money; when he had borrowed the limit on his insurance policies, he sold the house he had built at Smoke Tree Ranch in Palm Springs.

Roy Disney pointed out that the company remained in debt to the Bank of America and it was doubtful that any bank would lend for an amusement park. Walt would not be discouraged. One day he remarked to Hazel George, "If I were to go outside to finance Disneyland, would you contribute?"

"You bet I would!" the nurse replied.

"Find out how many others in the studio would do the same," Walt said. She canvassed studio workers, and most of them agreed they would be willing to invest in Disneyland; they even formed an organization, the Backers and the Boosters. Walt told Roy about it, and Roy agreed that it was a good sign. He began to view Disneyland with more sympathy.

Disneyland became a crusade with Walt, more so than sound cartoons, color, animated features and all the other innovations he had pioneered. He told a reporter the reasons for his zeal: "The park means a lot to me. It's something that will never be finished, something I can keep developing, keep 'plussing' and adding to. It's alive. It will be a live, breathing thing that will need changes. When you wrap up a picture and turn it over to Technicolor, you're through. *Snow White* is a dead issue with me. I just finished a live-action picture, wrapped it up a few weeks ago. It's gone. I can't touch it. There are things in it I don't like, but I can't do anything about it. I want something live, something that would grow. The park is that. Not only can I add things, but even the trees will keep growing. The thing will get more beautiful year after year. And it will get better as I find out what the public likes. I can't do that with a picture; it's finished and unchangeable before I find out whether the public likes it or not."

One day Roy Disney received a telephone call from a banker friend. "Walt was in my office today," the banker said.

"Oh?" Roy replied.

"It's about that park. We went over the plans he showed me. You know, Roy, that park is a wonderful idea."

"Did Walt try to borrow money from you?"

"Yes, he did. And you know what? I loaned it to him!"

Walt continued working quietly with his planning group, which occupied a small one-story building that had been moved to Burbank from the Hyperion studio. By the end of the summer of 1953, the money he had borrowed was running out, and he knew he would have to discover a way to finance the park. He found the solution while lying sleepless in bed.

"Television!" Walt told his brother the next morning. "That's how we'll finance the park—television!"

To Roy, it was the first thing Walt had mentioned about Disneyland that made sense. Like all major corporate decisions, this one had to face the approval of the board of directors of Walt Disney Productions. Walt usually prevailed, but the wisdom of entering two new fields—television and an amusement park—was questioned by conservative members of the board. Walt took the floor to explain his reasoning: Television was an important medium for acquainting the public with the Disney films; the two Christmas specials had demonstrated that. A weekly show would expend a vast amount of creative effort and money, with little or no profit except for creating bigger audiences for Disney films in the theater.

"If I'm going to devote that much talent and energy to a television show, I want something new to come out of it," Walt said. "I don't want this company to stand still. We have prospered before because we have taken chances and tried new things."

To board members who complained that Disney was not in the amusement-park business, he replied that the company *was* in the entertainment business—"and that's what amusement parks are." He admitted that it was hard for them to envision Disneyland the way he could, but he assured them, "There's nothing like it in the entire world. I know, because I've looked. That's why it can be great: because it will be unique. A new concept in entertainment, and I think—I *know*—it can be a success." When he finished, there were tears in his eyes. The members of the board were persuaded.

Roy agreed to go to New York to seek a contract with a television network. But he needed something to demonstrate what Disneyland would be like. Walt and the planners of WED had worked on many designs but there was no visualization of the park in a form to convince hard-headed businessmen. On a Saturday morning in September 1953, Dick Irvine telephoned Herb Ryman, whom he had known in the art department at Twentieth Century-Fox. Ryman had worked for Disney in the 1940s and had been on the South America trip; he had left the studio for other movie work and to pursue his own career as an artist. Irvine asked Ryman if he could come to the Disney studio as soon as possible.

Walt greeted him affably and told him, "Herbie, we're going to build an amusement park."

"That's interesting," Ryman replied. "Where are you going to build it?"

"Well, we were going to do it across the street, but now it's gotten too big. We're going to look for a place."

"What are you going to call it?"

"Disneyland."

"That's as good as anything."

"Look, Herbie, my brother Roy is going to New York Monday to line up financing for the park. I've got to give him plans of what we're going to do. Those businessmen don't listen to talk, you know; you've got to show them what you're going to do."

"Well, where is the drawing? I'd like to see it."

"You're going to make it."

Walt volunteered to stay with him through the weekend, and the astonished Ryman agreed to undertake the task. He began immediately, creating a schematic aerial view of the park from sketches and plans and Walt's own word pictures of what he wanted Disneyland to look like. The design was triangular, with the public entering the park at the bottom tip of the triangle. A berm surrounded the park to keep outside views from intruding; atop the berm traveled a small-size railroad which afforded the customers a look at the attractions within. Main Street acted as a funnel, drawing people toward the castle at the end of the street, where a hub led to the various realms.

By Monday morning, Herb Ryman had completed the drawing. Copies were made, and Dick Irvine and Marv Davis hastily colored them with pencils. The drawings were included in a folder with a description of the park written by Bill Walsh. For the first time, the idea of Disneyland was defined:

The idea of Disneyland is a simple one. It will be a place for people to find happiness and knowledge.

It will be a place for parents and children to share pleasant times in one another's company: a place for teachers and pupils to discover greater ways of understanding and education. Here the older generation can recapture the nostalgia of days gone by, and the younger generation can savor the challenge of the future. Here will be the wonders of Nature and Man for all to see and understand.

Disneyland will be based upon and dedicated to the ideals, the dreams and hard facts that have created America. And it will be uniquely equipped to dramatize these dreams and facts and send them forth as a source of courage and inspiration to all the world.

Disneyland will be something of a fair, an exhibition, a playground, a community center, a museum of living facts, and a showplace of beauty and magic.

It will be filled with the accomplishments, the joys and hopes of the world we live in. And it will remind us and show us how to make those wonders part of our own lives.

The realms were described in detail. True-Life Adventureland would feature a botanical garden with exotic fish and birds, and a ride "in a colorful explorer's boat with a native guide for a cruise down the Rivers of Romance." The World of Tomorrow would have a moving sidewalk, industrial exhibits, a diving bell, a monorail, a freeway children could drive, shops for scientific toys and a Rocket Space Ship to the Moon. Lilliputian Land included an Erie Canal barge ride through the famous canals of the world, passing miniature towns with nine-inch people. Fantasyland would be located within the walls of a great medieval castle, with a King Arthur carousel, Snow White ride-through, Alice in Wonderland walk-through and Peter Pan fly-through. Frontier Country would have an authentic frontier street, stagecoach, pony express and mule pack rides and a riverboat which "takes you downstream on a nostalgic cruise past the romantic river towns, Tom Sawyer's birthplace, and the old Southern plantations." Also included was Holiday Land, which would offer special attractions with the changing seasons—a one-ring circus in the summer, ice skating and bobsleds in the winter.

It was a boldly extravagant proposal, but the brochure declared flatly that "sometime in 1955, Walt Disney will present for the people of the world—and children of all ages—a new experience in entertainment."

21

Roy Disney flew to New York with his small burden, a six-page explanation of his brother's vision, together with a diagrammatic map of Disneyland and a fold-out aerial conception drawn by Herb Ryman under Walt's direction. Roy began discussions with the three television networks and with potential sponsors for an hour-long weekly television show. Roy stipulated that whoever wanted the television show would have to invest in Disneyland.

The Columbia Broadcasting System expressed little interest. General Foods saw the value of Disney to appeal to family consumers and offered a contract—if Disney would make a pilot film. Walt had established his policy: "We don't make samples."

Both the National Broadcasting Company and the American Broadcasting Company had long sought a television series from Disney. NBC, with the huge resources of its parent company, Radio Corporation of America, seemed the best prospect, and Roy had lengthy talks with the firm's founder, General David Sarnoff. Each time Sarnoff expressed his enthusiasm for a Disney series, as well as the park. But each time he handed over the negotiations to underlings, and Roy could get no commitment. After a long, frustrating meeting with RCA executives, Roy went back to his

hotel and telephoned Leonard Goldenson, president of
ABC.

"Leonard, a couple of years ago you expressed an
interest in working out something with us in television,"
Roy said. "Are you still interested?"

"Roy, where are you?" Goldenson asked. Roy told
him, and Goldenson said, "I'll be right over."

Goldenson and Roy Disney agreed that Disney would
supply a one-hour television series to ABC in return
for a $500,000 investment in the Disneyland park.
ABC would become a 35-percent owner of Disneyland
and would guarantee loans up to $4,500,000. The
arrangement was satisfactory for both parties. Disney
received much-needed cash and a credit line for the
park. ABC, which had been unable to compete in
ratings with the two older networks, would present a
prestigious show which could improve its standing in
the television marketplace.

In early 1954, Disneyland, Incorporated, which Walt
had founded three years before, was reconstituted with
Walt Disney Productions and American Broadcasting
Company-Paramount Theaters each owning 34.48 percent with investments of $500,000 apiece. Western
Printing and Lithographing, which had been associated
with Disney in publishing comics and books since 1933,
contributed $200,000 for a 13.79-percent interest. Walt
Disney acquired 17.25 percent by investing $250,000.

The plans for the Disneyland park and television
show were announced April 2, 1954. To demonstrate
the seriousness of his intentions, Walt declared the
series would begin in October of 1954 and the park
would open in July of 1955. He assigned veteran
Disney hands to production of the television show,
which would be patterned after the realms of Disneyland—Adventureland, Fantasyland, Frontierland, etc.
He moved the Disneyland park unit into a first-floor
wing of the Animation Building, and now the planning
gave way to practicability.

In July 1953, Walt had commissioned the Stanford
Research Institute to make two surveys: to find the

ideal location for Disneyland; and to determine Disneyland's economic feasibility. Walt had been offered a former police pistol range in Canoga Park in the northeast part of the San Fernando Valley. Stanford Research advised against it, reasoning that the San Fernando Valley was fifteen degrees hotter in the summer than the coastal areas, and ten degrees colder in the winter. Besides, visitors from cities to the south would have to travel across the Los Angeles urban sprawl to reach Canoga Park.

Harrison (Buzz) Price, Los Angeles director of the Stanford Research Institute, plotted the optimum location for Disneyland in terms of population centers and hotel-room availability. The ideal was the railroad terminal in downtown Los Angeles, but that was obviously the wrong place to acquire reasonably priced land. The future growth of the freeway system was plotted. Freeways would soon be spreading into the San Fernando and Pomona valleys and south to Santa Ana; those to Santa Monica and Long Beach would come later. Walt himself ruled out the location of Disneyland at the beach. He reasoned that the ocean would eliminate half the access to the park, creating a funnel effect. Besides, he had always disliked the honky-tonk atmosphere of amusement piers; and he didn't want people coming to Disneyland in bathing suits.

Price and his researchers discovered that the center of population in Southern California was moving south and east. They continued their hunt in that direction, arriving at Anaheim as the ideal location. It would be easily reached by the Santa Ana Freeway, then under construction, and twenty sites of 150 acres or more were available. The best one, Stanford Research decided, was a 160-acre orange grove near the junction of the freeway and Harbor Boulevard. (The selection was an accurate one; eighteen years later, the center of population of the eight Southern California counties would be in Fullerton, four miles away.) Walt and

Roy Disney were convinced. Negotiations began for purchase of the Anaheim property.

The feasibility survey by Stanford Research took more time. Researchers visited all the major amusement parks in the United States, as well as Tivoli Gardens and others in Europe. The American parks were found to be seasonal, unplanned, unimaginative attractions that appealed almost entirely to the local population, not tourists. The best research was accomplished at the San Diego Zoo, which had year-around attendance of two million. Thus the pattern of month-by-month patronage could be plotted.

Price and other Stanford researchers had a memorable encounter with the owners of amusement parks at their convention in Chicago in November of 1953. In a late-night session over whiskey and cigars, the park operators studied Walt Disney's concept of a new kind of amusement park. The decision was unanimous: It wouldn't work. There was not enough ride capacity. Too much of the park didn't produce revenue. The newfangled rides would cost too much in maintenance. Mechanical failure in a year-round operation would be epidemic. The park owners advised Walt Disney to save his money.

The results of the feasibility survey were encouraging to Walt. The figures were conservative: an estimate of 2,500,000 to 3,000,000 annual customers, with spending between $2.50 and $3 per person. Stanford Research accurately forecast the seasonal variation in attendance based on San Diego Zoo figures, and calculated the average attendance on the fifteen highest days as the proper yardstick for the size of the park. On the basis of its findings, an initial investment of $11,000,000 was recommended.

The original plan for Disneyland was being altered. Lilliputian Land, with its tiny mechanical figures, was put aside; Walt wanted larger figures and he needed time to develop new ways of making them move. The jungle ride was originally planned with live animals, but zoo keepers advised that would be impractical;

animals would be asleep or hidden much of the time. "We will need mechanical animals, so that every boatload of people will see the same thing," Walt said. The idea of walk-through attractions was dropped; amusement-park owners cautioned that patrons had to be transported in vehicles or they would bunch up and halt the flow of traffic.

All park operators contended that Walt's concept of a single entrance was faulty. It would create congestion and make parking difficult, they argued. Walt remained firm. He reasoned that people became disoriented when they entered by different gates. He wanted everyone to be channeled in the same way, to have their visit to Disneyland structured as part of a total experience. He was also insistent on the idea of the hub that led to the various areas of interest. "I'm tired of museums and fairs where you have to walk your legs off," he said. "I don't want anybody at Disneyland to get 'museum feet.'"

Throughout the planning, a familiar Disney word, "wienie," was used. A wienie was a lure, an inducement, in the same way that an animal trainer used a frankfurter to evoke tricks from a dog act. In Disneyland, the castle served as the wienie to draw the people down Main Street. Then, when they reached the hub, two other wienies would attract them to the right or to the left. In Tomorrowland it would be the towering Rocket to the Moon; in Frontierland, the Mark Twain steamboat.

Walt observed that other amusement parks had grown by accretion, often starting with a hot-dog stand and a merry-go-round, then adding features over the years with no design or pattern. World's Fairs, although conceived during a single span of time, were poorly planned; they were clusters of individual, highly competitive exhibits. The result was fatigue for the visitor. Most fatiguing of all were museums, Walt concluded, even great ones like the Louvre and the British Museum.

With his unique experience as a maker of animated

films, Walt Disney brought to the amusement park an extraordinary sense of continuity. He saw the need for Disneyland to flow, as did a movie, from scene to scene. The transitions should be gentle, he realized, with architecture and colors complementing each other in the area of change. Thus the visitor would be led from one attraction to the next without the jolt of adjustment, and he would remember everything he saw. That was not true of the visitor to a world's fair or a museum.

Walt had the ideal collaborators to help bring his vision to reality. They were men who had created the appearance of motion pictures—Dick Irvine, Harper Goff, Bill Martin, Bud Washo, Herb Ryman, Marvin Davis. They knew from long experience as art directors how to make sets pleasing to the eye, how to heighten drama by use of perspective and color. They had been accustomed to satisfying the desires of producers and directors, no matter how impractical they were. The average architect might not have been able to fulfill the wishes of Walt Disney. Walt wanted Main Street to be five-eighths scale, creating an air of nostalgic fantasy. But the stores along the street had to be practical ones where people could browse and shop. The art directors found the solution by making the ground floor 90 percent in scale, the second floor 80 percent and the third floor 60 percent. The result was a charming illusion.

There was one drawback in the use of studio art directors to plan Disneyland: they were accustomed to designing movie sets which were normally used for only a few days, then dismantled. They had no expertise in planning buildings that would resist the onslaught of weather, aging, and millions of visitors. And so Walt brought in an expert in civil, electrical and air-conditioning engineering, Sam Hamel, and hired the firm of Wheeler and Gray to assist as structural engineers.

Walt also needed a construction boss. He found him through C. V. Wood, the former head of Stanford Research Institute in Palo Alto who had joined Disneyland as General Director. Wood had been associated with Joseph Fowler, a consulting engineer and retired Navy admiral. One April Saturday in 1954, Wood telephoned Fowler at his home in Los Gatos, near Palo Alto. "I'd like to bring a friend over to meet you," said Wood. He arrived with Walt Disney, who had come north to inspect the miniature railroad of a local hobbyist.

"Look, Joe, I'd like to have you come down and get the feel of Disneyland," Walt remarked. Later Fowler told his wife, "Hell, I don't know anything about the motion-picture business, but I've got an invitation from the head of a studio, so I'll go down and stay a day or two." When he arrived at the studio, a secretary assigned him to an office, gave him keys to a car, and said, "We'd like you to talk to some contractors." It was three weeks before he returned home. He ended up supervising construction of Disneyland and managing the park for ten years.

Excavation for Disneyland began in August 1954, with the opening less than eleven months away.

The first step in preparing the property was removal of the orange trees. Morgan (Bill) Evans, whom Walt had hired to landscape Disneyland, had chosen trees he wanted to be spared and marked them by tying a colored rag around the trunks. Evans was upset to discover that the trees he selected had been removed with the others. It turned out that the man who operated the bulldozer was colorblind.

The announcement that Walt Disney was entering television with a weekly show stirred a rumble of controversy in the film industry. Most of the major producers had observed a strict hands-off policy toward the new medium, reasoning that collaboration would cause further decline in theater business. Theater owners bolstered that policy with threats to boycott the product of any studio that released its movies to television. Walt Disney expounded in an interview his reasons for entering television:

I've always had this confidence since way back when we had our first upsets and lost Oswald and went to Mickey Mouse. Then and there I decided that in every way we could, we would build ourselves with the public and keep faith with the public. We felt that the public were really the people we had to play to, you know? We didn't care about anybody in between. Once when I was trying to sell Mickey Mouse, a fellow told me something. He said, "Mickey Mouse? What is it? Nobody knows it. Why, I can get cartoons that I know for the same amount of money you're asking." Then he held up a package of Lifesavers. He said, "Now if you're inclined to sell me Lifesavers, that would be different. Because the public knows Lifesavers. They don't know you and they don't know your mouse."

That hit me. I said, "From now on, they're *going* to know. If they like a picture, they're going to know who made it. They're going to know what his name is." And I stuck Mickey Mouse so darn big on that title that they couldn't think it was a rabbit or anything else. The public has been my friend. The public discovered Mickey Mouse before the critics and before the theatrical people. It was only after the public discovered it that the theatrical people became interested in it. Up to that time the critics wouldn't be bothered to give it any space, you see?

So it all boils down that the newspapers and the people who write the newspapers are only interested in things after the public is interested —or if they think they can create some interest on the part of the public. So in all of our exploitation, everything from then on we kept directly at the public. I never went to motion-picture fan magazines. I said, "No, that is not the public. That's a segment of the motion-picture audience, but not the whole motion-picture audience." I always wanted to go for the big periodicals. I told my publicity boys, "Look, when you get the big magazines, then you're reaching a broader segment of the audience."

Now, when television came, I said, "There's a way we can get to the public. Television is going to be my way of going direct to the public, by-passing the others who can sit there and be the judge on the bench. Maybe they never see any more of the public than those in their offices or those they see at the cocktail hour. In other words, the world is that small to them."

I decided when we got into television, we would have to control it. Now everybody wanted to buy all our old product. We wouldn't sell it. We wouldn't hear of it. We wanted to handle it our-selves, make good use of it. Some of the old prod-uct that should not be shown we would not show. Some of it we would frame so it would have a proper presentation for today. . . . We won't throw any piece of junk at the public and try to sell 'em. We fight for quality. All we're trying to do through television is to let 'em know what we've done. And if they're interested in what we do, they'll come to the theaters to see it. There's a loyalty there. . . .

In two of the early television shows, Walt demon-strated his aim of acquainting the public with what his organization was doing. The series opened on October 27, 1954, with the *Disneyland Story,* which described coming attractions in both the *Disneyland* television show and the park itself. Two other progress reports on the park appeared during the first television season. On December 8, *Disneyland* presented *Operation Un-dersea,* a documentary about the filming of *20,000 Leagues Under the Sea.* The show was accused of being a "long, long trailer" to publicize the movie, as indeed it was; but *Operation Undersea* proved enter-taining enough to win the Television Academy's Emmy as the best show of the year.

Walt gave liberally of the studio's backlog of films to television in the first season, showing *Alice in Wonderland, Seal Island, So Dear to My Heart, Treasure Island, Wind in the Willows,* and *Nature's Half Acre,* as well as several of the short cartoons. He also presented original shows, all of which far exceeded the $100,000 budget. One of the most expensive was *Man in Space,* a prophetic view of space exploration which had been prepared with technical advice from Willy Ley, Heinz Haber and Wernher von Braun.

The television shows were introduced by Walt Disney himself; he agreed to appear after the network and advertising executives convinced him his presence was necessary to provide continuity and identification. He admitted to being "scared to death" when he had to face the camera, and he found fault with his performance, especially his voice. "It cracks," he complained in an interview. "I have a little laryngitis— because I smoke too much. And I talk too much; all day long I'm talking in meetings and wherever I go. I have a nasal twang, a Missouri twang. And my diction. I get sloppy and I say, 'Now we're gonna present something or other. . . .' Everybody says, 'That's fine, Walt, perfect,' but the little script girl says, 'Yes, but you said "gonna" instead of "going to." ' So I gotta do it over, because children are looking, and you can't have sloppy habits."

He grumbled over his dialogue and refused to talk about himself or praise his own product. His chief writer, Jack Speirs, a radio writer who came to the studio in 1952 and developed the knack of writing natural dialogue for Walt, sometimes misguessed Walt's desires. The writer provided a glowing introduction to a film that Walt recognized as one of the studio's lesser efforts. "It's a good idea to sell the picture," Walt told Speirs, "but I won't lie about it."

Walt's inability to lie extended to the television commercials, which he agreed to deliver on rare occasions. He would talk about the sponsor's product only if he believed in it, and he did a commercial about an

Eastman camera which he himself had found useful. But when the Eastman Company brought out newer models, he declined to extol them on television. "I like the old one," he insisted.

The hit of the first *Disneyland* season was *Davy Crockett*. Walt had been contemplating a series of television shows on legendary American heroes—Johnny Appleseed, Daniel Boone, Mike Fink, Big Foot Wallace, Davy Crockett and others. The first one concerned Crockett, and Bill Walsh prepared storyboards with a writer, Tom Blackburn. Walt liked the saga, which took Crockett from the frontier to Congress and finally to the Alamo. An outsized actor named James Arness was recommended to play Crockett, and Walt ran a science-fiction film in which he starred, *Them*. "That's Davy Crockett," Walt exclaimed, pointing not at Arness but another giant in the film, Fess Parker. He was hired, taught to ride a horse and sent off to film *Davy Crockett* in North Carolina.

Davy Crockett was designed to occupy three hour-long shows on *Disneyland*, but when the film was assembled, it fell short of the length. Walt first tried spacing out the gaps with sketches, but that proved ineffective. One morning Walt visited the office of George Bruns, a new composer at the studio, and mentioned the problem of bridging from one adventure to another. "George, can you get a little throwaway melody under the narration some way?" Walt asked. In half an hour, Bruns had composed a song that fit lines from Tom Blackburn's script: "Born on a mountaintop in Tennessee . . ." When Walt dropped by Bruns's office the next morning, the composer sang it for him.

"I can't tell much from your singing," Walt said, "but it sounds okay. Bring in a small group and make a demo." Tom Blackburn added more words to the song and Bruns made a demonstration record. Walt approved it, and the song was played and sung throughout the three segments.

The demand for "The Ballad of Davy Crockett" began when a small part of it was heard in the preview portion of the first *Disneyland* show. After *Davy Crockett, Indian Fighter* appeared on the ABC network on December 5, 1954, the avalanche began. The song was number one on the *Hit Parade* for thirteen weeks, and ten million records were sold. Fess Parker became a star, and Buddy Ebsen, who played Davy's sidekick, George Russel, gained a new career.

When the *Disneyland* television show was in the planning stages, the Disney merchandising department licensed manufacturers to issue products with the Frontierland imprint, presuming that the Davy Crockett films would be merely a transitory feature of the television series. However, Phil Sammeth of Disney merchandising believed that Crockett might inspire sales of coonskin hats, and he made inquiries in the industry. The results were discouraging. The fur-hat industry in America had almost disappeared; the biggest manufacturer, a Chicago firm, had stopped making fur hats after suffering a $200,000 loss on them. The only market for raccoon skins was Red China, and because of the trade embargo, a California warehouse had been filled with undeliverable skins. After much persuasion, and a 50-percent cut in the usual merchandising payment to Disney of $5,000 (to which was added 5-percent royalty on gross sales), a firm named Welded Plastics agreed to become licensee for Davy Crockett coonskin hats. Sammeth found a veteran fur cutter to oversee production of the hats.

The Crockett television shows brought an unprecedented demand for furry headgear. Manufacturers, Disney-licensed and otherwise, worked around the clock to produce hats. The wholesale price for skins jumped from fifty cents a dozen to $5. The warehouse in California emptied, and when raccoon skins disappeared, hat makers used anything from Australian rabbit to mink. More than ten million Davy Crockett hats were sold.

The Disney merchandising division quickly recovered from the surprise of the Davy Crockett boom. A new member of the Disney organization, Vincent Jefferds, sent telegrams to major department stores warning they would be liable for damages if they sold unauthorized merchandise. It was a bluff, but it gave Disney time to enfranchise manufacturers for products bearing the title "Walt Disney's Davy Crockett" and a picture of Fess Parker. Jefferds dispatched posters of Parker with rifle and frontier outfit to stores everywhere. Costumes, coloring books, toys of every kind, most of them bearing the Disney imprint, sold by the millions; it was the greatest merchandising sweep for any national craze, before or after. Disney offices in New York were so besieged by offers from hopeful licensees that the telephones had to be shut off for a time. One of the most popular items was a wooden Davy Crockett rifle, and the Disney merchandisers suggested a Davy Crockett Colt .45. "Absolutely not," Walt declared. "They didn't have Colt pistols in Crockett's time." He paid little attention to merchandising but he insisted on two things: All articles must be authentic to the period; and products had to be of good quality.

Walt had spent $700,000 on the Crockett films, even though he was assured of only $300,000 in revenue from television. The gamble paid off in other ways besides merchandising. Walt had an important star in Fess Parker. The three segments of *Davy Crockett* consolidated *Disneyland* as the most popular show in television, and merchandising provided substantial income. The Walt Disney Music Company, which had been formed in 1949 for sheet-music sales, thrived for the first time. The success of *Davy Crockett* led to formation of another subsidiary for phonograph records. Then the *Davy Crockett* films were spliced together and released in theaters. To charge money for an attraction that had already been seen free by ninety million people was inconceivable. Yet *Davy Crockett, King of the Wild Frontier* earned a theatrical profit of almost $2,500,000.

Diane Disney met Ronald Miller on a blind date during a football weekend in San Francisco. He was a handsome, towering, powerfully built football end for the University of Southern California, and his roommate arranged the meeting after the Stanford University game. Ron and Diane began dating on the U.S.C. campus, and Diane took him home to meet her parents at the family Christmas party. The dates developed into romance, and Diane and Ron talked casually about marriage. Both Walt and Lilly were impressed by Ron; they had expressed little regard for the boys Diane had brought home before. One evening as she was about to join Ron in his car, Walt remarked, "You know, Di, we like this fellow Ron." Her mother added, "Yes, if you want to marry him, it's all right with us."

Diane was flabbergasted. Her father had always told her and Sharon that they should wait until they were twenty-five before getting married; Diane was twenty. When she related to Ron what her parents had said, he was as startled as she was. When Diane arrived home later that evening, she told her parents, "He thinks it's a good idea, too."

Both Diane and Ron preferred a small wedding with close relatives and a few friends attending. So did Walt, but he also wanted the ceremony of a church wedding for his first-born. Diane and Ron picked the date, May 9, 1954, and the setting, a small Episcopal church in Santa Barbara. They were baptized in the church the week before, with Walt and Lilly as their witnesses.

Sharon came home from the University of Arizona to be her sister's maid of honor. Walt led Diane down the aisle, then stepped back as the ceremony began. As the minister intoned the ritual, Diane heard a little sob. She turned around and saw her father with tears rolling down his cheeks. She gave his hand a squeeze, and he looked at her soulfully.

"Who gives this woman to be married?" the minister asked.

"Her mother and I do," Walt replied falteringly. He recovered his composure at the wedding reception, held at the Santa Barbara Biltmore Hotel. While posing for photographs, he stood on his tiptoes in an effort to shorten the gap between himself and his new six-foot-five-inch son-in-law. The wedding cake had the Disney touch: the two figures on the top depicted Diane in Levi's, Ron in Bermuda shorts and bare feet—with a football helmet.

Ron was expecting to be drafted, and he dropped out of the university to go to work for his father-in-law, as liaison between WED and Disneyland. He was inducted in October and left for basic training at Fort Ord. Diane, who was expecting their first child, lived in Pacific Grove, near the camp. The baby arrived in the spring and was named Christopher Disney Miller. Walt was delighted to have a son in the family at last —although he was privately disappointed that Ron and Diane hadn't named the boy Walter.

22

TELEVISION PROVED its power to attract wider audiences for Disney films; both *20,000 Leagues Under the Sea* and *Lady and the Tramp* were immensely successful. At last the company no longer had to "live from one picture to the next." Also, the effectiveness of television as a selling medium permitted a wider range of story material for cartoon features. Formerly Walt had relied on universally known fairy tales for immediate audience recognition; he demonstrated with *Lady and the Tramp* that television could acquaint the public with entirely original plots and characters.

The movie profits added to the financial health of Walt Disney Productions, but they were not enough to accomplish the financing of Disneyland. The company sent emissaries to major corporations, seeking participation and advance payments. Some sparked to the promise of Disneyland and paid to have their corporate names associated with the park, others did not. Roy Disney and Larry Tryon, the company treasurer, made repeated visits to the downtown Los Angeles headquarters of the Bank of America to plead for new transfusions of funds to meet the Disneyland needs. Al Howe, who had succeeded Joe Rosenberg as the bank's liaison with Disney, was sympathetic to the project, but the Bank of America had no experience in financing amusement parks. The nation's unsettled economy in 1954 added to the bank's reluctance to continue pouring funds into Disneyland. As the budget rose from $7,000,000 to $11,000,000, Bank of America enlisted the Bankers Trust Company of New York to take a shared participation in the Disneyland loan.

To some of the bankers, Walt seemed profligate. "You can't put a price tag on creativity," he argued. That had been his theory from the beginning. He refused to make his cartoons on a strict budget because he wanted them to be better; making them better meant spending more money. When Roy argued that payments from distributors were not enough to cover production costs, Walt's answer was: "If we make better cartoons, we'll get more money next time." He was unable to establish budgets for *Snow White, Fantasia, Bambi* and other cartoon features because he was pioneering with new mediums, new techniques. The same with Disneyland. He set no budgetary limits on his planners and engineers. They were exploring unknown territory, and only at the end of the quest would Walt know what it cost.

In December 1954, Joe Fowler concluded that he could no longer get woodwork done outside the park with the speed and quality Walt demanded. Fowler proposed immediate construction of the Town Square Opera House so it could enclose the mill. The cost would be $40,000. "Gee, Joe, I just don't have the money," Roy Disney told Fowler, explaining that he had exhausted all possibilities for additional financing. But when Fowler returned the following day, Roy told him, "Yes, I've got your money. Go ahead."

Walt never doubted that his brother would find the money to build Disneyland. Walt's principal concern was meeting the impossible deadline that he had set for himself. By January 1, 1955, it seemed imperative that some compromises had to be made. Tomorrowland was the least developed section of Disneyland; Walt agreed to his staff's suggestion to board up Tomorrowland with an attractive fence, announcing that it would open later. No sooner was the decision made than Walt rescinded it. "We'll open the whole park," he told his staff. "Do the best you can with Tomorrowland, and we'll fix it up after we open."

The WED planners were working forty-eight hours a week, and Walt was with them every day, including Saturday. The studio commissary was closed on Saturday, so the group went to a nearby tearoom for lunch. The talk was always about Disneyland. Walt applied his concept to everything, from the overall philosophy of the park to the details of woodwork and landscaping. Nothing eluded his view, even the trash cans. He wanted them to be attractive additions to the decor, not utilitarian eyesores; hence each was decorated to fit its location—those in Frontierland were done in rustic style, etc.

At times it seemed that Walt was asking more than human ingenuity could provide. When the WED craftsman told him, "We can't make it work," he replied, "You guys are too close to this thing. Let's approach it from a different angle; maybe we can restage this show and *make* it work." He refused to compromise. Veteran operators of amusement parks viewed his plans and pointed out that the Town Square at the entrance to Disneyland would be wasteful; too much expense and space was being used in an area that would contribute little revenue. Walt listened to them and made no change. He intended the Town Square to set the

mood for visitors. It would be a place with flowers
and balloons, costumes and a brass band. Handsomely
wrought surreys, a fire wagon and a horse-drawn trolley
would take people down Main Street and to the rest
of the realms. The vehicles would not have enough
capacity to make a profit, but they contributed to the
entire experience. Walt insisted on fine furnishings for
the restaurants, even though they would be serving
reasonably priced meals. He believed that if a family
sat under a $50,000 chandelier and ate good food at a
fair price, the experience would add to their enjoyment
of the park.

After working with movie sets at the studio, Walt had
to accustom himself to the need for solidity in the Disneyland buildings. One day Walt came across a large mound
covered by a tarpaulin. He looked underneath and saw
hundreds of bags of cement. "What's all this?" he asked
of Robert (Bud) Washo, another art director recruited
from Twentieth Century-Fox for construction of Disneyland. Washo explained that he had acquired the
cement from several sources; he anticipated a shortage
because of the construction of a huge military airport
runway in Orange County. Walt grumbled. He scowled
as he watched the first pouring of cement for the
foundations of the Main Street buildings. John Wise,
structural engineer for WED, had specified concrete
pads four feet square, considering them the minimum
for such construction. Walt thought it profligate. "Wise
is wasting all my money underground," he complained
to Dick Irvine. Irvine argued the need for sturdy
foundations to withstand the impact of millions of
patrons.

Walt greedily absorbed everything the engineers told
him and soon could read mechanical drawings like an
expert. Sometimes the engineers told him that effects
he could easily accomplish in motion pictures were
impractical in an amusement park. They learned not
to say that to Walt Disney. To an engineer who pointed
out the impossibility of a Disney proposal, Walt replied: "You know better than to kill an idea without

giving it a chance to live. We set our sights high. That's why we accomplish so many things. Now go back and try again."

Those who worked closely with Walt learned never to say, "This can't be done." The right response was, "Well, Walt, this might be difficult because . . ." If an engineer exhausted every possibility and could not find a solution, Walt accepted the fact that it couldn't be done.

Problems arose with the Orange County building inspectors. They had no experience with a place such as Disneyland; if they had applied normal building codes, construction of the park would have been exorbitant. The standards for a high-rise office building did not apply to the Sleeping Beauty castle. Disney engineers explained their methods and their good intentions, and in most cases the inspectors were understanding. They were reassured of Disney's concern for safety when he installed automatic sprinklers in all the public buildings. Not only did the sprinklers ensure safety, they also permitted the use of materials that might otherwise have been considered a fire hazard.

The engineers argued that a water tower was needed to supply pressure for the sprinklers and fire hydrants. When an engineer tried to argue the absolute necessity of the water tower, Walt almost ejected him bodily from the office. He refused to have the ugly tank towering over Disneyland. "Find another solution," he insisted, and the engineers did. Water was piped in from more than one source, assuring an unchanging pressure. That cost extra money. So did the relocation of power lines on nearby properties. But Walt wanted no intrusion on the illusions he was conjuring.

Members of the park staff urged him to build an administration building. "No," he replied, "there isn't going to be any administration building. The public isn't coming here to see an administration building. Besides, I don't want you guys sitting behind desks. I want you out in the park, watching what people are doing and finding out how you can make the place more enjoyable for them."

When Joe Fowler proposed a drydock for the Rivers of America, Walt opposed it. He argued that it would be unattractive and would add nothing to the customers' enjoyment. Fowler with his Navy training realized that a drydock was necessary for maintenance of the big boats, and he argued persuasively. During the building stage, Walt referred to it derisively as "Joe's ditch." Later he turned the drydock into an asset by building a picturesque fish restaurant next to it. He named the drydock Fowler's Harbor and called the restaurant Maurie's Lobster House after Fowler's wife.

One of Walt's great concerns was trees. He wanted trees to be part of the beauty and the drama of Disneyland, and to play their roles, they needed to be big. Bill Evans hunted throughout Los Angeles and Orange counties to find specimen trees, scouting new subdivisions and freeway routes for trees that were to be removed. Walt sometimes accompanied Evans to inspect trees under consideration for Disneyland. Walt wanted each tree to fit its location—maples, sycamores and birches for the Rivers of America; pines and oaks for Frontierland, etc. He sometimes rejected a tree with the comment: "It's out of character." During an inspection tour of Nature's Wonderland, he rode the mine train, ordering it stopped from time to time so he could observe the vista. At one point he said, "Move all those trees back fifty feet. I want the people on the big trains to see what's going on in here. Those trees keep it hidden from them."

Always he wanted the trees bigger, despite the high cost of excavating and transporting them. One day Bill Evans found two trees that he was certain would impress the boss. He proudly exhibited them to Walt. "Where did you get the bushes, Bill?" Walt cracked. A staff member once questioned why Walt wanted big trees, since the buildings were scaled down to less than real size. "Trees have no scale," Walt replied flatly.

Walt rejected a design for a building with the comment: "I think the fellow was attempting a monument to himself rather than designing something that is for people." He impressed on his designers again and again that he wasn't seeking architectural masterpieces. "All I want you to think about," he told one of them, "is that when people walk through or ride through or have access to anything that you design, I want them, when they leave, to have smiles on their faces. Just remember that; it's all I ask of you as a designer."

Sometimes he did the designing himself. Marv Davis had labored over the contours of Tom Sawyer Island, but his efforts failed to please Walt. "Give me that thing," Walt said. That night he worked for hours in his red-barn workshop. The next morning, he laid tracing paper on Davis's desk and said, "Now *that's* the way it should be." The island was built according to his design.

The railroad, of course, was a special interest of Walt's. In the early stages of Disneyland, he considered buying an existing railroad from a hobbyist in Northern California. But he wanted the railroad, like everything else in Disneyland, to be fresh and new and his own. "Hell, we built a train before," he told Roger Broggie of the studio machine shop, "we can do it again."

The experience with the Carolwood-Pacific made the railroad one of the easiest projects at Disneyland. The Carolwood-Pacific locomotive, the *Lilly Belle*, was a standard-gauge engine reduced to one-eighth of full size; by multiplying its dimensions five times, Broggie arrived at an engine which was five-eighths normal, with a thirty-six-inch gauge—standard for narrow-gauge trains. The cab was slightly enlarged to accommodate the engineer. The engine and cars were build at the studio, and the railroad was one of the first Disneyland features to be completed.

The "dark rides" were also assembled at the studio. The talents of animators contributed to devising the stunts and the visual effects of the Snow White, Peter Pan and Mr. Toad rides, and mock-ups were laid out in a tin-roof shed so the planners could visualize space relationships. Other dark rides of amusement parks had steel wheels on the cars, but Walt considered them too noisy. "We're trying to tell a story in those rides; we need quiet cars," he said. He hired the Arrow Development Company to design a car that was both silent and highly maneuverable.

Walt visited the tin shed every day to see how the rides were progressing. His favorite was the Peter Pan, because it was an entirely new concept—a fly-through with cars suspended from the ceiling. As the rides came closer to completion, Walt himself rode them over and over again. Bob Mattey, who did the experimental work, and Roger Broggie, who completed the jobs, could always recognize Walt's reaction. If he was pleased, he got off the ride with a childlike giggle. If something went wrong, the eyebrow shot up and he muttered, "Fix this thing and let's get this show on the road."

Walt sought expert advice during the development stage. Dave Bradley ran a little amusement park where Walt had taken his daughters, and Walt invited him to comment on the new rides. Friendly help was also provided by George Whitney, who operated an amusement park in San Francisco. Walt listened to their suggestions, accepted some, rejected others. Whitney argued that the elevated railroad station at the park entrance was a mistake. "People won't walk up to the train," he contended. But Walt believed that the Main Street train station performed a vital function as marquee for the park; without elevation, it would have no significance.

"The people" were uppermost in his consideration. When an attraction pleased him, he said, "I think they'll go for this," or "They're going to eat this up." His expressions of rejection were: "That's not good enough for them," or "They'll expect something better."

He would not sell "them" short. Walt commissioned Owen Pope to construct two Conestoga covered wagons, three Yellowstones, two single-seat and two double-seat surreys and three buckboards for use in the park. Walt was unhearing of arguments that such rides would be too limited in capacity; he wanted them to lend authenticity and atmosphere to Main Street and Frontierland.

He also discarded contentions that vehicles would be vandalized. "Don't worry about it," he replied. "Just make them beautiful and you'll appeal to the best side of people. They all have it; all you have to do is bring it out."

Walt visited the Anaheim site during all phases of construction. He viewed the "stakeouts"—the plottings of building sizes by stakes and string. He made his suggestions as to sizes and proportions, always keeping the overall pattern in mind. Often he squatted down and commented, "Can you see little kids looking up at this?" Most of his planners had never considered looking at the park from the vantage point of a child.

The Disney vision was clear. Scale meant everything, whether it was the fairy-tale size of the railroad, or the nostalgic foreshortening of Main Street, or the romanticism of Frontierland.

"It's too heavy," he complained of the scale of Frontierland. His engineers explained that it was possible to make slim supports in iron and steel, but wood poles and fences had to be thick in order to support the weight. Walt wasn't satisfied. He replaced fences and poles with others that were thin and light, yet strong.

Everything had its proportion. The steamboat, the *Mark Twain,* had to seem as impressive as a Mississippi River paddlewheeler, yet it had to fit the scale of the Disneyland waterway. If the boat had been entirely scaled down, railings would have been at people's knees. The scale had to be adjusted to please the eye and remain functional. Walt approved the plans, and he ordered a scale model so he could judge the *Mark Twain*'s appearance. The superstructure was assembled at the studio and trucked one deck at a time to Anaheim. There it was assembled on the hull.

The *Mark Twain*'s hull was constructed at the Todd Shipyard in Long Beach. Nearly everything else was built by the various departments at the Disney studio. Almost from the beginning, Walt had designed the studio to be self-sufficient. In the early days, he established a laboratory to make black and white paints, so that the cartoons would have a uniform quality. When color film arrived, the studio had its own lab for making color paints. The Disney sound department created the multiphonic sound systems for *Fantasia,* and the machine shop perfected underwater cameras for *20,000 Leagues Under the Sea.* All of the departments were accustomed to dealing with the challenges that Walt gave them. When Walt wanted realistic hippos and giraffes for the jungle cruise, he knew his experts could provide them. Over the years he had learned the talents of his staff, including their hobbies. Animators who sculpted in their off hours were assigned to create scale models.

When the time came to fill the Rivers of America, Disneyland engineers explained they would need a special pump to move the water from wells. "No, just cut a flume to the river and turn the water on," Walt said. The engineers displayed their maps and pointed out that the water would have to travel uphill to reach the river. Walt insisted that they try it his way. To the amazement of the engineers, the water did flow as he had predicted. They didn't realize that a year before Walt had visited the property when it was still orange groves; he had questioned the growers about planting pruning, fertilizing—and irrigating. He remembered how the water flowed; the surveyors' maps were wrong.

Water poured into the Rivers of America, and then disappeared. The thirsty Orange County soil absorbed it all, and engineers searched for a way to hold the water above ground. They tried plastic liners and other substances, but nothing seemed to work. "Keep trying —you'll find something," Walt told them. Finally they located a clay soil nearby; an inch layer on the waterway formed a pad as hard as cement.

The day-to-day operation of Disneyland occupied the thinking of Disney executives, and they reported to Walt that their choice for management of the park had been narrowed to two companies. "What do we need them for?" he asked.

"To run the place," an executive replied. "We have no experience in running an amusement park."

"In the first place," said Walt, "this is not an amusement park. In the second place, we can run Disneyland as well as anyone. All you need are people who are eager, energetic, friendly, and willing to learn. They'll make mistakes, but we can learn from their mistakes."

By late spring, Disneyland seemed far from completion. Joe Fowler assured Walt that the July opening would be achieved—but then the Orange County plumbers and asphalt workers went on strike. C. V. Wood, Disneyland general manager, told Fowler, "We might as well postpone until September. We're not going to make it by July."

"Woody, we have to make it," Fowler replied. He knew how urgently the Disneys needed the summer business to start paying off their enormous debt. Besides, Fowler had been accustomed to meeting impossible deadlines; during the war he had supervised twenty-five shipyards. The plumbers returned to work after Fowler guaranteed them the same payment they would receive upon settlement of the strike. The asphalt situation was solved by hauling truckloads from San Diego at an immense cost.

With the July 17 opening approaching, money was getting scarce. The trees and shrubs which Bill Evans brought to the park became smaller as his budget shrank. By the time he reached his last landscaping task, on the northern side of the berm, no money was left. "I'll tell you what to do, Bill," said Walt. "You know all those fancy Latin names for plants. Why don't you go down there and put some Latin names on those weeds?"

Tomorrowland remained the least finished area. "Cover it up with balloons and pennants," Walt said.

To stage the pageantry for opening day and to supervise entertainment after the park opened, Walt hired Tommy Walker, who had achieved fame as both leader of the marching band and football conversion kicker for the University of Southern California. "If you have one idea in one hundred that works, I'll be satisfied," Walt told him. Among Walker's ideas for the opening was the release of hundreds of homing pigeons. Walker explained to Walt that ten days before the opening the pigeons would be released halfway between Los Angeles and Disneyland; thus the birds could familiarize themselves with half of the route home. When the pigeon owners assembled at the halfway point early one morning, Walt was there. He interrogated the owners about the birds' habits, and later he developed a television feature about pigeon raising.

One of Walker's assignments was to hire a leader for the band which would march down Main Street and play concerts at various locations in Disneyland. Walker avoided consideration of his father, Vesey Walker, a onetime Army bandmaster who had organized thirty high school bands. "Dammit, Tommy, I want you to hire the people who are most qualified," Walt grumbled. The elder Walker became a familiar figure with his elegant leadership of the Disneyland band. "Now, Veechy," Walt instructed him with his habitual mispronunciation, "I just want you to remember one thing: if the people can't go away whistling it, don't play it."

During the final days of construction, the Disney studio received a letter from a mother in an Eastern state. Her seven-year-old son had been stricken with leukemia, and he had expressed a desire to do two things: to meet the comedian Pinky Lee; and to ride on Walt Disney's train. The family had already left for California, hoping to fulfill the boy's wishes. When the family called the studio, they were told to report to Disneyland on Saturday morning. They arrived in their road-weary automobile, and Walt drove up shortly afterward.

"I understand you want to see my train—well, let's

go," Walt said, lifting the boy into his arms and striding off to where cranes were transferring the railroad cars from flatbed trucks to the rails. When the train was assembled and the engine fired up, Walt took the boy to the cab. It was the first trip around the park for the Santa Fe and Disneyland Railway and Walt pointed out the attractions that were still a-building.

When he returned to the administration building, he went to his car for a package. It was one of two gold-framed pictures that had been made from art work of *Lady and the Tramp;* the other had been sent to Grace Kelly and Prince Rainier of Monaco as a wedding gift. He gave the package to the boy. "Well, we really saw the place; he liked my train," Walt said to the parents. To a Disneyland employee, Bob Jani, who had witnessed the visit, he gave the order: no publicity.

The completion of Disneyland coincided with Walt's and Lilly's thirtieth wedding anniversary, and an invitation went to three hundred people for the "Tempus Fugit Celebration":

WHERE: Disneyland . . . where there's plenty of room . . .

WHEN: . . . Wednesday, July 13, 1955, at six o'clock in the afternoon . . .

WHY: . . . because we've been married Thirty Years . . .

HOW: . . . by cruising down the Mississippi on the *Mark Twain*'s maiden voyage, followed by dinner at Slue-Foot Sue's Golden Horseshoe!

Hope you can make it—we especially want you and, by the way, no gifts, please—we have everything, including a grandson!

Lilly and Walt

The guests arrived in the warmth of the July evening and were transported in surreys past the glittering lights of Main Street, through the gates of Frontierland and to the Slue-Foot Sue's saloon for cocktails. One of the early arrivals was Joe Fowler, who visited the *Mark Twain* for a final inspection. He encountered a lady who handed him a broom and said, "This ship is just filthy; let's get busy and sweep it up." And so the former admiral and Mrs. Walt Disney swept the sawdust and dirt from the deck of the *Mark Twain* in preparation for the guests.

Walt had been working all day at the park, and he welcomed the chance to relax with his friends and co-workers and show off Disneyland to them. He led the crowd across Frontierland Square to the dock where the *Mark Twain* awaited, all shiny and white and twinkling with old-fashioned electric bulbs that outlined the decks. A Dixieland band played brassy melodies and waiters circulated with trays full of mint juleps as the paddlewheeler pulled away from the dock with a whistle blast. Walt strolled among the guests and basked in their delight as the *Mark Twain* eased around the bend and sailed past the darkened Tom Sawyer's Island. He felt the weariness of the long months of planning and building, and the elation of seeing his dream almost completed. Those feelings combined with the juleps to make him gloriously high.

The party returned to the Golden Horseshoe for dinner and the frontier revue with high-kicking chorus girls and comic Wally Boag playing an antic Pecos Bill. As Boag began firing his blank pistols, Walt leaned over the balcony and fired back with his finger pointed like a gun. His daughter Diane recalled what happened thereafter:

"People below started to notice him. 'There's Walt,' they said. There was a little applause and general recognition from the audience. And with that, Daddy was off. He started to climb down the balcony, and every little bit of comment or applause would just keep him onward. At one point it got a little touchy—I thought he was going to fall from the balcony. But he made it down to the stage.

"He just stood there and beamed. Everyone started saying, 'Speech! Speech!' But there was no speech forthcoming. All he did was stand there and beam. Then everybody applauded and said, 'Lilly! Lilly! We want Lilly!' So Mother got up on stage, figuring, 'If I get up there, I can get Walt down.' Well, that wasn't the case. So Mother dragged Sharon and me up on the stage and still nothing happened. Dad was just planted there, and he was loving every minute of it.

"I guess someone must have sensed our plight, because the band started to play and Edgar Bergen came on stage and started to dance with me, and some others came up and danced with Mother and Sharon. Everybody started dancing, and my father was gently elbowed into the wings. He was loving every minute of it, just grinning at people.

"Everyone was worried about Dad's driving home. They were trying to steal his car keys and everything, but I just said, 'Daddy, can I drive you home?' He said, 'Well, sure, honey.' No problem at all. He was meek and mild and willing. He just climbed in the back seat of the car. He had a map of Disneyland, and he rolled it up and tooted in my ear as if with a toy trumpet. And before I knew it, all was silent. I looked around and there he was, with his arms folded around the map like a boy with a toy trumpet, sound asleep. I know he didn't have too much to drink, because the next morning he didn't have a hangover. He bounded out of the house at seven-thirty and headed for Disneyland again."

The hot July sun had barely risen as crowds began to gather for the grand opening of Disneyland. Within a few hours, every street within a ten-mile radius of the park was clogged with automobiles. The first-day event was invitational; tickets had been given to studio workers and those who had constructed the park, to press and dignitaries, to suppliers and officials of companies sponsoring exhibits. But there were many more who were uninvited; tickets to the grand opening had been cleverly counterfeited. Thirty-three thousand people poured through the gates. Rides broke down after the first onslaught of customers. Restaurants and re-freshments stands ran out of food and drink. A gas leak was detected in Fantasyland, and the entire area was closed to the public. Tempers flared as the sun grew hotter.

One of the young Disneyland workers retained three vivid memories of opening day: women's spiked heels sinking into the softened asphalt of Main Street; the Mark Twain steamboat with its decks awash because of too many passengers; parents tossing small children over the heads of the crowd to gain rides on the King Arthur Carousel.

Walt was spared the ordeal of watching the fiasco; he was being rushed from one part of the park to an-other for the making of a special television show. He didn't realize the failure of the opening until he read the press accounts the following day. Most of the re-ports were unfavorable, and one columnist accused Walt Disney of skimping on drinking fountains to pro-mote the sale of soft drinks. Walt telephoned the columnist to explain, off the record, that the plumbers' strike had required him to decide whether toilets or drinking fountains would be installed first. "People can buy Pepsi-Cola but they can't pee in the street," Walt said.

Ever afterward Walt referred to the opening day as "Black Sunday." Characteristically, he didn't dwell on the disappointment. He summoned his staff to deal with the pressing problems of increasing the capacity of the rides, handling the flow of people through the park, relieving the traffic jams in surrounding areas, serving food more expeditiously. He set about to repair press relations, inviting the staffs of newspapers, mag-azines and wire services to bring their families to Dis-neyland for special evenings. He appeared at each dinner to apologize for the inconveniences of opening day.

He spent his days at Disneyland and often slept overnight in his apartment over the firehouse on the Town Square. Night workers were sometimes startled to see Walt walking through the park in his bathrobe. Early one morning he encountered two carpenters making repairs on a Main Street building. "Hey, I got the key to the Sunkist store; come on over and we'll have a drink," he said. He unlocked the store, turned on the lights and discussed carpentry with the two workers over tall glasses of orange juice.

During the day he walked through the park, observing the people and their reactions, asking questions of the ride attendants, waitresses, store clerks, janitors. From the beginning, he insisted on utter cleanliness. Remembering the tawdry carnivals he had visited with his daughters, he told his staff, "If you keep a place clean, people will respect it; if you let it get dirty, they'll make it worse." He didn't want peanut shells strewn on the sidewalks; only shelled nuts were sold. No gum could be purchased inside the park. Young men strolled through the crowds, retrieving trash as soon as it was discarded.

He never seemed to tire of striding through the park and watching the people and their reactions to Disneyland.

"Look at them!" he enthused to a companion. "Did you ever see so many happy people? So many people just enjoying themselves?"

One day at twilight, a Disneyland engineer was strolling through Frontierland when he saw a solitary figure sitting on a bench. It was Walt Disney, savoring the sight of the *Mark Twain* pulling around the bend with a puff of white steam.

23

WITHIN SEVEN weeks, a million visitors had come to Disneyland. Predictions of attendance had been exceeded by 50 percent, and customers were spending 30 percent more money than had been expected. Disneyland was destined for enormous financial success, despite one temporary setback. After the park had opened, $1,000,000 worth of unpaid bills was discovered in a locked desk. An employee had been absentmindedly filing them away for months.

The *Disneyland* television series opened its second season on ABC September 14, 1955, with the screening of *Dumbo,* and the series continued to be the highest-rated television show. On October 3, 1955, Disney introduced a new concept in children's programming, *The Mickey Mouse Club.*

It was the first entertainment that Walt Disney had ever designed expressly for children. "But we're not going to talk down to the kids," he told his staff. "Let's aim for the twelve-year-old. The younger ones will watch, because they'll want to see what their older brothers and sisters are looking at. And if the show is good enough, the teenagers will be interested, and adults, too."

All of the Disney showmanship was poured into *The Mickey Mouse Club.* The show presented newsreels of what children were doing in foreign countries, and there were Mickey Mouse and Donald Duck cartoons. Daily serials were based on children's books: *The Hardy Boys,* with Tim Considine and Tommy Kirk; *Spin and Marty,* with Considine and David Stollery;

Corky and White Shadow, with Darlene Gillespie and Lloyd Corrigan. Jiminy Cricket gave entertaining, instructive lectures on hygiene and safety. All of the elements were tied together by the Mouseketeers, twenty-four talented youngsters joined by entertainer Jimmy Dodd and old-time Disney cartoonist Roy Williams.

Walt had seen enough of precocious child actors to know that he didn't want the usual Hollywood performers as Mouseketeers. He assigned Bill Walsh as producer and told him: "Look around at the local schools for nice-looking kids with good personalities. It doesn't matter whether they can sing or dance; we'll teach them at the studio. Watch the kids at recess. You'll find one who is the center of attention, who is leading all the action. That's the one we want."

The Mickey Mouse Club produced an audience response that television had never seen before. Three-quarters of the nation's television sets in service between five and six o'clock each weekday were tuned in to the Disney show. Children and adults everywhere were singing the club's anthem—"M-I-C, K-E-Y, M-O-U-S-E." The mouse-ear caps worn by the Mouseketeers sold at the rate of 24,000 a day; two hundred other items were merchandised by seventy-five manufacturers. The Mouseketeers became national figures, and millions of children could recite "Darlene," "Cubby," "Karen" and all the other names during the daily roll call. The most popular of the Mouseketeers proved to be Annette Funicello, a gasoline-station operator's daughter who had been discovered at a children's dance recital. She attracted the most fan mail—as many as six thousand letters a month.

Never before had quality programming for children been attempted on television, and the venture proved profitable for ABC; $15,000,000 in sponsorship was sold in the first season. The returns for Walt Disney Productions were not as good. ABC provided only half the $5,000,000 cost for thirty-six weeks of five hour-long shows. Disney made back some of the deficit in merchandising of the mouse-ear caps, phonograph records, a club magazine, etc. And *The Mickey Mouse Club* proved valuable in other, less measurable ways. By the mid-1950s, cartoon shorts had become unprofitable, and Disney was producing only half a dozen a year. A whole new generation was growing up with little acquaintance with Mickey Mouse, Donald Duck and the other Disney veterans. Now, because of television, the Disney cartoons were being seen by a larger audience each day than had seen them during their entire theatrical releases. Mickey's status as a folk hero was guaranteed for another generation.

After three decades in Hollywood, Walt Disney had finally achieved financial stability. Disneyland was successful beyond his own dreams. He had produced four hit movies in a row. Although the two television series did not provide profits, they contributed to the health of the Disney endeavors in other ways. Walt himself was slow to realize his new prosperity. He told the story: "One day I was driving home and as I was waiting at a stop signal I looked in a showroom and saw a beautiful Mercedes Benz coupe. 'Gee, I wish I could afford that,' I said to myself, and then I drove on. I had gone a couple of blocks when I said, 'But I *can!*' So I turned right around and went back and bought it."

Afterward he wrote his sister Ruth: "I may not be getting as excited over studio goings-on as I once did, but I haven't hit the rocking chair, either. No, sir. As a matter of fact, I bought myself a jazzy little sports car this year. . . . It's a car for a man who thinks young, and I'm just the guy for it. I thought for a while I was going to have to fight Sharon for possession of it. I loaned it to her one week while we were away and she threatened to steal it. It's a little beauty and almost as good as a blonde on each arm for getting a little envy from my fellow men."

But change in fortune had little effect on Walt's personal life. Nor did he glory in the company's financial health. "I've always been bored with just making money," he said. "I've wanted to do things, I wanted to build things. Get something *going*. People look at me in different ways. Some of them say, 'The guy has no regard for money.' That is not true. I *have* had regard for money. But I'm not like some people who worship money as something you've got to have piled up in a big pile somewhere. I've only thought of money in one way, and that is to do something with it, you see? I don't think there is a thing that I own that I will ever get the benefit of, except through doing things with it."

Walt realized that the company required growth and prosperity to keep faith with the stockholders. He and Roy always maintained the policy of paying minimal dividends to the shareholders, plowing the profits into the development of the company. "I have a regard for my stockholders," Walt said. "To me, it's a moral obligation, like the one I felt toward the people who helped me when I was having bad times in Kansas City. I worried and fretted about paying 'em back, and I paid them back in many ways. Like the little Greek Jerry, who loaned me money and let me eat in his restaurant on the cuff. After I was out here and got Mickey Mouse going, he wrote me. He had been in the automobile business, but he met another Greek in Phoenix and they wanted to start a restaurant. 'Walt,' he wrote, 'I need a thousand dollars.' Well, I had Mickey Mouse then, so I loaned him a thousand dollars, I sent him a check. After all, Jerry had let me eat on credit. My credit never got over sixty dollars, but I gave Jerry a thousand. Later I got a telegram from Jerry saying, 'Walter, I need another five hundred. We need air conditioning in Phoenix.' So I sent him five hundred. Then he wrote me, 'I'm having trouble with my partner; I want to buy him out.' I told him, 'Jerry, you've got to get along with your partner. I just can't loan you any more.' So my sixty dollars with Jerry cost me fifteen hundred dollars. I never saw it again. But I've tried, with everybody who befriended and helped me, to see that they came out all right."

During the early years of Mickey Mouse and the

Silly Symphonies, he had been amused but unswayed by the efforts of intellectuals to detect profundities in the Disney cartoons. Over the years he took a realistic, sometimes self-deprecating attitude toward the films. He once remarked, "When I was a kid, I read an art book and the author advised young artists to be themselves. That decided it for me. I was a corny kind of a guy, so I went in for corn."

He became inured to accusations of corn from critics, from scholars, even from his own children. Once he ran a new Disney film at home, and Diane remarked, "Gee, Dad, that's corny!" Her father replied, "Maybe so. But millions of people eat corn. There must be a reason why they like it so much." During a visit to France, a group of French cartoon makers met with Walt to seek his advice. "Don't go for the *avant garde* stuff," he told them. "Be commercial. What is art, anyway? It's what people like. So give them what they like. There's nothing wrong with being commercial."

After Walt had demonstrated his showmanship on television, leaders of the Academy of Motion Picture Arts and Sciences asked him to produce the Oscar telecast. The previous year's show had been a flop, and the industry's leaders saw Walt Disney as the savior of the Academy's prestige. The Academy delegation came to the studio for lunch with Walt. He listened politely to the arguments that only Walt Disney could rescue the Academy from its low estate. Then he replied, "Look, we live out here in the cornfield. All these years we've been turning out corny entertainment. I've never considered myself a big producer like Louis B. Mayer or Darryl F. Zanuck; I'm not in their class. I don't think our organization is cut out to make the kind of sophisticated entertainment that an Oscar show should be. And I think the public would resent it if I turned it into a Disney production. No, I think you'd better find someone else to put the show on for you."

Walt expounded his theories of film making during a studio conference to plan a book called *The Art of Animation*. He wanted the book to describe the history

of animation, with emphasis on what the Disney studio
had contributed to the art; he also wanted to pay
tribute to the artists whose talents had allowed him to
accomplish his goals. Among his remarks:

Don't get into any too-arty discussions. This has
been a very down-to-earth business. We can't go
off into those ivory towers. . . .

The mechanics are not what make this business. We can still get the idea over with nothing
but pencil drawings and without our present equipment. We don't need all this fancy stuff, actually.
A pencil reel will give you the story. The mechanics are secondary.

What is the difference between our product and
the other? We have never tried to hog anything.
The thing that makes us different is our way of
thinking, our judgment and experience acquired
over the years. Giving it "heart." Others haven't
understood the public. We developed a psycholo-
gical approach to everything we do here. We seem
to know when to "tap the heart." Others have hit
the intellect. We can hit them in an emotional
way. Those who appeal to the intellect only appeal to a very limited group. Let's not let the
mechanics get in here and foul the whole thing.
The real thing behind this is: we are in the motion picture business, only we are drawing them
instead of photographing them. We have got to
appeal to the whole population. All the famous
classical things always had this certain contact
with the public. . . .

My feeling about the early days and why the
cartoon lost out is that it was still a lot of
tricks. . . . For example, Felix the Cat had a personality but he didn't develop. They began re-
peating his tricks on which his personality was
based. Aesop's Fables caught on but never had
any real personality and began to die out. . . .

At first the cartoon medium was just a novelty,

but it never really began to hit until we had more
than tricks—until we developed personalities. We
had to get beyond getting a laugh. They may roll
in the aisles, but that doesn't mean you have a
great picture. You have to have pathos in the
thing. . . .

There is only one reason why "Walt Disney"
has been played up: because it adds personality
to the whole thing. It isn't "Ajax Films Presents"
—it is a personality. Actually, "Walt Disney" is
a lot of people. Let's put this in an honest way.
This is an *organization*. Each man is willing to
work with the other and share his ideas. This is an
achievement. . . .

Throughout the studio history, he resisted any dilu-
tion of "Walt Disney Presents." He relied on William
Anderson, Bill Walsh, Jim Algar, Winston Hibler and
Ben Sharpsteen to help prepare and produce film projects, but he insisted that each film remain "A Walt
Disney Production." He explained his philosophy to a
young employee, Marty Sklar, who was preparing a
slide presentation for the annual report. Sklar had pic-
tured key production personnel, and Walt commented:
"Look—Disney is a thing, an image in the public mind.
Disney is something they think of as a kind of entertainment, a kind of family thing, and it's all wrapped up
in the name Disney. If we start pulling that apart by
calling it 'a Bill Walsh Production for Walt Disney' or
'a Jim Algar True-Life Adventure for Walt Disney,'
then the name 'Disney' won't mean as much any more.
We'd be cutting away at what we've built up over all
these years. You see, I'm not Disney any more. I used
to be Disney, but now Disney is something we've built
up in the public mind over the years. It stands for
something, and you don't have to explain what it is to
the public. They know what Disney is when they hear
about our films or go to Disneyland. They know they're
gonna get a certain quality, a certain kind of entertainment. And that's what Disney is."

He was ever protective of "the Disney thing," and his scrutiny extended to every area of the company's operations. In 1957 he fired off an inter-office communication to one of his executives: "I hear that you gave permission, for a fee, to the agency that handles the Rheingold account to use 'Wringle, Wrangle' for a commercial. In the first place, I don't think that *any* of our music should be used for jingles, but above all, definitely not to exploit beer, cigarettes or such things. We should always be careful about what our music is used for because of our broad audience and also the timeless value of our films. In the past we have turned down several of these things, and this should be a continuing policy. What's happening—isn't the money coming in fast enough? Or as they say, 'Pig, don't make a hog of yourself.'"

His attitude was demonstrated in the way he showed dignitaries around Disneyland. As the fame of Disneyland spread throughout the world, royalty and heads of state visiting the United States insisted on including it in their tours. Walt showed off the park like a father with a new baby, and he never tired of answering the same questions: When did he first get the idea for Disneyland? Why did he locate it in Anaheim? How much did it cost?

The first foreign personage to visit Disneyland was President Sukarno of Indonesia. He was dazzled by the place, and as he and Walt stood on the prow of the *Mark Twain,* he remarked, "Mr. Disney, you must be a very wealthy man." Walt smiled and replied, "Yes, I guess I am; they tell me I owe about ten million dollars."

King Bhumibol and Queen Sirikit of Thailand were given the personal Disney tour, including the voyage on the *Mark Twain.* Walt pointed out some ducks paddling alongside the steamer and said to the king: "Your majesty, those are the only things I have here that didn't cost anything—they just moved in after we built the river." King Mohamed V of Morocco seemed to have trouble sorting out the real from the artificial during his tour with Walt. When the Jungle River boat passed under the waterfall, Walt commented, "It looks almost like real water, doesn't it?" King Mahendra and Queen Ratna of Nepal were given a dinner by Walt and Lilly at the Disneyland Hotel after their visit to the park. When dinner was over, Walt asked the king and queen if they had shopped during their tour. When they replied that they hadn't, Walt ordered the park reopened. The royal motorcade drove down Main Street to the Emporium, and the king and queen selected presents to take home.

Inevitably, Walt was recognized by the Disneyland crowds. He was embarrassed when his famous visitors were ignored, and he called to the crowd, "This is the King of Belgium—a real king!" or "My friend here is the Prime Minister of India, Mr. Nehru."

When Nikita Khrushchev, the Premier of Russia, visited the United States in 1960, he expressed his desire to see Disneyland. The Los Angeles police chief said he could not protect the premier in such crowds, and the visit was canceled. At a film-industry luncheon attended by scores of movie stars, Khrushchev ranted like a child who had been denied a toy. His outburst made headlines throughout the world.

Lilly Disney had wanted to meet the Russian premier and was disappointed that he hadn't come to Disneyland. So was Walt. He had planned to line up the eight ships of his new submarine ride and say to his visitor: "Well, now, Mr. Khrushchev, here's my Disneyland submarine fleet. It's the eighth largest in the world."

By the late 1950s, the Disney enterprises had undergone enormous growth. Walt's realm of activity now included Disneyland; the television series; live-action films; cartoon features and shorts; the True-Life Adventures and an outgrowth of it, People and Places; music publishing; records; books; magazines; and character merchandising. Commenting on the company's prosperity, Walt told a reporter, "Roy and I must have a guardian angel. We could never split up like Dean Martin and Jerry Lewis. Roy doesn't know whether it's my guardian angel, and I don't know whether it's his."

There was never a question of a split, but the relationship between the two brothers showed evidence of strain as the company's affairs grew more complex. Sometimes there was an explosion, usually caused by Walt, the younger, more impatient, artistically minded brother. And usually it was the volatile Walt who made peace. After one memorable clash, Walt arrived at Roy's office bearing a birthday present—an Indian peace pipe. Roy's pique vanished in laughter. Later that day Walt dictated a letter to Roy:

It was wonderful to smoke the Pipe of Peace with you again—the clouds that rise are very beautiful.

I think, between us over the years, we have accomplished something—there was a time when we couldn't borrow a thousand dollars and now I understand we owe twenty-four million!

But in all sincerity, Happy Birthday and many more—and—

I love you.

Roy's contribution to the building of the Disney empire was never underestimated by Walt. He often paid tribute to Roy's financial sagacity and his devotion to the family enterprise. Roy was performing an invaluable function for which Walt had neither the talent nor the appetite.

"I feel sympathetic toward Roy," Walt once said, "because he has to sit with the bankers. He has to sit with the stockbrokers who come in and harass you and say, 'I haven't turned any Disney stock in six months now; do something so I can turn it and make a profit.' I used to tell Roy, 'You've got to get away from those guys; they'll beat you down.' One time he called me from New York, and I told him, 'Come on back to California; the sun is shining here. Get away from those guys.' "

Roy realized the need to cultivate the financial marketplace. Each year he urged Walt to appear at the annual stockholders' meeting. Walt refused. "There's nothing I can do there," he argued. "It's a formality. We give 'em a report, tell 'em what we've got, and that's it. Who's sitting out there? Just representatives of brokerage houses and financial reporters. And maybe some little character who likes to attend stockholders' meetings like some people go to funerals. My real stockholders aren't out there."

One year when the company's fortunes were at a low ebb, Walt finally acceded to his brother's urgings. Walt addressed the meeting: "I don't know how many of you out there are stockholders. I've got a letter I want to read to you; it's from a lady in Florida. She writes, 'Dear Mr. Disney, I'm a Disney stockholder, and I'm very happy to be one. I don't care if you ever pay any dividends. I just hope you go on doing the fine work you've been doing.' " Walt folded up the letter and said, "Now *that's* the kind of stockholder I like. It's been very nice to appear before you. Now if you don't mind, I'd like to go back and try to get this company on its feet."

Walt also considered board of directors meetings a waste of time. He avoided the meetings except when Roy advised him: "Look, they're going to try to force us into something; you've got to be there." At such times, Walt and Roy Disney formed a solidarity that was fearful to oppose. When the stock was in a slump during the postwar period, influential stockholders urged the Disneys to announce a big expansion in order to inflate the stock price. The threat of stockholder suits was raised. The Disney answer: "Sue all you want. We're doing what we think we should do, and that's to take care of the best interests of the company, not any individual stockholder."

Even at times when the two brothers were at odds, they exhibited a mutual protectiveness. Many an employee learned the peril of agreeing with Walt when he was complaining about Roy, or with Roy when he grumbled about Walt. During a long plane flight Walt sat with an assistant and told how his plans had been thwarted by Roy's thrift. The aide replied he thought Roy had done everything he could to help Walt. Afterward the man reflected, "If I had agreed with Walt, he would have thrown me off the plane."

While Roy did not react as explosively as Walt during their disputes, he was no less disturbed. His wife, Edna, and son, Roy Edward, could always tell Roy's mood by the way he drove into the driveway of their Toluca Lake home. If the car came to an abrupt halt and the door slammed loudly, it meant that Roy had probably been arguing with Walt.

Like Walt, Roy was single-minded in his devotion to the studio. He generally arrived home with a briefcase bulging with letters, reports and memoranda to study in the evening. He and Edna had a small circle of friends, most of them not connected with the film business; his best friend was Mitchell Francis, Edna's younger brother, whom he had known from his early days in Kansas City. Roy had played polo with Walt during the 1930s and had bowled with studio teams in the war years. When Edna urged him in later years to take up golf as a relaxation from studio worries, he declined. "I don't want you to be a golf widow," he said. He preferred working in the garden.

Roy guarded his health. The tuberculosis in his twenties had influenced him deeply; he was determined to avoid another serious illness. Such was Roy's concern for his health that he had his appendix removed, not because it was troubling him but because he feared infection. In later years he installed exercise machines in the basement of his house and used them regularly. Like Walt, he was a poor sleeper, and he often used the machines to tire himself so he could return to sleep.

He enjoyed reading American history and amassed a large collection of works about Thomas Jefferson. But most of the time he read the nightly contents of his briefcase. When the company's fortunes improved in the late 1950s, his reading became more and more enjoyable, and often he would share his delight with Edna and young Roy. "Here, look at this," he said with a wide grin.

Roy remained modest about his own contribution to the company's prosperity. Late in his life he commented to an associate, "My brother made me a millionaire. Do you wonder why I want to do everything I can to help him?"

24

THE FIVE years that followed the opening of Disneyland were a period of great expansion for Walt Disney Productions, which had begun the 1950s with a gross income of $6,000,000 and had leaped to $27,000,000 in the first year of Disneyland operation. By the end of the decade, the figure was $70,000,000. Television production grew with the introduction in 1957 of a third series, *Zorro*. The project had been transferred to the studio from WED, and the half-hour adventure proved to be a popular attraction on the ABC network. *Disneyland* continued to be the top-rated series in television; in the second season Walt produced two more adventure episodes starring Fess Parker as Davy Crockett, again a television sensation and a moneymaker in the theaters. The second season of *The Mickey Mouse Club* was more successful than the first.

After two seasons of losing to *Disneyland* in the ratings, NBC scheduled the most expensive series in television, an hour-long western, *Wagon Train*. NBC lavished promotion on the show and it succeeded in toppling Disneyland from its number-one position. ABC, which was having success with Hollywood-made Western series such as *Cheyenne, Maverick* and *Wyatt Earp,* began importuning Disney: "Give us more Westerns! Give us more action!" A meeting was scheduled with top ABC officials at the Disney studio. Walt startled them by appearing at the conference room in full cowboy regalia. He twirled six-shooters and laid them down on the table. "Okay, you want Westerns— you're gonna get Westerns!" he exclaimed. But, he insisted, he was going to do the Westerns his way, depicting the true heroes and the true West. He recounted tales of Texas John Slaughter and Elfego Baca, and the ABC executives were totally convinced.

Walt disliked being forced to turn out product to fit an audience formula. He found himself competing with two dozen other television Westerns, and that wasn't the Disney style. He argued that his product had always succeeded by its uniqueness, not in following trends. But ABC told him: "Just keep giving us Westerns."

Despite its immense popularity, *The Mickey Mouse Club* ran into trouble. ABC claimed it couldn't find enough sponsors who wanted to appeal to the juvenile audience, and the show was cut to a half-hour for its third season, then discontinued. It had been a brave experiment, an attempt to present important programming to the young television audience; never again would it be done in commercial television. What killed *The Mickey Mouse Club?* Walt Disney hinted that it was greed; he believed the network's overloading of commercials caused viewers to lose interest.

The *Zorro* series had been an acknowledged hit for two seasons, but ABC declined to renew it. The reason was economic: the network could make more money with series which it owned, rather than those bought from independent producers. In canceling the series, ABC contended that Disney was barred from offering *Zorro* or *The Mickey Mouse Club* to other networks. Walt and Roy considered that unfair. They sued ABC, and after a lengthy negotiation, a settlement was reached. Disney would be able to take *Walt Disney Presents* (as it was called in its last two seasons on ABC) to another network. Disney would buy out ABC's one-third interest in Disneyland for $7,500,000. The settlement galled Walt—"What did they do to help build the place?"—but at least he was free. The purchase from ABC in 1960 gave Walt Disney Productions total ownership in Disneyland, the interests of Walt Disney and Western Printing having been acquired earlier.

When Walt returned from New York after the ABC settlement, he called Donn Tatum, former ABC West Coast television head who had joined the Disney organization in 1955. "Now we can go to NBC and talk about color," Walt said.

From the beginning of his career in television, Walt was convinced that the medium would some day move to color. Even though ABC had telecast his show in black-and-white, all of the new material was filmed in color. Other Hollywood producers considered that an unwise extravagance, but Walt was certain that color would add future value to the shows. NBC was the obvious place for him to test his theory. The network was promoting color because its parent company, RCA, manufactured color television sets. Tatum telephoned NBC president Robert Kintner, who expressed immediate interest in a color television series by Disney.

Both Walt and Roy Disney went to New York with Card Walker and Donn Tatum for the meeting with the RCA-NBC officials. The RCA board room in Rockefeller Center was decorated with brightly colored posters created by Disney artists, and Walt proceeded from one to the next, relating each story with emphasis on the use of color. It was a virtuoso performance, and the television executives were overwhelmed. All that remained was to work out the final details. When Walt dropped Walker and Tatum at their hotel, he told them: "Fellas, I want this deal. If necessary, I'll stand on my head in Macy's window."

Walt Disney's Wonderful World of Color made its debut on September 24, 1961, with a new character, Ludwig Von Drake, lecturing on how the Disney cartoons moved from silents to sound and from black-and-white to color. It was the beginning of a long and profitable relationship between Disney and NBC.

One day when the studio burdens seemed overwhelming, Walt muttered to his secretary, Dolores Voght Scott: "Let's shut down this office. We've got Disneyland. We don't need the studio." He wasn't serious, but it was an indication of his feeling about Disneyland. On one of his tours of the park with Joe Fowler, he remarked, "This is where I can get a real rest away from the humdrum of making pictures at the studio. This is *my* amusement area."

During the winter months when Disneyland was closed to the public on Monday and Tuesday, he inspected the refurbishing and building of new attractions. But he also liked to see how people were reacting to the park, and he usually toured the park every Saturday. Mobility became a problem, since television had made him readily recognizable. He seemed to enjoy the recognition, but he grew impatient with requests for autographs. Once when a grandmotherly tourist asked if he would give her an autograph, he replied, "No, but I'll give you a kiss," and he did. Sometimes he answered requests by handing out slips of paper on which he had previously signed his name. Occasionally there were hurt feelings, as when a mother wrote to Walt complaining that he had refused to sign her daughter's autograph book. He replied in a letter: "It isn't that I object to giving my autograph to fans while in the Park, but I have found that if I stop to sign autograph books, etc., for the youngsters, I usually get inundated with them and never get to where I was going nor accomplish what I had set out to do. So when they stop me I ask them to send me a note at the studio and their request will be fulfilled. This saves me endless time. If I failed to ask Tricia to do this, I am sorry, but perhaps you will give her the enclosed autographed photo taken of me and my little pet poodle, 'Lady.' "

During his visits to Disneyland, Walt was always "plussing"—looking for ways to improve the appearance of Disneyland and provide more pleasure for the customers. He would study an area and tell his staff: "Let's get a better show for the customers; what can we do to give this place interest?"

One Sunday, Dick Nunis, manager of Frontierland, was making out the weekly work schedule at the Chicken Plantation Restaurant when Walt came by on a strolling survey. The two men studied the traffic on the Rivers of America: the *Mark Twain* was pulling away from the dock, one keelboat was landing at the pier as another departed, two rafts were crossing to Tom Sawyer's Island, and three Indian canoes were racing around the bend. "Look at that!" Walt exclaimed. Nunis expected him to complain about the congestion, but Walt said, "Now there's a busy river! What we need is another big boat." The astonished Nunis asked him what kind of boat. "Not just another stern-wheeler," Walt said. "This time we need a sailing ship. I think we should have a replica of the *Columbia*. Did you know that was the first American vessel to sail around the world?" He delivered a history of the *Columbia,* which became the next addition to the Rivers of America.

As the principal feature of the Tahitian Terrace, which featured Polynesian dinners and entertainment, the Disney engineers had created a huge tropical tree of cement limbs and plastic leaves. When Walt first saw the tree in the restaurant, he commented, "Trunk's squatty." He climbed to the highest terrace and gazed at the stage. "You can't see the show from up here; the foliage is in the way," he said. "Let's do something about it."

After weeks of study, the engineers met with Walt

at the Tahitian Terrace and confessed their inability to raise the tree without great expense. Walt studied the huge tree and remarked, "This may sound silly—but why can't we just add six feet to the trunk?" That solved the problem. The trunk was severed, the tree raised by a crane, and six feet of cement and steel were added to the trunk.

Walt could be severe with employees who disturbed what he was trying to create at Disneyland. He reprimanded a publicity man for parking his car near the Frontierland railroad station. "When people come here, they expect to see the frontier," Walt said. "Your car destroys the whole illusion. I don't ever want to see a car inside the park again." Illusion was everything. A Disneyland television show was proposed in which Walt would soliloquize about the park as he walked down a deserted Main Street. Walt killed the idea in storyboard. "I don't ever want people to see the park empty," he said.

One evening Walt and Lilly were stopped by a guard while approaching a preview of the Monsanto exhibit. When Walt explained who he was, the guard said, "All right, you can go in, but she can't." Walt later ordered the guard fired—"If he treats me that way, imagine how he'll be with other people." Early in the operation of the park, he decided that Disneyland would have to train its own security people rather than use an outside agency. "You can't expect outsiders to give the courtesy that we want," he said. "We want the people who come here treated as *guests,* not customers."

Walt noticed that one of the railroad conductors treated the patrons curtly. He commented to an assistant, "See if you can't give that fellow a better understanding of the business we're in. Try to cheer him up. If you can't, then he shouldn't be working here. We're selling happiness. We don't want sourpusses here."

Walt often stopped to chat with ride operators about their problems. The more perceptive employees learned to recognize the nature of his visit to the park from his attire. If he wore a gray suit and sports shirt with his Smoke Tree Ranch neckerchief, he was there for pleasure; when he was on a business tour, he wore an old pair of gray pin-stripe trousers, an ancient leather jacket, a pair of clodhoppers and a farmer's straw hat. In his "business" clothes he sometimes went unrecognized by Disneyland workers. One day a Jungle Boat pilot failed to notice that he had a famous passenger. When Walt stepped off the boat, he walked up to the Frontierland superintendent, Dick Nunis, and asked, "What's the trip time on this ride?" Nunis replied that it was seven minutes. "I just got a four-and-a-half-minute trip," Walt said. "How would you like to go to a movie and have the theater remove a reel in the middle of the picture? Do you realize how much those hippos cost? I want people to see them, not be rushed through a ride by some guy who's bored with his work."

"Could I go on a trip with you?" Nunis asked. He and Walt rode one of the boats through Adventureland, and Walt explained how to conduct the trip—"Speed up in the dull stretches, then slow down when you have something to look at." For a full week, the Jungle Boat pilots were timed with stop watches until they perfected the length of the ride. When Walt arrived for his regular visit to Disneyland on the weekend, he walked through Adventureland without stopping. He did the same the following weekend. After three weeks, he took a ride on the Jungle Boat. When he returned to the dock, he entered the next boat for another ride. He went around four times, eliminating the possibility that the operators had "stacked the deck" by giving him the best pilots. When he emerged from the fourth trip, he provided his only comment: a thumbs-up sign to Nunis.

Tomorrowland remained a vexation to Walt; it had been neglected in the original planning because of lack of time and money. In 1959, Walt corrected the lapse with a $6,000,000 improvement of the Tomorrowland area.

The initial Disneyland plans included a monorail sweeping over the park, but the WED engineers couldn't lick construction problems. A couple of years after Disneyland had opened, Joe Fowler and Roger Broggie visited a monorail prototype in Cologne, Germany. Unlike other models, in which the car was suspended from the rail, this one rode piggyback, rubber wheels rolling noiselessly on a concrete ribbon. When Fowler and Broggie explained how the ride worked, Walt decided that was what he wanted.

Another addition for Tomorrowland was an underwater ride. The WED planners had suggested a glass-bottom boat, but Walt said, "No, let's give them a real submarine ride. We'll take them down in the water and let them look out of portholes. Give 'em a real show." The planners devised mock-ups of submarine ports and tested underwater stunts of giant squids, volcanic fire, etc. It all seemed feasible, and the Submarine Voyage was put into production. The United States Navy expressed a desire to sponsor the ride, but Walt declined, fearing interference if he became involved with government bureaucracy. Instead the General Dynamics Corporation became the sponsor.

The Matterhorn ride originated one day when Walt and Joe Fowler were sitting atop the wooded hill in the middle of Disneyland. "You know, Joe," Walt began, "why don't we make some snow and have a toboggan ride here?" Fowler explained that it would be difficult to maintain the snow, especially in the summertime; water drainage would also be a problem. Walt gave up the snow idea; instead, he built a replica of the Matterhorn with bobsleds racing through and around it.

The opening in June 1959 of the Matterhorn, the Disneyland-Alweg Monorail System and the Submarine Voyage, plus a Motor Boat cruise and a revamp of the Autopia, provided much-needed capacity for growing crowds. In the four years since the opening, Disneyland had attracted fifteen million visitors. Still Walt rejected complacency. When an elaborate Christmas parade was proposed, members of the Park Operating Committee spoke against it. They argued that it would be poor economics to spend $350,000 on the parade when holiday crowds would be attracted to Disneyland with or without the attraction. Walt rejected their arguments, declaring, "We can't be satisfied, even though we'll get the crowds at Christmastime. We've always got to give 'em a little more. It'll be worth the investment. If they ever stop coming, it'll cost ten times that much to get 'em back."

During the first season Walt offered a circus that proved a failure; the tent seated two thousand and no more than five hundred appeared at any performance. "People don't come to Disneyland to see a circus," Walt concluded, and he shut it down. The stagecoach ride had become a safety problem; the horses ran away three times and the top-heavy coach spilled. Joe Fowler suggested allowing no passengers on top of the coach. "If people can't ride on top, it's no show," Walt replied. "Let's discontinue it."

Walt's biggest disappointment was the periphery of Disneyland. Motels and restaurants sprang up, with eyecatching signs and sales gimmicks to attract the Disneyland millions. "I wanted to buy more land, but I couldn't," Walt told a reporter. "I had a helluva time raising the money as it was; I even put my family in hock by borrowing on my life insurance and stock. Believe me, if I ever built another Disneyland, I would make sure I could control the class and the theme of the enterprises around it."

Theatrical features remained the principal enterprise of Walt Disney Productions, and they thrived in the years following the opening of Disneyland. Walt Disney became the envy of other film producers because of his ability to pre-sell his movies on the television show, assured of a faithful audience that recognized the Disney trademark for wholesome entertainment. Producers were also envious of the gold that Disney could mine from his film vaults. Ever since *Snow White and the Seven Dwarfs,* he had designed the cartoon features to be timeless in nature. Thus they were unaffected by the transition of styles and could be released to each new generation. Buena Vista began the practice of bringing back the Disney classics every seven years; since the production cost on most of the features had already been paid, the re-releases represented almost total profit.

Walt was especially pleased when features that had failed in their first releases finally achieved vindication. When Card Walker told him that the 1957 re-release of *Bambi* would earn $2,000,000, Walt reflected, "You know, Card, I think back to 1942 when we released that picture and there was a war on, and nobody cared much about the love life of a deer, and the bankers were on my back. It's pretty gratifying to know that *Bambi* finally made it."

Walt sought a wider range of film material, and he bristled when the Story Department rejected a book because it was "not Disney material," implying that it wouldn't appeal to children. "Dammit, I'm making pictures for the *family,* not just children," he declared. "If I made pictures only for children, I'd lose my shirt."

Old Yeller marked a step toward greater realism in Disney films. The Fred Gipson story of life on a Texas farm in 1869 had been serialized in *Collier's* magazine and became a best-selling book. Bill Anderson thought it held promise as a Disney film; he also believed it could provide his chance to become a producer. Anderson had arrived at the studio during the war and had risen to become production manager of the studio.

Anderson poured out his enthusiasm for *Old Yeller* to Walt. That was a mistake. Walt did not like to be oversold on anything, and he viewed Anderson's pitch with a suspicious stare. Anderson continued his campaign, fearing that Walt would leave for Europe before reading the Gipson story. At eight o'clock on the Sunday morning of his departure, Walt awoke Anderson with a telephone call. "You buy that story," Walt ordered. "Don't let anybody get in your way. Buy that story. And since you've been bugging me on this, we'll see what kind of a producer you are. You can be my associate on this picture."

The rights to *Old Yeller* were purchased for $50,000, and Fred Gipson came to the studio to adapt his own story. A Hollywood writer enlarged the story, and Walt was displeased with it. In the book, the father of the family had left the farm for a cattle drive and was absent during the events of the summer. The cattle drive was added to the script, since the father was to be portrayed by Fess Parker; it seemed impractical to have the studio's important star appear only at the beginning and the end.

"The cattle drive will have to go," Walt decided. In one afternoon he eliminated thirty-five pages from the script, inserting dialogue from the book. "We bought this book because we liked it," he reasoned. "Why change it?"

In the book, the boy was forced to shoot his beloved dog because it had been bitten by a rabid wolf. Members of the production staff argued that such an ending would be too tragic for children. "This is a Texas farm in 1869 and the dog has rabies; there's no way he can be saved," Walt argued. "You gotta shoot him. It'll give the picture a touch of realism. The kids'll cry, but it's important for them to know that life isn't all happy endings."

Walt chose an Englishman, Robert Stevenson, to direct *Old Yeller*. He had been brought to America by David O. Selznick, and later made films for Howard Hughes at RKO. Walt admired one of Stevenson's television films and assigned him to direct a Revolutionary War film, *Johnny Tremain*, despite the director's English background. Walt's faith in Stevenson was justified, *Old Yeller* made a bigger profit than any previous live-action Disney film.

The Shaggy Dog had been around the Disney studio since the 1930s; it originated with a novel, *The Hound of Florence*, by Felix Salten, author of *Bambi*. The original plot concerned an apprentice of Michelangelo who turned into a dog, and in 1941 Walt designed it to be the studio's first live-action film. In a letter to George Schaefer, president of RKO, Walt suggested that the film "could be done in a high-class manner, with a fairly good cast, for less than $400,000. I believe it is the type of thing that would have the same appeal as *Topper, The Invisible Man* and other of those unusual pictures that have been so successful." The project lapsed with the outbreak of the war. In 1957, Walt asked Bill Walsh to hunt for film subjects to showcase the popular stars of *The Mickey Mouse Club.* Walsh suggested updating *The Hound of Florence* with Tommy Kirk as a teenager transformed into a shaggy dog by a mystic ring. The project was proposed to ABC as a television series. It was turned down as being too far-fetched. "All right, to hell with those guys," said Walt. "We'll make it as a feature."

He assigned Bill Walsh and Lillie Hayward to write the script, and Walt worked closely with them, contributing comedy business from his long experience with cartoons. For director he chose Charles Barton, a veteran of movie comedy. As father of the boy-dog, Walt cast Fred MacMurray, whose career had declined to the making of routine Westerns. The budget was established at a modest $1,200,000, and Walt decided to make *The Shaggy Dog* in black-and-white; he reasoned that color would add a disturbing note of reality to the supernatural comedics.

The Shaggy Dog proved a surprising success, earning more than $9,500,000 in the United States and Canada. It was an important film for the studio's history, proving that Disney could be as effective in live-action comedy as in cartoons. Fred MacMurray's career was re-established, and he served as star of a succession of Disney comedies. Walt was already planning another one during the filming of *The Shaggy Dog*. He visited the set one day and told MacMurray about a demonstration he had seen at the Brussels World's Fair; a science professor from an Eastern U.S. college had used puffs of carbon-dioxide gas and other dramatic devices to illustrate the interaction of elements. That was the inspiration for MacMurray's second Disney film, *The Absent-Minded Professor*.

Sleeping Beauty was put into production at a time when Walt was thoroughly engrossed in Disneyland, television and the live-action films. He kept an eye on the cartoon's progress, but he lacked time to lavish on its preparation, as he had done on all the previous features. As a result, the characters lacked the human touches that Walt always endowed; they also lacked his humor. The emphasis was on visual beauty and spectacular effects.

Sleeping Beauty continued in production for three years, and its cost mounted to an alarming $6,000,000. "I sorta got trapped," Walt admitted later. "I had passed the point of no return and I had to go forward with it." *Sleeping Beauty* lost money in its first release, and other Disney features—*Darby O'Gill and the Little People, Third Man on the Mountain, Toby Tyler, Kidnapped*—performed disappointedly at the box office. Another disappointment was *Pollyanna*. It was a beautifully wrought film, written and directed by David Swift with warm sentiment, and starring a brilliant young actress, Hayley Mills, daughter of the British star John Mills. Despite its excellence, *Pollyanna* earned less than $1,000,000. Walt theorized that he should have changed the title; the male segment of the film audience apparently balked at seeing a movie called *Pollyanna*.

Walt Disney Productions, which had a record profit of $3,400,000 for the fiscal year 1958–59, suffered a loss of $1,300,000 the following year, largely because of the cost of *Sleeping Beauty*. It was the first time in a decade that the company had lost money, and Walt found that he had to boost studio morale. He told his staff, "Look, we've been through this before. Why, we were just one step ahead of foreclosure when we lost our foreign market before the war. We might have gone under after the war if the bank hadn't agreed to carry us. We'll get out of this slump, too."

The reverse came soon. Walt authorized his biggest budget for a live-action feature—$4,500,000 for *Swiss Family Robinson*. He put $3,600,000 into his first cartoon feature with a contemporary story, *101 Dalmatians*. Fred MacMurray starred in *The Absent-Minded Professor,* Hayley Mills in a second film written and directed by David Swift, *The Parent Trap*. The four films produced a total profit of $19,000,000.

On April 25, 1961, Walt and Roy Disney marked a historic occasion in the history of their company: the loan from the Bank of America was finally paid off. For the first time in twenty-two years, revenue from the motion pictures would go directly to Walt Disney Productions instead of to the bank.

V

THE DISTANT REACH

1961–1966

25

HE SEEMED more than ever to be conscious of the passing of time. As he approached his sixtieth birthday in December of 1961, he became crotchety about it. His secretary, Dolores Scott, and the studio nurse, Hazel George, realized what was bothering him and they prepared a special gift: photographs of themselves twenty-five years before. Walt recognized the message: that he wasn't the only one who had aged. He was delighted with the gift.

He had long passed the age when the fortuneteller had predicted his early death, but he worked ever harder, fearful that he would die with things undone or in disarray. He once remarked to Hazel, "After I die, I would hate to look down at this studio and find everything in a mess." "What makes you think you won't be using a periscope?" she asked. "Smartass," he muttered.

His impatience to get things done contributed to his crankiness. He snapped at those who asked superfluous questions or failed to carry out his concepts. Executives and producers called Dolores or Tommie Blount, a new secretary in Walt's office, to inquire, "Is he in a good mood?" The studio password for a bad mood became: "Watch out—Walt's got his wounded-bear suit on."

Tommie Blount had to learn to deal with Walt's wounded-bear periods. During a two-day disgruntlement, he chided her for not reminding him of something he needed to do. "As I told you this morning—" she began, and he retorted, "You don't need to be so damned sassy about it." He stormed out of the office, and she went to her desk. Before walking out the door, he turned and grumbled, "You don't have to work here. There are other places where you can go."

Tearfully, she began cleaning out her desk. "It's all right," counseled Dolores, who had long experience with the Disney temper. "Don't go; he doesn't mean it." Tommie was convinced she had been dismissed, and she gathered up her belongings. When Walt returned to his office, he rang for her. "I didn't really mean that you had to go look for another job," he told her. "But you *did* sass me."

"No, I didn't," she replied.

"Yes, you did. Anyway, go buy yourself some flowers." He handed her a twenty-dollar bill. She refused it, but he insisted. She used the money to buy dinner with her favorite date, Thomas Wilck, who worked in the studio's public relations office. They were married in 1962, and Walt gave the bride away and paid for the reception. As he walked Tommie down the aisle of the church, Walt whispered to her, "I didn't tell Tom how sassy you are."

With the retirement of Dolores Scott, Tommie Wilck became Walt's number-one secretary, and she learned to understand her boss's moods and methods. Each evening she prepared a calendar of the following day's appointments for him. She tried to keep him on schedule, and one day when he continued talking with visitors past the twelve-thirty lunchtime, she rang a ship's bell, a gift from the Coast Guard. He was amused, and he instructed her to sound the bell every day at lunchtime. Tommie learned that the best way to get his attention for pending matters was to type the message in all capitals on three-by-five-inch note paper. He then wrote his terse decision on the paper in colored pencil.

Like Hazel George, Tommie Wilck was able to kid the boss and get away with it. Once she reported to Walt that a group of Marceline residents was visiting the studio. "Well, if I'm in the office when they finish the tour, show them in," Walt remarked. "After all, to the people in Marceline, I'm like God." Tommie replied, "We sometimes use that word in reference to you around here, too."

At five p.m., Walt was usually back in his office for Hazel's heat treatment and the Scotch mist that Tommie prepared for him (one day he changed his order without explanation to Scotch and soda, and that remained his evening drink). During one period, Walt, his secretary and the studio nurse used the treatment time to engage in a word game, selecting a new word each day and tracing its origin and meaning. Walt's use of words was sometimes curious. At a time when he was planning a Flying Saucer ride for Disneyland, he described how the saucer "hoovers" over jets of forced air. Tommie suggested that he meant "hovers." When he said "hoover" again, she remarked, "It really *is* 'hover.'" He continued, "And so this thing hoovers . . ." One day he caught her in a mispronunciation of "emeritus." He pounced on the error, declaring, "I pay you to be smarter than I am."

Hazel George's therapy at the end of each work day became more welcome to Walt; the pain of the old polo injury worsened with the years, causing almost unbearable agony. His constitution seemed strong, but he was subject to repeated colds and sinus infections. At times he developed a facial pain that was excruciating. Few people knew about it, but those who did could recognize when it occurred; Walt's complexion went pale and he began poking at his face. It happened during a press conference in Canada when Walt had been selected Grand Marshal of the Calgary Stampede; he continued answering questions despite the secret pain. He once suffered an attack during the night when he was sharing a stateroom on a Coast Guard cruise with a studio artist, Peter Ellenshaw. Walt tried to avoid disturbing Ellenshaw while running hot water for compresses to comfort his aching face.

Walt's fondness for chili and beans, hamburgers, potatoes and pie sometimes drove his weight to 185 pounds, and he forced himself to the discipline of diet.

But he still resisted all warnings that he should give up cigarettes. They had become too much a part of his life, too great a necessity for his restless hands. He smoked them until they were almost too short to hold, sometimes longer. When the Surgeon General of the United States announced that cigarettes were a cause of cancer, he tried switching to low-nicotine cigarettes. He couldn't stand them. Someone told him that brown French cigarettes were safe to smoke, and he tried them. He realized that they were no better for him, and he returned to his American brand. His wife, his doctors, Hazel and others urged him to give up cigarettes. He still smoked.

He worked constantly. He brought home stacks of scripts and read them by the hour in the living room or on the porch; because it pained him to sit up straight, he put the scripts in his lap and leaned over to read. Often in the middle of the night Lilly awoke to see Walt standing at his dresser, studying a script or making sketches, or talking to himself about a project.

Lilly found it exciting to receive a telephone call from Walt with the message: "Pack your things; we're going to Europe." Their travels were never aimless; Walt always had a mission in mind. When he was planning the Submarine ride, the Disneys flew to Switzerland to see a wave-making machine. Walt heard about a big coffee shop in a park in Milan, so they went there to study how the Italians made espresso. Then to Munich to see a new treadway for transporting people.

Often the Disneys journeyed to foreign countries to visit the company's film locations. One of Walt's favorite trips was for the film *Bon Voyage,* because it took him to Paris. He enjoyed visiting the places he had seen as a boy in 1918, and he grew impatient with taxi drivers. "He's going the wrong way," Walt complained. "I know, because I drove this route a hundred times when I was a driver for the Red Cross." Walt didn't like to have his sightseeing interrupted, and he grumbled when the studio publicist, Tom Jones, tried to arrange interviews. Finally Walt agreed to do them—"if you lump them all in two days." Walt endured two days of answering reporters' questions, charming all of them with his enthusiastic talk of future plans. He flagged only at the final interview, with a lady from Radio Luxembourg. He answered all her queries; then she asked if he would say a few words to the listeners in French. Walt thought for a moment, then said, *"Où est la toilette?"*

Walt and Lilly took trips to the West Indies with Welton Becket, architect, and his wife. They were supposed to be on vacation, but after two or three days Walt could not resist expounding about projects for the future. Inevitably, the trips were productive. The Disneys and the Beckets explored a volcanic island near Cuba where pirates were said to have made their home; this contributed to a future Disneyland attraction, Pirates of the Caribbean. Lilly liked to browse in antique shops, and in Puerto Rico, Walt bought a large cage with a mechanical bird; a later Disneyland attraction was the Tiki Room, with a chorus of singing birds.

The Disney family was growing; Diane and Ron Miller had four children in six years. After Ron left the Army, the Millers lived with the Disneys, but the house was not big enough for two families. There was too much clamor for Walt, and he became upset when Diane or Lilly rose from the dinner table to rock a squalling baby. He believed babies should not be coddled. He told Diane about an experiment in which a baby monkey grew to accept a stick tied with a rag as its mother. "See—you are expendable!" he cried.

After his Army service, Ron played a season as offensive end with the Los Angeles Rams professional football team, and it proved a punishing experience for both him and his father-in-law. Walt attended two games at the Coliseum in Los Angeles. In one, Ron was smashed from the side and knocked unconscious. In the other, he was kicked in the ribs. Ron hinted to Walt that he was bad luck, and Walt attended no more games. The road schedule required Ron to be away three weeks at a time, and Walt grumbled that he would like to see his son-in-law more often. Finally he told Ron, "You know, our studio is expanding, and there are a lot of opportunities for a young guy to learn the business. Why don't you take a job there?" After a battering season on the gridiron, the proposal sounded attractive to Ron.

Ron Miller worked as second assistant director on features and television shows, and his commanding presence helped make him effective in his job. Walt was pleased with Ron's progress and promoted him to associate producer. Walt had definite ideas about his son-in-law's future, as Ron discovered when he was working on *Moon Pilot*. Bill Walsh, who was producing, and James Neilson, the director, suggested that Ron direct the second unit—action scenes in which the principal actors were not used. Ron agreed.

Late one afternoon Ron was summoned to Walt's office. Usually Walt was in a pleasant mood after his traction and Scotch, but this time he was not. "What the hell is this about you directing a second unit?" he demanded. "Do you want to be a second-unit director or a producer?" Ron learned Walt's reasoning. At other studios, the director, who rehearsed the actors and supervised the day-to-day filming, was more important than the producer, who assembled all the elements and oversaw costs. At the Disney studio, where preparation meant more than the execution of a movie, the producer was pre-eminent. Walt could always hire a director to make his films; it was more important for him to train producers to prepare the Disney kind of picture. Any ambitions that Ron had for directing were soon forgotten.

As the Miller family grew, Walt became more upset with Diane. Finally he blurted out the reason: "You know, you're very selfish. You've named your children after everyone else, but you haven't named a single one after your father or your mother." That was remedied on November 14, 1961, when the fifth child

was born to Diane and Ron Miller. His name: Walter
Elias Disney Miller. On the evening of the day Walter
was born, Diane heard her father's cough down the
hospital corridor. He appeared at the door, and his
face was beaming. "Well, finally!" he said. At the
studio he passed out cigars with bands that read: "It's
a *grandson*—Walter Elias Disney Miller."

Sharon Disney did some modeling and played a
small role in *Johnny Tremain*. Friends arranged a blind
date with Robert Borgfeldt Brown, a designer with the
Charles Luckman architectural firm, and a romance
began. It proved to be a long courtship, Brown having
been reared in a staid, conservative Kansas City family. He was awed by Sharon's father, and, on one occasion, astounded by him. Brown and Sharon dined
one evening with Walt and Lilly at the Carolwood
house. It happened to be Walt's fifty-seventh birthday,
and he steadfastly ignored the fact. Lilly and Sharon,
who knew Walt's dislike of his birthdays, made little
mention of it. But Thelma, the Disney cook, hoped to
please him by preparing the only cake he enjoyed—
banana cream. Thelma piled whipped cream atop the
cake and carried it into the dining room.

"Who said I wanted a birthday cake?" Walt grumbled. Lilly responded by scooping up a handful of
whipped cream and tossing it in his face. He countered
with a handful aimed at her. Whipped cream was flying
through the dining room, splattering against the new
wallpaper. Sharon thought the scene was hilarious. Bob
Brown could only stare in astonishment.

Brown became accustomed to the Disneys' unor-
thodox ways, and after a year and a half of dating, he
proposed to Sharon. "Well, she's your problem now,
Bob," Walt told the bridegroom. Bob and Sharon were
married in a Presbyterian ceremony in Pacific Palisades
on May 10, 1959. To no one's surprise, Walt cried.

Walt immediately began trying to convince Bob
Brown to join the Disney organization. Brown was
determined to remain independent. Finally in 1963 he

agreed to become a planner in WED, and he proved to be a valuable member of the organization.

Another member of the Disney family was working at the studio, Roy Edward Disney, son of Roy. Young Roy had started in 1953 as an apprentice film editor for outside producers who rented space at the studio. When Roy was leaving for a location on a nature film, *Perri,* Walt suggested, "Why don't you take along a camera and shoot some behind-the-scenes stuff for the television show?" Roy did, and Walt was pleased with the results.

Roy worked for four years as assistant to Winston Hibler in the production of television shows. Then one day he walked into Walt's office and said, "I'd like to produce some of these TV shows myself." "Do you think you can handle it?" Walt asked. "Yes," Roy replied. "Okay, go ahead," said Walt.

Walt could be as tough with his nephew as with any of his producers. Roy produced a film about a white stallion, *The Legend of El Blanco,* and Walt's response was negative. "I hate that song," Walt began as he heard the theme music. He disliked other things about the film and kept saying, "I hate that song." Roy remarked, "Gee, I like it."

"Do you want to work on this show or not?" Walt snapped.

"I do," Roy said.

"Okay." Walt began suggesting how to convert the serious story into a more whimsical approach. "And for God's sake," Walt added, "change the music."

Roy reworked *The Legend of El Blanco* with a lighter touch and hired a Mexican quartet to record new music. He induced his uncle to appear on the lead-in with the quartet, and Walt wore six-shooters and a big sombrero. He liked the show so much that he chose it as the second film for the new television season.

Unless he had an eight-o'clock appointment in his office, Walt usually stopped by WED when he arrived at the studio in the morning. He once remarked to

Marc Davis, "Dammit, I love it here, Marc. WED is just like the Hyperion studio used to be in the years when we were always working on something new." He spent hours in the model shop, peering from all angles at three-dimensional replicas of future projects. Walt insisted that all additions to Disneyland be constructed in model form before being placed in production. He didn't trust blueprints; he wanted to see the height and scale of each new project and its relationship to the rest of Disneyland.

One of his major challenges for WED was to develop a method of animating three-dimensional figures in the same way that he had been able to give life to cartoon characters in films. The project had its origins in the miniatures with which Walt worked as relief from studio problems in the postwar years. Then came the Dancing Man, the nine-inch replica of Buddy Ebsen. The Barbershop Quartet was a step forward, affording songs and movement by a series of metal cams. The big drive to open Disneyland postponed the development; two of the early attractions, the Jungle Cruise and Nature's Wonderland, featured moving animals, but their actions were simplistic.

After Disneyland was operating successfully, Walt returned to the idea of animating figures with the realism of life. He told his WED designers, "Look, I want to have a Chinese restaurant at the park. Out in the lobby will be an old Chinese fellow like Confucius— not an actor, but a figure made out of plastic. Now, the customers will ask him questions, and he'll reply with words of wisdom. We'll have an operator in back of the figure answering the questions and making the lips move."

The system for animating the Dancing Man and the Barbershop Quartet had serious limitations. Cutting of the cams was a tedious process, and the action of the figure was limited to the diameter of the cam; also, the mechanism had to be placed within a foot or two of the figure. With the help of the studio's sound and electrical departments, a new system was devised to control the actions electrically by means of magnetic tape. A standard optical-sound-track tape sent signals to activate solenoid coils within the figure and produce the action.

The Chinese head, molded of latex, was able to blink and turn its eyes and open and shut its mouth. "Okay," said Walt, "now let's make him talk." He instructed the WED crew to watch television without sound, observing how people formed words. Wathel Rogers, who directed the project, recalled: "You could always tell who was working on the job; they never looked at your eyes when you were talking to them, always at your mouth." While working on the lip movements, the WED craftsmen also sought a better material for the figure. Latex deteriorated and cracked, and the surface resisted repair by vulcanizing. A hot-melt plastisol proved a far better substance; it had the flexibility and texture of human skin and could be repaired by soldering. The Chinese head was never finished. Walt had embarked on plans for a Disneyland exhibit that would dramatize American history. It would be called the Hall of Presidents, and every American President would appear in lifelike form. Now Walt's challenge to WED was to create a figure that would move and talk and look like Abraham Lincoln.

Since the new system combined sound, animation and electronics, it acquired the name of Audio-Animatronics. Its first application to Disneyland entertainment was the Enchanted Tiki Room, which opened in 1963. It was originally planned as a restaurant, with mechanical birds performing a concert at the end of the meal. Walt decided there wasn't enough time to serve the meals and perform the show, so the attraction was expanded to a seventeen-minute performance, with 225 birds, tiki gods and flowers singing, telling jokes, appearing and disappearing. As in cartoons, movements of animals were easier to reproduce convincingly in Audio-Animatronics than those of humans. Walt was convinced that his WED staff could do both. He checked the progress daily, and when disappointments came, he said, "Don't worry—it's going to work."

The overwhelming success of Disneyland inspired offers for Walt Disney to build theme parks in other parts of the country. "There will only be one Disneyland," he insisted, but there were hints that he had other plans in mind. Once he remarked to an associate, "Do you realize that we play to only one-fourth of the United States at Disneyland? There's a whole other world on the other side of the Mississippi."

Walt knew that his organization needed new goals —not only additions to Disneyland, but other challenges that would improve technology and stretch imagination. In 1960, he summoned his staff of planners and told them, "There's going to be a big fair in New York. All of the big corporations in the country are going to be spending a helluva lot of money building exhibits there. They won't know what they want to do. They won't even know *why* they're doing it, except that the other corporations are doing it and they have to keep up with the Joneses. Now they're all going to want something that will stand out from the others, and that's the kind of service we can offer them. We've proved we can do it with Disneyland. This is a great opportunity for us to grow. We can use their financing to develop a lot of technology that will help us in the future. And we'll be getting new attractions for Disneyland, too. That'll appeal to them: we can say that they'll be getting shows that won't be seen for just two six-month periods at the fair; those shows can go on for five or ten years at Disneyland."

He instructed a task force to visit the nation's top corporations and offer the Disney services for the New York World's Fair of 1964–65. If interest was expressed, Walt followed up personally. General Motors was the first to consider a Disney operation at the fair, and Walt journeyed to Detroit for discussions. General Motors executives were so convinced of the potential that they decided to develop their own organization to build an exhibit. "But you ought to try Ford," said one of the G.M. men. "They really need you."

Ford was responsive to Walt's proposal of an attraction that would carry fair visitors in Ford cars through Audio-Animatronic depictions of Man's development from the Stone Age to modern times. It didn't matter to Walt that Audio-Animatronics had not been perfected, and that there was no system for moving the cars through the exhibit at varying speeds. Walt was confident that his "imagineers," as they were called, would solve such problems.

General Electric, which was seeking to repair an image damaged by a price-fixing scandal, also hired Disney to create a world's fair exhibit. WED devised a revolutionary concept: a theater in which the spectators' seats would revolve around a series of stationary stages. Each of the stages would depict progress of the American home and electrical appliances. To coordinate the "Progressland" project, General Electric assigned a vice president whose previous expertise had been in heavy machinery. He listened impatiently as Walt outlined how the show would trace the American household from 1890 to the future. When Walt finished, the vice president remarked, "Well, that's not exactly what we had in mind. We're in the business of selling progress. What do we want with all that nostalgia?"

To the WED staff, the room temperature seemed to drop perceptibly. Walt replied with an edge to his voice, "Look, I built this studio on the basis of nostalgia, and we've been doing a pretty good job of selling it to the public all these years." Afterward he was so incensed that he ordered the legal department to determine if the General Electric contract could be broken. When the G.E. president, Gerald Phillippi, visited the studio on a vacation two weeks later, Walt told him, "I'm having trouble with one of your vice presidents." The man was instructed to stay out of Walt's way.

Robert Moses, president of the New York World's

Fair, visited Disneyland and the studio in 1963, accompanied by his executive vice president, William E. (Joe) Potter, a retired general and one-time governor of the Canal Zone. Walt showed them a slide presentation of the Hall of Presidents and displayed the working model of Abraham Lincoln. The astonished Moses exclaimed, "I won't open the fair without that exhibit!"

"Well, we couldn't get the entire Hall of Presidents together in time," said Walt. "But we might be able to finish Lincoln."

Moses negotiated with the state of Illinois to sponsor a lifelike representation of Abraham Lincoln at the World's Fair. Announcement of the exhibit brought criticism from a few Illinois citizens, who feared that the state's greatest citizen might be "cartoonized." Walt allayed such fears by appearing at a press conference in Springfield, Illinois, on November 19, 1963, to explain his good intentions. After all, he pointed out, he himself was a native of Illinois.

The last World's Fair attraction to be undertaken was "It's a Small World." Pepsi-Cola executives went to California to seek help from Disney in creating an exhibit to benefit UNICEF, the United Nations agency for children's welfare. A Disney executive, believing that three projects were more than enough to occupy WED, sent the Pepsi-Cola people to an engineering firm that specialized in children's playgrounds. Walt was angry when he heard about it. "I'm the one who makes those decisions!" he declared. "Tell Pepsi I'll do it."

His decision came less than a year before the May 1964 opening of the fair. Marc Davis, a Disney animator who had moved to WED, designed the animation for a boat ride through countries of the world, and Mary Blair provided the settings. The ride's effectiveness hinged on creating a song which could saturate each area and blend from one to the other. Walt gave the assignment to a pair of brothers, Richard and Robert Sherman, who had come to the studio to write songs for Annette Funicello and Hayley Mills to record. Walt drove the brothers to the WED headquarters, now located two miles east of the studio, and demonstrated the workings of the "It's a Small World" exhibit. "What I want," Walt explained, "is a song that is universal, that can be sung in any language, with any type of instrumentation, simultaneously." A large order, but the Shermans composed a simple two-part song that could be sung as a round or in counterpoint. It worked to perfection.

The WED crew worked night and day, combating impossible odds to prepare the four attractions for the fair opening. Walt made his own contributions to the show concepts. One of the scenes for the General Electric exhibit portrayed "Uncle Charlie" sitting in a bathtub with a cake of ice, trying to keep cool in the hot summer. Walt himself climbed into the bathtub to devise the action. "He shouldn't be reading a newspaper; it should be the *Police Gazette*," Walt mused as he sat in the tub. "There should be a glass of iced tea on the toilet seat there. And—let's see—his toes would be sticking up at the other end of the tub, and wiggling. Yeah, let's have his toes wiggling."

As always, Walt put himself in the position of the public. He realized that there would be a lot of waiting in line at the fair, and people wouldn't know whether or not a ride was shut down. "Let 'em see that something is going on," he said, and so the Ford cars and the "Small World" boats loaded outside the attractions. He even positioned the rest rooms to make them convenient for those in line. As at Disneyland, the queues were doubled back, so that those in line would have a sense of advancing toward their goal and would see a constantly changing human vista.

His technicians were astounded by the speed with which Walt absorbed the most complex of procedures. One morning he dropped in at the machine shop and asked a sound technician, Gordon Williams, to explain the workings of the tape machines that were being used for Audio-Animatronic figures. Williams took an hour to detail the functions of the transistors, recorders and other components of the highly complex system. That afternoon Walt returned with a group of General Electric executives. Williams expected to repeat his explanation of the tape system. Instead, Walt did it himself, using the precise terms and telling it all in ten minutes. It was a faultless performance.

The four World's Fair projects were assembled in mock-ups at the studio and shipped piece by piece to New York. As time grew short, some of the components were sent off whether they were working or not. Two hundred WED employees went east to complete the assembly and final tests for the exhibits. They encountered a multitude of unforeseen problems, including New York construction crews who resented the "outsiders" from California. Joe Bowman, who was supervising the building of the "Small World" ride, had won grudging acceptance from the construction workers, but progress was slow, and he was uncertain of meeting the opening-day deadline. With the building half completed, Walt arrived for an inspection. When he finished, he asked, "Joe, is there anything I can do to help?"

"It might help me get things moving around here if you met the men and talked to them," Bowman remarked. Walt chatted with the workers and inquired about their jobs, mentioning that his own father had been a carpenter on the Chicago World's Fair seventy years before. Bowman had no labor problems after Walt's visit.

The WED men themselves were working long hours to complete the exhibits. One evening four of the men were riding in a taxi to Walt's hotel after an inspection tour. "How are your wives getting along in New York?" Walt asked. There was silence, and he realized that the men had been working for weeks in New York, away from their families. The next day, the men began receiving telephone calls from California; their wives were joining them.

As opening day drew near, it appeared that Walt Disney might perform a miracle; the shows were beginning to perform as planned. Except for Mr. Lincoln. The Lincoln figure was by far the most sophisticated that the WED craftsmen had undertaken. Being Lincoln, it had to move with dignity, and Audio-Animatronics seemed too undeveloped to accomplish such a feat. On May 16, a week before opening day, "Great Moments with Mr. Lincoln" passed its test at the WED headquarters in California. The figure was shipped by air freight to New York the next day.

The arrival in New York was a portent of things to come. The delivery truck became ensnarled in the traffic for the opening of Shea Stadium, adjacent to the fair, and delivery was delayed until the following day. WED technicians set up the elaborate controls for the figure and discovered to their horror that it wouldn't work. "Mr. Lincoln" delivered his performance perfectly, then went into convulsions. The dampness of the New York air was suspected as a cause. Also the fluctuations of electrical current caused by the Shea Stadium lights and twelve-billion-candlepower beam in the Tower of Light Pavilion.

The temporary wiring in the Illinois building proved faulty, and electricians couldn't ensure a permanent installation until the day of the opening. A transformer broke down, and the show was without power for two days. Fuses blew and wires crossed, causing "Mr. Lincoln" to behave unpresidentially. Early one morning as the figure had failed for the hundredth time, Marc Davis turned to Jim Algar, who had written the script for the show, and remarked, "Do you suppose that God is mad at Walt for creating Man in his own image?"

Walt was present throughout the testing period, and if he experienced any concern, he didn't show it. He seemed confident that the show would be ready for a preview to be attended by Governor Otto Kerner, Adlai Stevenson and two hundred other Illinois dignitaries on April 20, two days before the fair opening.

For Walt Disney it was a crucial time. He was involved in a venture over which he did not have total control. He was putting his reputation and the skill of his organization in a mammoth arena where nations and corporations had spent millions of dollars in competition with each other. If he failed, he would evoke the scorn of Easterners to whom "Mickey Mouse" was an epithet for something made with eccentric skill. If he succeeded, he might win support for the future plans that were stirring in his mind.

"Mr. Lincoln" wouldn't work. Its electronic ills defied healing, even though the technicians worked around the clock. All of them understood the pressure that Walt faced. There were still rumblings of objections to a "fantasized" Abraham Lincoln, and members of the press were sniping at the project because Walt had decreed there would be no photographs.

On the day of the preview, the five hundred seats of the Lincoln Theater filled with the Illinois dignitaries and members of the international press. His face drawn, Walt watched as his technicians made one last, luckless attempt to master the faults of "Mr. Lincoln." Officials of the Illinois Pavilion spoke to the audience on the other side of the curtain, then Governor Kerner introduced Walt.

Walt lifted an eyebrow and told the audience with a half-smile, "There isn't going to be any show." The guests began to laugh. Walt continued, "It's true. We've worked like beavers to get it ready, but it's not ready, and I won't show it to you until it is. I'm sorry, but there's no point in showing a thing that might fall apart on us." He went on to explain in layman terms what the trouble seemed to be, and he assured the audience that "Great Moments with Mr. Lincoln" would open as soon as it worked.

A week later, "Mr. Lincoln" suddenly began functioning to perfection. On May 2, the Illinois Pavilion opened without fanfare, and it quickly became one of the most popular attractions at the fair. Among the industrial exhibits, General Electric's "Progressland" and Ford's "Magic Skyway" placed second and third in attendance during the first year; General Motors, with a much greater capacity and cost, was first. "It's a Small World" was rated the most charming attraction by most critics.

Before concluding the agreements with Ford and General Electric, Walt had suggested to his negotiator, Bill Cottrell, "Don't you think we ought to get something for the use of the Disney name?" Cottrell agreed, since the two corporations would benefit from association with Disney for the two years previous and the two-year duration of the fair. Cottrell returned from negotiations to report that both Ford and General Electric had agreed to a fee of one million dollars. "Do you think we should have asked for more?" Walt asked wryly.

At the conclusion of the World's Fair, he made a remarkable offer: If the two corporations established their exhibits at Disneyland, the million-dollar fee could be applied to moving expenses. The proposal was favorable not only to Ford and General Electric but to the stockholders of Walt Disney Productions; Disneyland would be the recipient of major attractions created and owned by Walt's personal company, WED.

General Electric's public-opinion surveys indicated that "Progressland" had helped improve the company's image in the wake of the price-fixing scandal—and had also increased sales. G.E. agreed to sponsor the show at Disneyland after the fair closed in 1965. Ford also had excellent results from its "Magic Skyway" but after much consideration decided against the move to Disneyland; executives reasoned they could not afford so large an outlay for promotion in one marketing area. The prehistoric monsters from the Ford show were transferred to the Disneyland train ride; the rest of the figures were scrapped. "It's a Small World" and "Great Moments with Mr. Lincoln" moved to Disneyland intact.

Walt was pleased with the results of his ventures at the New York World's Fair. He had acquired new attractions for Disneyland at minimal cost. He had established an impressive record of working with large corporations for common goals. And by stretching the creative muscles of his imagineers, he had achieved in a brief time what might have taken years to accomplish. Time, to Walt Disney, was important.

26

THE WALL of Walt Disney's conference room was dominated by an aerial map of Disneyland. Next to it was an enlarged reproduction of *Variety*'s annual list of the biggest moneymaking films of all time. By the early 1960s, seven of the top fifty were Disney pictures. One or two more joined the list each year, as Disney grew more dominant in the field of family movies, which the major companies had largely abandoned. "I put that up there to study what are the big moneymakers," Walt said to a reporter as he studied the list. "Most of them aren't the sensational pictures with a lot of sex; they're attractions for the whole family." Walt was careful to avoid any film material which might be offensive to families. He strayed from his principle only once. In *Bon Voyage,* he permitted a scene in which an attractive Parisian girl propositioned Fred MacMurray at a sidewalk cafe. "I caught hell for it," Walt said. "Never again."

In 1964, Walt Disney produced the greatest of his successes, *Mary Poppins*.

The project had had its beginnings twenty years before when Walt picked up a book on the bedside table of his daughter Diane. "What's this?" he asked. She explained that it was a collection of stories about an English nanny who could fly. Walt read the book and recognized immediately that it was Disney material. The author, P. L. Travers, didn't agree. She was an Australian lady who had lived in England and had taken her son to New York to escape the London Blitz of World War II. Walt asked Roy, who was going to New York in early 1944, to call on Mrs. Travers and express the company's interest in acquiring the Mary Poppins stories.

"We had a very nice talk, and she seemed glad to see me," Roy wrote to his brother. "She said in years back she was a contributor to several English magazines, and on a couple of occasions she had written about Disney pictures." Mrs. Travers told Roy that she owned the copyright, but her American publishers had an interest in what she did in motion pictures. "I had a hunch that this was a 'stall' at the moment, for the way she said it, it didn't seem logical to me," Roy said. "It seemed to me that she was fencing."

Roy added in his letter: "Mrs. Travers said she could not conceive of Mary Poppins as a cartoon character. I tried to tell her that this was a matter that should be left for future study—that it might be best for *Mary Poppins* to be produced in a combination of live action and cartoon, using the animation to get the fantasy and illusion of the Mary Poppins character. I told her that we were thoroughly qualified and equipped to produce either medium, and, as a matter of fact, are producing such types of pictures."

Walt followed up Roy's visit with a letter to Mrs. Travers inviting her to visit the studio and discuss what kind of production she had in mind. She remained interested but noncommittal. That continued to be her attitude over the years. When Walt visited England during the making of his first live-action films there, he paid a call at Mrs. Travers's home in Chelsea and discussed the filming of *Mary Poppins* over tea. Still she refused to relinquish the movie rights. It was not until 1960 that Mrs. Travers finally agreed to deal with the Disneys. By this time, Walt's eagerness for the property had grown so acute that he paid an extraordinary price: he gave her approval of the screen treatment.

Robert Stevenson, who had proved with *Old Yeller*, *The Absent-Minded Professor* and *In Search of the Castaways* to be the most serviceable of Disney directors, declared himself to be the obvious choice to help prepare and to direct *Mary Poppins*. After all, he had been a boy with an English nanny in an upper-middle-class family in Edwardian England. Bill Walsh, who was to co-produce, and Don DaGradi, a veteran Disney story man, were charged with devising a script from the series of Travers stories.

Once again Walsh employed a technique which had proved successful: he injected Walt Disney into the script. The father of the London family became the important figure instead of the mother, and he was instilled with the same qualities Walsh recognized in Walt: Mr. Banks was outwardly a strong-willed person, though he was soft underneath; he was cunning and resourceful and got along well with the children; and he was "always in trouble with the bank."

Walt assigned Robert and Richard Sherman to write the songs for *Mary Poppins*. They returned in two weeks with sketchy versions of five songs that could fit into the script, including "Feed the Birds" and "Supercalifragilisticexpialidocious." Walt liked them, especially "Feed the Birds." "That song'll replace Brahms' Lullaby," he declared, and he cried every time he heard it. The Sherman brothers were told to work closely with Don DaGradi, and Walt gave them an office near his. "Any time you want to talk to me, call my secretary and come on over," he said.

Mrs. Travers made two journeys to Burbank to view the storyboards for *Mary Poppins*. She objected to many of the liberties that had been taken with her characters, and adjustments had to be made. Walt Disney exercised his own considerable powers of persuasion to win Mrs. Travers's approval. By the time she returned to England, she seemed convinced that the Disney innovations had originated in her own books.

Walt closely followed the writing of the script, making contributions from his intimate knowledge of London. He had become an anglophile during the making of his four English features and in his revisits of London. He loved to prowl the old streets, visiting antique shops and apothecaries and chatting with the proprietors. Once he pressed an unwilling Lilly into a search for a Disney Street; when they finally found it, Lilly was amused to learn that it had once been called Dunghill Lane. Walt was fascinated with the buskers who made a precarious living by entertaining in pubs and on the London streets. He introduced the idea of having Bert, Mary Poppins's exuberant friend, make music as a one-man band. Walt remembered the chalk artists who drew scenes on the sidewalk in front of the National Gallery, and the script included Bert's sidewalk mural. Walt also suggested a fantasy sequence in which horses leaped off a carousel and raced through the countryside.

During the planning stages, Bill Walsh and Don DaGradi sought a theme for the chimney sweeps' dance atop the London roofs. They explained their need to Peter Ellenshaw, the British-born matte artist and designer whom Walt had brought to the studio after his work on *Treasure Island*. Ellenshaw described a ritual he shared with other students during his college days in London. Returning from a day at the seaside, the young men stopped at pubs along the route back to the city. After a pint or two, they locked arms and performed a dance to the time of "Knees Up, Mother Brown." It consisted of raising knees as high as possible, then racing to the other side of the pub. The owner usually ejected the roisterers because of the disruption.

"Can you do it for us?" Walsh asked. Ellenshaw could, and did. Walsh and DaGradi were charmed by the exuberant dance, and they hastened to show it to Walt. This time both Ellenshaw and DaGradi performed it in Walt's office.

"Hey, that's great!" Walt responded. "Let me try it."

Now the three men plunged across the room, knees high, to the chant of "Knees Up, Mother Brown." Walt immediately sent for the Sherman brothers and demonstrated the dance to them. They were assigned to write an adaptation of the old song, and they produced "Step in Time" in half an hour. It provided the background for the liveliest number in *Mary Poppins*.

Walt's total control of the script process can be seen in the various drafts of the *Mary Poppins* screenplay. The pages are marked by the familiar Disney handprinting as he made additions and deletions in the scenes. In the opening sequence of the first-draft screenplay, dated July 12, 1961, these emendations appear:

Camera follows Mr. Banks down street on his way home from work—Let him open door on the upset household. . . . Nanna's dialogue: "It's not only the children but the adolescent adults, etc." The cook and maid should be peeking out doors at this scene . . . (eliminating screams of Jane and Michael). This makes kids brats. Let Nanna Kate do all the screaming . . . She has packed in such a hurry that some of her clothes stick out of the bag. . . . [Mr. Banks's] bowler, umbrella and brief case are very English. . . . Mr. Banks brings money home in evening in his brief case—takes his lunch to work in it each morning. . . . [of the exchange between the departing Nanna and Mrs. Banks:] We see all of this thru Mr. Banks' eyes. . . . Mr. Banks hangs up bowler hat and umbrella and carries brief case and evening paper. . . . [substituting dialogue:] Mr. Banks: "What! Another position?" Nanna: "Yes! To get a little rest I have just accepted a position in a lunatic asylum (or boiler factory). Good day, Mr. Banks." . . . [Mr. and Mrs. Banks compose an advertisement for a new nanny:] As Mrs. Banks starts to read it back, dissolve to front page of *London Times* which is all want-ads—camera zooms in to Mr. Banks' ad. Mrs. Banks continues to read—or a chorus of nannies' voices reading—the complete advertisement. Dissolve to morning shot, exterior Banks house with scores of nannies, etc.

Walt's editing continues throughout the script, changing a word of dialogue, eliminating whole scenes, adding visual touches. Subsequent versions of *Mary Poppins* received the same treatment. A script dated December 31, 1962, contains comments on almost every page:

Played to camera . . . They forget camera and play to each other. . . . Bad taste [eliminating a line about the cook's cold—". . . wheezing and drizzling like a broken dredge pump"] . . . Is this the only use of kitchen set? . . . Use mechanical robins here. . . . Do we need Mary in this? . . . This is sad; use later. . . . Would Mary have a nanny? . . . Father should sing part of this. . . . Background music: "Tuppence the bag" . . .

Mrs. Travers had portrayed Mary Poppins as a middle-aged woman, and Walt first considered Bette Davis for the role. But as the score by the Sherman brothers developed, it appeared that the role would require a singing actress. Mary Martin was a candidate, but she decided against a return to films. Walt began thinking that Mary Poppins could be played by a younger actress, and he was receptive when his secretary, Tommie Wilck, suggested Julie Andrews, who had starred in the musical *My Fair Lady* and was then appearing on Broadway in *Camelot*. He asked to see film of Miss Andrews and was told that a screen test she had previously made had been destroyed; it had made her seem unsuitable for movies. Walt attended a performance of *Camelot* on his return from Europe late in 1961. He was impressed by her stage presence, her beauty, and her clear, lyrical soprano; he was overwhelmed by her loud, sure whistle in the number

"What Do the Simple Folk Do?" He met her backstage after the performance and proceeded to relate the entire plot of *Mary Poppins*. She was impressed with such attention from Walt Disney, but she was not certain that she wanted to make her film debut as a flying nanny.

On February 26, 1962, Walt wrote Miss Andrews: "We would still like to have you consider playing the role of 'Mary Poppins' in the Pamela Travers story, and I have just asked our Casting Department to contact your agent to see if some workable arrangements can be made. As it is difficult to visualize a story of this type from a written script, I thought you might fly out to Hollywood the early part of June and then you could sit down with us and get a first-hand idea of what the finished story will be. We can play the songs, lay out the story line and I am sure after seeing this sort of presentation you will be able to make your own decision. . . . We definitely feel in our own minds that, with your talent, you would create an unforgettable Mary Poppins, and we hope you will want to portray this wonderful character after you have seen the presentation which we can have ready for you in June. . . ."

Miss Andrews and her husband, Tony Walton, came to the studio after she completed her contract for *Camelot*. She saw the storyboards and heard the Sherman brothers' songs and liked the material, although she had some reservations. She returned to England to await the birth of her first child. Walt wrote her on June 22 that "the 'go-ahead' from you and your manager to start negotiations on *Mary Poppins* . . . made all of us here very happy. In the meantime, we are revamping *Mary*—putting in better songs—and the story is shaping up much better. Your helpful criticism has inspired the boys to dig in, which I feel is going to pay off very well. So before long, we will have a new approach to the story. . . ."

A girl named Emma Kate was born to Julie and Tony Walton in November, and they came to California in February to begin preparations for *Mary Poppins*. Walton was assigned to design the costumes in the film. Miss Andrews's agreement with the studio stipulated that she would be released from the film if Warner Brothers should cast her as Eliza Doolittle in the movie version of *My Fair Lady*. Jack L. Warner, who was producing the film, chose Audrey Hepburn instead.

With Julie Andrews cast as Mary Poppins, Walt sought an American actor for the role of Bert, the cheerful chimney sweep. Walt didn't want the film to be too British, and mixtures of accents never bothered him—he had successfully cast Hayley Mills as an American girl. When Dick Van Dyke was suggested for Bert, Walt admitted he had never seen him on television. He viewed a segment of *The Dick Van Dyke Show* in a projection room and decided immediately to cast Van Dyke as Bert. Ed Wynn, whom Walt had used in several comedies, was assigned to play the eccentric Uncle Albert. The rest of the cast was mostly English: David Tomlinson, whom Bill Walsh had seen in a British comedy, *Up the Creek;* Glynis Johns, who had appeared in *Sword and the Rose* and *Rob Roy;* Hermione Baddeley; Reginald Owen; Elsa Lanchester; Arthur Treacher; and two talented youngsters, Karen Dotrice and Matthew Garber.

The filming of *Mary Poppins*, although lengthy, proved to be as smooth and pleasant as had been the making of *Dumbo*. Some of the sequences were designed for combination live action and cartoon, and Walt instructed Robert Stevenson not to concern himself about the animation that would be filled in later. "Don't worry," Walt said, "whatever the action is, my animators will top it." He was challenging them, and they knew it.

Walt made a habit of "walking through" the sets after they had been built, searching for ways to use them. Bill Walsh described a visit by Walt to the Bankses' living room in search of reaction to the firing of Admiral Boom's cannon: "Walt got vibes off the props. As he walked around the set he said, 'How about having the vase fall off and the maid catches it with her toe?' Or, 'Let's have the grand piano roll across the room and the mother catches it as she straightens the picture frame.' "

In the early stages of production, Van Dyke was being tested in various makeups for later sequences. To relieve the boredom, he delivered snatches of comedy routines. One of them was his impression of an aged man desperately striving to step down from a sidewalk curb without injury. When Walt viewed the test in a projection room, he decided immediately to cast Van Dyke as the antediluvian Mr. Dawes, board chairman of the bank. "And build a six-inch riser on the board-room set," Walt instructed, "so Dick can do that stepping-down routine."

Mary Poppins was premiered at Grauman's Chinese Theater in Hollywood on August 27, 1964. The industry audience responded with cheers, and Walt realized that he had a hit of immense proportions. He was enjoying the triumphant glow at the post-premiere party when Mrs. Travers approached him. "It's quite nice," she began. "Miss Andrews is satisfactory as Mary Poppins, but Mr. Van Dyke is all wrong, and I don't really like mixing the little cartoon figures with the live actors. When do we start cutting it?"

Walt smiled indulgently. "The contract says that when the picture is finished, it's my property," he replied. "We aren't going to change a thing."

Movie critics, many of whom had deprecated the postwar Disney films, devoted columns of praise to *Mary Poppins*. Bosley Crowther wrote in the New York *Times*: ". . . the visual and aural felicities (Disney and company) have added to this sparkling film —the enchantments of a beautiful production, some deliciously animated sequences, some exciting and nimble dancing and a spinning musical score—make it the nicest entertainment that has opened at the Music Hall this year." Judith Crist in the New York *Herald Tribune*: "The performers surpass even the technical wizardry of the film . . . Miss Andrews is superb at song and dance and the heart of the matter." Hollis Alpert in *Saturday Review:* "One of the most magnificent pieces of entertainment ever to come from Hollywood." Even Disney-hating *Time* magazine conceded: "To make a good show better, Disney employs all the vast magic-making machinery at his command. The sets are luxuriant, the songs lilting, the scenario witty but impeccably sentimental, and the supporting cast only a pinfeather short of perfection."

Although he claimed to be indifferent to critical response, Walt Disney could not conceal his pleasure at the outpouring of praise. The box-office figures mounted astonishingly, and in its first release *Mary Poppins* amassed worldwide rentals of $44,000,000. Walt was delighted when the film drew thirteen Academy nominations; it was the first time that a Disney movie had contended in the leading categories. *My Fair Lady* won the Oscar as best picture of 1964, but Julie Andrews, who had evoked sympathy by being overlooked for the film version of the Eliza Doolittle role she had created, was named best actress for her role in *Mary Poppins.*

Walt refused to entertain suggestions for a sequel to *Mary Poppins,* clinging to his old theory that "you can't top pigs with pigs." To devote a year or two of his creative life to a sequel was unthinkable. "Time is getting on, and I still have things left to do," he remarked. "I don't want to go back and cover the same ground."

The extraordinary success of *Mary Poppins* prompted renewed awe for the achievements of Walt Disney. While he enjoyed recognition of his talents, Walt distrusted an excess of praise. Among his associates, he responded with an expletive. In the presence of strangers, he was polite but uneasy. One noon he entertained a group of industrialists at his table in the commissary, and they were extravagant in their praise of Walt Disney. Donn Tatum recognized Walt's discomfiture and tried to relieve the situation by remarking, "Well, Walt, there's only one thing left for you to do, and that's to walk on water."

Walt's eyes twinkled and he answered, "I've already tried that and it doesn't work."

His creative touch extended to everything, from a new cartoon feature based on Kipling's *The Jungle Book* to a projected Disneyland attraction, the Haunted Mansion, to a musical film based on a Broadway play, *The Happiest Millionaire*. He even found time to write an original story for a film to star Dick Van Dyke, *Lt. Robin Crusoe, U.S.N.* The idea came to him on an airplane, and he jotted the plot down on a scrap of paper. Later he insisted on screen credit for his contribution. It read: "Original story by Retlaw Elias Yensid," a backward version of his own name.

With all his activities, he found time for small kindnesses. He invariably sent notes of condolence to friends and employees whose parents died. When old schoolmates and teachers and business associates from his Midwest years wrote him, he responded with long, reminiscing letters. He supported many charities, particularly those that benefited children. He maintained a warm relationship with St. Joseph's Hospital, across the street from the studio, donating to fund drives and ordering decoration of the children's wing with Disney characters.

Christmas was a time of trial for Walt's secretaries. He maintained a file of hundreds of children of his personal friends, members of the press, studio workers, film executives, etc. To each child went gifts of Disney character merchandise—one important item apiece, plus a few little ones. The gifts continued until the child reached the age of twelve, then he or she was dropped from the list and received a Christmas card instead. Walt's secretaries were charged with assembling the packages, and each had to be wrapped separately. A room in a studio warehouse was converted to a Santa's workshop, and Walt dropped in to inspect the packages and make sure that his specifications were observed.

Walt usually left his family shopping until a day or two before Christmas, and his secretaries were enlisted to help. Often he settled on expensive perfumes for Lilly and their daughters. Finding gifts for him was a recurring problem; after opening packages he often grumbled, "I don't need that." One year his daughters presented him with a handsome volume of the complete works of Leonardo da Vinci. "What are you trying to do—educate me?" he muttered. But later that day Sharon and Diane saw him in a corner poring over the book. Walt often found more delight in the simplest of gifts than in the lavish presents from industry leaders. Hazel George had a good sense of what would please the boss, and she rarely spent over a dollar. One Christmas she gave him a dime-store kaleidoscope, and it fascinated him. He insisted that visitors to his office peer at the changing patterns of light and color.

He enjoyed sharing his enthusiasms with others. When Robert Stevenson and his son were journeying eastward on the Santa Fe Super Chief, the director was surprised to receive an invitation to ride in the locomotive. Knowing that Stevenson was a railroad buff, Walt had arranged the treat with the president of Santa Fe.

In the 1960s, Walt acquired a new toy—a company airplane. Since his activities were taking him all over the country, he concluded that a private plane would prove a convenience. As he did with most projects he contemplated, he ordered a survey by Harrison (Buzz) Price, the Stanford Research Institute executive who had been encouraged by Walt to form his own company, Economics Research Associates. The survey established the wisdom of Walt's plan for a company airplane, and he made the proposal to Roy. Roy thought it a bad idea, and Walt countered by saying, "Well, I've got a little money; I'll do it myself." Roy finally agreed to the purchase of a Queen Air Beechcraft.

Walt took delight in planning each trip, plotting the itinerary on maps in his office over his evening Scotch.

When passengers arrived at the plane's home base at Lockheed Airport, he loaded their luggage aboard. During the flight he served the drinks and supervised the galley. For years Walt had yearned to pilot a plane, and on occasion the company pilot, Chuck Malone, allowed Walt to take over the controls. Walt insisted that Ron Miller and Bob Brown learn how to land the plane, in case of emergency when they were flying with their families. After Chuck Malone became ill while piloting the plane alone, Walt established the rule that two pilots would be required during all flights.

Walt was determined to overcome Roy's opposition to the plane, and he planned a trip to the redwood country of Northern California and to Sun Valley, Idaho, for himself, Lilly, Roy and Edna. Roy was an uneasy passenger at first, but Walt persuaded him to assume the role of navigator. Roy, who had served as a navigator in the Navy in World War I, took over the task with enthusiasm, and he became a convert to the company plane.

Walt was convinced that the plane was an efficient tool for the company, not merely a frill for the executives. He grew more impatient with the claims of bankers and journalists that he was a profligate. He firmly believed he was not. He chastised producers who exceeded their budgets, and he was always seeking means to cut down production costs. Walt kept himself apprised of the company's fiscal matters by means of a weekly memorandum he received from Orbin V. (Mel) Melton of the business department. Each Friday, Melton sent Walt a message consisting of three subjects written in capital letters, followed by a single sentence. Melton's succinctness was purposeful; he realized that Walt would not take the time to absorb anything longer. Usually the three sentences contained enough information; rarely did Walt call Melton for a detailed explanation.

While he respected the financial needs of the company, Walt refused to be limited by them. At a meeting to discuss some major changes in Disneyland, Marc

Davis, who had worked on the plans, began his presentation by saying, "Well, I've got an expensive way and a cheap way of doing this." Walt rose from his seat and walked to where Davis was standing. Placing a hand on Davis's shoulder, Walt said, "Marc, you and I do not worry about whether anything is cheap or expensive. We only worry if it's good. I have a theory that if it's good enough, the public will pay you back for it. I've got a big building full of all kinds of guys who worry about costs and money. You and I just worry about doing a good show."

As Disneyland began its tenth year, it had grown from twenty-two attractions to forty-seven, from an investment of $17,000,000 to $48,000,000. Forty-two million people had passed through the main gate. Walt and Roy Disney appeared at a tenth-anniversary dinner attended by those who had helped them build Disneyland into one of the showplaces of the world.

Roy was characteristically modest in his remarks to the audience: "Well, a lot of you probably don't even know me or didn't know me, but I *have* been here. And along with the rest of you, I've had my nervous moments, too. But it has been a wonderful ten years. And while we have the public to thank for their wonderful attendance, we also have to thank you people that were the key gang in handling that public and in giving them satisfaction, pleasing them, and making them come back like they have—and having the word-of-mouth go around the world as it has. I have seen in my travels far and wide that the reputation of Disneyland stands out primarily, even beyond the show itself, for the courtesy of the people handling the public, and the cleanliness and friendliness of the place. I've always said, in my end of the work, that it takes people to run a business. You people have been the heart and soul of this business and we appreciate it no end. And we say congratulations to *you* for doing the grand job that you have done all these ten years."

Walt was in a mellow, reminiscing mood when he spoke. He talked about hiring the singer Donald Novis to appear in the Golden Horseshoe Revue, and how Novis recommended a young comic he had worked with in Australia, Wally Boag. Walt recalled his first meeting with Joe Fowler, the retired admiral, and how "little by little we sort of got him trapped" into taking over the building and operating of Disneyland. Walt continued:

Well, we had a lot of problems putting this thing together. There was pressure about money. A lot of people didn't believe in what we were doing, and we were putting the squeeze play where we could. I remember that we were dealing with all three networks. They wanted our television show, and I kept insisting that I wanted this amusement park. And everybody said, "What the hell does he want that damned amusement park for?" I couldn't think up a good reason—except that I wanted it. . . .

ABC needed a television show *so damn bad* that they bought the amusement park! Well, five years later, my brother figured we'd better buy those guys out. They had a third interest; they had only a half million dollars invested in that park. But my brother figured, "If we don't buy them out now, we're going to be paying them a lot more later." He paid them, after five years, seven and a half million dollars for their five-hundred-thousand-dollar investment. And it was a smart move.

Well, my brother's had the worries of getting this money and fighting the bankers and things; and there was a time, I think it was after we opened the park, that our bankers said to my brother, "About that amusement park—we're not going to let you put another nickel into it." And my brother said, "Well, if you're going to start running our business, we're going out and find another place to borrow money." And by gosh, they finally gave him the money.

But it's been nip-and-tuck. I mean, when we opened, if we could have bought more land, we would have. Then we'd have had control and it wouldn't look too much like a second-rate Las Vegas around here. We'd have had a little better chance to control it. But we ran out of money, and then by the time we did have a little money, everybody got wise to what was going on and we couldn't buy anything around the place at all! . . .

This time, after ten years, I want to join my brother and thank you all who have been here with us and have been a part of making this thing come across. But I just want to leave you with this thought: that it's just sort of been a dress rehearsal, and that we're just getting started. So if any of you start to rest on your laurels, I mean, just forget it. . . .

Honors continued to shower on Walt Disney. The highest came on September 14, 1964, when President Johnson presented him with the Medal of Freedom at the White House.

Walt flew east in the company plane with a few of his lawn-bowling cronies from Palm Springs. They paused for a lawn-bowling tournament en route, then went on to Washington. Walt had ample time before the ceremonies, so he asked his driver to stop at the Lincoln Memorial. Walt stood before the heroic statue of Lincoln for minutes, reading the measured words carved in marble as his eyes filled with tears. Then he went on to the White House, where Lyndon Johnson gave him the nation's highest civilian honor. The citation: "Artist and impresario, in the course of entertaining an age, Walt Disney has created an American folklore."

The accomplishments of Walt Disney impressed even his own grandchildren. He delighted in telling the story of how he and Lilly were babysitting with the children of Diane and Ron Miller when a thunderstorm struck during the night. The children came scrambling to the grandparents' bed and one of them pleaded after a clap of thunder: "Turn it off, Grandpa."

He related the story to Hazel George during one of their therapy sessions. She replied, "And did you?" Walt grunted and said, "You know what my next project is going to be? An Audio-Animatronic nurse."

27

LIKE MOST of Walt Disney's projects, CalArts had a long history. It dated back to the early 1930s, when Walt decided to train a new generation of cartoonists so he could accomplish his goals in animation. The result was a liaison with the Chouinard Art Institute, and Walt continued to support the school long after he had discontinued classes for animators. Chouinard had flourished after World War II because of large numbers of veterans who studied there under the G.I. Bill of Rights. But poor management and an embezzling employee brought the school to the edge of insolvency in the late 1950s.

Nelbert M. Chouinard, who had founded the school in 1921, asked Marc Davis, a Disney animator who had been a teacher at the school, if he thought Disney would donate a scholarship. Davis knew of Walt's respect for Mrs. Chouinard and suggested asking for a luncheon appointment to explain the school's plight. Walt met with Mrs. Chouinard and was immediately responsive; he remembered that Chouinard Art Institute had given Disney artists free classes when the studio could not afford to pay for them. He responded with money to help the school in its troubled period, and he contributed the studio's financial expertise. Walt realized that Chouinard's problems required more than periodic infusions of cash. He worked with his staff on ways to modernize the school, proposing a widened curriculum and a showcase where students could display and sell their art.

Walt's own taste in art leaned toward the dramatic paintings of Rembrandt, Goya, Velázquez and El Greco, as well as the illustrations of Paul Gustave Doré; he had also been influenced in his youth by the Ashcan School of American artists, particularly Robert Henri. But Walt was not opposed to abstract art (indeed, portions of *Fantasia, Dumbo* and other Disney cartoons featured abstractionism). He believed students should find their own mode of expression—*after* they had been schooled in the fundamentals of art. During a visit to Chouinard, he was irritated to see first-year students using paint rollers on canvases.

He believed in an intermingling of the arts: "What young artists need is a school where they can learn a variety of skills, a place where there is cross-pollination." Walt's plan had a practical side; such a school could provide future talent for his own as well as other Hollywood studios, fulfilling in a more formalized and broadened way the function of the Disney school for animators in the 1930s. Walt commissioned Economics Research Associates to survey the problems of Chouinard Art Institute and offer possible solutions. In time there were twenty studies, offering a variety of proposals including a City of the Arts, a cluster of interrelated schools where students could polish their skills and market their works to help support their studies.

The school project began to take form when Walt learned that the Los Angeles Conservatory of Music was in the same condition as Chouinard. The conservatory, founded in 1883 when Mrs. Emily Valentine brought the first grand piano to Los Angeles, had been victimized by an embezzler, was declining rapidly because of faulty management, and was being supported largely by a single patron, Mrs. Richard Von Hagen,

wife of a Los Angeles lawyer and businessman. Walt
lunched with Mrs. Von Hagen, and they had an animated discussion about their problem schools. She
proposed the concept of a college patterned after the
California Institute of Technology, encompassing all
the arts in the same manner that Caltech included the
sciences; the new school would be called the California Institute of the Arts. CalArts began its history in
1962 with the merger of Chouinard Art Institute and
the Los Angeles Conservatory of Music.

Walt embarked on planning a college for artists
with the same thoroughness he had employed in con-
ceiving Disneyland. He sent researchers across the
country to visit art schools and conservatories, studying the curricula and facilities, measuring classrooms
and corridor space. Walt sought advice from such ad-
ministrators as Lee DuBridge of Caltech and Franklin
Murphy of UCLA. He commissioned his own artists
to create brochures and sketches of prospective cam-
puses.

As the concept of CalArts grew, he considered
where the school should be located. He became enthusiastic about hilltop property across the Cahuenga
Pass from the Hollywood Bowl. The land belonged to
the County of Los Angeles, and the County Supervisors agreed to release it for CalArts. All that was
needed was permission by the State Legislature; and
the Democratic leader of the Assembly, Jesse Unruh,
assured that would be forthcoming. But at the last moment Walt decided against the property. He concluded
that the steep slopes would make construction difficult.
Most of all, he did not want to deal with government
bureaucracy. His wartime experiences remained vivid
and painful.

Thirty-six other locations were considered until Walt
and Roy decided on a simple solution: Walt Disney
Productions would donate thirty-eight acres of its Golden Oak Ranch, a 728-acre spread in Placerita Canyon, north of the San Fernando Valley. The ranch,
where gold had been discovered by a Spaniard in 1842,

had been bought by the studio in 1959 as a site for
film locations.

Walt talked about CalArts in a 1964 press interview
in his office:

> We've got to fight against bigness. If a school gets
> too large, you lose an intimacy with the students;
> they begin to feel they're just part of a big com-
> plex. I don't think you can create as well in too
> big a plant. That's why I always tried to avoid
> bigness in the studio. . . . I like the workshop idea,
> with students being able to drop in and learn all
> kinds of arts. You know, a kid might start out
> in art and end up as a talented musician. A school
> should offer a kind of cross-pollenization that
> would develop the best in its students. . . . I
> started out to be a political cartoonist. I grew up
> on my dad's socialist paper, *Appeal to Reason,*
> and I thought sure I was going to draw political
> cartoons. But then I took some children's classes
> at the Kansas City Art Institute; I went two
> winters, three nights a week, and my ideas about
> my future began to change. I learned a lot from
> professional teachers at the Institute—they were
> more professional artists than teachers. . . . Imag-
> ination is an intuitive thing; I think it's some-
> thing you're born with. But it has to be developed.
> I learned a lot as a kid by going to vaudeville
> houses. The father of a friend of mine in Kansas
> City owned one, and we saw the shows three
> nights a week. When I moved to Chicago, I went
> to the vaudeville and burlesque shows more often.
> One house had eighteen acts of vaudeville; I saw
> every one and built my gag file. . . . I might have
> become a political cartoonist, except that I was ex-
> posed to movie cartoons at the Kansas City Film
> Ad Company. There were a lot of cartoonists
> there, but none of them had my ambition to do
> anything else. The artist just did his work and
> turned it over to the cameraman to photograph.

But I wasn't satisfied with that. I watched the cameraman do his work, and I asked questions: "What's your exposure?" "Why do you shoot it that way?" He was secretive at first, but then he told me all about it, and he let me run the camera myself. So I learned. . . . The trouble with universities is that they restrict students from learning about a lot of things. The young people have to get so many credits toward their degree, and they don't have a chance to delve into other subjects. That won't be true at CalArts. Students will be able to take anything—art, drama, music, dance, writing. They'll graduate with a degree of Bachelor of Fine Arts, and if they want a Bachelor of Arts they can go to other colleges and acquire a few more credits. . . . The student body of CalArts shouldn't be over two thousand, and as many as possible should reside on campus. There should be some allowance for those who are talented, yet are not students; they should be able to express themselves without worrying about grades. There will be a lot of scholarships at CalArts. Those who can pay will pay; those who can't will get scholarships. We don't want any dilettantes at CalArts. We want people with talent. That will be the one factor in getting into CalArts: talent.

Walt's opposition to a second Disneyland weakened as his organization at WED matured in its skills. Walt saw the chance of doing something beyond duplication of a theme park. He concluded that another Disneyland could be used as the "wienie" to accomplish his greater goal: planning and building a new kind of city that would show how people could live in a clean, handsome and stimulating community.

The beginnings of his thinking might be traced to the building of the Burbank studio in the late 1930s. Walt was able to plan the Burbank plant in every detail, down to the contour of the animator's chair. Disneyland was again the product of meticulous planning, and, within the confines of the park, it worked. But Walt was appalled by how the promoters made a "second-rate Las Vegas" out of the periphery.

After spending his adult life in Los Angeles, he had witnessed how the automobile had changed a sunny, attractive town into a concrete-paved, smog-choked metropolis. He wanted to combat the tyranny of the car and restore a degree of the comfortable life that his generation had known earlier in the century.

Research began in 1958, when Walt commissioned Economics Research Associates to determine the most favorable location in the East for another Disneyland. The answer confirmed Walt's thinking: Florida. The weather allowed a year-round operation, which was necessary for such a large investment. The single drawback was Florida's population. Disneyland had been attracting between 60 to 65 percent of its 5,000,000 annual visitors within the state; whereas Florida's entire population was 6,500,000. Walt wasn't concerned. "We just gotta get the folks up north to want to come down," he reasoned.

Two more surveys were made in 1959: one to determine the best place within Florida, the other to evaluate the possibility of a City of Tomorrow to surround the theme park. The research suggested Palm Beach as the most favorable location. RCA, which wanted to join with Disney in a theme park, began negotiations for twelve thousand acres in North Palm Beach. But the two parties couldn't reach an agreement, and Palm Beach was dropped as a potential site. That suited Walt, who retained his prejudice against placing his park near the ocean. He didn't want to compete with the beach atmosphere; furthermore, the Florida coast was subject to humidity and hurricanes. "I want to be inland," he declared. "We'll create our own water."

In 1961, Walt ordered another survey to determine the ideal location. Ocala was the number-one choice; second, Orlando. Again the Florida Project was put aside as Walt embarked on the planning for the New

York World's Fair. In 1963, when design of the four exhibits neared completion, Walt decided to begin preparing another challenge for WED. He ordered a third evaluation of the Florida site. Previous findings had overlooked an important future route of the Florida freeway system. The new data pointed to Orlando as the ideal location.

In November 1963, Walt made a fateful flight to the East. Along with Donn Tatum, Card Walker, Joe Potter, Buzz Price and Jack Sayers, a Disneyland executive, Walt sought a final location of the company's next theme park. The party stopped at St. Louis, where civic leaders had been seeking Disney's participation for a riverfront park as part of the rejuvenation of the downtown city. But there was too little land, and the financial risk seemed too great. Next came Niagara Falls, where Disney had been asked to join a development on the Canadian side. The long, cold winter precluded a profitable operation there. A site between Washington, D.C., and Baltimore was also rejected because weather would not permit year-round operation.

The plane headed south. Walt directed the pilot to fly along the coast of Florida so he could satisfy himself that he did not want to build a park on the ocean. The travelers headed inland, flying at a low altitude—Walt always liked to fly as low as possible to study the landscape. The plane circled over the limitless swamps and forests near Orlando, and Walt peered down with calculating eyes. Then he ordered the pilot to New Orleans. As the Disney executives drove from the airport to their hotel, they noticed crowds of people huddled around radios and watching television sets in store windows. When Walt arrived at the hotel he learned what had happened: President Kennedy had been shot.

Walt was shocked and saddened, and he said little on the gloomy return flight to California. Before the plane arrived in Burbank, he remarked, "Well, that's the place—central Florida."

Walt and Roy agreed to seek enough property in

central Florida so the new project could be developed as a totality, avoiding the visual ruin of Anaheim. Robert Foster, secretary and general counsel of Disneyland, was assigned to the delicate operation of acquiring the land in a quiet manner that would prevent prices from soaring. He studied geodetic survey maps, searched Orlando, Ocala and Lakeland newspapers for land offerings, read circulars from real-estate dealers. In February 1964, Roy Disney and several executives flew to Florida; Walt was left behind for fear that he would be recognized. The travelers registered at hotels under assumed names and made unobtrusive surveys of the areas. They reported to Walt that several large parcels of land were available. "Okay, let's go after some land," he said.

Robert Foster began operations in Florida, functioning with the secrecy of a James Bond. Through the New York law firm that represented Disney—Donovan, Leisure, Newton and Irvine—he located a Miami lawyer, Paul Helliwell, who had important connections in the state. Without identifying his company, Foster told his purpose: "To acquire a large parcel of land for recreational purposes, large enough for land use as well." Helliwell referred Foster to Roy Hawkins, a real estate dealer with statewide experience. Foster identified himself to Hawkins as Robert Price, his first two names. Although he later disclosed his real identity and that of his employer to Hawkins, Foster remained "Bob Price" in negotiations with landowners.

In May 1964, Foster and Hawkins had narrowed their choices to three areas—one between De Land and Daytona Beach, another near Osceola City, a third in Orange County near Orlando. Foster made a presentation to Disney executives in Burbank, arguing for the De Land-Daytona Beach property. Walt ended the proposal by interrupting, "Bob, what in the hell are you doing way up there?" He reminded Foster of surveys that showed the northern location would be too cold for a year-round operation and for the park's vegetation.

The Osceola City property was owned by a state senator, Irlo Bronson, who had a commitment to sell 2,500 of his 10,000 acres. The Disney efforts were centered on Orange County. There were three major areas: 12,000 acres owned by two cousins; Bay Lake property owned by twelve Orlando couples; another lake area of 1,200 acres belonging to a pair of brothers. Forty-eight small parcels, called outages, had separate owners. By August, the three major holdings were tied down with options. Senator Bronson decided to sell his entire 10,000 acres at Osceola City, and the property was acquired by Disney as an alternative if the Orange County operation foundered.

A crisis developed with the discovery that the owners did not control mineral rights; they belonged to a mineral company and Tufts College. After lengthy negotiations, both agreed to a settlement and relinquished their rights.

The major problem was the outages. The lake property had been subdivided in 1913 and plots had been sold through mail-order catalogues. A fifty-person task force traced descendants of the original buyers and offered to purchase the property. A conference room in Burbank contained a huge map of Orange County, and each day the state of acquisitions was plotted, like territory won by troops in a war. Walt visited the room daily.

Placing his palm over the intersection of two highways, he said, "Now this is very important to our future development. If we can get all the property here, we can do something imaginative with it. If we can't get it all, then we'll be stuck with something conventional."

During one of the meetings, Bob Foster mentioned a large parcel that was available. "Buy it," Walt said. Roy protested that they had already committed themselves to a huge amount of acreage. "Yes, Roy," Walt replied, "but wouldn't you love to own seven thousand acres around Disneyland now? And anyway, we can always sell this parcel later if we have to."

Walt couldn't resist seeing the property himself, even though he realized the danger if he were recognized. He flew off to Florida in the company plane with a few of his executives. When the plane stopped to refuel at a Florida airport, all of the travelers started heading for the terminal. One of them said to Walt, "You can't go; you'll be spotted." Walt grudgingly agreed to remain on the field. A young mechanic stared at him and remarked, "Are you Walt Disney?" "Hell, no," Walt replied. "I get mistaken for him all the time, and if I ever run into that s.o.b., I'm going to tell him what I think of him."

Walt viewed the proposed site from the air. The land was a broad vista of cypress groves and black-watered swamps, and it seemed a forbidding task to raise a theme park and a city of the future from the wilderness. But Walt was immensely pleased. "Yeah, it's going to be fine," he said.

Rumors continued to circulate in Orlando about who was buying options on the vast property. Some said it was Ford Motor Company, others suspected McDonnell-Douglas or Disney. When Roy Hawkins sent postcards from Seattle to friends in Orlando, many citizens were convinced that Boeing was the mysterious purchaser.

By October of 1965, less than three hundred acres remained to be acquired. News reporters from the East were visiting the studio, and in a press conference a representative of the Orlando *Sentinel* asked Walt if his company was buying land in Florida. He could have dodged the question with a half-truth; instead, he replied, "I'd rather not say."

That weekend Bob Foster made a trip to Orlando with Joe Potter, the Army general who had been Robert Moses's chief aide at the New York World's Fair and had recently joined the Disney organization. Using assumed names, they registered at a hotel, viewed the site from a helicopter and tramped over the ground. When they returned to the hotel on Sunday, they saw a headline on the Orlando *Sentinel:* "WE SAY IT'S DISNEY."

Still hoping for secrecy, Potter used a pay telephone to call Card Walker and report that the news was leaking. Walt made the decision to announce the Florida Project. Potter and Foster flew to Miami to meet with the Governor of Florida, Haydon Burns, who wanted to make the announcement himself the following day at a convention luncheon.

And so the news was out, with land acquisitions unfinished. The price on the remaining parcels of land quickly rose from $180 per acre to $1,000. But Disney had been able to acquire options on 27,000 acres of Florida at a price of $5,000,000.

On November 15, a press conference was held at the Cherry Plaza Hotel in Orlando. With a politician's flourish, Governor Burns introduced Walt Disney as "the man of the decade, who will bring a new world of entertainment, pleasure and economic development to the State of Florida." The Governor termed Roy Disney "the financial wizard of Walt Disney Productions."

"This is the biggest thing we've ever tackled," Walt began. "I might, for the benefit of the press, explain that my brother and I have been together in our business for forty-two years now. He's my big brother, and he's the one that when I was a little fellow I used to go to with some of my wild ideas, and he'd either straighten me out and put me on the right path—or if he didn't agree with me, I'd work on it for years until I got him to agree with me. But I must say that we've had our problems that way, and that's been the proper balance that we've been needing in our organization. . . . In this project, though, I'd just like to say that I didn't have to work very hard on him. He was with me from the start. Now whether that's good or bad, I don't know."

Members of the press asked about a model community for the employees of the Florida Project, and Walt disclosed publicly for the first time his thinking about a city of the future: "I would like to be part of building a model community, a City of Tomorrow, you might say, because I don't believe in going out to this extreme blue-sky stuff that some architects do. I believe that people still want to live like human beings. There's a lot of things that could be done. I'm not against the automobile, but I just feel that the automobile has moved into communities too much. I feel that you can design so that the automobile is there, but still put people back as pedestrians again, you see. I'd love to work on a project like that. Also, I mean, in the way of schools, facilities for the community, community entertainments and life. I'd love to be part of building up a school of tomorrow. . . . This might become a pilot operation for the teaching age—to go out across the country and across the world. The great problem today is the one of teaching."

Walt set up a Florida Project planning committee at WED consisting of himself, Joe Potter and Marv Davis, who had a rare knack of putting Walt's ideas into form. Only the three men had keys to the room where the Florida plans were kept. Throughout the planning, Walt concerned himself with the overall concept of the Florida Project and the design of the City of Tomorrow, paying scant attention to the theme park. He asked his planners: "If you were going to build another Disneyland, how would you do it?" They decided they would build it exactly as before. The design for Disneyland was perfect; the only alteration would be better access between Fantasyland and Frontierland. The finding confirmed Walt's belief that he should concentrate his thinking on the City of Tomorrow. "We know how to build a theme park," he said. "The new one will be no different from Disneyland—except we'll have more water."

The City of Tomorrow became an obsession. He wanted it to include every possible scientific advance, and he commissioned Joe Potter, "Find out what industry is thinking about the future. What's going on in the research laboratories, in the think tanks? Let's take advantage of their know-how in our own planning." Letters of inquiry were sent to five hundred corporations, and over the months Potter and others visited a hundred factories, research centers and foundations.

Walt read omnivorously on city planning. Among the fourteen surveys he ordered from Economics Research Associates was one on model cities. It revealed that planned communities had existed since 1900 B.C., when one was established in Egypt for builders of a pyramid. Of the 125 new cities that had been built in the United States by the mid-1960s, few could be considered successful; most had repeated or compounded the errors of old cities. Walt was impressed by the New Towns program of postwar England, yet it seemed to have produced communities that were dull and drab. Walt was not discouraged. His natural optimism convinced him that environments of high quality could be planned so that people could "live like human beings" in the modern world.

Nor was he discouraged by the failure of big corporations in efforts to create model cities. One major company had spent $100,000,000 in research for a plan to establish ten such cities, but the project came to nothing. Archaic building codes, protective labor unions, building material contractors, and shortsighted politicians inevitably made progressive change impossible. With his customary distrust of politicians, Walt Disney sought unprecedented freedom to develop a model city without interference. Donn Tatum pointed out that what he really wanted was "an experimental, absolute monarchy." Walt raised an eyebrow and asked puckishly, "Can I have one?" "No," Tatum replied.

Walt needed a name for his future city. One day at lunch with his WED staff he mused, "What we're talking about is an experimental prototype community of tomorrow. What does that spell? E-p-c-o-t. EPCOT. That's what we'll call it: EPCOT."

28

ON NEW Year's Day, 1966, Walt Disney was seen by millions on television as Grand Marshal of the Tournament of Roses parade in Pasadena. To the generation who had seen him weekly on his television series, he seemed little different. The same straight hair and trimmed mustache—perhaps a little grayer—and the same wide grin and upraised eyebrow. But those who worked closely with Walt could see changes. He had passed his sixty-fourth year in December, and his once-limitless energies were beginning to flag. More and more he complained that he was feeling "gimpy" and that the day's activities left him "pooped."

The old polo injury had grown worse. Pain shot down his back and into his left leg, and the nightly treatments by Hazel George brought little relief. Facial pain continued to afflict him; the attacks came at bedtime, and he spent hours in the night applying hot compresses to his face. A chronic sinus problem required weekly treatments. He was subject to colds and on at least two occasions probably had walking pneumonia. He developed a kidney ailment and entered St. John's Hospital in Santa Monica for examinations. His desk calendar for 1966 shows a series of doctor's appointments and hospital visits. He spent more long weekends at Smoke Tree Ranch, where the Disneys had bought another house, and sometimes he remained a week.

The illnesses seemed to reinforce the old premonition that he would die before finishing his work. Late one evening at Disneyland, Walt walked with three of his longtime associates to his parking space in the service area behind the firehouse apartment. They had been to a dinner party attended by the key figures who had helped Walt build the park, and Walt commented warmly, "I really enjoyed that. It was one of the nicest evenings I've spent."

His companions agreed, and one of them said, "It was a good time. We'll have to arrange more just like it."

"No," Walt said, "there won't be any more."

"Sure, there will," the man insisted.

"No. I'm sixty-four now, and I'm not getting any younger, you know."

His companions predicted many more years for Walt and more parties. "No, I won't live forever," he said quietly. The others fell silent, and he said with a smile, "Let's just say this was a wonderful evening and I won't forget it." He climbed into his car and drove off.

Walt grew closer to his family. He delighted in his grandchildren, and by early 1966 he had seven. Diane and Ron Miller now had six children—Christopher, Joanna, Tamara, Jennifer, Walter and Ronald; in January 1966, a daughter, Victoria, was born to Sharon and Bob Brown. Walt was pleased with the way both his sons-in-law were progressing in the company. Ron had demonstrated his talent and leadership as a producer, and Bob proved a creative force at WED.

A deeper bond seemed to develop between Walt and Lilly. Studio workers noted how they strolled hand in hand as he showed off a new movie set or demonstrated the latest Audio-Animatronic marvel. Walt took pride in her sense of style and commented to Diane, who was inclined to casualness in her attire: "Kid, why don't you let your mother show you how to dress?" Walt admired Lilly's taste in antiques and never complained about her shopping expeditions during their trips.

Lilly continued to express concern over Walt's grandiose schemes, but she was immensely proud when they succeeded. She was pleased with the homage Walt received. After she and Walt had attended a New York dinner for America's astronauts, she telephoned Diane in California to report that Walt received the most attention. "Everyone seems to think that your father is the most important man in the world," Lilly said.

Walt enjoyed teasing Lilly. She disapproved of his taking over the controls of the company plane on their cross-country flights, but he continued to do so. During a flight to Orlando, Walt went forward to the cabin and told the pilot, Jim Stevenson, "Hand me the mike." Walt announced over the loudspeaker: "This is your captain speaking." As he had expected, Lilly leaped up and started toward the cabin. Walt boomed over the loudspeaker: "No, not the captain. This is the commander-in-chief of the whole damned outfit!"

Walt also seemed closer to Roy, and they worked together in greater harmony than ever before. Roy was wholeheartedly in favor of the Florida Project, and he plotted the means to finance it. Still, Roy kept mentioning his wish to retire from active participation in the company. That was something that Walt could not countenance. He actively plotted against Roy, telephoning Edna to remark, "You don't want Roy hanging around the house all day, do you?" In conversations with Roy, Walt argued that it would be unthinkable for him to attempt the huge Florida undertaking without the daily support of Roy. As usual, Walt won. Roy postponed his plans for retirement.

In frequent pain and impatient to get things done, Walt became more short-tempered at the studio. Spotting a man from the business department at a WED meeting, Walt snapped, "What the hell are you doing here?" He wanted only his creative people present during planning sessions.

When Walt was conferring with Joe Potter on the contour of a bay area at the Florida Project, Potter remarked, "Now the bay could be extended, but that would cost a million and a half dollars." Walt exploded. "Dammit, Potter, why do you waste my time talking about unimportant matters?" he muttered. For ten days Walt passed Potter in the hall without speaking. Then Potter received a call from Tommie Wilck: "Walt would like to have you come over at four to chat a while." The retired general reported to the office and for an hour Walt discussed people in the organization, how he had met them and what they contributed. On the following Monday, Walt's secretary called again, and Potter appeared for another conversation. Finally he remarked, "Walt, you know me. But I'm still the same guy I was before, and you'll have to accept me as I am." Walt replied, "I couldn't sleep Friday night. I kept asking myself, 'Why the hell do I kick Potter around like that.' "

Honors continued to pour in, and none pleased him more than having schools named after him. The first was in Tullytown, Pennsylvania. When his train arrived at the station, Walt waved to the crowd from the locomotive cab. He also arrived by train for the dedication of an elementary school in Marceline. It was a double occasion: an honor for the famous home-town boy; and the first time the Santa Fe Super Chief had ever stopped at Marceline.

The third Walt Disney school was at Anaheim. At the ceremonies, Walt responded by inviting all the children in the school to be his guests for a day at Disneyland. "Of course, it wouldn't be a real celebration unless you could come to Disneyland on a school day," said Walt, astonishing the school officials by declaring a school holiday.

Despite his slackening energies, Walt seemed to accomplish more than ever before. He visited WED daily, overseeing the planning for the Florida Project, as well as new developments for Disneyland. He prepared *The Happiest Millionaire* and viewed rushes on films in production. He continued planning CalArts. He appeared in television lead-ins, and he found time for a variety of charities and to serve on the boards of the Performing Arts Council of the Los Angeles Music Center and the California Angels baseball team.

He devoted more time to animation. Starting with

Sleeping Beauty, his supervision of the cartoon features had necessarily been curtailed, and the studio's animators felt neglected. *The Jungle Book* changed that. Walt had long considered a feature based on the Rudyard Kipling stories, but the project was abandoned again and again for lack of a plot line. Bill Peet, with whom Walt had known a stormy but productive association, worked on a treatment, but his temper clashed with Walt's for the last time. In a quarrel with Walt over the story, Peet announced: "It's going to be done my way!" Only one person made final judgments at the Disney studio. Bill Peet left.

Another writer assigned to *The Jungle Book* was Larry Clemmons, a former gag writer for Jack Benny and Bing Crosby. Walt handed him a book with the remark, "Here is the original by Rudyard Kipling. The first thing I want you to do is not to read it."

With Woolie Reitherman as director and the veteran crew of reliables doing the animation, the early sequences developed satisfactorily. The voices of Phil Harris, George Sanders, Louis Prima, Sebastian Cabot and others who were new to Disney cartoons brought freshness and inspiration to the animators. Walt himself had suggested Harris. "I heard him at a benefit in Palm Springs; he's great," Walt said.

Milt Kahl and Frank Thomas animated the boy Mowgli and Bagheera the Panther, John Lounsbery developed the elephants, and Ollie Johnston drew Baloo the Bear. While the animators were pleased with the individual sequences, they worried about the storyline. They still had painful memories of *Pinocchio,* which was half completed when Walt recognized its deficiencies and ordered a costly overhaul. At the end of a story meeting, Milt Kahl expressed the general concern: "Walt, don't you think we should get some kind of overall storyline, so we can know where we're going?"

"No," Walt replied. "You can get all bogged down with these stories." He slapped Kahl on the leg and said, "It will be all right." His instinct proved correct;

the richness of the characters carried *The Jungle Book* from one sequence to another, and a strong storyline wasn't needed. Walt made contributions to the storyboard sessions with the zest of the Mickey Mouse days. After an exhilarating meeting he commented to the animators, "You guys ought to have me down more often. I'm the least-paid gag man in the studio."

Walt continued his travels in the company plane through most of 1966. He flew to Pittsburgh and spent three days at the Westinghouse Research Center, inspecting the company's rapid-transit system and other developments for the future. He surveyed new shopping centers, visiting Rochester, Philadelphia, Washington, D.C., Baltimore and Dallas. He strolled through the clusters of stores, observing the flow of traffic, whether people seemed stimulated by the surroundings, whether they came as families. He was disappointed in most of the centers; they seemed cheerlessly functional. Only in Dallas did he find one that impressed him; he admired the use of a glassed ceiling to admit natural light.

The plane took Walt to film locations and to Denver, where the company had invested in the Celebrity Sports Center. He flew to St. Petersburg, Florida, to observe the functioning of a new composting system. He visited the site of Disney World, as the Florida Project was now called, and viewed it from a helicopter and from the ground, using gas-filled balloons to test elevations of future buildings. He delighted in the vastness of the property. "You know," he reflected to Dick Nunis during a visit, "it's like standing on the top of the Matterhorn and looking seven miles in one direction and eleven miles in another. It's all ours. Why, we could not only have our own Disneyland, but our own Sea World, our own Knott's Berry Farm, as well as a couple of cities. And we'll run it all the way it should be run."

In July, Walt rented a 140-foot yacht for a cruise through British Columbia waters. Walt insisted that the entire family go along on the thirteen-day voyage—

Lilly; Diane and Ron and their six children; Sharon and Bob and their six-month-old baby. All flew to Vancouver in the Disney plane, and Walt supervised the transfer of baggage and people by taxi to the yacht.

The boat turned out to be less roomy than expected. At times thirteen persons crowded into the single living room, and wrangles resulted. Walt served as peacemaker, an unusual role for him. But he was determined that the trip would be a success, and he settled squabbles with a serenity that his family had never seen before. When things quieted down, he retired to the windy upper deck and hunched over his reading. He had brought a mound of things to read—scripts, mostly, but also books on city planning and one on how to select a college president.

Walt's physical condition worsened during the cruise. His voice grew huskier, and his leg stiffened. His family noticed he had great difficulty getting in and out of boats. By the end of the trip he was impatient to return, and he couldn't understand why Ron and Bob had to stop at a cannery for the smoking of the salmon they had caught.

Walt resumed his schedule at the studio, but the pain grew worse. After the dedication of the New Orleans Square at Disneyland on July 24, he entered the UCLA Medical Center for tests. X rays showed that calcification of the old neck injury had increased; an operation could help relieve the condition. Walt decided he would wait until after the end of the year.

He had much to occupy him. A new project was the development of Mineral King Valley as a ski resort. Walt had become interested in skiing when he made *Third Man on the Mountain* in Switzerland in 1958. With his customary curiosity, he chatted with ski instructors, asked skiing tourists for their likes and dislikes, studied the traffic patterns up and down the slopes. In 1960, he commissioned Economics Research Associates to survey the ski potentials at San Gorgonio Mountain, in the San Bernardino range, and at Mineral King Valley, near the big-tree country of Sequoia Na-

tional Park. Later, he ordered surveys of Aspen, Colorado, and Mammoth Mountain in California.

When Walt was asked to stage the ceremonies at the
Winter Olympics in Squaw Valley in 1960, he accepted.
He sent three of his top aides—Ron Miller, Dick Nunis
and Tommy Walker—to Squaw Valley two months
before the opening to plan the festivities. The proposals
included ice sculptures throughout the valley, a thou-
sand-piece band for the opening ceremonies, entertainment nightly for the athletes, steel poles for the flags
of all nations. When Olympic authorities started complaining about costs, Walt declared, "Either we're going
to do it the right way, or Disney will pull out." The officials acquiesced.

At the Olympics, Walt met Willy Schaeffler, a Bavar-
ian ski expert who had become a coach at Denver
University. The two men sparked to each other, and
Walt hired Schaeffler to help him scout a location and
develop plans for a ski resort. Walt's choice narrowed
to Mineral King, and Schaeffler confirmed that it had
an excellent potential. So did a survey by Economics
Research Associates. It showed that Southern California facilities accommodated only one skier per day for
each hundred citizens, compared to three for the San
Francisco area and nine for New England. Obviously
restless, athletic Southern Californians needed a ski
resort within easy distance. Mineral King would be
only four hours away by car, and it had a variety of
skiing bowls with five-mile runs and four-thousand-
foot drops, comparable to the best in Switzerland.

In 1965, the United States Forest Service placed
Mineral King on the market for bids from companies
seeking to develop it for skiing. The Disney offer of
$35,000,000 was accepted. The thirty-year lease was
contingent on getting a commitment for a state highway for access to Mineral King and completing a master plan by January 1969.

While Schaeffler plotted ski courses, Walt began his
plans for the settlement in Mineral King Valley. They
included an alpine village, skating rink, hotels, dor-

mitories for young people, ten restaurants, etc. Automobiles would be banned from the valley; visitors would be brought in by train or other conveyances. California officials were impressed by the earning potential of the Mineral King project; Economics Research Associates estimated a $600,000,000 addition to the state's economy in the first ten years of operation. Governor Edmund G. Brown assured his support of the highway, and the federal government offered $3,000,000 for road construction. Brown and Disney were scheduled to announce plans for the highway at a press conference at Mineral King on September 19, 1966.

Fair weather had been predicted, but gray clouds rolled over the Sierra peaks, sending the temperature to twenty degrees. Walt flew from Burbank to Visalia in the Disney plane, then he and other executives motored to the valley for the noon conference. Governor Brown was late, and the press had been delayed in their climb up the mountain in a bus traveling narrow roads. Walt had worn wool pants and a heavy camping jacket, but he seemed affected by the cold. His face was drawn and deeply lined. When the press arrived, reporters remarked that Walt did not look well. Bob Jackson, who was handling public relations for the Mineral King project, explained that the altitude and cold had caused Walt's pallor.

Governor Brown made his appearance, and he and Walt delivered their statements at a makeshift table between two huge trees on the floor of the valley. Both expressed hopes for a successful conclusion of the project, and Walt answered questions about the nature and timing of his plans. Then Walt retired to the rustic general store to warm himself by the stove. Bob Jackson entered to ask if Walt could return outside to pose for some photographs with the Governor against the backdrop of mountains.

"Could you wait a few minutes until I catch my breath and rest a while?" Walt asked wearily. When he emerged from the store, he was smiling again, and he stood with Brown for photographs. By two o'clock, the ceremonies were over, and Walt got into the car for the drive back to Visalia. It had been his last press conference.

As work progressed on the master plan for Disney World, Walt expanded the original committee of himself, Joe Potter and Marv Davis. Regular meetings were held in the Disney World conference room, the biggest at WED. Walt often came to the session with a paper napkin stuffed in his coat pocket; on the napkin would be notes and diagrams he had made over breakfast at home. Marv Davis sometimes succeeded in preserving the napkins; usually Walt crumpled and discarded them.

In early October, Walt came to the Disney World planning meeting with a sketch. It was an outline of the Florida property, and on it in the Disney script were marked such locations as "Park—Hotels," "Lake," "Camps and Motels," "Tourist Trailer Camp," "Main Entrance," "Air Port and Motels," "Industrial Entrance." Also the notation, "Truck route always under monorail."

"This is how we'll do it," Walt announced to the WED planners. His sketch, which was called the Seventh Preliminary Master Plot Plan, remained the basic pattern for developing the Florida Project.

A plan for governing Disney World was needed for presentation to the Florida legislature. Obviously the territory, twice the size of Manhattan, needed some kind of governmental structure to provide services and fulfill the needs of its citizens. Research showed that the Florida statutes permitted special assessment districts to perform the proprietary functions of government: water, sewers, fire protection, etc. Bob Foster, who was in charge of preparing the plan, argued that a municipality was also required to protect civil rights. Walt resisted. Jules Stein, head of the Music Corporation of America, had advised him to avoid a municipality; Stein drew from his experience in the MCA-owned Universal City, a part of Los Angeles. At a meeting in the Disney World conference room, Foster made his presentation. He had printed all the governmental powers on foot-long cards: drainage, zoning, inspection, gas, water, power, roads, etc. As he defined each power, he placed the card under the improvement district. But then he had several cards, principally civil rights, which did not fit in the improvement district. "Dammit, you speak slowly, Bob," Walt said finally. "Why don't you put those in a city?" The governmental proposal, including a municipality, passed the Florida legislature with only minor changes.

During the planning meetings, Walt became impatient over talk about operation of the theme park. "You guys know *that* by now," he snapped. "I don't want to discuss what we learned in the past; I want to talk about the *future*." He devoted most of his own thinking to EPCOT, and he discoursed about it in an October interview:

"It's like the city of tomorrow ought to be, a city that caters to the people as a service function. It will be a planned, controlled community, a showcase for American industry and research, schools, cultural and educational opportunities. In EPCOT there will be no slum areas because we won't let them develop. There will be no landowners and therefore no voting control. People will rent houses instead of buying them, and at modest rentals. There will be no retirees. Everyone must be employed. One of our requirements is that the people who live in EPCOT must help keep it alive."

Walt remarked that EPCOT would be only one of two prototype cities. The other, which was forming in his mind, would be an experimental laboratory for administering cities. Retired persons and others could buy property in the second city.

"I happen to be an inquisitive guy," Walt continued, "and when I see things I don't like, I start thinking, why do they have to be like this and how can I improve them? City governments, for example. We pay a lot of taxes and still have the streets that aren't paved or are full of holes. And city street cleaners and garbage collectors who don't do their jobs. And property owners who let dirt accumulate and help create slums. Why?"

The reporter commented that Walt seemed to have enough to manage without taking on experimental cities.

"Oh, you sound just like my wife," he replied with a chuckle. "When I started on Disneyland, she used to say, 'But why do you want to build an amusement park? They're so dirty.' I told her that was just the point—mine wouldn't be."

On October 29, Walt flew east to receive the American Forestry Association award at Williamsburg for "outstanding service in conservation of American resources." With Sharon and Bob Brown, he toured the colonial houses of Williamsburg, which he admired for its authentic reproduction of early America. He signed autographs for tourists and posed for photographs with his hands and legs in prisoner's stocks. He fretted over his speech for the award banquet, finally ignored it and spoke extemporaneously about his own love of nature.

When Walt returned to California, he realized he could no longer postpone surgery. His breath was short, and the pain almost rendered his leg useless. On Wednesday, November 2, he entered St. Joseph's Hospital for more tests. This time X rays revealed a spot the size of a walnut on the left lung. Doctors told him surgery was imperative.

He returned to the studio on Thursday for conferences on national developments in theater arts. On Friday, he joined the full board of CalArts for a four-hour meeting at which architectural plans for the campus were revealed for the first time. Afterward Walt remarked to a fellow board member, "Now it's time to select a president, broaden the board and get rolling." Walt reviewed footage of *The Gnome-mobile*, had a haircut and manicure in the barbershop and watched forty-three minutes of rushes of films in production. He was scheduled to attend a banquet in honor of his friend Jules Stein, but he felt too tired to go.

Walt went to a house in Encino which the Miller

family had occupied before they moved to a bigger home nearby; the Disney house on Carolwood was being remodeled. He rested on Saturday, and the next morning he drove himself to St. Joseph's. On the way, he stopped by the Millers' new house and for a few minutes he watched Ron play football with neighborhood youngsters. Walt waved to Ron and then drove on.

Surgery was scheduled for Monday morning. Walt didn't want any fuss made over him, and he told Lilly not to come to the hospital. But Diane insisted that the family should be there, and she and Sharon and their mother sat in the hospital room to await the outcome of the operation. When the surgeon entered, he was grimfaced. He said the left lung had been cancerous and had been removed. The lymph nodes were oversized, and the outlook was poor. "I would give him six months to two years to live," the surgeon said.

The women were stunned, and Lilly seemed unwilling or unable to accept the news. Her daughters, too, could scarcely believe it. When Diane returned to the hospital that night in a driving rainstorm, she somehow convinced herself that her father had a chance, and she was able to face him hopefully. Her father was still in the intensive-care unit, and he was beginning to regain consciousness. "Were you there?" he asked weakly. She nodded, and he said knowingly, "Your mother was there, too."

When Lilly arrived, he was optimistic. "Sweetheart, I'm a new man," he said. "I've only got one lung, but otherwise I'm good as new."

During the stay in the hospital, Walt seemed to regain some of his vigor, and he was cheerful with family visitors. To his nephew, Roy Edward Disney, he remarked: "Whatever it is I've got, don't get it." The studio had announced only that Walt Disney had undergone surgery to correct an old polo injury, but reports of the severity of the surgery circulated. John Wayne, who had also had a lung removed, sent Walt a tele-

gram: "WELCOME TO THE CLUB—THE ONLY PROBLEM
IS HEIGHT," meaning that high altitudes were to be
avoided. Walt was delighted with the message and
showed it to the nurses and visitors.

After two weeks in the hospital, Walt was bored and
eager to return to work. The doctors said he could
leave, and he telephoned Tommie Wilck to come and
get him. He insisted on going to his office, and he read
reports on the company's projects and had a few brief
conferences. Winston Hibler, who sought Walt's advice on a script of *The Horse in the Gray Flannel Suit*,
was startled to find Walt weak and drawn. But as they
conversed, his voice grew stronger.

"I had a scare, Hib," Walt said. "I never had this
sort of thing before. But I'm going to be okay—just off
my feet for a little while. You guys will have to carry
on with the motion-picture product. I'll be around to
help you; when you get stuck on something, I'll be
here." After making suggestions for the movie script,
he added: "Get the story. The story's the most important thing. Once you've got the story, then everything else'll fall into place."

At lunchtime he went to the Coral Room, but instead of sitting at his traditional table in the northeast
corner, he joined the men at the WED table. They,
too, were shocked by his appearance. Walt explained
that part of his left lung had been removed and it had
been cancerous. But he was certain he would be back
to normal as soon as he got some rest. Talking about
the illness seemed to bore him, and he inquired about
the projects at WED. After lunch, he accompanied his
staff to the WED building to look at the works in progress. He asked Roger Broggie about the state of the
Pirates of the Caribbean ride for Disneyland. It had
been completed and shipped to the park, Broggie said,
but more tests were needed. The business faction in the
company was pressing for a Christmas opening. "Broggie, don't you tell them you can do it; that show isn't
ready," Walt insisted.

Walt sat down to talk with Marc Davis, who had been with him from the creative years of the early features through the imagineering of Disneyland and Disney World. Mel Melton, whom Walt had made president of WED, came by, anticipating that Walt might have some business matters to discuss, as he usually did on his visits. "I'm not working now," Walt said, giving Melton a pat on the stomach. "I just want to sit here and talk to Marc."

Walt laughed heartily at sketches Marc had drawn for an Audio-Animatronic bear-band show at Mineral King. Walt kidded Marc about losing weight, and Marc replied, "Well, one thing—they sure knocked a hell-uva lot of weight off you." He regretted saying it and quickly mentioned that a mock-up of a moon-ride show was ready for viewing. Walt and Davis, along with Dick Irvine, John Hench and other WED engineers, inspected the mock-up, and Walt made suggestions for improvements. Then he turned to Irvine and said, "I'm getting kinda tired; do you want to take me back to the studio?" Walt walked to the door and turned to say to Davis, "Goodbye, Marc." Davis had never heard Walt say goodbye before.

Walt returned to the studio on Tuesday and Wednesday, holding meetings and visiting departments. He dropped in at the set of *Blackbeard's Ghost,* surprising Bill Walsh, who was producing the film. "I thought you were across the street at the hospital, Walt," said Walsh. Peter Ustinov, who was starring in the film, joined the conversation, and Walt remarked that surgeons had removed a rib to get at a problem—"some damned thing they're fooling around with." He spoke to the director, Robert Stevenson, about the picture's progress. Then he left.

There was one last goodbye. Hazel George had sent him a get-well card in the hospital with the note, "I'll see you in the 'Laughing Place.' " On his final day at the studio, he sent for her, and they met in the room where they had spent hundreds of hours talking and laughing about a myriad of studio matters while she treated him for the ever-present pain.

"Well, here we are in the 'Laughing Place,'" he said, studying her reaction to his gaunt appearance.

"There's something I want to tell you—" he said, but the words wouldn't come. Instead, they embraced each other, weeping.

The following day was Thanksgiving, and Lilly drove Walt to the Millers' house for an afternoon dinner. Walt enjoyed being among the children, and watching movies of the Canadian voyage. He talked reflectively with Ron. "Boy, I had the biggest scare of my life," Walt said. "Even though I'd had warnings all these years, I never thought it would happen to me." He admitted that he would have to slow down his pace. "I'm going to turn over the picture-making to you producers. I think you guys can work as a team, 'cause you've been showing it for the past three years. I'm gonna devote all my time to Disney World and EPCOT." He added with a grin, "That doesn't mean I'm not going to read those scripts."

Walt thought he might feel better if he went to the desert, and he and Lilly flew to Palm Springs. But he stayed only one night at the house at Smoke Tree Ranch. He grew weaker, and he returned to St. Joseph's Hospital on November 30.

He was beginning to fail more quickly than doctors had anticipated. Cobalt treatments diminished his strength and robbed his appetite. He grew concerned about the future of his family and ordered his personal attorney to sell a block of Disney stock for Diane's benefit. When she asked him why, he said, "Kid, I'm worried about you and Ron with that big mortgage to pay for."

Roy brought him reports of developments in the company, and Ron told him of good business for *Follow Me, Boys* at the Radio City Music Hall. Small things pleased him, as when Diane brought a basket of delicacies. Walt enjoyed the visits with his family, but at times he seemed to seek solitude, as if he didn't want Lilly and the girls to see him in such pain.

He grew weaker, and the drugs sometimes made him confused. "Don't be late for the plane," he said to Sharon for no reason at all. Once he saw reporter Nancy Dickerson on television and said, "Oh, there's Jackie Kennedy. Isn't she lovely?"

His sixty-fifth birthday fell on December 5, but he was too ill for any observance. His strength continued to wane, and his voice became weak and raspy. On the afternoon of December 14, Lilly visited him and she telephoned Diane later to say, "Oh, he's so much better. He got out of bed. He kept putting his arms around me, and his grip was so strong. I know he's going to get well. I know he's going to be all right."

Roy visited him that evening, and Walt seemed weak but lucid. The two brothers talked quietly about company matters, and Walt was intent on discussing Disney World and EPCOT. He stared at the ceiling, which was covered with foot-square acoustical tiles, and he raised a faltering hand to point out the design of the Florida property. Roy, too, was encouraged by Walt's appearance, and he remarked to Edna that night that he thought Walt had a good chance to recover.

Walt Disney died at nine-thirty-five the next morning of an acute circulatory collapse.

Sorrow and disbelief encircled the world. Newspapers in every country in the world reported the news of Walt Disney's death, and citizens everywhere felt the loss. Presidents, premiers and kings expressed their sympathy, and editorials hailed the Disney achievements. The Los Angeles *Times* called him "Aesop with a magic brush. Andersen with a color camera. Barrie, Carroll, Prokofief, Harris—with a genius touch that brought to life the creatures they had created . . . No man in show business has left a richer legacy." The London *Times* reported that he "produced work of incomparable artistry and of touching beauty."

The New York *Times* commented: "Starting from very little save a talent for drawing, a gift of imagination that was somehow in tune with everyone's imagination, and a dogged determination to succeed, Walt Disney became one of Hollywood's master entrepreneurs and one of the world's greatest entertainers. He had a genius for innovation; his production was enormous; he was able to keep sure and personal control over his increasingly far-flung enterprise; his hand was ever on the public pulse. He was, in short, a legend in his own lifetime—and so honored many times over. Yet none of this sums up Walt Disney...."

A Paris newspaper said, "All the children in the world are in mourning. And we have never felt so close to them." Another in Holland called Walt Disney a king who "reigned for several decades over the fantasy of children in all the world." A Mexico City paper reported the sadness of the country's children, "and more than one tear was seen in the eyes of grown men." Disney was described by an editorialist in Turin as "a poet-magician who brought the world of fable alive," and a Düsseldorf newspaper said Disney's Oscars "were of less value than the shouts of joy from the young and old."

His friend Dwight D. Eisenhower commented, "His appeal and influence were universal. Not restricted to this land alone—for he touched a common chord in all humanity. We shall not soon see his like again." From the White House, President Lyndon B. Johnson wrote to Lilly: "It is a sad day for America and the world when a beloved artist leaves us. Millions of us lived a brighter and happier life by the light of your husband's talents. We mourn him and miss him with you. Mrs. Johnson and I pray that you will find some comfort in the knowledge that beauty, joy and truth are immortal. The magic of Walt Disney was larger than life, and the treasures he left will endure to entertain and enlighten worlds to come."

Eric Sevareid on the *CBS Evening News* seemed to express the feelings of most Americans over their loss:

It would take more time than anybody has around the daily news shops to think of the right thing to say about Walt Disney.

He was an original; not just an American original, but an original, period. He was a happy accident; one of the happiest this century has experienced; and judging by the way it's been behaving in spite of all Disney tried to tell it about laughter, love, children, puppies and sunrises, the century hardly deserved him.

He probably did more to heal or at least to soothe troubled human spirits than all the psychiatrists in the world. There can't be many adults in the allegedly civilized parts of the globe who did not inhabit Disney's mind and imagination at least for a few hours and feel better for the visitation.

It may be true, as somebody said, that while there is no highbrow in a lowbrow, there is some lowbrow in every highbrow.

But what Walt Disney seemed to know was that while there is very little grown-up in a child, there is a lot of child in every grown-up. To a child this weary world is brand new, gift wrapped; Disney tried to keep it that way for adults. . . .

By the conventional wisdom, mighty mice, flying elephants, Snow White and Happy, Grumpy, Sneezy and Dopey—all these were fantasy, escapism from reality. It's a question of whether they are any less real, any more fantastic than intercontinental missiles, poisoned air, defoliated forests, and scraps from the moon. This is the age of fantasy, however you look at it, but Disney's fantasy wasn't lethal. People are saying we'll never see his like again.

The news was shattering to everyone in the Disney organization—in the studio, at WED, at Disneyland and in the growing outpost in Florida, in the Buena Vista offices throughout the world. Some had worked with Walt for thirty years, some were newcomers; all had felt his presence as the guiding intellect of the company. Now it was time for Roy to assume control and maintain the destiny that his brother had charted.

Roy issued a statement which told of the loss that everyone felt. Walt was irreplaceable, said Roy, adding, "As President and Chairman of the Board of Walt Disney Productions, I want to assure the public, our stockholders and each of our more than four thousand employees that we will continue to operate Walt Disney's company in the way that he has established and guided it. Walt Disney spent his entire life and almost every waking hour in the creative planning of motion pictures, Disneyland, television shows and all the other diversified activities that have carried his name through the years. Around him Walt Disney gathered the kind of creative people who understood his way of communicating with the public through entertainment. Walt's ways were always unique and he built a unique organization. A team of creative people that he was justifiably proud of."

The funeral was as Walt had specified—private. The body was cremated, and only the immediate family was present for the simple service at Forest Lawn Memorial Park in Glendale on the day after he died. Instead of flowers, the family requested that contributions be made to the California Institute of the Arts.

Walt had wanted to keep the gravity of his illness secret because he feared that the news would depress the company stock. Astonishingly, it rose ten points in the weeks following his death. Roy attributed the rise to the fact that the stock had long been underpriced; also, Wall Street reacted to rumors that Disney was being sought for acquisition by large corporations. A new owner could sell the studio's backlog of films to television for a huge immediate profit. Roy admitted that there had been inquiries, but he said, "God help us if we had to be absorbed into some big conglomerate mess. We'd have to be running pretty scared to agree to that sort of thing. And we're not scared."

The company had to be run the Disney way, and Roy, who had been trying to retire, reluctantly took full charge at the age of seventy-three. He acquainted himself with the workings of WED and ordered the planning for Florida to continue without delay. Film production would be dealt with by a committee of those who had worked intimately with Walt—Card Walker, Ron Miller, Roy E. Disney, Bill Anderson, Bill Walsh, Winston Hibler, Jim Algar and Harry Tytle. Roy admitted that a committee was not the best way to run an organization, "but we will have to do it that way until the new leadership develops."

In the spring of 1967, the Florida legislature passed the statutes that allowed Disney World to proceed. In the following years, Roy made frequent visits to Florida, watching the property change from brackish swamps to blue lakes with white-sand beaches. He was working harder than he ever had during Walt's lifetime, and he promised Edna, "As soon as I finish Walt's dream, I'll quit and let the younger guys take over." With all his work, Roy maintained the Disney humor. One day in Florida, after bouncing in a jeep over rutted roads and slogging through a muddy field, he gazed skyward and cried, "Walt, what have you gotten me into?"

Roy declared that the official name of the Florida Project would be Walt Disney World. He reasoned, "Everybody knows the Ford car, but not everybody knows it was Henry Ford who started it all. It's going to be *Walt* Disney World, so people will always know that this was Walt's dream."

His associates were astonished by the ease and skill with which Roy accomplished the financing of Walt Disney World. They were also dismayed when in the midst of negotiations with the moneymen, Roy confided to his financial staff, "Wait a minute, let's give them a better deal. They've been good to us, and we may have to go back to the well again. Besides, the offering will be oversubscribed." His staff felt they had lost their negotiating power, but Roy's strategy proved correct. He had made friends, as well as lenders, of the Eastern banks.

At last, in October 1971, Walt Disney World was opened to the public, and Roy felt he could slow down. He was seventy-eight, and he wanted to cut his duties in half. He and Edna were planning to take a long cruise to Australia, and she hoped the vacation would help improve Roy's spirits. He had never quite recovered from the depression he felt over Walt's death.

Roy was in a reflective mood when he finished his day's work on a December Friday. As he sometimes did when his appointments were over, he poured himself a Scotch and water and came out to chat with Madeleine Wheeler, who had been his secretary for twenty-eight years. He talked for a long time about events of the past and remarked that he was scheduled for full retirement in a year, "But I might stay on another half-year; that would be my fiftieth year in the picture business," Roy said. "Will you stick with me?" Madeleine, who herself had remained two years past retirement to assist Roy, said she would.

"I may see you at the Disneyland Christmas parade," he said as he left the office.

Roy and Edna had planned to take three of their grandchildren to Disneyland on Sunday, but Roy wasn't feeling well. He had been having examinations for new glasses and complained of a cloud over one of his eyes. Young Roy and his mother took the children to the Christmas parade. When they returned, they found Roy lying dazed on the floor beside his bed. An ambulance rushed him to St. Joseph's Hospital. He died of a cerebral hemorrhage the following day.

The new leadership took over. Donn Tatum became chairman of the board, and Card Walker assumed the office of president; both had worked closely with Roy during the five years after Walt's death. Ron Miller had become executive producer.

Roy had lived long enough to see most of Walt's

dreams fulfilled. Walt Disney World had been built. CalArts had become a reality on a sixty-acre site in Valencia, its handsome buildings financed largely by bequests in Walt Disney's will. Mineral King was stalled because of legal maneuvers by conservationists. And EPCOT awaited a practical approach to its complexities.

And yet the foundations of EPCOT, Walt's vision of the City of Tomorrow, could be seen in Disneyland and Walt Disney World. The noted designer James Rouse, in a commencement speech at the Harvard School of Design in 1963, observed: "I hold a view that may be somewhat shocking to an audience as sophisticated as this, and that is, that the greatest piece of design in the United States today is Disneyland. If you think about Disneyland and think of its performance in relationship to its purpose—its meaning to people more than its meaning to the process of development—you will find it the outstanding piece of urban design in the United States. It took an area of activity—the amusement park—and lifted it to a standard so high in its performance, in its respect for people, in its functioning for people, that it really became a brand-new thing. It fulfills the functions that it set out to accomplish unself-consciously, usefully and profitably. I find more to learn in the standards that have been set and the goals that have been achieved in the development of Disneyland than in any other single piece of physical development in the country."

Walt Disney World carried the EPCOT vision one step forward. The monorail whisks visitors noiselessly from parking lots to the theme park and right into the lobby of the Contemporary Resort Hotel. Utilities and service facilities are in underground corridors, so there is never a need for the street excavation that plagues modern cities. Garbage and trash disappear into pneumatic tubes and are speeded a mile a minute to a compacting plant. The waste is burned in incinerators so filtered and water-scrubbed that only steam escapes from the smoke stack. A plant removes nearby all the suspended solids from sewage, chlorinates the water and pour it into the swamps. A hundred-acre Living Farm uses part of the water for a laboratory for the growth of trees and plants. The many other innovations have brought planners and conservationists to Walt Disney World to study ways to make cities more livable.

Futurist Ray Bradbury once predicted that the influence of Walt Disney would be felt for centuries to come. Certainly in the years following his death, Disney remained a presence to the world's millions. The classic films were being seen by greater audiences than ever before. Even the early Mickey Mouse cartoons were being rediscovered and cherished, and such features as *Fantasia* and *Alice in Wonderland*, commercial failures in their first releases, had been vindicated by a new generation. If Walt Disney had only made film entertainment, his place in American history would be assured.

But he did more. He created Disneyland, and he laid the foundations for Walt Disney World and EPCOT, with their limitless potential for bettering the human condition.

It had been a long distance from Laugh-O-Grams to Walt Disney World. Walt did not complete the journey; he had died as he feared he would, with his work undone. But those he had trained completed it, and the result of their labors was seen by the public for the first time on October 23, 1971. Beneath the spires of Cinderella's Castle, Arthur Fiedler conducted the World Symphony with 145 musicians representing sixty-six countries. The family was all there—Lilly, Roy and Edna; Diane and Ron Miller and their seven children; Sharon and her husband, William Lund (Bob Brown had died of cancer a year after Walt's death), and her three children; Roy Edward Disney and his wife Patricia and their four children.

Roy Disney stepped to the microphone and gazed beyond the festive crowd, past the brightly painted buildings of the theme park and to the vista beyond—

the massive Contemporary Resort Hotel, the deep-blue lakes and green forests. Roy expressed gratitude to the thousands who had helped build Walt Disney World, and then he reminisced:

"My brother Walt and I first went into business together almost a half-century ago. And he was really, in my opinion, truly a genius—creative, with great determination, singleness of purpose and drive; and through his entire life he was never pushed off his course or diverted to other things. Walt probably had fewer secrets than any man, because he was always talking to whoever would listen. Talking of story ideas or entertainment projects. My banker one day said, 'How is such-and-such a picture progressing?' And I said, 'Joe, I don't think we have a picture of that name in work.' He repeated the name and said he saw little sketches of the story. I said, 'Joe, Walt was just using you as a good guinea pig to see how you would react to the story. We don't have any picture like that in work.' And that was the way Walt went through his life."

Roy then spoke of the woman who "was with him at all times, cheering him on, giving him an argument when she thought he was wrong." As the castle's carillon played "When You Wish Upon a Star," Lilly walked down a ramp accompanied by Mickey Mouse. She stood in the spotlight beside Roy, and he said to her, "Lilly, you knew all of Walt's ideas and hopes as well as anybody; what would Walt think of it?"

"I think," Lilly replied, "Walt would have approved."

on the gloomy return flight to California. Before the plane arrived in Burbank, he remarked, "Well, that's the place— central Florida."

Walt and Roy agreed to sock enough property in

SOURCES

A LARGE part of this book was drawn from interviews with relatives and co-workers of Walt Disney, and the author is grateful for their help. They include:

James Algar, Ken Anderson, Bill Anderson, George L. Bagnall, Ruth Disney Beecher, Roger Broggie, George Bruns, Harriet Burns, Candy Candido, Les Clark, Larry Clemmons, William H. D. Cottrell, Jack Cutting, Marc Davis, Marvin Aubrey Davis, Edna Francis Disney, Roy E. Disney, Ron Dominguez, Buddy Ebsen, Tim Elbourne, Peter Ellenshaw, Bill Evans, Richard Fleischer, Robert P. Foster, Joseph W. Fowler, Hazel George, Gerry Geronimi, Harper Goff, Floyd Gottfredson, John Hench, Winston Hibler, Al Howe, Dick Huemer, Richard F. Irvine, David Iwerks, Wilfred Jackson, Robert F. Jani, Fred Joerger, James A. Johnson, Ollie Johnston, Tom Jones, Milt Kahl, Ward Kimball, Eric Larson, John Lounsbery, Irving Ludwig, Sharon Disney Lund, Jim Macdonald, Fred MacMurray, Chuck Malone, C. G. Maxwell, Mel Melton, Diane Disney Miller, Ron Miller, Margaret Winkler Mintz, Tom Nabbe, Richard A. Nunis, Ken Peterson, Walt Pfeiffer, Dolly Pope, Owen Pope, William E. Potter, Harrison Price, Sandy Quinn, Woolie Reitherman, Wathel Rogers, Herbert Ryman, Dolores Scott, Robert Sewell, Leonard Shannon, Ben Sharpsteen, Sal Silvestri, Martin A. Sklar, Paul Smith, Jack Speirs, Robert Stevenson, James L. Stewart, William Sullivan, Donn Tatum, Herb Taylor, Frank Thomas, Norman Tokar, Lillian Disney Truyens, Lawrence E. Tryon, Card Walker, Tommy Walker, Bill Walsh, Bud Washo, Madeleine Wheeler, Thomas Wilck, Tommie Blount Wilck, Roy Williams, John Wise.

The Archives of Walt Disney Productions, directed by David R. Smith, provided invaluable material. Both Walt and Roy Disney seem to have possessed a sense of history, and their care in preserving their own and the company records proved helpful to the biographer. I have used Walt Disney's words wherever possible; hence the original copies of his New York letters to Roy, the transcriptions of story meetings, Walt's annual letters to his sister, etc., were of great value. In 1956 Walt recorded a series of long interviews about his past history for the book Diane Disney Miller wrote with Pete Martin. Roy Disney also reminisced in three lengthy interviews shortly before his death.

As a news reporter, the author interviewed Walt Disney scores of times over a twenty-five-year period and consulted with him on two previous books about the studio and his life. I have drawn from that material, as well as from the hundreds of magazine and newspaper interviews given by Walt. I also viewed home movies and Disney films dating back to the Alice Comedies and Oswald. Special thanks are due to Card Walker, Vincent Jefferds, James Stewart and the Disney family.

INDEX

393